Irish Philosophy in the Age of Berkeley

ROYAL INSTITUTE OF PHILOSOPHY SUPPLEMENT: 88

EDITED BY

Kenneth L. Pearce and Takaharu Oda

CAMBRIDGE
UNIVERSITY PRESS

PUBLISHED BY THE PRESS SYNDICATE OF THE UNIVERSITY OF CAMBRIDGE
The Pitt Building, Trumpington Street, Cambridge, CB2 1RP,
United Kingdom

CAMBRIDGE UNIVERSITY PRESS
UPH, Shaftesbury Road, Cambridge CB2 8BS, United Kingdom
32 Avenue of the Americas, New York, NY 10013–2473, USA
477 Williamstown Road, Port Melbourne, VIC 3207, Australia
C/Orense, 4, planta 13, 28020 Madrid, Spain
Lower Ground Floor, Nautica Building, The Water Club, Beach Road,
Granger Bay, 8005 Cape Town, South Africa

Printed in Great Britain by Bell & Bain Ltd, Glasgow.
Typeset by Techset Composition Ltd, Salisbury, UK

A catalogue record for this book is available from the British Library

ISBN 9781108970822
ISSN 1358-2461

Contents

Notes on the Contributors

Manuel Fasko (manuel.fasko@philos.uzh.ch) *is a graduate student at the University of Zurich currently working on his dissertation about George Berkeley's conception of nature funded by the Swiss National Science Foundation (http://p3.snf.ch/Project-172060). Apart from George Berkeley his research interests include Early Modern philosophy in general and the British and Irish tradition of the 17th-18th century in particular. Along with Peter West, he co-won the 2019 Colin and Ailsa Turbayne International Berkeley Essay Prize and his most recent publication is 'A Scotist nonetheless? George Berkeley, Cajetan, and the Problem of Divine Attributes'.*

Peter West (westp@tcd.ie) *is a PhD Candidate at Trinity College Dublin. His research focuses primarily on Early Modern epistemology, especially Berkeley. He is currently working on a project tracing 'anti-representationalist' thought throughout the seventeenth- and eighteenth-century in thinkers such as John Sergeant, Berkeley, and Thomas Reid. Recent publications include 'Reid and Berkeley on Scepticism, Representationalism, and Ideas' and 'Berkeley on the Relation Between Abstract Ideas and Language in Alciphron VII'.*

Eric Schliesser (nescio2@yahoo.com) *is Professor of Political Science at the University of Amsterdam and Visiting Scholar at Chapman University. His recent publications include* Adam Smith: Systematic Philosopher and Public Thinker *(Oxford University Press, 2017).*

Marc A. Hight (mhight@hsc.edu) *is Elliott Professor of Philosophy at Hampden-Sydney College. He is the author of* The Correspondence of George Berkeley *(Cambridge University Press, 2013),* Idea and Ontology *(Penn State University Press, 2008), and numerous articles in early modern philosophy and the philosophy of economics.*

Samuel C. Rickless (srickless@ucsd.edu) *is Professor of Philosophy at the University of California San Diego, and Affiliate Professor at the University of San Diego School of Law. He is the author of* Plato's Forms in Transition: A Reading of the Parmenides *(Cambridge University Press. 2007),* Berkeley's Argument for Idealism *(Oxford University Press, 2013), and* Locke *(Wiley-Blackwell, 2014). Recent published work includes articles on Locke on akrasia (with*

Notes on the Contributors

Leonardo Moauro), on Hume's distinction between impressions and ideas, and on Mary Shepherd's criticisms of Berkeley.

Ruth Boeker (ruth.boeker@ucd.ie) *is Assistant Professor in Philosophy at University College Dublin and Affiliated Member of the UCD Centre for Ethics in Public Life. Her recent publications include 'Shaftesbury on Liberty and Self-Mastery'* (International Journal of Philosophical Studies, *2019*), 'Shaftesbury on Persons, Personal Identity and Character Development' (Philosophy Compass, *2018*), and 'Locke on Personal Identity: A Response to the Problems of his Predecessors' (Journal of the History of Philosophy, *2017). She is also guest editor of a recently published special issue on* New Perspectives on Agency in Early Modern Philosophy (International Journal of Philosophical Studies, *2019*).

Kate Davison (kate.davison@sheffield.ac.uk) *is a lecturer in eighteenth-century history at the University of Sheffield, specialising in the social and cultural history of Britain. She is currently working on her first book, which focuses on humour and laughter in early eighteenth-century London, and she has also published in* The American Historical Review *and* The Historical Journal.

Christine Gerrard (christine.gerrard@lmh.ox.ac.uk) *is Professor of English Literature at the University of Oxford, and Barbara Scott Fellow in English at Lady Margaret Hall, Oxford. Her recent publications include 'Laetitia Pilkington and the Mnemonic Self',* The Review of English Studies 70, *(June 2019), 489–508; 'Memory and the Eighteenth-Century Female Poet', in* Memory in Western Literature, *3 vols. (Sivas, Turkey, 2018), Vol. 1, 1–23; 'Senate or Seraglio? Swift's "Triumfeminate" and the Literary Coterie',* Eighteenth-Century Ireland *31 (2016), 13–28. She is currently completing an edition of* Jonathan Swift, The History of the Four Last Years, *for Cambridge University Press, and working on a book on women and memory in the long eighteenth century.*

Ian Leask (ian.leask@dcu.ie) *is a Lecturer in Philosophy in the School of Theology, Philosophy, and Music, Dublin City University. He is the editor of a modern, annotated, edition of John Toland's* Letters to Serena *(Dublin: Four Courts, 2013).*

Kenneth L. Pearce (pearcek@tcd.ie) *is Ussher Assistant Professor in Berkeley Studies in the Department of Philosophy, Trinity College Dublin. He is the author of* Language and the Structure of Berkeley's World *(Oxford University Press, 2017) and co-editor* *(with Tyron Goldschmidt) of* Idealism: New Essays in Metaphysics *(Oxford University Press, 2017)*.

Jacob Schmutz (jacob.schmutz@uclouvain.be) *is Associate Professor of Philosophy at Université Catholique de Louvain. He teaches medieval and Renaissance philosophy. He has widely published on early-modern scholasticism, and is currently preparing a comprehensive catalogue of French college notebooks of the 1500–1800 period.*

Takaharu Oda (odat@tcd.ie) *is a PhD Candidate and Provost's Scholar at Trinity College Dublin. He is currently working on his thesis on Berkeley's pragmatist theory of causation, especially in the 1721 treatise* De motu. *Recent publications include 'Semiotics against Transubstantiation: Peirce's Reception of Berkeley' (forthcoming) and 'Izutsu's Zen Metaphysics of I-Consciousness vis-à-vis Cartesian* Cogito' *(co-authored,* Comparative Philosophy, *2020)*.

Preface

Over the past several decades, scholarship in the history of early modern philosophy has undergone a major methodological shift. Historians of philosophy once focused almost exclusively on the logical analysis of philosophical arguments presented in a handful of canonical 'Great Books' with only very limited attention to historical context or the specific interests and concerns of the philosophers under discussion.[1] While this kind of logical analysis is clearly important, most historians of philosophy today believe that contextual factors must play a much larger role. The 'contextualist revolution' (as Christia Mercer (2019) has called it) has led to greater attention to texts and authors outside the traditional canon and opened up new possibilities for interdisciplinary research, building greater connections to fields such as intellectual history, history of science, theology, and religious studies.

John Locke (1632–1704) was an early beneficiary of this shift. Beginning from John Yolton's *John Locke and the Way of Ideas* (Yolton, 1956), there has been significant interest in the historical context of Locke's philosophy, including volumes such as *Locke's Philosophy: Context and Content* (Rogers, ed., 1994) and *English Philosophy in the Age of Locke* (Stewart, ed., 2000). These studies have contributed to a deeper understanding of Locke's philosophy and its connections to the scientific, political, and religious issues of his day, and also brought to light fascinating philosophical work by Locke and others that had previously been neglected.

To date, George Berkeley (1685–1753) has not received the same level of benefit. Although scholars such as Bertil Belfrage (1986), David Berman (1994; 2005), Stephen Daniel (2011), and José Antonio Robles (2001) have advocated for the importance of Berkeley's historical context and the influence of Irish thinkers such as John Toland, William King, Peter Browne, and Robert Boyle, Berkeley's context has yet to receive the kind of sustained scholarly attention that has been paid to Locke's. This is closely connected with the fact that most scholars of early modern philosophy are still unaware of the complex and sophisticated philosophical and religious debates that took place in Ireland in the 17th and 18th centuries.

---

[1] For an example of this kind of approach see Bennett (1971).

doi:10.1017/S1358246120000181   ©The Royal Institute of Philosophy and the contributors 2020

Kenneth L. Pearce and Takaharu Oda

Today, Berkeley's *Principles* (1710) and *Three Dialogues* (1713) are among the standard texts for the study of European philosophy. No other Irish philosopher, and no other work of Berkeley's, has achieved this 'canonical' status. However, Ireland was a major centre of philosophical activity in Berkeley's lifetime, and Berkeley was far from the only contributor. Studying this broader Irish philosophical discussion will improve our understanding of Berkeley and also of early modern philosophy more generally. This is in line with a new approach to the history of philosophy focused on philosophical conversations, rather than on the 'grand systems' of individual thinkers.[2]

To promote this much needed study, we proposed to hold a conference on the topic Irish Philosophy in the Age of Berkeley, with papers to address the Irish context of Berkeley's philosophy; the philosophical work of other Irish thinkers active during Berkeley's lifetime; the reception within Ireland of other philosophical figures, ideas, and movements; and the reception of Irish philosophy outside Ireland. Three papers were invited, and an additional nine chosen by anonymous review of abstracts.

The Irish Philosophy in the Age of Berkeley conference took place at Trinity College Dublin 5 and 6 April 2019, with the generous support of the Royal Institute of Philosophy, the Mind Association, the Trinity Long Room Hub Arts and Humanities Research Institute (Making Ireland Research Theme), the Trinity College Dublin Faculty of Arts, Humanities, and Social Sciences Event Fund, and the Trinity College Dublin Department of Philosophy. We are pleased to present in this volume ten of the twelve papers given at the conference. The papers discuss the philosophical work of a wide variety of Irish writers, including Robert Boyle (1627–1691), William King (1650–1729), William Molyneux (1656–1698), Robert Molesworth (1656–1725), Peter Browne (c. 1665–1735), Jonathan Swift (1667–1745), John Toland (1670–1722), Thomas Prior (1680–1751), Mary Barber (c. 1685–1755), Samuel Madden (1686–1765), Arthur Dobbs (1689–1765), Francis Hutcheson (1694–1746), Constantia Grierson (c. 1705–1733), Laetitia Pilkington (c. 1709–1750), Elizabeth Sican (fl. 1730s), and John Austin (1717–1784). The range of topics addressed is also quite wide, including philosophical reflections on mind, science, religion, economics, beauty, free will, laughter, education, motherhood, gender, and knowledge.

---

[2] This approach is exemplified, for instance, by Hutton (2015).

2

The first section, comprising the first four chapters, sheds light on the early modern Irish context of Berkeley's philosophy. We begin with 'The Irish Context of Berkeley's "Resemblance Thesis"' by Peter West and Manuel Fasko. Berkeley's resemblance thesis states that 'for one thing to *represent* another, those two things must *resemble* one another' (p. 7). The authors argue that this principle – which plays a central role in Berkeley's immaterialist arguments – must be understood against the specifically Irish background of Berkeley's thought. In particular, they show that this principle plays an important role in the philosophical work of Molyneux and King.

In Chapter 2, 'Does Berkeley's Immaterialism Support Toland's Spinozism? The Posidonian Argument and the Eleventh Objection', Eric Schliesser, considers Berkeley's 'clockwork' argument from design in the eleventh objection against his own principles (*Principles* §§60–66), as it invoked a scholarly debate between Daniel Garber and Margaret Wilson. Schliesser argues that Berkeley's response to this objection must be understood against the background of what he calls the 'Posidonian argument', a form of design argument derived from Cicero's *On the Nature of the Gods*. Schliesser discusses the versions of this argument that were advocated by Boyle and Samuel Clarke (1675–1729) and criticized by Toland.

In Chapter 3, 'Poverty and Prosperity: Political Economics in Eighteenth-Century Ireland', Marc Hight aims to situate Berkeley's arguments about social and economic policy in *The Querist* (1736) with respect to contemporary mercantilist wisdom and three other Irish thinkers of the same period: Madden, Dobbs, and Prior.

In Chapter 4 'Berkeley's Criticisms of Shaftesbury and Hutcheson', Samuel Rickless elucidates the nature and purpose of Berkeley's metaphysical and moral arguments in Dialogue 3 of *Alciphron* (1732). In this dialogue, Berkeley criticises the moral theories of Anthony Ashley Cooper, the Third Earl of Shaftesbury (1671–1713) and Hutcheson. Rickless argues that Berkeley's disagreements which Shaftesbury and Hutcheson in ethics and aesthetics can be linked directly to Berkeley's idealism.

The second section, comprising the remaining six chapters, sheds further light upon other Irish philosophers in Berkeley's lifetime. The first two of these chapters continue the discussion of Hutcheson.

Chapter 5, 'Francis Hutcheson on Liberty' by Ruth Boeker, focuses on Hutcheson's Latin textbook on metaphysics, *Metaphysicae synopsis: ontologiam, et pneumatologiam, complectens* (1742), which was probably composed in Dublin in the 1720s. Boeker argues that this underexplored text, which contains

Hutcheson's most detailed commentary on philosophical debates about liberty, is best understood by positioning it within the Irish context, and particularly the views of King and the views discussed in Molesworth's circle.

In Chapter 6 "'Plainly of Considerable Moment in Human Society": Francis Hutcheson and Polite Laughter in Eighteenth-Century Britain and Ireland', Kate Davison reveals another aspect of Hutcheson's philosophy by examining his *Reflections upon Laughter* (1725), originally published in the *Dublin Journal*. Hutcheson was one of the earliest proponents of what is now known as the 'incongruity' theory of laughter. Drawing on contemporary views, such as those of Shaftesbury and Swift, Davison considers Hutcheson's philosophy of laughter in the context of early eighteenth-century British and Irish conceptions of gentlemanly politeness in order to understand the moral and social role of laughter according to Hutcheson's theory.

The following two chapters concern the place of women in early modern philosophy. In Chapter 7 'What the Women of Dublin Did with John Locke', Christine Gerrard spotlights the writings of a group of Dublin women, often known as the 'triumfeminate' of their mentor Jonathan Swift. Despite the name, the 'triumfeminate' actually had four women as members at different times: Barber, Pilkington, Grierson, and Sican. Gerrard argues that the literary output of these women shows deep engagement with Locke's philosophy, particularly Locke's views on motherhood, education, and memory.

In Chapter 8 'From Serena to Hypatia: John Toland's Women', Ian Leask examines the role of women in the thought of the religious and political radical John Toland. Leask chiefly focuses on two of Toland's works: his 1720 biography of Hypatia of Alexandria and his *Letters to Serena* (1704). Leask argues that in these texts a feminist (or at least proto-feminist) polemic is intertwined with Toland's critique of priestcraft.

Chapter 9, Kenneth L. Pearce's 'Peter Browne on the Metaphysics of Knowledge', examines the philosophy of one of Toland's most vigorous opponents. Browne originally developed his theory of analogical language in order to answer Toland's objections against religious mysteries. However, Pearce shows that Browne employs analogy much more broadly in his theory of mind. In particular, Pearce argues that Browne's analogical account of knowledge has important similarities with functionalist theories in contemporary philosophy of mind.

The final chapter concerns Irish philosophy in exile. Jacob Schmutz's 'John Austin SJ (1717–84), The First Irish Catholic Cartesian?' provides an analysis of a previously unknown manuscript of a metaphysics course conducted in Rheims in 1746–1747 by an Irish Jesuit. Schmutz shows that the course is not so conservative and Scholastic as might have been expected, but instead shows significant Cartesian influence particularly in the theory of mind and knowledge.

The papers in this volume represent only a small sample of Irish philosophy as it existed in Berkeley's lifetime. It is our hope that this sample might serve to demonstrate how much is to be gained by further attention to this topic and, more broadly, how much value there is to interdisciplinary history of philosophy beyond the canon.

Kenneth L. Pearce and Takaharu Oda

Department of Philosophy, Trinity College Dublin
PEARCEK@tcd.ie
ODAT@tcd.ie

References

Bertil Belfrage, 'Development of Berkeley's Early Theory of Meaning,' *Revue Philosophique de la France et de l'Etranger*, 176 (1986), 319–330.

Jonathan Bennett, *Locke, Berkeley, Hume: Central Themes* (Oxford: Clarendon Press, 1971).

David Berman *George Berkeley: Idealism and the Man* (Oxford: Clarendon Press, 1994).

David Berman, *Berkeley and Irish Philosophy* (London: Continuum, 2005).

Stephen Daniel, 'Berkeley's Rejection of Divine Analogy,' *Science et Esprit*, 63 (2011), 149–161.

Sarah Hutton, *British Philosophy in the Seventeenth Century* (Oxford: Oxford University Press, 2015).

Christia Mercer, 'The Contextualist Revolution in Early Modern Philosophy,' *Journal of the History of Philosophy*, 57 (2019), 529–548.

José Antonio Robles, 'Filosofía natural y religión. Los casos de Newton, Boyle y Berkeley,' *Revista Patagónica de Filosofía*, 2 (2001), 43–56.

Kenneth L. Pearce and Takaharu Oda

G. A. J. Rogers (ed.), *Locke's Philosophy: Context and Content* (Oxford: Clarendon Press, 1994).

M. A. Stewart (ed.), *English Philosophy in the Age of Locke* (Oxford: Clarendon Press, 2000).

John Yolton, *John Locke and the Way of Ideas* (Oxford: Oxford University Press, 1956).

The Irish Context of Berkeley's 'Resemblance Thesis'

MANUEL FASKO AND PETER WEST

Abstract
In this paper, we focus on Berkeley's reasons for accepting the 'resemblance thesis' which entails that for one thing to represent another those two things must resemble one another. The resemblance thesis is a crucial premise in Berkeley's argument from the 'likeness principle' in §8 of the *Principles*. Yet, like the 'likeness principle', the resemblance thesis remains unargued for and is never explicitly defended. This has led several commentators to provide explanations as to why Berkeley accepts the resemblance thesis and why he also takes his opponents to do so too. We provide a con-textual answer to this question, focusing on epistemological discussions concerning resemblance and representation in Early Modern Irish Philosophy. We argue that the resemblance thesis is implicit in early responses to William Molyneux's famous example of the 'man born blind made to see' and trace the 'Molyneux man' thought experiment as it is employed by Irish thinkers such as William King and Berkeley himself. Ultimately, we conclude that Berkeley's acceptance of the resemblance thesis can be explained by the Irish intellectual climate in which he was writing.

Introduction

One of Berkeley's most direct arguments against materialism, and the representationalist epistemology which he takes the likes of Descartes and Locke to subscribe to, comes in §8 of the *Principles*.[1] There, Berkeley puts forward what scholars refer to as the 'likeness principle' (LP) which states that 'an idea can be like nothing but an idea'. From LP, Berkeley argues that since the qualities which inhere in an unper-ceivable material substance could never resemble our ideas our ideas could not possibly *represent* those qualities.[2] If Berkeley's argument is

---

[1]   With the exception of his correspondences all references to Berkeley are to Luce & Jessop's edition of *The Works of George Berkeley, Bishop of Cloyne* (London: Nelson, 1948–1957), 9 vols. Unless mentioned, we refer to the version which was last published in Berkeley's lifetime.
[2]   Hill reads the argument in PHK §8 in much the same way (Hill, 2011). See also Cummins (1966); Cummins also coined the term 'the likeness principle'.

doi:10.1017/S1358246120000089   © The Royal Institute of Philosophy and the contributors 2020

Manuel Fasko and Peter West

successful, then it undermines the widely held view that our knowledge of external things in the sensible world comes via ideas in our
minds which represent them. The likeness principle is one of the
key premises in Berkeley' argument in §8 of the *Principles* and there
are several interpretations of Berkeley's treatment of it.[3] However,
as several commentators have pointed out, another premise is
required to reach Berkeley's conclusion that ideas could not possibly
represent unperceivable qualities of material substances.[4] To establish that conclusion, Berkeley requires his readers to accept that 'for
one thing to *represent* another, those two things must *resemble* one
another'. This premise is what we call the 'resemblance thesis' –
and it appears to be similarly unargued for.

Various attempts have been made to explain why Berkeley accepts
the resemblance thesis and why he fails to provide an explicit case for
its defence. Most notably, Jonathan Hill has argued that Berkeley's
acceptance of the resemblance thesis finds its roots in Cartesian discussions surrounding scepticism and intentionality. In what
follows, we argue that there is a more local explanation – namely,
the intellectual environment in *Ireland* and debates amongst *Irish*
thinkers in which Berkeley was actively engaged. Our aim is not to
undermine Hill's reading and we do not contest the claim that
Cartesian thought influenced Berkeley's philosophy – on the
contrary, Berkeley's *De Motu* clearly suggests that Berkeley *was* influenced by Cartesianism. We simply contend that, before looking far
and wide for the source of Berkeley's views on representation and resemblance, one ought to begin this search locally; in Dublin and
Ireland. Ultimately, we conclude that Berkeley's views on the relation

---

[3]　For a metaphysical reading of the likeness principle – that is, one
which entails that ideas *could not possibly* resemble material objects – see
Cummins (1966). For an epistemological reading – which entails that we
could not possibly *know* that ideas resemble material objects – see Winkler
(1989) or Dicker (1985). More recently, Todd Ryan has argued that the likeness principle is a claim about the nature of relations in Berkeley's system
(Ryan, 2006). Ryan's argument lead Dicker to modify his reading in
Dicker (2011, chap. 7). For a recent discussion of the LP and an overview
of previous readings, see Frankel (2016). Frankel ultimately prefers a metaphysical reading.

　　Clearly, Berkeley himself took the LP to be an important part of his philosophy as he explicitly refers to it throughout the *Principles*. See (PHK §§9,
pp. 18–20, 25, 27, 47, 50, 57, 61, 87, 90, 135, 137–38). In all of these sections
the principle is treated as explicitly relevant. It is also repackaged and put
forward in (DHP 1.203-207).

[4]　See Hill (2011); Winkler (1989, p. 138); Carriero (2003).

8

The Irish Context of Berkeley's 'Resemblance Thesis'

between representation and resemblance *were* influenced by the immediate Irish context in which he was writing and that this has so far been underappreciated in the relevant scholarship.

We believe the resemblance thesis was more widespread in Early Modern Irish thought than we are able to demonstrate in this paper, but for the time being focus on tracing it through William Molyneux, William King, and Berkeley's engagement with both the Molyneux problem and debates in Ireland concerning the problem of divine attributes. Our contention is that Molyneux's problem of the 'blind man made to see', and early responses to it, make it evident that the resemblance thesis was an underlying and often implicitly accepted principle in Irish thought.[5] We thus aim to build on and substantiate David Berman's claim that the Molyneux problem is the 'root metaphor' of Early Modern Irish philosophy.[6]

The structure of our argument is as follows. Firstly, we argue that early responses to Molyneux's problem of a blind man made to see established the resemblance thesis as an underlying principle in Early Modern Irish philosophy. The two earliest responses, from Molyneux himself and Locke,[7] emphasise the extent to which the objects of sight were seen to be *unlike* anything with which a blind man is familiar. In section two, we focus on William King's account of human knowledge of the divine attributes.[8] King draws on Molyneux's example, arguing we are no more familiar with God's attributes than a blind man is with the objects of sight. King also explicitly advocates an account of representation by means of

[5] In a forthcoming paper, we focus explicitly on the employment of the example of a 'man born blind' amongst Early Modern Irish thinkers. See Fasko & West (forthcoming). The two papers, alongside one another, are an attempt to substantiate Berman's claim that the Molyneux man is the 'root metaphor' of Early Modern Irish philosophy.

[6] See Berman (2005, p. 87). For a more recent discussion of the Molyneux problem in Irish thought, see Jones (forthcoming).

[7] While Locke was not Irish, he played a crucial role in disseminating Molyneux's question and was highly influential on Irish thought in general. See, for example Berman (2005, p. 87).

[8] For the purposes of this paper, we focus on King's views. We do so on the basis of the greater influence that King demonstrably exerted on Berkeley compared to other Irish thinkers. Yet, Berkeley could have found – and most likely did find – similar views across the Irish Anglican religious spectrum in (e.g.) Edward Synge or Peter Browne. While their views differ in important ways, there are notable similarities in their treatment of the resemblance thesis in general and its application to the problem of divine attributes in particular.

9

likeness, thus suggesting that it is the failure of our knowledge of divine attributes to adequately *resemble* the true nature of those attributes that entails the former is only ever an inadequate representation. In section three, we consider Berkeley's response to King. Berkeley disagrees that our knowledge of divine attributes is comparable with a blind man's notion of the objects of sight, arguing that we use the knowledge we have of ourselves, as spirits, as an imperfect but nonetheless appropriate *representation* of the divine. Despite their disagreement, we emphasise that neither disputes the plausibility of the resemblance thesis itself. This suggests that both Berkeley and King found themselves working under the constraint of explaining how we can represent the divine attributes to ourselves *by means of resemblance*. Finally, we point to the fact that Berkeley uses Molyneux's original problem to defend his claim that the objects of touch and sight are fundamentally heterogenous (i.e., unalike) as further evidence that his acceptance of the resemblance thesis is rooted in Irish thought.

As we see it, there at least are two advantages to focusing on the resemblance thesis in Irish thought. Firstly, this discussion provides an insight into the more local influences on Berkeley's philosophy. There is no doubt that Berkeley took himself to be engaging with influential figures from across Europe including Descartes, Malebranche, and Locke. After all, the 'materialism' he opposes is, as he puts it, a 'strangely [i.e. widely] prevailing' view (PHK, §4). But the impact of other Irish thinkers on Berkeley's views should not be underestimated. Indeed, at least once Berkeley explicitly identifies himself *as an Irish thinker.*[9] Secondly, we see this discussion as beneficial to Early Modern scholarship more generally. By focusing on the local influences on Berkeley, a 'canonical' figure in Early Modern scholarship, this paper will shed light on Ireland's wider contribution to important epistemological debates concerning representation and knowledge via ideas.

1. The Resemblance Thesis

In this section, our aim is to establish the importance of the resemblance thesis in Berkeley's argument in §8 of the *Principles* and

---

[9]   In the *Notebooks* he writes: 'There are men who say there are insensible extensions, there are others who say the Wall is not white, the fire is not hot &c We Irish men cannot attain to these truths' (NB, 392). See also (NB, pp. 393–94; *Works* VI, 236f.; Querist, q. 19, pp. 455, 526 or 540).

outline the interpretative problem that arises from his failure to justify or defend it. The resemblance thesis, as we previously stated, is the claim that 'for one thing to *represent* another, those two things must *resemble* one another'. Before proceeding, it is worth clarifying our own construal of 'representation' in Berkeley's writing. Berkeley himself uses the term 'represent' in both a strict and a loose sense. In a strict sense, Berkeley understands representation as literal *re-presentation* of an object – such as when I imagine an idea which is an 'image' or 'copy' of something I have perceived via the senses (PHK, §33; see also PHK, §27). It is this *re-presentation* which requires resemblance and since Berkeley deems resemblance to be a necessary relation (NTV, §§45; TVV, §42–43 & §61), in what follows, when we refer to representation in a *strict sense* it should be taken to refer to a non-arbitrary relation. This non-arbitrariness is what distinguishes it from Berkeley's use of representation in a *loose sense*. When Berkeley uses the term 'represent' in a loose sense it is used synonymously with 'signify'.[10] Signification relations are those shared between a sign and a thing signified and, importantly, in contrast with representation in a strict sense, they are *arbitrary* relations. In this paper, we are primarily concerned with Berkeley's employment of the term 'represent' in a *strict* sense as outlined above. By attributing the resemblance thesis to Berkeley, then, we take him to accept that representation, in this strict sense, requires resemblance.[11]

At least two passages make it clear that Berkeley both accepts the resemblance thesis *and* takes his opponents to accept it too. Firstly,

[10] See e.g. (PHK Intro §15). We discuss this further in what follows.

[11] It might seem implausible, especially from a contemporary point of view, to reduce representation (in a *strict sense*) to resemblance because the latter is a symmetrical and the former an asymmetrical relation. However, it should be noted that we do not attribute to Berkeley the view that representation is *reducible* to resemblance. Rather, we claim, for Berkeley, resemblance (a necessary relation) between two objects is a pre-requisite for one representing the other. Furthermore, we suggest that in a sense Berkeley thinks that representation *is* symmetrical in as much as there is a resemblance between an original (an archetype) and its copy (an ectype). It seems reasonable to attribute to Berkeley the view that we do not tend to *say* that an original resembles a copy, since the latter is made in the image of the former, but that, given that they do share a relation of resemblance, one *could* say that an original represents a copy. Thanks to Tom Stoneham for raising concerns regarding the symmetry of representation relations.

Manuel Fasko and Peter West

the following passage from the unpublished *Manuscript Introduction* to the *Principles:*

> There is no similitude or resemblance betwixt words & the ideas that are marked by them. Any name may be used indifferently for the sign of any idea, or any number of ideas, it not being determin'd by any likeness to represent one more than another. *But it is not so with ideas in respect of things, of which they are suppos'd to be the copies & images. They are not thought to represent them any otherwise, than as they resemble them.* Whence it follows, that an idea is not capable of representing indifferently any thing or number of things it being limited by the likeness it beares to some particular existence, to represent it rather than any other. (MI, §12, our emphasis)

Berkeley claims the key difference between (i) words and their objects, and (ii) ideas and their objects is that a word can arbitrarily signify any idea, without resembling it, while ideas themselves can only represent that which they resemble.[12] Words, Berkeley explains, can signify 'indifferently'. However, the representational capacity of an idea is 'limited by the likeness it [bears]'. Even the terminology that Berkeley uses is important: the relation between words and ideas is one of 'signification', an arbitrary relation, whereas the relation between ideas and their objects is one of 'representation' which depends entirely upon what a certain idea does and does not resemble.[13] This passage is not repeated in Berkeley's published Introduction to the *Principles*, and there is no obvious counterpart in any of his published works.[14] Nonetheless, as Kenneth Winkler emphasises, that does not mean he ceased to believe that there is a difference between representation in a *strict* sense and signification, i.e. between a non-arbitrary and an arbitrary relation (Winkler, 1989, p. 12).

---

[12] In this instance, Berkeley seems to subscribe to a Lockean conception of the relation between words and ideas. It is contested whether Berkeley held on to this view in his published works, although this is not crucial to our current discussion. For recent discussion of the development of Berkeley's early views on language and an argument to the effect that Berkeley does *not* accept the Lockean view, see Pearce (2017, chap. 2). For an overview of this debate, see West (2018, esp. p. 58).

[13] For further discussion of the difference between 'signification' and 'representation' (in both Locke and Berkeley) see Winkler (2005); Saporiti (2006); Daniel (2008).

[14] However, Berkeley does seem to draw a similar distinction in (NTV, §144) and (Alc., 4.7, p. 149).

The Irish Context of Berkeley's 'Resemblance Thesis'

In §8 of the *Principles,* the resemblance thesis clearly informs both Berkeley's characterisation of his opponents' view and his response to that view. There he writes:

> But say you, though the ideas themselves do not exist without the mind, yet there may be things like them whereof they are copies or resemblances, which things exist without the mind in an unthinking substance. I answer, an idea can be like nothing but an idea; a colour or figure can be like nothing but another colour or figure. If we look but ever so little into our thoughts, we shall find it impossible for us to conceive a likeness except only between our ideas.

Hylas also puts forward a similar view in the *Three Dialogues*, maintaining that 'real things or external objects [are] perceived by the mediation of ideas, which are their images and representations' (DHP, 1.203). The first thing to note is that Berkeley presents his opponents (materialists who accept a representationalist epistemology) as holding the view that even if our ideas are the only things we immediately perceive – a claim which Berkeley takes himself to have established in the preceding sections – those ideas might simply be 'copies or resemblances' or 'pictures or representations' of qualities inhering in unthinking, material substances. The second thing to note is that Berkeley takes it that he can refute this position simply by emphasising that ideas can *only* resemble other ideas. Berkeley does not consider any other way in which an idea might *represent* its object beyond resemblance. While this might not be surprising in light of the view expressed in MI §12, it would be likely to surprise those of his opponents who held that the relation between ideas and material things is a *causal* one. As Jonathan Hill puts it:

> [Berkeley] does not ever seem to consider the possibility that there might be material substances that do not resemble the objects of direct perception [i.e. ideas] at all, but which nonetheless cause them. (Hill, 2011, p. 49)

It is also important to note that the kind of 'representationalists' that Berkeley is primarily concerned with also accept the 'resemblance thesis'. Ideas, according to Berkeley's opponents, are 'representations' of 'real things' which Berkeley takes to be synonymous with saying they are 'copies', 'images', or 'pictures' of those things (PHK, §8; DHP, 1.203). It is clear, then, that according to Berkeley's reading of his opponents, ideas *represent* by means of *resemblance.* In Philonous' words, according to representationalists,

Manuel Fasko and Peter West

material objects are 'represented or painted forth' by ideas in our minds (DHP, 1.206).[15]

John Carriero argues Berkeley's treatment of the relation between representation and resemblance is drawn from Medieval, Aristotelian accounts of sensible knowledge (Carriero, 2003). The Aristotelian view, broadly speaking, is that likeness is key to knowledge of the sensible world: 'species' that come to exist in the mind resemble what exists, and we get to know about what exists thanks to that resemblance relation. Berkeley's aim, on Carriero's reading, is to emphasise that without resemblance it is very difficult to consistently maintain we get to know what the world is really like. This is largely consistent with Kenneth Winkler's explanation of Berkeley's acceptance of the resemblance thesis. Without identifying any specific roots in scholastic thought, Winkler nonetheless focuses on establishing, for Berkeley, ideas which represent other objects do so in virtue of being *images* of those objects.[16]

Such readings may help us to understand *what Berkeley's view is*, but they do little to explain Berkeley's treatment of the resemblance thesis in *Principles* §8 and why he (seemingly) did not feel the need to justify it. In that regard, a contextual reading is more helpful. Hill provides such a reading, charting the rise of the resemblance thesis after Descartes – for whom, 'resemblance and causation cannot be separated' – through later Cartesians such as Foucher, Du Hamel, and Malebranche. For all these thinkers, Hill argues, 'The conclusion is evident [...] representation *must* be about resemblance' (Hill, 2011, p. 56). Hill's claim is by taking Berkeley to be a part of this Cartesian tradition, and engaged in these debates, it is possible to explain why he never saw the need to justify his employment of the resemblance thesis.

Our aim is not to refute Hill's account. Nor do we think our explanation of Berkeley's acceptance of the resemblance thesis should displace Hill's. However, we do contend that our reading fills a gap in

[15] This is worth stressing. It was suggested to us by Samuel Rickless that Berkeley might not necessarily be combatting a view whereby ideas *represent* since he often talks about ideas as 'images' or 'resemblances.' However, we hope to have made it clear that Berkeley is tackling the view that ideas *represent* by *resembling* objects. This is also suggested by his claim in PHK §27 that 'an agent [i.e. a mind] cannot be like unto, or represented by, any idea whatsoever.' Here, Berkeley clearly thinks that *if* an idea represented a spirit it would be by means of resembling it.

[16] See Winkler (1989, p. 10). Indeed, Berkeley consistently refers to ideas as 'images' throughout his writings (cf. NB, pp. 706, 818 & 823; NTV, §44; PHK, §§27, pp. 33 & 137; DHP, 3.231).

current literature surrounding this issue. It may well be the case that Berkeley also inherited the resemblance thesis from Cartesian thinkers and as far as he was engaging in their debates there was, thus, no need to explicitly justify its employment. However, as Hill's own discussion shows, even by the time Berkeley was writing, it was far from being a universally accepted axiom and Berkeley did not only engage himself in debates of the Cartesian tradition. Why, then, did Berkeley more generally take himself to be writing in an intellectual climate in which the resemblance thesis could be left unargued for – at least explicitly? Hill's reading offers one explanation as to why Berkeley saw it as unnecessary to defend resemblance in certain contexts. Our claim, however, is that it would be amiss *not* to also consider Berkeley's immediate, local context – in Ireland. We thus work on the reasonable assumption that Berkeley's immediate intellectual context is just as likely to have shaped his philosophical views as the wider context of eighteenth-century Europe. Our cause is strengthened by the fact that, throughout his career, many of Berkeley's philosophical views were explicitly and directly developed as responses to debates amongst Irish thinkers such as John Toland, William Molyneux, and William King.[17] This provides a compelling reason to search for the roots of Berkeley's resemblance thesis in Early Modern Irish philosophy. Thus, in what follows, we argue that Berkeley's acceptance of the resemblance thesis was likely to have been influenced by his engagement with William Molyneux, William King, and, more generally, thinkers in Ireland who were engaged in debates concerning representation and human knowledge of the divine attributes.

2. The Molyneux Problem

The aims of this section are to give an exposition of the Molyneux problem and to establish that the resemblance thesis is at least implicit in the two earliest responses to the problem; those of Molyneux himself and Locke. We thus trace the beginning of the 'man born blind's' journey through Early Modern Irish thought.

Molyneux first proposed the problem to Locke in a letter in 1688. There is no indication that Locke responded to this first letter and

---

[17]   See Fasko & West (forthcoming). We do not discuss Toland in what follows, but there are good reasons to think Berkeley's discussion of language in dialogue VII of *Alciphron* is a response to Toland's *Christianity Not Mysterious*. For more on this see Pearce (2017, pp. 54–56 & 152–157).

Molyneux sent another in 1693. Eventually, the problem was included in Locke's *Essay* from the second edition onwards. There, he quotes a section of Molyneux's letter verbatim, which reads:

> Suppose a man born blind, and now adult, and taught by his touch to distinguish between a cube and a sphere [...] Suppose then the cube and sphere placed on a table, and the blind man to be made to see; query; 'Whether by his sight, before he touched them, he could now distinguish and tell, which is the globe, which the cube?' (*Essay* II.ix.viii)[18]

The problem Molyneux lays out is determining whether such a 'blind man made to see' would, based on his tactile experience of cubes and spheres, be able to tell the difference between a cube and sphere just by looking at them. Molyneux's answer is no. Locke agrees, citing the fact that the blind man made to see has no prior experience of how his visual experiences correspond with his tactile experiences. As he puts it, he has no experience 'that what affects his touch so and so, must affect his sight so and so'. Locke adds to this that those who are not blind are 'beholden to experience, improvement, and acquired notions' (*Essay* II.ix.viii) in their ability to do what the Molyneux man cannot – namely, relate our visual experiences to our tactile ones (and vice versa). The more overt principle that underlies Molyneux and Locke's response to the problem, then, is that one needs to have *experienced the correspondence* between sensations of one kind and sensations of another to know that it exists.

Our contention is that there is an implicit principle at work here; namely, the resemblance thesis. For Molyneux and Locke, it is impossible for the blind man made to see to distinguish between a cube and a sphere by sight alone, because his representational capacities are restricted by likeness. The visual sensations which he begins to perceive as soon as he is 'made to see' do not *represent* anything to him, because they are not *like* anything he knows (up to that point). More specifically, the visual sensations with which he is now bombarded do not resemble any of the tactile sensations with which he has previously been acquainted. Prior to being made to see, cubes and spheres, for the blind man, are shapes that can be discerned by *tactile* sensation alone. In fact, it would be true to say that, for the blind man (before he is made to see), cubes and spheres *just are*

[18] Any reference to Locke's *Essay* in what follows refers to the fourth edition published in 1694. The first iteration of the Molyneux problem can be found in a letter from July 7th 1688 (that Locke never replied to) in Locke (1978, p. 482).

things that are felt – assuming that shapes cannot be heard, smelt, or tasted. Without the 'experience' or 'acquired notion' that cubes and spheres can be *seen* as well as felt, it is just not possible, Molyneux and Locke take it, for the blind man to see cubes and spheres. The visual sensations that the blind man is 'made to see' *represent* nothing to him, prior to the experience that 'what affects his touch so and so, must affect his sight so and so', because they do not *resemble* anything with which he is currently familiar.

In this way, we contend that it is at least *prima facie* plausible that Molyneux and Locke's reactions to the 'blind man made to see' thought experiment were read in this way by subsequent Irish thinkers. This *prima facie* plausibility will suffice for our current purposes. As will become evident, we take it that the proof is in the pudding; by looking at how Molyneux's example came to be employed in subsequent Irish thought it becomes clear that it was taken to be a matter of representation and resemblance. Discussions concerning the relation of representation and resemblance would come to a head in the midst of a defining Irish debate; the issue of divine attributes. In the next section, we focus on William King's contribution to that debate, and argue that his own employment of the 'Molyneux man' indicates that he took it as illustrative of the resemblance thesis.

3. King and Divine Attributes

In this section, we demonstrate that the resemblance thesis plays a crucial role in the account of human knowledge of the divine attributes that William King puts forward in his *Sermon*. We also show that King's own employment of the example of a man born blind ties his own views, regarding representation and resemblance, to those of Molyneux and Locke. In this way, we begin to chart the progression of the resemblance thesis in Irish thought and the increasingly important role that the man born blind plays.

Despite the fact that the significance of William King in Irish history tends to go underappreciated, his influence within the context of Irish thought was quite significant.[19] He was not only the Archbishop of Dublin (1703-1729) and personally acquainted with both Molyneux and Peter Browne (Berkeley's provost at Trinity College), he was also a member of the *Dublin Philosophical*

---

[19] See Fauske (2011, pp. 1–10 & 173–184). For more on this and King's position on the problem of free will, see Pearce (2019).

Society which Molyneux founded in 1683.[20] However, it is King's influence on Berkeley that is most significant for our current purposes. On March 1st, 1710, Berkeley wrote to his friend Percival about his *New Theory of Vision*, explaining that he has made some adjustments in light of King's (harsh) criticisms. He writes:

> I met with some who supporting themselves on the authority of Archbishop of Dublin's [i.e. King] sermon concerning the prescience of God, denied there was any more wisdom, goodness or understanding in God than there were feet or hands, but that all are to be taken in a figurative sense; whereupon I consulted the sermon and to my surprise found his Grace asserting that strange doctrine. (Letter 12 [8], 35, [31f.])[21]

While a consideration of the extent of King's influence on the early development of Berkeley's thought is beyond the scope of the present paper, the analysis of the sermon Berkeley mentions in the second part of the quote is important.

In his sermon on *Divine Predestination and Fore-knowledge, consistent with the Freedom of Man's Will*, King was concerned to defend the 'Doctrine of Predestination' (King, 1709, §1) against its apparent inconsistency with the 'contingency of events' (King, 1709, §6). While King agrees that humans could not consistently possess both infallible foreknowledge and free will, he thinks this inconsistency does not arise in the case of the divine. This is explained by the fundamentally different nature of God and the divine attributes compared to our own:

---

[20]   There is evidence that King was a member from of the DPS as early as October 1683 (Hoppen 1970, p. 43). Thus, it is very likely he was one of the 'divers very ingenious men' Molyneux claims to have discussed the problem with (Locke, 1978, p. 482). By the time Berkeley presented his *On Infinites* (1707), King was the DPS' vice-president. In 1707 the DPS was re-founded by Berkeley's confidant Samuel Molyneux (1689–1729), son of William, who at the same time helped to ensure his father's correspondence with Locke, including the letter that prompted Locke to include Molyneux's problem in the *Essay* in 1693, were published (see *Some Familiar Letters between Mr Locke and Several of his Friends* appeared in 1708). For more on the chequered history of the DPS, see Hoppen (1970). For more on the personal relationship of King and Browne, see (Winnett, 1974, pp. 4–6 & 29–36; Fauske, 2011, pp. 114–15).

[21]   Page numbering in square bracket from *Works* VIII and the other from Hight (2013).

The Irish Context of Berkeley's 'Resemblance Thesis'

[I]t is in effect agreed on all hands, that the Nature of God, as it is in it self, is incomprehensible by human Understanding; and not only his Nature, but likewise his Powers and Faculties, and the ways and methods in which he exercises them, are so far beyond our reach, that we are utterly incapable of framing exact and adequate Notions of them. (King, 1709, §3)

According to King virtually everyone agrees that the divine nature and attributes are incomprehensible for humans and hence that we have no proper notion of them. It is in this context that the man born blind makes it first appearance in the sermon:

And if God's Foreknowledge and Predetermination were of the same nature with ours, the same Inconsistency would be justly infer'd. But I have already show'd that they are not of the same kind, and [...] that they are quite of another nature, and that we have no proper Notion of them, any more than a Man born blind has of Sight and Colours; and therefore that we ought no more to pretend to determine what is consistent or not consistent with them, than a blind Man ought to determine, from what he hears or feels, to what Objects the Sense of Seeing reaches. (King, 1709, §7)

King uses the man born blind to illustrate his point that we have no proper notion of God and his attributes. This, in turn, is supposed to solve the apparent inconsistency. King's solution is, simply put, that it only *seems* like an inconsistency to us because we have only inadequate knowledge of the divine attributes (King, 1709, §30). As King sees it, just as a man born blind has no adequate notion of light and colours, *we* have no adequate notion of divine foreknowledge. Thus, we are in no better a position to give an accurate account of divine foreknowledge than a blind man is to give an accurate account of the nature of light and colours.

Admittedly, some of the details of King's description of a man born blind differ from Molyneux's original example (for example, King's blind man is not, at first, made to see). However, upon closer inspection it is clear these differences are superficial, and that King's use of the man born blind is more than a mere verbal coincidence. For example, King takes up what seems like a reversed version of the Molyneux problem when he denies the blind man could infer from tactile perceptions anything about what visual perceptions would be like. Moreover, King *does* draw a comparison with a blind man made to see several sections later. In §12, he explains that our knowledge of the divine attributes is, *at first*, equal to the blind

Manuel Fasko and Peter West

man's knowledge of light and colours. However, our prospects with regard to God's attributes are more promising than a blind man's with regard to light and colours because we can hope to attain knowledge of the divine attributes in the next life (King, 1709, §12).

So far, we have shown that King employs Molyneux's example of the man born blind in relation to his account of our knowledge of divine attributes. This is not enough in itself to establish that King accepts the resemblance thesis. However, that this is indeed the case becomes clear if we consider his account of representation. Shortly after introducing the 'man born blind' in §7, King points out that

> when we would help a Man to some Conception of any thing, that has not fallen within the reach of his Senses we do it by comparing it to something that already has, by offering him some Similitude, Resemblance or Analogy, to help his Conception. (King, 1709, §8)

In what follows, King illustrates this point by using the example of a map which, he argues, is a representation of the depicted country, in just the same way as our attributes are representations of the divine. As King points out, a map may represent the depicted country – a three-dimensional assembly of mountains, rivers and so on – despite being a two-dimensional sheet of paper. He explains that no one in their right mind would assume that countries are made of paper or that '*China* is no bigger than a Sheet of Paper, because the Map, that represents it [is]' (ibid., §8). King argues that there need only be a 'faint resemblance' or a 'little likeness", as he later puts it, between two things in order for one to represent the other. Note, however, he thinks that such a resemblance must exist. In general, King thinks the resemblance between 'Similitudes and Representations' and what they represent

> lies not in the Nature of them, but in some particular Effect or Circumstance that is in some measure common to both; we must acknowledge it very unreasonable to expect, that they should answer one another in all things. (King, 1709, §8)

For our purposes, it is not important to discern exactly what King means by 'particular Effect or Circumstance'. What is important is that §8 clearly shows that King accepts the resemblance thesis. This should be clear from the fact that King advocates two claims. Firstly, when we wish to provide someone with a conception of that with which they are not acquainted, we use a *resemblance* or similitude of that thing. Secondly, a map's ability to represent is determined by the resemblance (however faint) it bears to a particular country.[22]

What's more, we are now in a position to appreciate that King's treatment of the man born blind is grounded in his acceptance of the resemblance thesis. According to King, to a man born blind, ideas of light and colours do not fall 'within the reach of his senses'. Thus, we can only attempt to provide a conception of light and colours to him by virtue of weak representations thereof. However, as King explains, these will inevitably be 'imperfect Representations' (King, 1709, §12). Like a map and the country it represents, there is no likeness *in nature* between sensations of light and colour and the notions of them had by a man born blind. The best that can be hoped for is similarity in 'Effect and Circumstance'. What we have seen, then, is that King develops an account of knowledge of divine attributes grounded on the assumption that representation requires resemblance. Moreover, King uses the example of the blind man made to see to elucidate that account. In the next section, we demonstrate that despite challenging King's account, Berkeley likewise accepts the resemblance thesis and similarly draws on Molyneux's example.

4. The Resemblance Thesis in Berkeley

4.1 Divine attributes

In this section, we consider the influence of both Molyneux's man born blind and King's use of it in the context of knowledge of the divine attributes on Berkeley's own views. In this way, we trace the roots of the resemblance thesis in Berkeley's engagement with these

---

[22] For this King was heavily criticized by Anthony Collins. In his *Vindication of the Divine Attributes* (1710) Collins argues the marks on a map do not solely represent by resemblance (i.e. like an image) but in the same way words do (pp. 23–24). For example, a blue line cannot represent water (the way an image would do) and for that reason cannot give someone previously unacquainted with it an idea of water. However, it can represent the turning and bending of the river. While Collins does not explicitly say so, it seems obvious that this is due to the resemblance it can bear to it. Most tellingly for our purpose, Collins does not attack the resemblance thesis. Rather, it underlies his own argument. Hence, there is another protagonist in Berkeley's immediate intellectual environment who Berkeley deemed important and who seems to accept the resemblance thesis (see (Letter 38 [27], 79 [58]; TVV §6, *Siris* § 354)).

Manuel Fasko and Peter West

two discussions which shaped the Irish intellectual milieu in Berkeley's time.

Although the previously quoted letter to Percival confirms Berkeley's early interest in the problem of divine attributes, Berkeley waited until the first publication of *Alciphron* (1732) to comment on it publicly and explicitly. In §§16–22 of the fourth dialogue Berkeley argues that the difference between divine and human attributes is one of degrees rather than one in nature. As one of his spokespersons Crito puts it:

> But for your part, Alciphron, you have been fully convinced that God is a thinking intelligent being, in the same sense with other spirits, though not in the same imperfect manner or degree. (Alc. 4.22, p. 171)

Berkeley's use of the phrase 'the same sense' is important here, and indicates that, as he sees it, when we refer to either ourselves or God as 'thinking intelligent being[s]' we are doing so univocally which, in turn, is possible because the attributes are of the same nature. This is confirmed by several remarks in his earlier works. For example, in the *Three Dialogues,* he argues we can represent the nature of God to ourselves, via the immediate knowledge we have of our own minds (DHP, 3.231).[23] As Berkeley's spokesperson Philonous in the *Three Dialogues* explains:

> my soul may be said to furnish me with an idea, that is, an image, or likeness of God, though indeed extremely inadequate. For all the notion I have of God, is obtained by reflecting on my own soul heightening its powers, and removing its imperfections. I have therefore, though not an inactive idea, yet in my self some sort of an active thinking image of the Deity. (DHP, 3.231–232).

Although Berkeley admits that it is to take the word idea 'in a large sense' when we understand our soul as an image of God (an infinite mind), the crucial point for our purposes is twofold. Firstly, this procedure only makes sense if human and divine attributes are of the same nature.[24]

---

[23]   Berkeley thus agrees with King that we can only gain knowledge of God 'by resembling him with something we do know and are acquainted with' (King, §8). The difference is that Berkeley, unlike King, thinks the knowledge we have of our own spirit can play this role. For more on Berkeley's position, its historical context, and a recent overview on the secondary literature, see Fasko (2018).

[24]   This line of thought is also applied to other finite minds in PHK §140. See Pearce (2018, pp. 186–88).

The Irish Context of Berkeley's 'Resemblance Thesis'

In other words, this only makes sense if Berkeley is using the term 'mind' or 'spirit' univocally as applied to God *and* ourselves.[25] Secondly, the procedure only makes sense if it is a case of representation in a *strict sense* – i.e. if it is not a case of signification. Yet, this does not entail that the *resemblance* relation is *exactly the same* as when ideas are concerned. Otherwise, Berkeley would not stress that we cannot 'represent' God or any other (finite) minds by ideas (DHP, 3.231).[26] However, it is equally evident that Berkeley thought that minds (finite or infinite) are alike. Berkeley explicitly connects the notions of 'likeness' and 'image' in relation to our knowledge of God.[27] In other words, the kinds of things as well as their likeness may be of a different kind when it comes to minds and ideas. Nonetheless, in each case representation requires resemblance and hence both are instances of representation in a *strict sense*.

In short, Berkeley, like King, accepts the resemblance thesis and brings it to bear on the problem of divine attributes. Berkeley agrees with King that human attributes can be considered as 'representations' of their divine counterparts *precisely because* there is some resemblance between them. However, while the two authors agree about the mechanism of representation, they fundamentally disagree about the nature of this resemblance. King does not distinguish between representation as instantiated in ideas and minds respectively the way Berkeley does. Moreover, he argues the 'faint resemblance' between God's attributes and our own is not grounded in a shared nature but in 'circumstances and effects' (King, 1709, §8). Berkeley, however, is happy to accept that God and finite spirits are similar in nature. He takes this to provide him with firmer foundation on which to argue that there is a relation of representation between the two. In fact, he claims to have rejected King's account for precisely this reason – viz., according to Berkeley, King's position does not allow us to prove the existence of (a wise and benevolent) God

---

[25]   This is confirmed by the fact that he repeatedly highlights 'finiteness' as the key difference between humans and the divine, both of which he calls minds (e.g. PHK, Intro, §2; PHK, §§33&117; DHP, 2.219 & 3.236; Alc., 4.21). That Berkeley takes human and divine spirits to be of the same nature is also confirmed in the aforementioned letter to Percival (Letter 12 [8], 36, [32]).

[26]   The reason for this impossibility is that minds are unlike ideas which is explicitly stated in PHK §25. There, Berkeley writes (with reference to §8 and the likeness principle) that an idea cannot be the 'resemblance or pattern of any active being' (i.e. of a mind) (see also PHK, §139).

[27]   Again, this line of thought is applied to other finite minds in (PHK, §140). For more on the connection between images and likeness, see (DHP, 1.203, 1.205 & 3.246).

Manuel Fasko and Peter West

(Letter 12 [8], 36, [32]; Alc., 4.17–18, pp. 163–66).[28] Thus, Berkeley's approach constitutes a robust denial of King's account of our knowledge of the divine attributes.

It is therefore safe to assume when Berkeley refers to a 'man born blind' in the conclusion of §21, it is again more than a mere verbal coincidence:

> This doctrine, therefore, of analogical perfections in God, or our knowing God by analogy, seems very much misunderstood and misapplied by those who would infer from thence that we cannot frame any direct or proper notion, though never so inadequate, of knowledge or wisdom, as they are in the Deity; or understand any more of them than one born blind can of light and colours. (Alc., 4.21, p. 171)

The conclusion of §21 certainly looks like a thinly veiled criticism of King. Contrary to King (1709, §12) Berkeley thinks we have a better notion of the divine attributes than someone born blind can have of light and colours. The disagreement between King and Berkeley, therefore, lies in the nature of, and extent to which, divine attributes *resemble* our own. However, neither contests that in order for us to represent to ourselves the divine attributes we need to be acquainted with something *like* them.

Berkeley's usage of the man born blind clearly illustrates how his solution differs from King's. Moreover, it is evidence of his engagement with his immediate intellectual milieu in Ireland in which, we have argued, the resemblance thesis was widely accepted. This engagement becomes more explicit in Berkeley's optical writings (the *New Theory* and *Theory of Vision Vindicated and Explained*) where the 'man born blind' resurfaces and plays a crucial role in his argument for the heterogeneity of the objects of vision and touch.

4.2 The heterogeneity thesis

Our final aim is to demonstrate that in discussions concerning Berkeley's acceptance of the resemblance thesis, we ought to broaden

[28] Note also §17 where Berkeley writes: 'Suppose, for instance, a man should object that future contingencies were inconsistent with the foreknowledge of God' (Alc., 4.17, p. 164). While this was not King's position it is the problem his sermon deals with (e.g. King, 1710, §§7&11). That Berkeley *does* attack King in the fourth dialogue is widely accepted in the secondary literature, see O'Higgins (1976, pp. 93–94); Berman (1976, p. 23); Pearce (2018, pp. 177–80).

the scope beyond just the argument in §8 of the *Principles*. We have already demonstrated Berkeley's account of human knowledge of the divine attributes, developed in response to King's own account, is grounded upon the assumption that representation requires resemblance. In this section, our aim is to show that the resemblance thesis is also central to Berkeley's argument for the heterogeneity of visible and tangible objects in the *New Theory of Vision* (NTV) – despite the resembling things (i.e. ideas) being radically different than in the case of the divine attributes. Furthermore, Berkeley's frequent employment of Molyneux's example of a man born blind demonstrates that he is once again drawing on issues that have arisen in debates amongst Irish thinkers such as Molyneux and King in developing this argument.

Berkeley sets out with two aims in the *New Theory*, the second of which is to 'consider the difference there is betwixt ideas of sight and touch, and whether there be any idea common to both senses' (NTV, §1).[29] Ultimately, his answer is a negative one; there are no ideas common to both senses. Berkeley's claim, which he establishes over the course of the text, is that the constant connection that we perceive between certain visual experiences (e.g. seeing shapes with corners) and certain tangible experiences (e.g. the feeling of sharpness) is only a 'habitual connexion that experience has made us to observe between them' (NTV, §147). What is significant, for our current purposes, is that Berkeley frequently employs the man born blind example in order to illustrate the impossibility, as he sees it, of objects that are common to both senses.[30]

In §132, Berkeley explains that his conclusion is confirmed by 'the solution', as he puts it, 'of Mr. Molyneux's problem'. Berkeley is

---

[29]   The first aim is to 'show the manner wherein we perceive by sight the distance, magnitude, and situation of objects.' (NTV, §1) Only the second is relevant to our current concerns. For an insightful discussion of NTV in general and the heterogeneity thesis in particular, see Atherton (2020, chap. 2) and Atherton (1990, chap. 10).

[30]   For the sake of brevity, we will focus on NTV. Yet, Berkeley also uses the example repeatedly in *Theory of Vision Vindicated* (TVV, §§44–45&51). Most notably Berkeley concludes the book by quoting from a report of William Cheselden about an actual man born blind made to see which he thinks shows 'by fact and experiment, those points of the theory which seem the most remote from common apprehension were not a little confirmed, many years after I had been led into the discovery of them by reasoning' (TVV, §71). See William Cheselden (1728, VII) 'An account of some observations made by a young gentleman, who was born blind, or lost his sight so early, that he had no remembrance of ever having seen, and was couch'd between 13 and 14 Years of age'.

clearly convinced by Molyneux's and Locke's negative response to the question of whether a blind man made to see could differentiate between a cube and a sphere by sight. With that in mind, he explains,

> if a square surface perceived by touch be of the same sort with a square surface perceived by sight, it is certain the blind man here mentioned might know a square surface as soon as he saw it. (NTV, §133)

For, if a tangible square and a visible square were of the 'same sort', presenting the (no longer) blind man with a cube would simply be 'introducing into his mind by a new inlet an idea he has already been well acquainted with'. We are left with a dilemma, although not a very difficult one to get out of. Berkeley claims; either we allow that 'visible extension and figures are specifically distinct from tangible extension and figures, or else that the solution of this problem given by those two thoughtful and ingenious men is wrong' – the latter option is never seriously entertained. It is clear from this instance that Berkeley places considerable weight on the response to the problem provided by Molyneux and Locke.

In this way, Berkeley uses the 'root metaphor' of Early Modern Irish philosophy to confirm his conclusion that the object of sight and touch are entirely heterogeneous. The heterogeneity of tangible and visible objects, Berkeley goes on to explain, has important ramifications regarding the nature of representation. For example, he considers the potential objection that, since tangible squares are 'liker' (i.e. more similar) to visible squares in virtue of having 'four angles and as many sides', it follows that they *are* 'of their own nature fitted to represent them, as being the same sort' (NTV, §141). In response, Berkeley explains:

> I answer, it must be acknowledged the visible square is fitter than the visible circle to represent the tangible square, but then it is not because it is liker or more of a species with it, but because the visible square contains in it several distinct parts, whereby to mark the several distinct corresponding parts of a tangible square, whereas the visible circle does not. (NTV, §142)

His point is that, in this case, the term 'represent' can only be used loosely in reference to an *arbitrary* relation; that is, one grounded on experience and custom. *Only once it is agreed* that a particular visible idea 'represents' a particular tangible idea in this way, can it be said of certain visual ideas that they are 'fitter' to stand for certain tangible ideas. However, this is not a case of representation in a *strict sense*, for it is not grounded in any relation of, what

The Irish Context of Berkeley's 'Resemblance Thesis'

Berkeley later calls, 'likeness or identity of nature' (NTV, §147). The relation between the ideas of sight and touch is, then, not one of re-presentation (in a *strict sense*) but of signification.[31]

One reason for this is that by perceiving a certain visible shape (say, a visible square) one is not automatically imparted with a *conception* of the corresponding tangible shape (a tangible square). Berkeley goes on to confirm this by once again drawing on the example of a blind man. If a blind man were warned by a sighted person that he had come to 'the brink of a precipice', then he would justifiably be surprised by this apparent foreknowledge.[32] As Berkeley puts it,

> He cannot *conceive* how it is possible for mortals to frame such predictions as these, which to him would seem as strange and unaccountable as prophesy does to others. (NTV, §148, our emphasis)

Berkeley's claim is the blind man cannot possibly conceive, or represent to himself, how this ability, of seeing what is ahead of oneself, could work. For he has neither prior experience of such an

---

[31] Hence, the conclusion that vision is the language of God in the same passage (NTV, §147). For this see also (PHK, §43; TVV, §§38–40; Alc., 4.10–12). See Fields (2018) for a discussion of the relation between Berkeley's employment of the Molyneux man and his argument for the divine language thesis.

It is important to note that this distinguishes Berkeley's point here from his qualifications of 'represent' in the case of other minds. It obvious from the context that Berkeley uses *represent* here synonymously with *signify* see Winkler (1989, p. 138). In §143 it is evident that 'fitter' refers to properties of visible ideas considered as signs. Visual ideas are signs for tactile ideas the same way written letters are signs for sounds. Once *a* is assigned to signify a certain sound it is fitter to represent spoken words containing this sound. Yet, Berkeley thinks no one would claim that *a* in virtue of its nature was fitter to 'represent' (Berkeley actually means 'signify' here) this sound rather than *b*. The relation *seems* to be non-arbitrary but that is simply because we have been repeatedly exposed to the correspondence of sign and thing signified (NTV, §51). The same holds for visual ideas and tangible figures. God designed the world in such a way that visible ideas are signs for tactile ideas and God assigned certain visible figures to signify certain tactile figures by giving them a corresponding number of parts. However, neither the parts nor their combination are of the same nature and hence there is no resemblance between them. We want to thank Margaret Atherton for her help with this difficult passage and Clare Moriarty and Ville Paukkonen for pressing us on the question of Berkeley's use of the term 'fitter'.

[32] See also (Alc., 4.15, p. 161) where Berkeley is making a similar point by supposing a 'nation of men blind from their infancy'.

Manuel Fasko and Peter West

ability nor any ideas, conceptions, or experiences that are of the same nature or kind. The blind man's ability to represent the world to himself, Berkeley argues, is restricted by what he has experienced it to be *like*. Moreover, this is precisely the point he is making in Alc. 4.21 which can be understood as him saying that our notion of the divine may be inaccurate but not inexistent because light and colours are the proper objects of sight (PHK, §46; Alc., 4.10) and in virtue of lacking the ability to see and the heterogeneity of ideas, there is nothing the blind man could use to represent them to himself. In Berkeley's own words: 'a blind man, when first made to see, [...] would neither perceive nor imagine any resemblance or connexion between these visible objects [i.e. light and colours] and those perceived by feeling [i.e. distance]' (TVV, §44).

Conclusion

We set out to explain Berkeley's acceptance of the resemblance thesis by placing his views concerning representation and resemblance in the context of debates that were happening in his immediate intellectual environment in Dublin and Ireland. Thus, we outlined the Irish roots of a principle which plays a crucial role in Berkeley's argument against representationalist epistemology in §8 of the *Principles*. We did so on the basis that if a contextual explanation is available, then before looking to the Cartesian or Aristotelian traditions, we ought to consider Berkeley's immediate intellectual context in Ireland. We then charted the progress of the resemblance thesis through Molyneux, King, and Berkeley's own active engagement in debates that shaped this Irish intellectual milieu. Molyneux's example of the blind man made to see, we argued, brought to the surface the notion that in order to conceive of an object one must already be familiar with something that *resembles* that object. We then suggested that the example of a 'man born blind' was employed by both King and Berkeley in their respective accounts of human knowledge of the divine attributes. While King and Berkeley disagree over the extent to which humans can be said to have knowledge of the divine attributes, neither contests the fact that this knowledge must be grounded on a relation of resemblance. Finally, we argued Berkeley's acceptance of the resemblance thesis plays a key role in his argument for the heterogeneity of the objects of sight and touch. It became evident that while things represented are of a different kind in each instance, in both cases, their representational relation requires resemblance, i.e. that these are cases of representation in a

28

strict sense. In this way, we demonstrated that the resemblance thesis, while often implicit, can be identified in some of the most immediate and earliest influences on Berkeley's thought as well as important discussions within his work which, at first sight, may not seem connected. Thus, without ruling out alternative explanations, we conclude that Berkeley's acceptance of the resemblance thesis is rooted, primarily, in Irish thought.[33]

University of Zurich
manuel.fasko@philos.uzh.ch
Trinity College Dublin
westp@tcd.ie

References

Margaret Atherton, *Berkeley's Revolution in Vision* (Itaca and London: Cornell University Press, 1990).

Margaret Atherton, *Berkeley* (Hoboken NJ and Chichester: Wiley-Blackwell, 2020).

George Berkeley, *The Works of George Berkeley, Bishop of Cloyne* (London: Nelson, 1948–1957).

David Berman, 'Introduction' in: D. Berman and A. Carpenter, *Archbishop King's Sermon on Predestination* (Dublin: Cadenus Press, 1976).

David Berman, *Berkeley and Irish Philosophy* (London and New York: Continuum, 2005).

John Carriero, 'Berkeley, Resemblance, and Sensible Things', *Philosophical Topics*, 31.1/2 (2003), 21–46.

William Cheselden, *Philosophical Transactions of the Royal Society of London* 35.402 (1728), 447–50.

Phillip Cummins 'Berkeley's likeness principle', *Journal of the History of Philosophy* 4.1 (1966), 63–69.

---

[33] Thanks to the editors Kenneth Pearce and Takaharu Oda for their helpful comments. Moreover, we appreciated the instructive feedback and criticism of the participants at the *Irish Philosophy in the Age of Berkeley* conference held at Trinity College Dublin – especially Lisa Downing, Marc Hight, Clare Moriarty, Ville Paukkonen, Sam Rickless, and Tom Stoneham. Thanks also to Margaret Atherton and Todd DeRose for their thoughts on earlier drafts of this paper.

Manuel Fasko's research on this chapter was carried out in the context of his funding by the Swiss Science Foundation for which he extends his sincere gratitude.

Stephen H. Daniel, 'Berkeley's Semantic Treatment of Representation', *History of Philosophy Quarterly* 25.1 (2008), 41–55.

Georges Dicker, 'An Idea Can Be like Nothing but an Idea', *History of Philosophy Quarterly*, 2.1 (1985), 39–52.

Georges Dicker, *Berkeley's idealism: a critical examination* (Oxford: Oxford University Press, 2011).

Manuel Fasko, 'A Scotist Nonetheless? George Berkeley, Cajetan, and the Problem of Divine Attributes', *Ruch Filozoficzny* 74.4 (2018), 33–50.

Manuel Fasko & Peter West 'Molyneux's Question: The Irish Debates', in Gabriele Ferretti & Brian Glenney (eds.) *Molyneux's Question* (Routledge: London [forthcoming]).

Christopher A. Fauske, *A Political Biography of William King* (London and New York: Routledge, 2011).

Keota Fields, 'Berkeley's Semiotic Idealism' in *Berkeley's Three Dialogues: New Essays*, Stefan Storrie (ed.) (Oxford: Oxford University Press, 2018), 63–84.

Melissa Frankel, 'Berkeley on the "Twofold state of things"', *International Journal for Philosophy of Religion*, 80.1 (2016), 48–53.

Marc A. Hight, *The Correspondence of George Berkeley* (Cambridge: Cambridge University Press, 2013).

Jonathan Hill, 'Berkeley's Missing Argument: The Sceptical Attack on Intentionality', *British Journal for the History of Philosophy*, 19.1 (2011), 47–77.

Theodore K. Hoppen. *The Common Scientist of the Seventeenth Century: A Study of the Dublin Philosophical Society, 1683–1708* (London: Routledge & Kegan Paul, 1970).

Darrell Jones, 'The Molyneux Problem and Irish Enlightenment', in: Moyra Haslett, *Irish Literature in Transition vol. I 1700–1780* (Cambridge: Cambridge University Press, 2020), 110–28.

John Locke, *The Correspondence of John Locke*, ed. E. S. De Beer, 8 vols. (Oxford: Clarendon Press, 1976–89), vol. 3 (1978).

James O'Higgins, 'Browne and King, Collins and Berkeley: Agnosticism or Anthropomorphism?', *The Journal of Theological Studies* (1976).

Kenneth L. Pearce, *Language and the Structure of Berkeley's World* (Oxford and New York: Oxford University Press, 2017).

Kenneth L. Pearce, 'Matter, God, And Nonsense', in: Stefan Storrie, *Berkeley's Three Dialogues: New Essays* (Oxford: Oxford University Press, 2018), 176–90.

Kenneth L. Pearce, 'William King on Free Will', *Philosopher's Imprint* (19) 2019, 1–15.

The Irish Context of Berkeley's 'Resemblance Thesis'

Todd Ryan, 'A new account of Berkeley's likeness principle', *British Journal for the History of Philosophy*, 14.4 (2006), 561–80.

Katia Saporiti, *Die Wirklichkeit der Dinge* (Frankfurt a. M.: Vittorio Klostermann, 2006), 102–109.

Peter West, 'Berkeley on the Relation Between Abstract Ideas and Language in Alciphron VII', *Ruch Filozoficzny* 74.4 (2018), 51–70.

Kenneth P. Winkler, *Berkeley: An Interpretation* (1989).

Kenneth P. Winkler, 'Berkeley's Doctrine of Signs', in: Winkler, Kenneth P., *The Cambridge Companion to Berkeley* (Cambridge and New York: Cambridge University Press, 2005).

Arthur R. Winnett, *Peter Browne, Provost, Bishop, Metaphysician* (London: SPCK, 1974).

Does Berkeley's Immaterialism Support Toland's Spinozism? The Posidonian Argument and the Eleventh Objection

ERIC SCHLIESSER

Abstract
This paper argues that a debate between Toland and Clarke is the intellectual context to help understand the motive behind the critic and the significance of Berkeley's response to the critic in PHK 60-66. These, in turn, are responding to Boyle's adaptation of a neglected design argument by Cicero. The paper shows that there is an intimate connection between these claims of natural science and a once famous design argument. In particular, that in the early modern period the connection between the scientific revolution and a certain commitment to final causes, and god's design, is more than merely contingent. The details of PHK 60-66 support the idea that the critic is responding to concerns that by echoing features of Toland's argument Berkeley undermines the Newtonian edifice Clarke has constructed.

1 Introduction

In this paper I return to a brief exchange in the 1980s between two influential scholars, Daniel Garber[1] and Margaret Dauer Wilson[2] over the implications of Berkeley's handling of the eleventh objection at *Principles of Human Knowledge* (PHK), 60-66.[3] While the exchange has attracted some modest attention,[4] the import of the question they were debating, namely what exactly is at stake in Berkeley's response to the hypothetical critic in *Principles* 60-66, has eluded full clarification. This hypothetical critic argues that Berkeley's immaterialism makes the hidden parts of nature and the hidden organs of

[1]   See Garber (1982).
[2]   See Wilson (1985/1999). My references are to the page numbers in the 1999 reprint.
[3]   All references to Berkeley are to Luce & Jessop's edition of *The Works of George Berkeley, Bishop of Cloyne*, 9 vols. (London: Thomas Nelson & Sons, 1948–1957). I have used the following abbreviation: *Part I of A Treatise concerning the Principles of Human Knowledge* (*Works*, vol. 2), section x = PHK x.
[4]   See Downing (2005).

doi:10.1017/S1358246120000090   © The Royal Institute of Philosophy and the contributors 2020

Eric Schliesser

plants and animals dispensable:[5] 'why does not an empty case serve as well as another?' (PHK, 60; in context Berkeley is using the clockwork metaphor to talk about nature). The critic worries that the hidden structure of nature and its organisms becomes vacuous. The question I wish to answer is, why care about that?

The main point of my paper is that a debate between Toland and Clarke is the immediate intellectual context to help understand the motive behind the critic and the significance of Berkeley's response to the critic in PHK 60-66. These, in turn, are responding to Boyle's adaptation of a neglected design argument by Cicero.[6] I end up siding with Garber for reasons distinct from his.[7] So, while I do not disagree with the now standard interpretation that this critic expresses 'the rival claims of corpuscularian science' (Atherton 2020, p. 79), I argue that this understates what is at stake. For, the critic does not limit herself to corpuscularian science. For, I show, there is an intimate connection between these claims of natural science[8] and a once famous design argument.

In particular, I show how in the early modern period the connection between the scientific revolution and a certain commitment to final causes, and god's design, is more than merely contingent.[9]

I first briefly discuss PHK 60-66 and the competing interpretations by Garber and Dauer Wilson. I agree with Winkler (1989) and Atherton (2020) that providence seems crucial to the argument, but they fail to explain fully what would have motivated the critic. In the third section, I introduce a neglected design argument presented in a

[5]   See Winkler (1989, p. 265).
[6]   But see Hunter (2009, pp. 235–45); Schliesser, (2017, 281ff). My discussion below deviates a bit from Hunter and my own earlier treatment.
[7]   This way of construing my argument originates a paper given in his honor at Garberfest in September 2014 at Princeton. This paper has benefitted greatly from the audience comments. In addition, the paper was presented at conferences at York (in honor of Catherine Wilson) and Dublin in 2019. I am grateful to comments by learned audiences in all these venues as well as to Daniel Moerner, René Brouwer, and the editors of this volume on earlier drafts.
[8]   Using 'science' without warning is a bit anachronistic. As it happens most of my own use of 'science' involve examples from and discussions about observational, geometric, physical astronomy (which has always been thought a science), so if one wishes one can substitute 'astronomy' or, when appropriate, 'natural philosophy' whenever I use 'science'.
[9]   On the significance of final causes in early modern science, see Osler (1996). My argument explains why this is so.

once prominent place in Cicero and I offer some natural reconstructions of it. In section 4, I show how Boyle used this argument. In section 5 I focus on Toland in order to set up the crucial section on Clarke (section 6), and the way in which the argument figures in a controversy between Clarke and Toland. In section 7, I return to Berkeley and show how the details of PHK 60-66 support the idea that he is responding to concerns that by echoing features of Toland's argument he undermines the Newtonian edifice Clarke has constructed.

2 The Garber-Dauer Wilson Debate

In his 1982 article, Garber concluded that:

> never once in the course of [Berkeley's] lengthy response [to a hypo-thetical critic in PHK 60-66] does he suggest that the objects in question do not really have internal parts. Berkeley takes it for granted that they do and attempts to explain why God may have made things in the way in which he did....there is no suggestion that the mechanisms that Berkeley is talking about are any less real than tables or chairs. The mechanisms that must exist are not presented as fictional, instrumental things, terms in a mathematical theory of nature that have no significance outside of that theory, a status that he explicitly gives forces and attractions...It seems clear that Berkeley meant to include the hidden corpuscular sub-structure of things as well. (Garber, 1982, pp. 182–184)

In Quine-ean terms one may say that on Garber's reading that in Berkeley's philosophy the visible and the indispensable, hidden qual-ities of things have ontological parity.[10] By contrast Margaret Dauer Wilson denies that Berkeley accepts imperceptible or insensible cor-puscles (even if they are ideational) or the reality of hidden mechan-ical structure. For, in the intellectual culture of the mechanical philosophy corpuscles are by definition insensible so there is no reason why he would have to accept these into his ontology.[11]

While both Garber and Wilson draw on many of Berkeley's texts, the underlying debate seems to turn on to what degree Berkeley's re-sponse to his hypothetical critic expresses his own all things

[10]   On the significance of indispensability arguments in Berkeley, see Schliesser (2005, p. 45).
[11]   I pretend here that the claims about hidden corpuscles and hidden mechanisms are on par. But, of course, the latter are not by definition insensible.

considered views (as Garber contends) or accepts premises only for the sake of argument to refute this kind of critic (as Dauer Wilson contends). As Winkler notes PHK 60-66 has 'a complex structure' (1989, p. 265). So, it is no surprise that part of Dauer Wilson's charge against Garber is that he 'overreads' the passage.[12]

In refuting Dauer Wilson's criticism,[13] Winkler usefully points out that the central issue in the response to the hypothetical critics in Principles 60-66 is not one of ontology, but with the complexity hidden behind the visible world – a complexity that seems unnecessary on a natural reading of Berkeley's principles. In Winkler's terms, the critic 'wants the immaterialist to explain why "God should make us, upon a close *inspection* into his works, *behold* so great variety of *ideas*, so artfully laid together"' (Winkler, 1989, p. 268, quoting PHK 64, emphasis in Winkler). Winkler recognizes the real issue here is the question of God's providence (1989, p. 275). But given that Berkeley endorses God's providence, Winkler does not explain why the hypothetical critic could have been worried about the drift of Berkeley's immaterialism. Berkeley reports the objection as, 'how upon our principles, any tolerable account can be given, or any final cause assigned of an innumerable multitude of bodies and machines, framed with the most exquisite art, which in the common philosophy have very apposite uses assigned them, and serve to explain abundance of phenomena?' (PHK, 60). So, the critic is both interested in how on Berkeley's account the diversity of phenomena can be explained and how final causes are assigned. Crucially for my present purposes the critic intimates a tight link between these two tasks in 'the common philosophy'.

In my contribution to the debate, I show that the hypothetical critic expresses a concern that touches on the status of an extremely important and once influential design argument. This argument had been adopted by quite diverse schools of natural philosophy in the period. And while Berkeley's immaterialism also provides support for a

---

[12]   Downing, who sides with Dauer Wilson, concurs but softens it: 'thus I agree with Wilson that Garber overreads PHK 60-6 somewhat.'

[13]   Atherton (2020, p. 81) also sides with Garber, but she thinks the point of Berkeley's 'reformulated...account of the order of nature' is to move 'from a causal account' (associated with the mechanical philosophy) 'into one in terms of signs and signifiers, ideas and their meanings. On such an account, the order of nature is explicitly for us, it is an order that exists through the understanding of creatures and requires, as Berkeley says, the "wisdom and beneficence" of the creator'. I agree with her, but I would emphasize, perhaps, even more than she would the significance of God's wisdom and beneficence to the argument.

distinct design argument, it does seem to undermine the more natural one embraced by the hypothetical critic, who, on my reading stands for the main current of the scientific culture of the age. On my proposed reading then, Berkeley really has no choice but to accept the premises that he needs in order to refute the hypothetical critic.

3 The Posidonian Argument

In this section, I introduce the once famous design argument transmitted, and perhaps invented by Cicero's *On the Nature of the Gods* (composed ca. 45BC).[14] In this section I offer two interpretations of this argument: (1) a prima facie interpretation; (2) a 'neglected' [15] one. In the subsequent section (4) I offer what I call (3) a 'transcendental interpretation', I show that it is very familiar to seventeenth and eighteenth centuries authors.

After discussing other kinds of design arguments, Cicero's Stoic character, Quintius Lucilius Balbus, says,

> But if all the parts of the universe have been so appointed that they could neither be better adapted for use nor be made more beautiful in appearance, we must investigate whether this is chance, or whether the condition of the world is such that it certainly could not cohere unless it were controlled by intelligence of divine providence. If, then, nature's attainments transcend those achieved by human design, and if human skill achieves nothing without the application of reason, we must grant that nature too is not devoid of reason. It can surely not be right to acknowledge as a work of art a statue or a painted picture, or to be convinced from distant observation of a ship's course that its progress is controlled by reason and human skill, or upon examination of the design of a sundial or a water-clock to appreciate that calculation of the time of day is made by skill and not by chance, yet none the less to consider that the universe is devoid of purpose and reason, though it embraces those very skills, and the craftsmen who wield them, and all else beside?
>
> Our friend Posidonius has recently fashioned a planetarium; each time it revolves, it makes the sun, moon, and planets reproduce the movements which they make over a day and a night in

---

[14] On the history of design arguments more generally, see, especially, Hurlbutt (1985), Manson (2003), Del Ratzsch & Jeffrey Koperski (2016).
[15] Inspired by Hunter (2009), op. cit.

Eric Schliesser

the heavens. Suppose someone carried this to Scythia or to Britain. Surely no one in those barbarous regions would doubt that that planetarium had been constructed by a rational process. Yet our opponents [the Epicureans] here profess uncertainty whether the universe, from which all things take their origin, has come into existence by chance or some necessity, or by divine reason and intelligence. Thus, they believe Archimedes more successful in his model of the heavenly revolutions than nature's production of these, even though nature's role is considerably more ingenious than such representations. (*On the Nature of the Gods*, 2.87-88)[16]

There are many arguments from design. Let's dub the main one articulated in the quoted passage by Balbus, the 'Posidonian argument'. It deploys – in David Sedley's felicitous phrase – the 'structural resemblance of state-of-the-art-planetary mechanism to the celestial globe.'[17] For, it relies, to simplify, on the supposition that everybody (even barbarians) will grant that if a sophisticated complex machine, which is a scientific representation of nature, is the product of intelligent design, then (once granted) it turns to suggest that the represented complex (beautiful, well-adapted, etc.) machine must itself also have an intelligent author.[18]

I stipulate that despite the presence of minor variants, we are dealing with the Posidonian argument when (i) a presentation of a design argument is accompanied (as it is in Cicero's text) by (ii) a reference or allusion to Archimedes' planetary sphere; (iii) a reference to Posidonius' portable planetarium (iv) and some uneducated foreigner (ignorant barbarian, savage, etc.).[19] If all four of these are present in

[16]   Cicero, *The Nature of the Gods*, trans. P.G. Walsh Oxford: Oxford University Press, (1978, pp. 78); I have made some minor modifications. For the Latin after Cicero, *De natura deorum* 2 and 3, ed. A.S. Pease Cambridge MA.: Harvard University Press (1958), pp. 763–769.

[17]   See Sedley (2007, p. 207).

[18]   As Sedley notes the represented world need not be itself a mechanism (Sedley, 2007, p. 207).

[19]   According to (Sedley 2007, p. 207, n. 6), Archimedes' sphere is 'likely to be the original Stoic example', and the naming of Posidonius' a 'localizing touch' (Posidonius was one of Cicero's teachers). In addition, see Kidd (1988, pp. 74–75). See also the useful discussion in Berryman (2010, pp. 150–55). Details on Archimedes' sphere can also be gleaned from (among others) Cicero (e.g., Republic 1.21-22; Tusculan Disputations 1.63), Sextus Empiricus, M. 9.115, and Proclus (A Commentary on the First Book of Euclid's Elements, Book I, Chapter XIII). (All available to early modern readers.) For more such references see: http://www.math.nyu.edu/~crorres/Archimedes/Sphere/SphereSources.html.

later texts we can be sure that the (original) source is Cicero. However, as I note below, there are variants of this design argument in which either (ii) or (iii) is dropped or different machines are used as examples. In these cases we may still be dealing with versions of the Posidonian argument (especially if Cicero is mentioned or knowledge of him can be presupposed). Of course, sometimes technical works on planetariums and astronomy (and their history), may note Cicero's mention of Posidonius' or Archimedes' planetarium without intending to offer a design argument (which is why (i) is necessary condition).[20]

Before I offer a modest reconstruction and evaluation of the argument,[21] I note a few features related to (i-iv). Balbus suggests that there are three ordering principles of the universe: chance, necessity, or intelligence.[22] The chance option is historically associated with the epicurean position, an identification that continued in subsequent history through the eighteenth century.[23] Sometimes I treat this option as synonymous with 'brute fact'. Berkeley sometimes uses 'blind chance' (PHK, 93; it's called 'blind' because of the denial of providence and final causes). The necessity option (which also denies final causes), I'll associate with Spinozism. Berkeley calls it 'fatalism' or 'fatal necessity' (PHK, 93). Thanks to Cudworth and Bayle, Strato became the ancient figure associated with the system of necessity in the early modern philosophy.[24] It is not altogether

---

[20] See, for example, this entry of Beeckman's diary in 1629: http://adcs.home.xs4all.nl/beeckman/IIIv/1629vhtml#105, or Huygens' description of his planetarium: http://dbnl.nl/tekst/huyg003oeuv21_01/huyg003oeuv21_01_0110.php?q=Posidonius (Huygens, 1944, p. 588).

[21] For a very careful and illuminating rational reconstruction of Cicero's argument, see Hunter (2009, pp. 235–45). Hunter's aim is to show how Cicero's argument is an instance of a 'non-trivial valid argument leading from the admission that certain artifacts require a designer to the conclusion that certain natural entities, or the natural world as a whole, also require one' (p. 236) Hunter thinks that in Cicero's version the 'reference to Archimedes is a mistake' (p. 239, n. 12), presumably by a scribe. I disagree with Hunter, but for my present argument this does not matter; sometimes early modern readers did bring the Posidonian argument and Archimedes' sphere together.

[22] Notice that I speak of 'ordering principle', because for a Stoic it would be unintelligible to allow that the universe could be caused by nothing. I return to this in the text when I discuss the role of the Principle of Sufficient Reason (PSR) in the argument.

[23] For evidence, see Schliesser (2013).

[24] The systems of Hylozoistic atheism (Cudworth's polemical description of Strato) and divine fate (Stoics) are run together in the wake of the Spinoza controversy. See Brooke (2006, 391ff).

Eric Schliesser

unlikely that the system of necessity was associated with Stoicism itself in Cicero's day.[25] Finally, Balbus asserts that a divine mind is the final option. He clearly associates the products of a divine mind with a providential order. Often I'll simply use, following Berkeley, 'God' or 'the Intelligence that sustains and rules the ordinary course of things' (PHK, 62) to refer to this option. Without explanation, Balbus seems to think that chance, divine mind, and necessity exhaust the genuine possibilities.

If one takes Balbus' exposition at face value,[26] the argument relies on the analogy between the apparent beauty of the well-adapted, manufactured (etc.) machine and the beauty and well-adapted nature of the heavens to infer an intelligence behind the universe.[27] Moreover this argument may be read to rely on a further aesthetic premise, 'nature's attainments transcend those achieved by human design,'[28] and in conjunction with the empirical assertion that human craft produces nothing without reason and art to argue for the existence of a higher excellent intelligence behind nature's

[25] Divine fate works through an open-ended series of causes. While most Stoics insisted they believed in a providential order, it is no surprise that 'According to Epicurus, Letter to Menoeceus, preserved in Diogenes Laertius at 9.133 (LS 20A), the Stoic doctrine of fate would involve an "inexorable necessity"'. Quoted from Brouwer (2019, p. 36). See also Cicero, *De Divinatione* 1.125-126.

[26] For example, Lewis Ezra Hicks, quotes the same passage at length but without comment as an illustration of how Cicero anticipates modern arguments. Without analysis, he treats the argument as relying fundamentally on 'analogy' (Hicks, 1883, p. 64).

[27] Hunter nicely describes the 'logical motor' of 'standard' design arguments as follows: it 'motivates its conclusion with a "how much more so" question' (p. 236). Hunter does not attribute the standard version to the Ciceronian passage under discussion because he wishes to interpret the passage as exemplifying a 'new' argument. But the Ciceronian passage can plausibly be interpreted as articulating both the 'standard' as well as the 'new' arguments (as Hunter admits 'even the "how much more so" comparison of the standard version is not entirely absent' (p. 240)). Nothing hinges on my disagreement with Hunter here.

[28] One need not understand 'excellence' (*perfecta*) in strictly aesthetic terms. One can interpret it in terms of magnitude, size, or power (etc.). But this is not to deny the presence of aesthetic elements in Cicero's argument ('beautiful'). These aesthetic issues, especially in terms of the inhabitants of planets of other solar systems, matter a lot to Clarke and Newton (see the General Scholium to the *Principia*), but for present purposes this can be left aside.

order.[29] I do not foreground the significance of this analogy, but it is not irrelevant (cf. PHK, 106-109).

Posidonius was a famous Stoic philosopher active on Rhodes, where he was almost certainly met by Cicero.[30] It is very likely that Cicero encountered a portable planetarium designed by Posidonius. Neither Cicero nor Balbus explains what the function of the barbarian in the argument is. But I take it that it is meant to be the imagined judgment of untutored (because uncivilized) humanity, that is, a kind of lowest denominator judgment. If the thought experiment does its job – 'even a barbarian will consent to X' – then nobody can object to X. In the context of the Posidonian argument, it seems to entail that if a machine is of sufficient complexity and artificiality everybody will agree it is the product of highly rational design and artifice.[31]

Okay, with that in place, I offer a rational reconstruction of Balbus' argument. My reconstruction is not meant to be exhaustive (again I drop the role of analogy), but I intend for it to capture the gist of the implied argument and for it to be a valid argument.

1. All of nature's parts are ordered; they exhibit apparent design and beauty.
2. Artificial, complex machines are the product of rational design.
3. A planetarium is a complex machine or concrete representation of the heavens.
4. Nature's complexity is greater than the complexity of a planetarium.
5. Posidonius' planetarium is a successful representation of the heavens.
6. Even a barbarian will acknowledge that Posidonius' planetarium is a complex machine (when she is confronted by it)

---

[29] Jantzen (2014) treats Balbus' argument primarily as an argument by analogy. In the argument by analogy, nature (represented by the machine) is also a machine (or machine-like). Jantzen offers two more interpretations of Balbus' argument: in one it is assimilated to another argument for the improbability of order; in the other it is assimilated to a Socratic argument from purpose. Given the structure of Cicero's text it is indeed likely that the argument for the improbability of order is in the background of Balbus' exposition.

[30] Plutarch, (*Life of Cicero*) 4.5. They stayed in touch: for their later correspondence, see Cicero, (*Letters to Atticus*) 2.1.1. I thank René Brouwer.

[31] Presumably Cicero is trying to screen off debates over human artifacts that may seem imperfect in various ways.

7. So, even a barbarian, who correctly accepts premise (2), will acknowledge that Posidonius' planetarium is produced by rational design.
8. Nature's order is caused either by chance, or by necessity, or by a divine mind.
9. Nature's order is not caused by necessity or chance because it is impossible that something less complex can be the product of rational design while the more complex thing (i.e., nature) it represents is not.
10. For if you thought otherwise, then the designer of the less complex concrete model would be superior to the cause of the thing represented by the model (nature). That is, if nature's order has greater complexity than the clock and the clock is a product of design then so is nature's order.
11. Therefore, nature's order is caused by the divine mind's rational design.

Strictly speaking the conclusion does not require premises (2) through (7). But the particular appeal of this argument rests on these premises. The obvious weak spot in the argument is (8); Balbus assumes without argument that (8) is exhaustive. If it is not exhaustive, then the argument is obviously not sound. In addition, I have formulated (8) so as to take the *origin* of *nature* off the table. That's because due to the embrace of a version of the PSR – *ex nihilo nil fit* – for a Stoic, and most ancients,[32] nature must be caused. Obviously when we deal with a later, Christian context, the status of (8) and the acceptance of PSR which it presupposes, needs to be investigated.

The universal quantifier – 'all of nature's parts are ordered' – in premise (1) also seems rather strong.[33] In addition, even if one were

---

[32] Strictly speaking, the Stoics may not have embraced *ex nihilo nihil fit*, but they did embrace various causal principles that clearly rule out uncaused motion and, in some instances, un-caused existence. For very helpful discussion, see Bobzien (1998, section 1.3.3). Given their theology, it seems the question of the origin of cosmic existence does not quite arise in the crisp way it does for Lucretius or Aristotelian thinkers, and later Christians (see Bobzien, 1998, p. 412). Cicero's De *Divinatione* 1.125-126 is worth reading on fate. Cf. Lucretius on his principle at *De Rerum Natura*, 1.149-156. http://www.perseus.tufts.edu/hopper/text?doc=Lucr.+1.150&fromdoc=Perseus%3Atext%3A1999.02.0130, accessed 9 January, 2019. I thank Eric Brown for helpful discussion.

[33] In Newton's general scholium, one of the arguments from design also appeals to it: 'All that diversity of natural things which we find, suited to different times and places.'

to grant that all of nature is beautiful, not everybody will naturally agree with (1) – as Diderot would argue, defective animals (so called 'monsters') are born not infrequently.[34] This suggests that not all individual parts of nature are best adapted for use. How to think about (1) in light of such naturally occurring imperfections is no easy matter. There are ways to account for nearby versions of (1) in which some apparent imperfections turn out to be very beneficial in light of the overall beauty and aptness of the universe.[35] Even so, it is no surprise that modern presentations of so-called deductive, abductive, and inference to the best explanation design arguments tend to require only that 'some things in nature...exhibit exquisite complexity.'[36]

While (1) is characteristic of arguments *from* design, one may well wonder if (1) is really required in Balbus' version of the argument. For one can derive the conclusion (11) without it. That is to say, the real work in this reconstruction of the argument is not being done by the existence of apparent design (1), but by (a) the (partial) morphism between the concrete model and reality and (b) the relational complexity of model and reality (that is, (3), (4),(10)).[37] Versions of the argument that continue to appeal to (1), I'll treat as '*prima facie* versions of the Posidonian argument'. Versions of the Posidonian argument that drop (1), I'll call the 'neglected Posidonian argument'.[38]

Of course, some modern readers may also think that there is something fishy about (9–10). Surely, some artifices are better than their natural counterparts? One can grant that (perhaps easier now in age of precision tools), and still think that (9–10) can survive scrutiny. In fact, I would argue that Balbus' point here is a more subtle.[39] Even the very best concrete models of reality are imperfect because they must leave out or abstract away from some of the intricacy of nature. This point is basically stipulated in (4). This is not to deny that one can imagine successful concrete representations of nature where the concrete model is (say) unnecessarily more complex than nature (e.g., by adding an extra gear); but, leaving aside questions

[34] See Wolfe (2005, pp. 187–204).
[35] Leibniz is fond of such arguments.
[36] See Ratzch & Koperski (2016). Of course, if one is in the grip of the PSR, one may well wonder why it's only some parts that appear as designed.
[37] See Hunter (2009).
[38] In deference to the spirit of Hunter (2009). The details of his reconstruction different from mine.
[39] Again Hunter (2009) has done excellent work on this.

Eric Schliesser

about to what degree such complexity must be functional and efficient, even *that* concrete model will leave out other bits of the machinery of nature or the phenomena it tracks. So, the stipulation (4) can be defended and survive scrutiny.

But that it is stipulated suggests that (9–10) may be dispensable. Here's a thought: premise (3) relies on the idea that the model inherits its features, or at least many of its significant ones, from reality *in virtue* of the effort in representing reality. That is to say, the particular complexity it has may be built by humans, but it is meant to track nature. The particular machine is built by humans, but – and this captures the intuition behind premise (10), the morphism it exhibits with reality is not original in the human designer, but extrinsic to it.[40]

Note that due to technological developments (2) can increasingly seem less plausible, if we insist that it is only humans can build artificial machines. Artificial machines that design and create other artificial machines (can) exist now.[41] It is conceivable, even likely, that in the fullness of time such artificially designed machines by other machines will prompt people, or even the machines themselves, to assert that 'such exquisitely crafted machines could never have been designed by feeble creatures like humans!'[42] Of course, as stated (2) makes no mention of humans (even if the implied referent may well be humans), and, in fact, the argument would work just as well if one were to think, as Paley suggests, of machines or robots engineering other machines.

I offer one final observation on the reconstruction of the prima facie argument. Premise (6) is a bit redundant if you accept premise (3). And premise (7) is redundant if you simply accept premise (2). In both cases a rhetorically arresting thought experiment is used to provide evidence for something one is likely to accept anyway. So, one may consider premises (6–7) dispensable.

So, to sum up the situation so far: the prima facie version of the Posidonian argument, which is an argument from design (and so contains (1)), contains within it – if we drop (1), (6), and (7) – a very clever argument for the existence of God. The 'neglected' Posidonian argument goes like this:

A.   Artificial, complex machines are the product of rational design.

---

[40]   Again, this idea is inspired by Hunter (2009).
[41]   William Paley (1813) considers the possibility of an infinite chains of watches producing watches (Paley, 1813, Chapter 2, paragraph IV).
[42]   The idea was inspired by Dennett (2017).

44

B.   A planetarium is a complex machine or concrete representa-
     tion of the heavens (and the complexity of the planetarium
     that it has in virtue of being a model of nature is derived
     from nature.)
C.   Nature's complexity is greater than the complexity of a
     planetarium.
D.   Posidonius' planetarium is a successful representation of the
     heavens.
E.   Nature's order is caused either by chance, or by necessity, or
     by a divine mind.
F.   Nature's order is not caused by necessity or chance because it
     is impossible that something less complex can be the product
     of rational design while the more complex thing (i.e., nature)
     it represents is not.
G.   Therefore, nature's order is caused by the divine mind's
     rational design.

As Hunter notes, this 'neglected' version of the Posidonian argument
(so without (1)) does not become obsolete through the rise of
Darwinism or, as I have suggested, even robots. That's because it
does not make any explicit claim about the appearance of design in
nature. It's not an argument *from* design, but an argument *to* design.

Of course, there is a reason why this 'neglected' argument is neglected. A-D are dispensable. It's also not obviously sound because
either (E) is incomplete, that is, there may be alternative ways to
explain the origin of nature's complexity or order without a deist
God; or the argument for necessity and/or chance can be made
more robust and seem more explanatory than appeal to a divine
mind. And (F) may be thought begging the question. In the next
section I show that there was widespread familiarity with the
(prima facie version) Posidonian argument in the early modern
period in which the significance of premises (2-5)/(A-D) get
re-conceptualized.

4 Early Modern Posidonian Arguments, especially Boyle

It is well known that Hume's *Dialogues Concerning Natural Religion*
(1776) are modeled on, and often borrow heavily from, Cicero's
On the Nature of the Gods.[43] In fact, most learned readers would

---

[43]   There is a huge literature on this. But see Sessions (2002); Battersby
(1979, pp. 239–52).

Eric Schliesser

have been familiar with the Posidonian argument, because Cicero and *On the Nature of the Gods* continued to be read and quoted approvingly throughout the early modern period.[44] That Berkeley knew his Cicero is exemplified by the fact that he took the very idea of minute philosophers from Cicero as is mentioned on the cover-page and in the first dialogue of *Alciphron*.[45] Another quote from Cicero graces the cover-page of *Passive Obedience*.[46]

On the Nature of the Gods is, in fact, quoted in *An Essay towards preventing the Ruin of Great Britain*.[47] In *Passive Obedience* (Section XIV), Berkeley explicitly quotes one of Balbus' claims from Cicero's *De Nature Deorum*, that man is created to contemplate and imitate nature.

Perhaps more surprising is that Cicero is prominent among works that fit squarely in the modern canon of works at the intersection of philosophy and natural philosophy. More important, even when he is critical, Samuel Clarke calls Cicero 'that great Master' (*A Discourse*, 209) and 'the greatest and best philosopher, that Rome, or perhaps any other nation has ever produced' (*A Discourse*, pp. 292–293).[48] It's not just Cicero's moral philosophy that is read; in drawing on Newton, Clarke quotes approvingly from *On the Nature of the Gods* in his important Boyle lectures (1705), *A Demonstration of the Being and Attributes of God* (e.g. p. 110, where Toland is being mocked, and p. 229, where, as I discuss later, the Posidonian argument is explicitly discussed).

In fact, there were lively, high profile debates in the early modern period over Cicero's true philosophical views in *On the Nature of the Gods* (which anticipate the debates over Hume's views in the Dialogues.) For example, in his response to Collins's notorious (1713) *Discourse on Free Thinking* (which includes an epigraph

[44] For the origin of this in Renaissance thought, see Glacken (1967, pp. 54ff. & 376).
[45] Berkeley, *Alciphron, or The Minute Philosopher in Seven Dialogues* (*Works*, vol. 3).
[46] Berkeley, *Passive Obedience* (*Works*, vol. 1).
[47] See Stuart-Buttle (2019, p. 206). Berkeley, *An Essay towards preventing the Ruin of Great Britain* (*Works*, vol. 6).
[48] I am quoting Samuel Clarke's *A Discourse concerning the Unalterable Obligations of Natural Religion and the Truth and Certainty of the Christian Revelation* from the 1732 edition of *A discourse concerning the being and attributes of God: the obligations of natural religion, and the truth and certainty of the Christian revelation* (London: Knapton). I am using this edition (rather than earlier ones) because in it Clarke's reliance on the authority of Newtonian physics is most pronounced.

from Cicero's *On the Nature of the Gods*),[49] Richard Bentley, who had a much discussed correspondence with Newton and one of the leading classicists of the age, does not merely criticize Collins' arguments and positions, but has a lengthy analysis of how to interpret Cicero properly. (Collins had treated Cicero as a free-thinker).[50] The same strategy, including a motto quoting Cicero, is followed in *The Guardian*'s critical review of Collins's book (published on March 14, 1713) attributed to Berkeley by his son.[51]

But the most famous version of the prima facie Posidonian argument during the early modern period is probably to be found in Boyle. It occurs on a variant of a more familiar argument. First, I quote the familiar argument:

> 'tis like a rare Clock, such as may be that at Strasbourg, where all things are so skilfully contriv'd, that the Engine being once set a Moving, all things proceed according to the Artificers first design, and the Motions of the little Statues, that at such hours perform these or those things, do not require, like those of Puppets, the peculiar interposing of the Artificer, or any Intelligent Agent imployed by him, but perform their functions upon particular occasions, by vertue of the General and Primitive Contrivance of the whole Engine. (*A Free Enquiry*, in *The Works of Robert Boyle*, vol. 10, p. 448)

Boyle uses the world-clock analogy in order to drive home the idea that God's *general* providence works by general and original (this captures the sense of Boyle's 'primitive' in light of the 'first design') causes.[52] It presupposes Boyle's voluntarist treatment of God's agency.[53] Boyle's argument seems familiar to us, educated as we are

---

[49]   For excellent background on Collins' and Toland's interest in Cicero, and the practice of quoting Cicero, see Tarantino (2016, pp. 81–100).
[50]   See Bentley (1734), 'Phileleutherus Lipsiensis' *Remarks on a late Discourse of Freethinking*. I have inspected the seventh edition online (see 246ff): https://books.google.nl/books?id=4HtPAAAAYAAJ&hl=nl&pg=PA246#v=onepage&q=Cicero.
[51]   It is, however, likely penned by Steele. And my argument does not rely upon it.
[52]   To modern eyes it is tempting to read the 'general' causes as laws of nature. But in this passage Boyle could also be relying on the traditional idea that the clock has a real essence (the hidden from sight 'contrivance') from which effects follow in exception-less fashion (such a world would also be amenable to description by laws of nature, of course).
[53]   See Henry (2009) but also Harrison (2002).

Eric Schliesser

to see Darwinism, in part, as a response to Paley's watch.[54] For my present purposes I want to focus on the Strasbourg clock because Boyle uses it elsewhere that reveal his debt to Cicero (or some intermediary source).

For, on the *Usefulness of Natural Philosophy*, Boyle adds two claims to his treatment of the Strasbourg clock:[55] (i) 'the various motions of the wheels and other parts concur to exhibit the phenomena designed by the artificer in the engine...'; (ii) 'and might to a rude Indian seem to be more intelligent than Cunradus Dasypodius himself.' (Essay IV)[56] Here I ignore Boyle's low regard for the intellectual achievements of native Americans. The phenomena exhibited by the (second) Strasbourg clock were primarily astronomical, that is, it was a gigantic, massive planetarium in which heavenly motions and phenomena were faithfully represented.[57] In context, Boyle is explicitly rejecting local final causes (and action at a distance). That Cicero is probably his inspiration is confirmed not just by the great similarities in tropes, but also by the fact a few pages later he explicitly cites *On the Nature of the Gods* (for different purposes).

Boyle's version of the Posidonian argument (astronomical clock, ignorant foreigner) was familiar enough such that Locke would offer his own variant of a discussion of the Strasburg clock (without mention of Boyle) at *Essay* 3.6.3 and 3.6.9 but with 'a gazing countryman' and no Indian. The Essay also has a quote from Cicero's *De Natura Deorum* on its cover. Rather than piling on further examples, I'll treat it as established fact that the prima facie Posidonian argument was widely known in the early modern period.

Now I want to offer a more speculative ascription to the Early Moderns of recognition of a different version of the Posidonian argument. I have been unable to find an explicit statement of it. But it arises rather naturally upon reflection, and it illuminates the debate between Toland and Clarke.

Recall that the 'neglected' version of the Posidonian argument goes like this:

A.   Artificial, complex machines are the product of rational design.

---

[54]   See, for example, Boyle (1991, p. xvi).
[55]   In his works Boyle uses the Strasbourg clock to offer many different kinds of arguments to design. Many of these are logically distinct from the Posidonian Argument.
[56]   Conrad Dasypodius was the designer of the famous Strasburg clock.
[57]   Check out this wonderful image: https://www.atlasobscura.com/places/strasbourg-astronomical-clock, accessed 1 February, 2020.

B. A planetarium is a complex machine or concrete representation of the heavens (and the complexity of the planetarium that it has in virtue of being a model of nature is derived from nature.)

C. Nature's complexity is greater than the complexity of a planetarium.

D. Posidonius' planetarium is a successful representation of the heavens.

E. Nature's order is caused either by chance, or by necessity, or by a divine mind.

F. Nature's order is not caused by necessity or chance because it is impossible that something less complex can be the product of rational design while the more complex thing (i.e., nature) it represents is not.

G. Therefore, nature's order is caused by the divine mind's rational design.

Recall that (F) seems to beg the question. And that the PSR seems to be presupposed in E. I made no effort to suggest that there is an important link between the PSR and F. But in the early modern period, they get linked together in a very famous passage:

> It follows from this both that (a) something cannot arise from nothing, and also (b) that what is more perfect – that is, contains in itself more reality – cannot arise from what is less perfect. And this is transparently true not only in the case of effects which possess (what the philosophers call) actual or formal reality, but also in the case of ideas, where one is considering only (what they call) objective reality. (Descartes, *Meditations on First Philosophy*, AT VII 40-41; CSM II 28-29; letters added to facilitate discussion).[58]

In the context in which this passage is taught and discussed in the scholarly literature, the main interest is in connecting the two causal principles (a&b) to Descartes's theory of ideas, the relationships actual, formal, and objective reality, and understanding how these connect to his argument for the existence of God. Later in the book Descartes treats (a&b) as clearly linked.[59]

---

[58] Quoted from Descartes (1988, p. 91).

[59] It seems one can derive (b) from (a). If something with more reality arose from something with less reality, then the quantity (more reality–less reality) would have arisen from nothing.) I thank David Gordon for discussion.

Descartes claims to derive or infer (a&b) from another principle, 'Now it is manifest by the natural light that (c) there must be at least as much (reality) in the efficient and total cause as in the effect of that cause.' This (c) is pretty much treated as axiomatic by Descartes. It has its roots in neo-Platonic conceptions of emanation which merged with Aristotelian ideas about efficient causation. The underlying idea is that an effect receives its qualities from a cause and these (cause and effect) are conceived hierarchically.[60]

I'll call (a-c), 'Descartes' causal principles'. The relationship between (a) and (c) is easy to discern (although one may wonder which one is truly the more fundamental principle). In addition, it's clear that with his embrace of (a)/(c) that Descartes is clearly committed to something akin to the PSR. That (b) follows from (c) is also pretty clear.

Obviously (b) is not identical to (F) in the neglected Posidonian argument. But if we are allowed to treat complexity as a species of perfection, as Descartes does in the First Replies,[61] then (b) underwrites (F). For (b) and ((C), from which (F) is derived) rely on the same intuition that the model or copy derives its key, effective properties, the ones that track or are morphic with reality, from reality. And reality is more perfect or nobler than a copy. What I assume, however, is that these causal principles are more widely shared in the early modern period until we see them explicitly challenged.

Of course, these reflections entail that (A-B) are misleading if we think of (to use Descartes' terminology) the total cause of a complex machine that tracks nature (say a portable planetarium) as limited to the human artificer that designed and built the concrete model. *Crucially, on the interpretation pursued here, the total cause of a planetarium includes something of, or presupposes, the natural order which it tracks.*

Now, how much of nature's order is presupposed in a concrete model of it, is worth careful consideration. But if we import these Cartesian causal principles into the Posidonian arguments we have been considering, we get a new premise:

(I) A condition of the possibility of (an intended) successful (concrete) scientific representation of nature is that nature is orderly.

---

[60] See Lin (2004, p. 32).
[61] See also Dennett (2008).

With this premise (I) we can drop (A-C) and doing so will be the basis of what I call a 'transcendental Posidonian argument'. Before I articulate the full version of it I motivate it by looking at critic of Cartesianism, Samuel Clarke. I argue that this – possibly even more anachronistic – transcendental interpretation of the Posidonian argument is a natural outgrowth of reflection on the scientific revolution in progress. The transcendental interpretation focuses on the fact that a scientific model of the world plays a crucial role in the Ciceronian argument.

An important aspect of the enduring attraction of the prima facie version of the Posidonian argument in the early modern period depends on the fact that *if* one is committed to the idea that science can reveal design of nature then progress in the sciences aided by, say, microscopic and telescopic technology keeps revealing new and ever more sophisticated evidence of design.[62]

To see how such an argument plays out, I discuss Samuel Clarke's Boyle lecture, *A Demonstration of the Being and Attributes of God* (1705). This is presented as a response to Hobbes and Spinoza and their followers, but the only follower mentioned is Toland, to whom I turn first.[63]

5 Toland's Appropriation of Newton.

Toland's *The Letters to Serena* (1704) is a rhetorically complex work in five letters.[64] The first three letters include a genealogy of the idea

[62]   I suspect the first post-Copernican person to make *this* move was the unusual Leuven Jesuit, Leonard Lessius (Leys) in 1612. See Leonard Lessius, *De prouidentia numinis* (1612, p. 25). I have discussed the passage and its broader significance in my blog, https://digressionsnimpressions. typepad.com/digressionsimpressions/2019/01/on-the-discovery-of-progress-lessius-on-a-dutch-glasstelescope.html.

[63]   I have discussed the complex relations among Clarke, Toland, and Newton in Schliesser (forthcoming) and Schliesser (2012).

[64]   On Toland's philosophy, see Daniel (1984), and Dagron (2009). For, a useful introduction to Toland's views, especially as they relate to the reception of Newton and Newtonianism see Jacob (1969). Jacob treats Toland as a sincere critic of Spinoza and as a follower of Bruno. As my argument notes there are non-trivial differences between Toland and Spinoza (see Dagron, 2009, chapter vii), but I do not doubt that in the fifth letter to Serena, Toland is what I have been calling a Spinozist. This is not the place to explore the commonalities between Bruno and Spinoza or the ways in which Toland's criticism of Spinoza is a mere smokescreen. On these

Eric Schliesser

of immortality of soul, a proto-feminist tract, and an account of justice amongst other themes discussed. The fourth letter is a self-styled 'confutation of Spinoza'[65] – like other English critics of Spinoza, Toland finds Spinoza's account of motion wanting – often using the authority of Newton's then recent *Principia* in the process; the fifth letter, by contrast, advances Spinozist themes by rejecting Newton's account of the vacuum, space, and God (amongst other doctrines).[66] Among the Spinozist positions that Toland adopts as his own is that God's immanence in nature (and the denial of the immateriality of the soul).[67]

Here I focus on a key feature of *Letter* four. In order to do justice to Toland's position, I introduce some anachronistic terminology: by '*anti-mathematicism*' I mean the expressed reservations about the authority and/or utility of the application of mathematics. Such anti-mathematicism can come in many guises and strands. Here I focus only on what I call '*The global anti-mathematicist strategy*' by which I mean to pick out those arguments and positions that challenge and de-privilege the epistemic authority and security of mathematical *applications as such*. To avoid misunderstanding, this strategy is compatible with allowing some subservient uses (for bits) of mathematics in one's physics (and praise for *pure* mathematics). The position pre-dates Toland. The canonical late seventeenth century expression of the global anti-mathematicist strategy can be found in Spinoza's so-called 'Letter on the Infinite' addressed to Lodewijk Meyer and published in his *Opera Posthuma*.[68]

---

points, see Leask (2012). (Leask turns Toland into a Leibnizian of sorts, a topic that transcends this paper.) Recently, Toland has been read as interpreting Newton with a Lockean epistemology, see Wigelsworth (2003). For present purposes I can remain agnostic about Wigelsworth's main thesis, for he, too, recognizes Spinozism in Toland (see, especially, Wigelsworth, 2003, p. 530).

[65] *Letters*, 5.1, 163. I am quoting by letter, paragraph, and page-number to the original 1704 edition. There is a nice recent edition of John Toland's *Letters to Serena*, (Toland, 2013) which also provides original page-numbers.

[66] See Daniel (1984, op. cit., p. 11).

[67] It is useful to note that Toland coined the term 'pantheism' shortly after the *Letters* in 1705, in the title of his work, *Socinianism Truly Stated, by a pantheist*. See Jacob (1981).

[68] For a lot more details on Spinoza's position, see Schliesser (2018). Throughout the seventeenth century in response to the aspirations of what we may dub 'Galilean science,' there were informed criticisms of the

In order to understand what is at stake in Clarke's response to Toland it is indispensable that we have some features of Toland's *global anti-mathematicist strategy* in view. Toland expresses a key aspect of his position as follows: 'The Mathematicians generally take the moving force for granted, and treat of local motion as they find it, without giving themselves much trouble about its original [cause]; but the practice of the philosophers is otherwise, or rather *ought* to be' (*Letters* 4.8, p. 141, emphasis added).[69]

This passage presupposes a hierarchically organized intellectual division of labor between the 'mathematicians' who, Toland explains, find 'rules of motions' by 'observations learnt from...experience'; they only deal with 'local motion' (or a 'change in situation') in order to generate the 'ordinary rules of motion' by 'probable calculations' (*Letters* 4.8, p. 141). That is to say, these 'mathematicians' are primarily engaged in what we would call 'empirical induction' and 'instrumentalist description'.[70] Higher in status are the 'philosophers', who assign causes and the (causal) 'principles' of 'true' motion (*Letters* 4.8, p. 140).[71]

There are three key features of the hierarchical intellectual division of labor:

(i) it is normative ('ought to be');
(ii) mathematicians, or we might say, mathematical natural philosophers do not have last word on their own analysis (*qua* mathematician);
(iii) mathematicians are incapable of supplying what we really want – a causal understanding of how the world operates.

It is the combination of (i-iii) that makes Toland's position instantiate a global anti-mathematicist strategy. (That's compatible with him allowing a pragmatic or instrumental role for mathematics in physics.) In context, and throughout the *Letters*, Toland implies that the methodological stance of (the first edition of) the *Principia* explicitly recognizes a distinction between the discovery

---

utility and application of mathematics to natural philosophy. For an inventory of such arguments, see Tamás Demeter & Eric Schliesser, eds. (2019). See, especially, Nelson (2019).

[69] Daniel (1984 op. cit., p. 102), also notes the significance of this.

[70] Toland's position allows that 'mathematicians' may not realize that they are doing no more than this.

[71] The distinction is functional; it's of course possible that the very same person acts as a 'mathematician' and as a 'philosopher'.

Eric Schliesser

of *local* forces (which, Toland grants, are discovered by Newton) and the 'general or moving force of all matter' (see *Letters* 5.29, p. 233–34). Toland may thereby be the first to interpret the methodological stance of Newton's *Principia* in an instrumentalist fashion – something that only becomes fashionable after the addition of the General Scholium and Clarke's exchange with Leibniz. For this precedes the changes to the *Principia* in response to the controversy over the status over action at a distance.[72] Here I leave aside the question to what degree Toland's interpretation of Newton can be defended in light of the details of the *Principia*.[73] Toland's strategy may well have inspired Berkeley's in *De Motu*.[74] But for present purposes another key move by Toland is to reject what we would call the invocation of a 'God of the gaps'.[75] He does so by appealing to the authority of Cicero. He then goes on to imply that one reason to favor the idea that motion is essential to matter is that it minimizes such invocation of gap-filling-God:

> [T]hey are forc'd at last to have recourse to God, and to maintain that as he communicated Motion to Matter at the beginning, so he still begets and continues it whenever, and as long as there's occasion for it, and that he actually concurs to every Motion in the Universe....As Cicero observes when the philosophers are ignorant of the cause of anything, they presently betake themselves for refuge and sanctuary to God, which is not to explain things, but to cover their own negligence or short-sightedness...
>
> I hold then motion is essential to matter...as inseparable from its nature as impenetrability or extension. (*Letters* 4.15-16, pp. 157-58)

In these passages, Toland is not merely criticizing occasionalist views, but all views, including even the concurrentist,[76] that require any activity by God. Toland contrasts two (coherent)

[72] Of course, there are modern interpreters that also claim that Newton was an instrumentalist. The most insightful defense of this view is McMullin (2001, pp. 279–310); for criticism see Smith (2001), Ducheyne & Weber (2008); cf. Schliesser (2011).
[73] There is often a conflation between Newton's stance toward action at a distance and his stance toward causal explanations as such. Recent Newton scholarship has done much to make some necessary distinctions, see Smeenk & Schliesser (2013).
[74] Berkeley, *De Motu* (*Works*, vol. 4).
[75] For discussion see Del Ratzsch (2014).
[76] See McDonough (2008, pp. 567–90).

54

positions: first, one claims that matter is passive and requires God to be the first and concurring cause. Second, one aims to minimize God's role altogether and, thereby, opts for active matter and 'activity' is an essential quality of matter. The second view dispenses with God's role as the first cause of motion and has a tendency to insist that the universe must have existed forever.

In a nutshell: Toland adopts the second position: 'I deny that matter is or ever was an inactive dead Lump in absolute Repose, a lazy and unwieldy thing…I hope to evince that this Notion alone accounts for the same Quantity of Motion in the Universe, that it alone proves there neither needs nor can be any Void, that Matter cannot be truly defin'd without it, that it solves all the Dificultys about the moving force, and all rest which we have mention'd before.' (*Letters* 5.16, pp. 159–60). By contrast, in a *Demonstration* Clarke adopts the former position (matter is passive, etc.), strongly implying that this is also Newton's position.[77]

So, the way to understand Toland's challenge is as follows: the mathematical structure of the *Principia* is ultimately neutral on matter being truly active or passive and what the general source of motion is. While Newton qua mathematician *talks* of forces as causes in order to help keep track of observed regularities, these do not pick out genuine explanatory causes in nature – that's the task of the philosopher and by Toland's lights Newton acknowledges this division of labour. Toland takes up the task to offer a philosophical conception of matter that coheres with the *Principia*; one in which matter is essentially active and, with a nod to Cicero's authority, that dispenses with a need for God (beyond a vague immanent substance monism in which God gives being to matter).[78] If, by contrast, you insist that matter is passive then you introduce the 'god of the gaps'.

Now, while the next section is devoted to analyzing Clarke's response to Toland, I do not have space to explain Clarke's response to Toland's matter theory here (or Berkeley's attitude toward Newton). But, while I do not want to downplay their differences, notice how much Toland anticipates features of Berkeley: they both think there is a hierarchical division of labor in which the

---

[77] There is a lively debate among Newton scholars on how to understand Newton's position on the activity and passivity of matter: see Kochiras (2009); Schliesser (2011); Ducheyne (2014); Chen (2020); Parker (2020).

[78] Despite Toland's criticism of Spinoza in *Letters* 4, the position is decidedly Spinozistic. See for very good work on Spinozistic active materialism, Wolfe (2010).

Eric Schliesser

metaphysician/philosopher assigns causes while the work of the natural philosopher/geometrician can be interpreted as a mere tracking of the relations of the phenomena (for Berkeley, see *De Motu*, pp. 71–72; PHK, p. 107)). They are both in a non-trivial sense global anti-mathematicists (while allowing the use of mathematics for evidential reasons) and, perhaps, even instrumentalists about Newtonian natural philosophy. They do not take the self-understanding of the new sciences as authoritative in first philosophy.

Moreover, Toland's move is essential for understanding why people would have thought that the stance one takes about the nature of matter theory has significant effects on how one views the status of providence/Intelligence. In response to Toland, Clarke uses the Posidonian argument to link a particular conception of matter theory and scientific progress to the existence of Intelligence. By the end of the next section it should be clear that Berkeley's immaterialism undermines Clarke's framework.

6 Clarke responds to Toland

In the context of a polemic with Toland, who in the *Letters to Serena* with his own appeal to Cicero's authority rejects what we would call the invocation of a 'God of the gaps',[79] Clarke points out that when in Ancient times, 'Epicurus and his follower Lucretius' imagined 'finding fault in the frame and constitution of the Earth' this was somewhat plausible due to the 'infancy of natural philosophy' (although Clarke notes with satisfaction that even then the 'generality of men' were not persuaded). Clarke can point to recent discoveries in anatomy and physiology such as 'the circulation of the blood, the exact structure of the heart and brain' as well as the discovery of a number of veins and other vessels neither known nor imagined in ancient times. (*A Demonstration* pp. 227–28; cf. Hume's *Dialogues*, 11.11). Then Clarke writes:

> If Tully, from the partial and very imperfect knowledge in astronomy, which his times afforded, could be so confident of

[79] 'As Cicero observes when the philosophers are ignorant of the cause of anything, they presently betake themselves for refuge and sanctuary to God, which is not to explain things, but to cover their own negligence or short-sightedness.' (See John Toland, *Letters to Serena*, L4.15-16, pp. 157–58) While elsewhere in the *Letters,* Toland quotes Cicero's *On the Nature of the Gods*, here Toland gives no specific reference; he seems to echoing Cicero's *De Divinatione* 1.125-126.

the heavenly bodies being disposed and moved by a wise and understanding mind, as to the declare that in his opinion, whoever
asserted the contrary, was himself[80] void of all understanding:
What would he have said, if he had known the modern discoveries in astronomy? The immense greatness of the world (I mean of
that part of it, which falls under our observation), which is now
known to be as much greater than what in his time they imagined
it to be, as the world itself, according to their system, was greater
than Archimedes' Sphere? (*A Demonstration of the Being and
Attributes of God*, pp. 228–29)

The history of scientific progress becomes an added argument for the
plausibility of the Posidonian argument.[81] In the *narrow* sense this is
so because on Clarke's account, science discovers more evidence of
apparent design where previously there just had been mystery or
lack of knowledge and, thus, is capable of ever more refined representations of nature covering an increasing domain of nature. This fact
feeds into a broader argument that Clarke makes in context: the
history of scientific progress *itself* becomes a further argument for
the existence of a designing and benevolent God. In fact, after
listing a large number of Newton's then recent discoveries, Clarke in-
terprets the history of scientific progress as an unfolding Biblical
prophecy:

We now see with how great reason the author of the Book of
Ecclesiasticus after he had described the beauty of the Sun and
Stars, and all then visible works of God in heaven and earth,
concluded ch. 43, v 32 (as we after all the discoveries of later
ages, may no doubt still truly say,) 'There yet hid greater
things than these, we have seen but a few of his Works.'
(*A Demonstration* XI, pp. 232–33)[82]

[80]   Clarke quotes here book 2 of *The Nature of the Gods* in Latin. The
passage is a few paragraphs removed from the Posidonian argument. The
reference to 'Archimedes' sphere' reminds us that we are still in the ambit
of the Posidonian argument.
[81]   Gibbon seems to have had this point in mind in his 'Address' collected
in Gibbon (1797, vol. 3, p. 469), and the footnote that calls explicit attention
to Cicero. See https://books.google.nl/books?id=17E8AAAAYAAJ&pg=
PA469&dq=Newton+Posidonius.
[82]   This is a rare occasion where Clarke appeals (against his official purposes) to a Biblical text at all in a *Demonstration*. Given the non-canonical (or
deuteron-canonical) status of *Ecclesiasticus*, Clarke's choice is worth exploring, but I cannot pursue the question here. (But since Clarke is not deriving

Eric Schliesser

Newton's then recent discoveries become an important evidentiary signpost for understanding scientific progress as an open-ended, unfolding and confirmation of confident Biblical prophecy.

Now we can return to the Posidonian argument in order to explore the transcendental interpretation of it. As I have emphasized the Posidonian planetarium is more than a time-keeper; it is capable of predicting other heavenly phenomena, especially eclipses. So, rather than viewing the heavenly phenomena as portents of danger (revolution, omens, etc.) the scientific representation fits them into an ordered universe.[83] That is, the empirical success of the planetarium points to the significance of predictable order; the designer of a planetarium presupposes an orderly celestial globe.[84] For example, In Newton's *Principia* this orderliness is crowned by the original closing pages of the book, Newton's ability to predict the orbits of comets.[85]

So, we can put the significance and true intuitive force lurking within all elements of the Posidonian argument in anachronistic fashion: a condition of the possibility of (an intended) successful scientific representation of nature is that nature is orderly or ordered. Then *a history* of successful scientific representations, and technologies of representation relying on these, becomes a distinct and over time increasingly compelling argument for an orderly nature.[86] This leads me to the promised transcendental interpretation of the Posidonian argument.[87] The form of the transcendental intrpretation is as follows:

---

doctrine, it should not raise too many eyebrows.) I thank Peter Anstey and David Gordon for discussion.

[83] This is noted in Adam Smith, 'The History of Astronomy' (3.1, EPS, p. 48). All my references to Adam Smith's History of Astronomy are to paragraph and page-numbers in *Essays on Philosophical Subjects* in the Glasgow edition.

[84] This point stands even if one insists that the design of the planetarium is based on empirical data.

[85] The classic paper is Kriloff (1978, p. 640). For the contextual meaning, see Albury (1978).

[86] This is so, even if the representations do not track the causal order of nature, but merely track or predict the phenomena. Hunter (2009) puts the point very precisely: 'It is the complexity internal to both the model and its original. Let us call it the pattern (P) which both the original and its model instantiate. By virtue of P the original and the copy are partially isomorphic' (p. 244).

[87] Clerk Shaw was the first to remind me of the significance of Kant's *Critique of Judgment*, where the logical purposiveness of nature is

I. A condition of the possibility of (an intended) successful scientific representation of nature is that nature is ordered.
II. Science has a history of success.
III. The world's order is not produced by nothing.
III *. The same cause or principle is responsible for the existence of the world and its order.
IV. Order is produced by necessity, or by chance, or by designing mind.
V. The particular order science finds is not the subject of chance or necessity.
VI. ∴ So nature's order must be produced by a designing mind (or nature is designed).

I make three claims about this version of the argument. First, most early moderns who were interested in such arguments were interested in re-affirming that God was the cause of the world. For Christians it is natural to assume (III*) there is a tight link because the cause of the existence of nature and the cause of its order are taken to be the very same.[88]

Second, the transcendental version of the Posidonian argument changes the significance of the history of science and the character of science more generally. For, on the prima facie approach to the Posidonian argument when it comes to the question of intelligent design in nature, science is, in principle, perceived to be a neutral means in order to establish the nature and existence, if any, of the God(s). However, on the transcendental version of the Posidonian argument, science is not neutral at all about the existence of an Intelligence, because science itself presupposes for its very possibility and intelligibility that there is order and a source of order. So, while the scientist has a kind of privileged access to the hidden features of nature, she has it in virtue of a commitment to finding the hidden order of God's design in our discoveries.

Third, on the transcendental version, the force of the Posidonian argument does not rely anymore on the (perhaps dubious to post-Humeans or post-Darwinians) explicit assumptions of the original

---

presupposed as a 'regulative principle', but not constitutive principle, in one's science (see the antinomy of the Judgment).
[88] In the 'Preface' to (Nieuwentyt, 1719, ix), Nieuwentyt asserts that in Cicero the 'existence' of the gods are taken for granted, but that the debate turns on the nature of the gods. A few pages later, Nieuwentyt introduces a version of the argument that is now attributed to Paley (see Jantzen 2014, pp. 168–69 with great material).

Eric Schliesser

argument in Cicero (such as 'nature's attainments transcend those achieved by human design') and the role of Descartes' causal principles in the neglected version of the argument. Moreover, now the Posidonian argument stresses the structural resemblance between state-of-the-art-planetary mechanism and the celestial globe, but does not appeal to aesthetics more generally nor claims about analogies between the designer of the planetarium and heavens.[89] As in the neglected version of the Posidonian argument, this argument does not appeal to apparent design to motivate the argument nor mentions it in its premises.

Of course, the premises of the transcendental version of the argument are not without controversy. Premise (I) may be thought too strong in two ways. First, it may be the case that all that is required is to presuppose in a scientific practice that a relevant region of nature is ordered. So one can imagine rewriting premise (I) as follows:

I*. A condition of the possibility of (an intended) successful scientific representation of a region of nature is that a region nature is ordered.

While this would require reformulating other premises (e.g., III), it does not undermine the conclusion of the argument. In fact, as it turns out that ever more bits of nature are orderly (comets, geology, etc.), it may well strengthen the overall argument. Even so, to what extent all regions of nature share the same order or whether the same region remains orders is also not obvious (something Newton and Hume worried about).

Premise (II) is hard to evaluate – a lot depends on one's baseline and one's expectations. But it is no surprise that as the scientific revolution unfolds this premise seems very secure, despite the development of pessimistic meta-induction arguments (offered, say, by Aristotle's Ghost in Swift in *Gulliver's Travels*).[90]

Premise (III) relies, in its most general sense on a version of the causal principle or on the PSR. Not all thinkers embraced the PSR

[89] Hunter puts the insight very nicely: 'The new argument does not make the mistake of comparing unconnected instances of complexity. Its very different strategy is to exploit the fact that one and the same instance of complexity is found simultaneously in two places.' (p. 242) To be clear: Hunter's 'new' argument is not my 'anachronistic' argument, but akin to what I have called the 'neglected' version; Hunter's 'new' argument preserves the neutrality requirement.

[90] See Schliesser (2005, pp. 705–706).

in the early modern period, but I am unfamiliar with anybody that denies the causal principle. As I noted above (III*) is in one sense controversial – there were lots of debates over the relationship between God and secondary causes –, but in other sense not so controversial (because God's omnipotence was simply assumed). In addition, there are hidden simplicity and parsimony assumptions packed into (III*).

Premise (IV) is inherited from the ancients. After Berkeley, philosophers start to explore new sources of order (e.g., the mind's imposition, emergence, and even the development of a science that deals with the nature of order, entropy, etc.) and start to challenge the naturalness of this premise.

Premise (V) requires argument. There are some philosophical proponents of chance (most notably Hume) as a source of order. And once probability theory is developed, the argument for chance is made in sophisticated fashion (by D'Álembert and Laplace) in the context of Enlightenment debates over cosmology and cosmogony in the generation after Berkeley. But in Berkeley's life most of the philosophical debates center on the challenges of Spinozism to this premise. In a nutshell critics of Spinozism (Clarke, Newton, MacLaurin) argue that while it predicts (by stipulation) necessary variety, it fails to predict the *particular* variety we observe. But as cosmogony starts developing (from Kant onward), the Spinozist position gets recast and becomes more plausible again. But in so doing another premise (III*) starts to become less likely.

That is, even if one is distinctly reserved about final causes or God's providence, the transcendental version of the argument tightly links scientific progress to God's or nature's order. If you accept this argument then, with scientific progress, you get a providential deism for free. It also motivates commitment to the possibility of scientific progress.

Before I return, in closing, to Berkeley, let me note one more feature about Clarke's version of the transcendental version of the Posidonian argument. Above I quoted Clarke on Tully and Archimedes' sphere, and the fact that the history of scientific progress makes the Posidonian argument even more compelling now than it was in Cicero's time. On the preceding page, Clarke had expressed a version of the thought as follows:

> If Galen so many ages ago could find in the construction and constitution of the parts of a Humane body, such undeniable marks of Contrivance and Design; as forced him Then to

Eric Schliesser

acknowledge and Admire the Wisdom of its Author; What
would he have said, if he had known the Late Discoveries in
Anatomy and Physick, the Circulation of the Blood, the exact
structure of the Heart and Brain, the Uses of Numberless
Glands and Valves for the Secretion and Motion of the Juices
in the Body, besides several Veins and other Vessels and
Receptacles not at all known, or imagined for so much as to
have any Existence in his Days, but which Now are discovered
to serve the Wisest and most exquisite Ends imaginable?
(Demonstration, p. 226)

Here Clarke relies on modern discoveries about the hidden structure
of living things, plants and animals. That is to say, the larger context
of Clarke's Posidonian argument treats the natural and living world
symmetrically. Our inquiry of nature generated, compared to the
by no means mean achievements of the Ancient world, hitherto
unimaginable signs of order and functionality.

7 Berkeley's Hypothetical Critic

Let's, finally, return to the eleventh objection. My claim is now
straightforward. In Berkeley's presentation of the eleventh objection,
we can discern that this objection involves anxiety that Berkeley's
philosophy is undermining appeal to Clarke's version of the
Posidonian argument. I quote:

[I]t will be demanded to what purpose serves that curious organization of plants, and the animal mechanism in the parts of
animals; might not vegetables grow, and shoot forth leaves of
blossoms, and animals perform all their motions as well
without as with all that variety of internal parts so elegantly con-
trived and put together; which, being ideas, have nothing powerful or operative in them, nor have any necessary connexion with
the effects ascribed to them? If it be a Spirit that immediately
produces every effect by a fiat or act of his will, we must think
all that is fine and artificial in the works, whether of man or
nature, to be made in vain. By this doctrine, though an artist
hath made the spring and wheels, and every movement of a
watch, and adjusted them in such a manner as he knew would
produce the motions he designed, yet he must think all this
done to no purpose, and that it is an Intelligence which directs
the index, and points to the hour of the day. If so, why may
not the Intelligence do it, without his being at the pains of

making the movements and putting them together? Why does not an empty case serve as well as another? And how comes it to pass that whenever there is any fault in the going of a watch, there is some corresponding disorder to be found in the movements, which being mended by a skillful hand all is right again? The like may be said of all the clockwork of nature, great part whereof is so wonderfully fine and subtle as scarce to be discerned by the best microscope. In short, it will be asked, how, upon our principles, any tolerable account can be given, or any final cause assigned of an innumerable multitude of bodies and machines, framed with the most exquisite art, which in the common philosophy have very apposite uses assigned them, and serve to explain abundance of phenomena? (PHK, 60)

In the first sentence of the quote we see a clear allusion to Clarke's use of Galen in the Demonstration. In the third sentence, there is a clear allusion to Clarke's extension of Boyle's prima facie version of the Posidonian argument. And further down the paragraph, the hypothetical critic echoes Clarke by reminding the reader of Berkeley that there is still a great deal to be discovered of nature ('the clockwork of nature, great part whereof is so wonderfully fine and subtle as scarce to be discerned by the best microscope'). So, while it is true that the characteristic features of the Posidonian argument are not mentioned, PHK conveys central features of Clarke's particular presentation of it.

The connection to the Posidonian argument is reinforced and even strengthened by Berkeley's restatement of the objection in paragraph 64:

that what has been objected in sect. 60 amounts in reality to no more than this: ideas are not anyhow and at random produced, there being a certain order and connexion between them, like to that of cause and effect; there are also several combinations of them made in a very regular and artificial manner, which seem like so many instruments in the hand of nature that, being hid as it were behind the scenes, have a secret operation in producing those appearances which are seen on the theatre of the world, being themselves discernible only to the curious eye of the philosopher. But, since one idea cannot be the cause of another, to what purpose is that connexion? And, since those instruments, being barely inefficacious perceptions in the mind, are not subservient to the production of natural effects, it is demanded why they are made; or, in other words, what reason can be assigned why God should make us, upon a close inspection into His works, behold so great variety of ideas so artfully laid together, and so much according to rule; it not being credible that He would be at the expense (if one may so speak) of all that art and regularity to no purpose. (PHK, 64)

The restatement makes clear that the critic's worry is really about Berkeley's immaterialism reopening the door to chance ('ideas are not anyhow and at random produced'). And also, by undermining the argument for final causes, even the system of necessity ('all that art and regularity to no purpose'). The whole point of securing Intelligence in the Posidonian argument, is to rule out necessity and chance. In addition note, too, that the critic is concerned that Berkeley's position makes pointless the scientist's effort to find hidden structure. The cultural significance of the Posidonian argument is precisely that scientific activity is an act of faith *and* strengthens it rationally. Finally, the restatement of the hypothetical critic also reveals the commitment to something like the PSR in making scientific enquiry intelligible ('what reason can be assigned why God should make us, upon a close inspection into His works, behold so great variety of ideas so artfully laid together, and so much according to rule').

Now Margaret Dauer Wilson had claimed that 'in these sections Berkeley is confronting an opponent who simply argues that on his principles the organization of nature as we know it makes no sense. Berkeley contends that this organization does have a point, though not a causal role' (Dauer Wilson, 1999, p. 247). This is right in so far that Berkeley does deny that that this organization involves efficient causes. Instead he proposes his doctrine of signs to explain nature's regularity. But Berkeley does insist that his argument leaves room to conclude the 'wise contrivance' of nature's order. For he has no doubt that the 'order and connexion between' our ideas (PHK, 64) is a sign of the order imposed by Intelligence. That is to say, the eleventh objection turns on the relationship between the hidden order of nature and the order and functionality science finds in providing evidence for the working of providence.

Conclusion

I have used the exchange between Garber and Dauer Wilson to illustrate the benefits of my interpretation of this larger context. For, the larger historiographical point I wish to illustrates that even after a long generation of work in the so-called contextual revolution,[91] the philosophical context of even quite canonical texts is sometimes not yet sufficiently grasped.

I have argued that the eleventh objection expresses anxiety over the status of the Posidonian argument in light of Berkeley's immaterialism. I do not mean to suggest that Berkeley's response to the hypothetical critic who is anxious to defend the existence and operation of Intelligence leaves everything untouched. Berkeley's response reiterates that nature is law-governed.[92] And, in fact, Berkeley articulates a rather modern (in Cassirer's sense) conception of what can be discovered by science:[93] 'There are certain general laws that run through the whole chain of natural effects; these are learned by the observation and study of nature, and are by men applied as well to the framing artificial things for the use and ornament of life as to the explaining various phenomena: which explication consists only in showing the conformity any particular phenomenon has to the general laws of nature, or, which is the same thing, in discovering the uniformity there is in the production of natural effects' (PHK, 62).

But Berkeley also re-orients the end of scientific discovery of nature's hidden complexity and order. This need not lead to the denial of (contemplation of) Intelligence (even if the point is 'the use and ornament of life' or providing 'signs for our information' (PHK, 66)).

Of course, that nature is orderly, even law-governed, is a key feature of the Posidonian argument is. If anything, in the Transcendental version of the argument it is of central importance. So, Berkeley's argument does not undermine the legitimacy of using the history of scientific success as support for Intelligence. In fact, to somebody with an eye toward the Posidonian Argument, PHK 60-66 reveals the centrality of order/law-governedness to the whole argument. Berkeley's response to the eleventh objection gave Hume the clear target he needed.

University of Amsterdam & Chapman University
nescio2@yahoo.com

---

[91]   See Mercer (2019).
[92]   See Ott (2019).
[93]   Cf. Ducheyne (2006).

Eric Schliesser

References

W.R. Albury, 'Halley's Ode on the Principia of Newton and the Epicurean Revival in England,' *Journal of the History of Ideas* 39.1 (1978), 24–43.

Margaret Atherton, *Berkeley* (Oxford: Wiley Blackwell, 2020).

Christine Battersby, 'The *Dialogues* as Original Imitation: Cicero and the Nature of Hume's Scepticism,' in *McGill Hume Studies*, ed. D.F. Norton, N. Capaldi & W.L. Robison (San Diego: Austin Hill Press, 1979), 239–252.

Richard Bentley [7th, enlarged edition] *Remarks on a Late Discourse of Freethinking: in a Letter to N.N.* by Phileleutherus Lipsiensis, (London: Knaptons, 1734 [1713]).

George Berkeley, *The Works of George Berkeley, Bishop of Cloyne*, 9 vols. (London: Thomas Nelson & Sons, 1948–1957).

Sylvia Berryman, *The Mechanical Hypothesis in Ancient Greek Natural Philosophy* (Cambridge: Cambridge University Press, 2010).

Susanne Bobzien, *Determinism and Freedom in Stoic Philosophy* (Oxford: Oxford University Press, 1998).

Robert Boyle, *Selected Philosophical Papers of Robert Boyle*, ed. M.A. Stewart (Indianapolis: Hackett, 1991).

Robert Boyle, *The Works of Robert Boyle, Vol. 10*: Notion of Nature and other publications of 1684–6 Michael Hunter and Edward B. Davis (eds) (London: Pickering & Chatto. 2000).

Christopher Brooke, 'How the Stoics Became Atheists,' *The Historical Journal* 49.2 (2006), 387–402.

Rene Brouwer, 'The Stoics on Luck,' in *The Routledge Handbook of the Philosophy and Psychology of Luck*, ed. Ian M. Church & Robert J. Hartman (London: Routledge, 2019), 34–44.

Cicero, *De Senectute De Amicitia De Divinatione*. With An English Translation. William Armistead Falconer. (Cambridge: Harvard University Press, 1923).

Cicero, *The Nature of the Gods*, trans. P.G. Walsh (Oxford: Oxford University Press, 1978).

Cicero *The Letters of Cicero; the whole extant correspondence in chronological order, in four volumes*. Evelyn S. Shuckburgh. (London: George Bell and Sons, 1908-1909).

Samuel Clarke, 'A Discourse concerning the Unalterable Obligations of Natural Religion and the Truth and Certainty of the Christian Revelation' in *A discourse concerning the being and attributes of God: the obligations of natural religion, and the truth and certainty of the Christian revelation* (London: Knapton, 1732).

M. Tvlli Ciceronis *De natvra deorvm: bimillenial edition*. 2. Libri secundus et tertius. Edited by A.S. Pease, (Cambridge MA.: Harvard University Press, 1958).

Elliott D Chen, 'Newton's early metaphysics of body: Impenetrability, action at a distance, and essential gravity.' *Studies in History and Philosophy of Science Part B: Studies in History and Philosophy of Modern Physics* (2020).

Tristan Dagron, *Toland et Leibniz: l'invention du néo-spinozisme* (Paris: Vrin, 2009).

Stephen H. Daniel, *John Toland: His Methods, Manners, and Mind*, vol. 7 (Kingston: McGill-Queen's Press-MQUP, 1984).

Tamás Demeter & Eric Schliesser (eds.) 'The Use and Abuse of Mathematics in Seventeenth and Eighteenth Century Natural Philosophy,' *Synthese* (special issue) 196.9 (2019), 3461–64.

Daniel C. Dennett, 'Descartes's Argument from Design.' *The Journal of Philosophy* 105.7 (2008), 333–45.

Daniel C. Dennett, *From Bacteria to Bach and Back: The Evolution of Minds* (New York: WW Norton & Company, 2017).

Rene Descartes, *Descartes: Selected Philosophical Writings*, trans. John Cottingham, Robert Stoothoff, & Dugald Murdoch (Cambridge: Cambridge University Press, 1988).

Lisa Downing, 'Berkeley's Natural Philosophy and Philosophy of Science,' *The Cambridge Companion to Berkeley*, ed. Kenneth M. Winkler (Cambridge: Cambridge University Press, 2005), 230–265.

Steffen Ducheyne, 'Reid's Adaptation and Radicalization of Newton's Natural Philosophy.' *History of European Ideas* 32.2 (2006), 173–89.

Steffen Ducheyne & Eric Weber, 'The Concept of Causation in Newton's Mechanical and Optical Work,' *Logic and Logical Philosophy* 16.4 (2008), 265–88.

Steffen Ducheyne, 'Newton on Action at a Distance,' *Journal of the History of Philosophy* 52.4 (2014), 675–702.

Daniel Garber, 'Locke, Berkeley, and corpuscular skepticism,' in *Berkeley: Critical and Interpretive Essays*, ed. Colin Murray Turbayne (Mineapolis: University of Minnesota Press, 1982).

Clarence J. Glacken, *Traces on the Rhodian Shore: Nature and Culture in Western Thought from Ancient Times to the End of the Eighteenth Century*, vol. 170 (Berkeley: University of California Press, 1967).

Edward Gibbon, *Miscellaneous Works of Edward Gibbon* (Dublin, 1797).

Eric Schliesser

Peter Harrison, 'Voluntarism and Early Modern Science,' *History of Science* 40.1 (2002), 63–89.

John Henry, 'Voluntarist Theology at the Origins of Modern Science: A Response to Peter Harrison.' *History of Science* 47.1 (2009), 79–113.

Lewis Ezra Hicks, *A Critique of Design-arguments: A Historical Review and Free Examination of the Methods of Reasoning in Natural Theology* (New York: Scribner, 1883).

Graeme Hunter, 'Cicero's Neglected Argument from Design.' *British Journal for the History of Philosophy* 17.2 (2009), 235–245.

Robert H. Hurlbutt, *Hume, Newton, and the Design Argument* (Lincoln: University of Nebraska Press, 1985).

Christiaan Huygens, *Oeuvres complètes*, Tome XXI, Cosmologie, ed. J.A. Vollgraff (Den Haag: Martinus Nijhoff, 1944).

Margaret Candee Jacob, 'John Toland and the Newtonian Ideology,' *Journal of the Warburg and Courtauld Institutes* 32 (1969), 307–331.

Margaret Jacob, *The Radical Enlightenment* (London: Allen & Unwin, 1981).

Bernard C. Jantzen, *An Introduction to Design Arguments* (Cambridge: Cambridge University Press, 2014).

I.G. Kidd, *Posidonius II. The commentary: (i) Testimonia and Fragments 1–149* (Cambridge: Cambridge University Press, 1988).

Hylarie Kochiras, 'Gravity and Newton's Substance Counting Problem,' *Studies in History and Philosophy of Science Part A* 40.3 (2009), 267–280.

A.N. Kriloff, 'On Sir Isaac Newton's Method of Determining the Parabolic Orbit of a Comet,' *Monthly Notices of the Royal Astronomical Society* 85 (1925), 640.

Ian Leask, 'Unholy Force: Toland's Leibnizian "Consummation" of Spinozism.' *British Journal for the History of Philosophy* 20.3 (2012), 499–537.

Leonard Lessius, *De prouidentia numinis* (1612), 25, in *Ravvleigh his ghost. Or a feigned apparition of Syr VValter Rawleigh to a friend of his, for the translating into English, the booke of Leonard Lessius (that most learned man) entituled, De prouidentia numinis, & animi immortalitate: written against atheists, and politi- tians of these dayes.* Translated by Edward Knott in 1631, https://quod.lib. umich.edu/e/eebo/A05370.0001.001/1:6?rgn=div1;submit=Go;subview=detail;type=simple;view=fulltext;q1=Cicero, accessed 10 January, 2019.

Martin Lin, 'Spinoza's Metaphysics of Desire: The Demonstration of IIIP6.' *Archiv für Geschichte der Philosophie* 86.1 (2004), 21–55.

Lucretius, *De Rerum Natura*, http://www.perseus.tufts.edu/hopper/text?doc=Lucr.+1.150&fromdoc=Perseus%3Atext%3A1999.02.0130, accessed 9 January, 2019.

Neil A. Manson, ed., *God and Design: The Teleological Argument and Modern Science* (London: Routledge, 2003).

Jeffrey K. McDonough, 'Berkeley, Human Agency and Divine Concurrentism,' *Journal of the History of Philosophy* 46.4 (2008), 567–90.

Ernan McMullin, 'The impact of Newton's *Principia* on the Philosophy of Science,' *Philosophy of Science* 68.3 (2001), 279–310.

Christia Mercer, 'The Contextualist Revolution in Early Modern Philosophy,' *Journal of the History of Philosophy* 57.3 (2019), 529–48.

Alan Nelson, 'Descartes on the Limited Usefulness of Mathematics,' *Synthese* 196.9 (2019), 3483–504.

Bernard Nieuwentyt, *The Religious Philosopher* (London, 1719, second corrected edition, trans. John Chamberlayne).

Walter Ott, 'Berkeley's Best System: An Alternative Approach to Laws of Nature,' *Journal of Modern Philosophy* 1.1 (2019), 1–13.

Margaret J. Osler, 'From immanent natures to nature as artifice: The reinterpretation of final causes in seventeenth-century natural philosophy.' *The Monist* 79.3 (1996), 388–407.

William Paley, *Natural theology: Or, evidence of the existence and attributes of the deity*. [14th edition] (London, 1813 [1802]).

Adwait A. Parker, 'Newton on active and passive quantities of matter', *Studies in History and Philosophy of Science Part A* (2020) https://doi.org/10.1016/j.shpsa.2020.03.006.

Plutarch. *Plutarch's Lives*. with an English Translation by Bernadotte Perrin. (Cambridge, MA.: Harvard University Press, 1919).

Del Ratzch & Jeffrey Koperski, 'Teleological Arguments for God's Existence,' *The Stanford Encyclopedia of Philosophy* (Winter 2016 Edition), https://plato.stanford.edu/archives/win2016/entries/teleological-arguments/.

Eric Schliesser, 'On the Origin of Modern Naturalism: the Significance of Berkeley's Response to a Newtonian Indispensability Argument.' *Philosophica* 76 (2005), 45–66.

Eric Schliesser, 'Wonder in the Face of Scientific Revolutions: Adam Smith on Newton's "Proof" of Copernicanism,' *British Journal for the History of Philosophy* 13.4 (2005), 697–732.

Eric Schliesser

Eric Schliesser, 'Newton's Challenge to Philosophy: A Programmatic Essay.' *HOPOS: The Journal of the International Society for the History of Philosophy of Science* 1.1 (2011), 101–128.

Eric Schliesser, 'Newton's Substance Monism, Distant Action, and the Nature of Newton's Empiricism,' *Studies in History and Philosophy of Science Part A* 42.1 (2011), 160–166.

Eric Schliesser, 'Newton and Spinoza: on Motion and Matter (and God, of Course),' *The Southern Journal of Philosophy* 50.3 (2012), 436–458.

Eric Schliesser, 'On Reading Newton as an Epicurean: Kant, Spinozism and the Changes to the Principia.' *Studies in History and Philosophy of Science* 44.3 (2013), 416–428.

Eric Schliesser, *Adam Smith: Systematic philosopher and public thinker* (Oxford: Oxford University Press, 2017).

Eric Schliesser, 'Spinoza and the Philosophy of Science.' *The Oxford Handbook of Spinoza* Michael Della Rocca (ed.) (Oxford: Oxford University Press, 2018), 155–89.

Eric Schliesser, 'Newton's Polemics with Spinozists in The General Scholium,' (forthcoming).

David Sedley, *Creationism and Its Critics in Antiquity* (Berkeley: University of California Press, 2007).

William Lad Sessions, *Reading Hume's Dialogues: A Veneration for True Religion* (Bloomington: Indiana University Press, 2002).

Adam Smith, *The Glasgow Edition of the Works and Correspondence of Adam Smith: III: Essays on Philosophical Subjects* (Oxford: Oxford University Press, 1980 [1795]).

Christopher Smeenk & Eric Schliesser, 'Newton's *Principia*,' in *The Oxford Handbook of the History of Physics*, ed. Jed Z. Buchwald & Robert Fox (Oxford: Oxford University Press, 2013), 109–165.

G.E. Smith, 'Comments on Ernan McMullin's "The Impact of Newton's Principia on the Philosophy of Science",' *Philosophy of Science* 68.3 (2001), 327–38.

Tim Stuart-Buttle, *From Moral Theology to Moral Philosophy: Cicero and Visions of Humanity from Locke to Hume* (Oxford: Oxford University Press, 2019).

Giovanni Tarantino, 'Collins's Cicero, Freethinker,' in *Atheism and Deism Revalued: Heterodox Religious Identities in Britain, 1650–1800*, ed. Wayne Hudson, Diego Lucci, & Jeffrey R. Wigelsworth (London: Routledge, 2016).

John Toland, *Letters to Serena*, ed. Ian Leask (Dublin: Four Courts Press, 2013).

Jeffrey R. Wigelsworth, 'Lockean Essences, Political Posturing, and John Toland's Reading of Isaac Newton's Principia,' *Canadian Journal of History* 38.3 (2003), 521–35.

Margaret Dauer Wilson, 'Berkeley and the essences of the corpuscularians,' in John Foster & Howard Robinson (eds.), *Essays on Berkeley: A Tercentennial Celebration* (Oxford: Oxford University Press, 1985); reprinted in her *Ideas and Mechanism: Essays on Early Modern Philosophy*. (Princeton: Princeton University Press, 1999), 243–56.

Kenneth P. Winkler, *Berkeley: An Interpretation* (Oxford: Oxford University Press, 1989).

C.T. Wolfe, 'The Materialist Denial of Monsters,' in *Monsters and Philosophy*, ed. C.T. Wolfe (London: King's College Publications, 2005).

C.T. Wolfe, 'Endowed Molecules and Emergent Organization: the Maupertuis-Diderot Debate,' *Early Science and Medicine* 15.1–2 (2010), 1–2.

Poverty and Prosperity: Political Economics in Eighteenth-Century Ireland

MARC A. HIGHT

Abstract

I draw attention to a group of thinkers in Ireland in the first half of the eighteenth century that made significant contributions to the philosophy of political economy. Loosely organized around the Dublin Philosophical Society founded in 1731, these individuals employed a similar set of assumptions and shared a common interest in the well-being of the Irish people. I focus on Samuel Madden (1686-1765), Arthur Dobbs (1689-1765), and Thomas Prior (1680–1751) and argue for two main theses. First, these Irish thinkers shared a number of commonalities with the English mercantilist thinkers of the eighteenth century, and to the degree that they did, their proposals to aid Ireland and reduce poverty were largely doomed to failure. Second, these Irish thinkers also importantly *diverged* from typical eighteenth-century mercantilist thinking in several ways. These modifications to mercantilism resulted in large part from the unusual political situation of Ireland (as a nation politically dependent on England) and helped orient their economic thinking along more institutional lines. In particular, the emphasis of the Irish on full employment and on the modification of social as well as political institutions is an early step forward in making political economy more sophisticated.

1. Introduction

Descriptions of eighteenth-century Ireland as an oppressed and impoverished island, enduring misery at the hands of the English Parliament, are common. Writing in 1918, George A. T. O'Brien provides a typical account of the state of Ireland. 'Ireland started the eighteenth century with as poor an economic outfit as can well be imagined. As we shall see, all the efforts which were made to improve her condition were fruitless, so long as the power of the English Parliament prevailed' (O'Brien, 1918). Although some dispute the level of economic hardship that the Irish endured,[1] there is no doubt that the plight of the Irish poor was the subject of

---

[1]   See Cullen (1967).

doi:10.1017/S1358246120000107   © The Royal Institute of Philosophy and the contributors 2020

Marc A. Hight

considerable discussion at the time. I wish to renew attention on a group of thinkers in Ireland in the first half of the eighteenth century that made significant contributions to the philosophy of political economy. Loosely organized around the Dublin Philosophical Society founded in 1731 (later the Royal Dublin Society after 1820 with the patronage of King George IV), these individuals employed a similar set of assumptions and shared a common interest in the well-being of the Irish people. I here focus on just three thinkers active in the first half of the eighteenth century: Samuel Madden (1686–1765), Arthur Dobbs (1689–1765), and Thomas Prior (1680–1751). Although occasionally known individually, the importance and reach of these individuals has been underestimated if not often ignored in the shadow of more famous figures.[2] Adam Smith, for instance, owned a copy of the *Observations* of the Dublin Society and there is some reason to think Smith might have been inspired by his Irish predecessors.[3] If Adam Smith constitutes the most famous early critic of mercantilism (even coining the term), then the history of similar insights with his Irish compatriots deserves closer attention. Although in the grips of mercantilist thinking, as a group these Irishmen were an important intellectual force pushing *away* from mercantilism in the first half of the eighteenth century, especially in their proposals for the amelioration of poverty. I argue for two theses.

First, these Irish thinkers shared a number of commonalities with the English mercantilist thinkers of the eighteenth century, and to the degree that they did, their proposals to aid Ireland and reduce poverty were largely doomed to failure. These thinkers share a commitment to a favorable balance of trade, the importance of population in producing the wealth of a nation, and what I call the 'moral defect' theory of poverty (the claim that poverty is the result of a poor work ethic and other defects of character). Thus, these Irish thinkers all argue that Ireland should seek to develop domestic industries that do not

---

[2]   One notable exception is Salim Rashid, who explicitly argues that these thinkers constitute a 'school' of Irish political economy (Rashid, 1988; Rashid, unpublished).

[3]   According to Smith's own 1781 manuscript catalog of his library, he owned a copy of the Scottish edition of the society's weekly observations: *The Dublin Society's Weekly Observations* (Dublin: R. Reilly, 1739), reprinted in Glasgow as *The Dublin Society's Weekly Observations for the Advancement of Agriculture and Manufactures* (Glasgow: R & A Foulis, 1756). See Mizuta, (ed.), (2000, p. 19). As for the speculation that Smith might have been inspired by the work of these Irish thinkers, I have not the space to carefully defend that view here.

compete with already established industries (in England) in order to avoid punitive measures from the English. These industries should aim at enlarging the productive population, and overarching everything must be a commitment to a moralizing national spirit. The basic idea is that developing industries (such as the production of linen and hemp) that do not rival English manufactures can actually improve the wealth of England as well as Ireland. Furthermore, this rising tide can create wealth in a fashion that is no political challenge to Britain. I contend, however, that these strands in their thinking undermined the effectiveness of their proposals as the logic of mercantilist thinking was not ultimately consistent with their aims. Nonetheless, the manner in which they tested the coherence of contemporary political economic thought arguably laid the foundation upon which Smith and others would build.

Second, these Irish thinkers also importantly *diverged* from typical eighteenth-century mercantilist thinking in several ways. These modifications to mercantilism resulted in large part from the unusual political situation of Ireland (as a nation politically dependent on England) and helped orient their economic thinking along more institutional lines. In particular, the emphasis of the Irish on full employment and on the modification of social as well as political institutions is an early step forward in making political economy more sophisticated. The emphasis that the Dublin Philosophical Society placed on the role of spreading practical knowledge, for instance, is under-appreciated. Instead of focusing simply on balance of trade, these philosophically minded men sought to reorient economic thinking in terms of wealth generation, especially in terms of the role of the larger population. As a result, there is a clear progression in the thought of early eighteenth-century Irishmen away from characterizing poverty as a 'moral defect trap' and instead thinking of poverty in terms of the institutions and incentives that govern the lives of people.

Drawing demonstrably on the work of others in the Dublin Philosophical Society, George Berkeley arguably advances the most philosophically savvy theory of political economy that recognizes the importance of crafting social and political institutions that provide proper incentives for people to escape poverty. One might reasonably think of Berkeley as learning from his fellow Irishmen and then presenting those insights in a particularly effective manner in his works of political economy. The present essay, however, focuses on Berkeley's contemporaries.

Marc A. Hight

2. Seventeenth and Eighteenth Century Mercantilism

'Mercantilism' is no longer a term with a broadly well-accepted definition, but arguably some central tenets remain fairly clear. As Jonathan Barth notes,

> Today, there is very little agreement on any precise definition for the word *mercantilism*, and an aura of ambiguity now surrounds it.... Diversity, however, arose out of consensus: out of the common supposition that a favorable balance of trade and the resulting influx of money into a country – the balance-of-trade doctrine and specie objective – were the principal means to power and plenty' (Barth, 2016, p. 257).

This alleged consensus should not obscure the significant differences in economic thought in the eighteenth century. There were debates about how best to promote favorable balances of trade and promote the well-being (variously characterized) of nations. Those debates reveal differences large enough for some scholars to deny that the concept has any meaningful use as a historical category at all.[4] For my purposes, however, the underlying commonalities are sufficient to ground my argument and provide a platform for discussing political economy in the context of eighteenth-century Ireland.

The most widely accepted exemplar of English mercantilist thinking is the seventeenth-century thinker Thomas Mun. Printed in 1664, Mun's *Englands Treasure by Forraign Trade, or The Balance of our Forraign Trade is The Rule of our Treasure* has an apt title. Under the guise of advice to his son, Mun advances his core thesis early: 'The ordinary means therefore to encrease our wealth and treasure is by Forraign Trade, wherein wee must ever observe this rule; to sell more to strangers yearly than wee consume of theirs in value'.[5] One appropriate if slightly oversimplified way of characterizing conventional economic wisdom at the time is through the phrase 'balance of trade'. The logic of the view depends on the assumption that the possession of specie – in particular silver and gold – constitutes (national) wealth or is at a minimum a reasonable surrogate for such wealth. Thus, when one exports more than one imports, there is more specie coming into the country, and some of that comes into the treasury through a variety of taxes and duties. That all of England (and later Britain) operated under this conventional wisdom is evident by the continual repetition of its core themes

---

[4] See Pincus (2012) and Stern and Wennerlind (2014, pp. 3–22).
[5] See Mun (1664, Ch. 2, 3).

throughout the first half of the eighteenth century. The most orthodox repository of mercantilism is probably *The British Merchant*,
first published in 1713 and reprinted several times, including a
large third edition in 1748. The author provides a summary of his
main points early in the work, of which I reproduce the initial five
propositions to serve as a representative example.

1.   That the Prosperity and Happiness of this Kingdom depend
     very much upon our foreign Trade.
2.   That we have no Gold or Silver of our own growth; that all we
     have is imported from abroad, in exchange for the Product and
     Manufactures of our own Country.
3.   That we gain Gold and Silver from those Countries which do
     not sell us so great a value of Manufacture as they take from
     us; for in this case the Balance must be paid in Money.
4.   That we must pay a Balance in Money to such Countries as sell
     more Manufactures than they take from us; and that the capital
     Stock of Bullion is diminished by such a Commerce, unless the
     Goods we import from an over-balancing Country shall be re-
     exported.
5.   That we are most enriched by those Countries which pay us the
     greatest Sums upon the Balance; and most impoverish'd by
     those which carry off the greatest Balance from us.[6]

The underlying concept of wealth that motivates this thinking is
not entirely unreasonable for the period, even if now largely
thought to be mistaken. The physical possession of specie was
thought important for a number of reasons. First, most believed
that the prosperity of a nation was dependent on its supply of
capital in a system where the total (global) volume of trade was
essentially static. Trade, as it were, was essentially thought of as a
zero-sum game. This idea ties in well with the presumption in
favor of economic self-sufficiency. As an example, a nation dependent
on agricultural imports was viewed as being at a strategic disadvantage in times of conflict. Although many with a passing familiarity
with mercantilism associate it with protectionism with respect to
manufactured goods, agricultural protectionism was equally as important. Second, having a reserve of specie was considered essential
in case of emergency, to include the threat of war. Third, large
stocks of circulating specie facilitate domestic trade essential for the
proper functioning of the economy. Finally, the possession of
specie was more or less a demonstrable sign of wealth and economic

---

[6]   See King (1721, I. 21).

success. It was a visible measuring stick of relative power and political robustness.

Mercantilist England thus had a number of major aims in their economic policy throughout the 17th and 18th centuries, all in the service of accumulating as much specie as possible through maintaining a favorable balance of trade. I want to emphasize four of them that resonate particularly strongly with the themes of our Irish thinkers.

(1)   Protect English manufactures from foreign competition
(2)   Protect English agriculture
(3)   Encourage the growth of a native merchant fleet
(4)   Correct the moral defects of the populace, to include fighting inappropriate luxury as well combating the special defects of the poor, insofar as those defects adversely impacted balance of trade

The lengths to which England (and then Britain) went to pursue these goals should not be underestimated. For instance, the English forced their colonies to pay for everything in hard currency where possible. This policy ensured that specie would dominantly remain at home. Since that policy quickly removed hard currency from the colonies, local economies often operated by payment in kind with other products in lieu of cash. American colonial money was not legal tender in England. The Irish pound was a metal coin and was allowed to trade in England (the rate was set at 13 Irish pounds per 12 pounds sterling in 1701), but similar policies applied to them also typically saw specie in short supply in Ireland. By design, the colonies were starved of official British coinage. As evidence of the larger point, in 1715 the colony of North Carolina made seventeen different forms of money legal tender, ranging from tobacco to Spanish and Portuguese coins to wampum copied from natives. In general, the policy of England towards its colonies was one of forced dependence. To give a sense of the expansiveness of the mindset, most colonies were not even allowed to have their own local Anglican bishops. Clergy were forced to return to England for ordination. Although Ireland had its own bishops, most of the colonies (including the American colonies) did not.

The Navigation Act was similarly designed to protect mercantile interests. The Act, passed in 1651 and renewed in various forms throughout the remainder of the 17th century, required that goods from Asia, Africa, or the Americas be transported only in English ships. The Scots were exempted from the policy after union in 1707, but Ireland was excluded from the benefits of the laws until 1779 (the laws were not repealed until 1849). The Wool Act of

1699 and the previous Importation Act of 1667 are common examples of mercantilist thought at work in England. The latter banned Irish cattle from being sold in England (it was eventually repealed in 1863). These and similar acts were largely the result of internal domestic politics in England, but they were driven and enabled by conventional economic wisdom.[7] What matters for our purposes here is that justification for these acts were largely along the lines of promoting balance of trade through the protection of domestic industries. What is demonstrably *not* present in the goals of the mercantilist is much reference to the wealth of the *people*. In short, the welfare of the populace is at best a means to the ends of national wealth, and not an end in itself.

3. Conventional Wisdom in Ireland

Faced with mercantilist policies, the educated Protestant Irish were forced to find new ways to develop and defend their interests in the eighteenth century. At the same time, these Protestant elites in Ireland considered themselves *both* essentially English *and* Irish, which placed them in an unusual position. The result is a group of thinkers trying to bend conventional economic wisdom to their own ends, which includes the well-being of Ireland, broadly considered.

What makes this group of Irish thinkers interesting and important is that they were generally all personally linked (including Berkeley). Most were members of the Dublin Society of 1731[8] or operated within its social sphere,[9] they were all Anglicans with a commitment

---

[7] The Importation Act, for instance, was strongly contested in Parliament by representatives in London, who consumed much Irish beef, and graziers in England who supplied feed to the Irish cattle industry. The bill is also widely believed to be a political ploy by Lord Ashley and the 2nd duke of Buckingham against the interests of the duke of Ormond – Lord Lieutenant of Ireland at the time – and the earl of Clarendon, the lord chancellor. The ploy worked; Ormond was removed as Lord Lieutenant of Ireland shortly thereafter and his faction lost favor with the king.

[8] There were previous societies created in Dublin with similar or identical names. The earliest is the Dublin Philosophical Society founded in 1684 by William Molyneux.

[9] Prior and Dobbs were founding members. Madden was active within the society and listed amongst its members by 1734. Berkeley was a close friend of Prior, and was invited to formal membership but declined.

to certain similar moral and religious worldviews, and they had a common cause, namely the economic development of Ireland. Here I argue that these men were bound, often implicitly, by the conceptual constraints of the general concept of mercantilism as just outlined.[10] They recognized the critical role of balance of trade, they endorsed the moral defect theory of poverty, and they accepted the need to accumulate hard currency. That said, they also diverged from the dominant mercantile thinking by emphasizing the need for a development program that made critical use of knowledge and trade skills, by noting the need to encourage population growth, and by advancing an alternative conception of wealth production that took better account of the interests of the general population. Berkeley's insistence, for instance, that money should be re-conceptualized as a 'ticket' or 'counter' was aimed at focusing economic policy on monetary circulation (in a closed national system). His view, however, fell short of the dynamic monetary analysis that would emerge at the end of the century.[11] Nonetheless, instead of simply accepting that hard currency *just is* national wealth, these Irish thinkers advanced a more comprehensive understanding of wealth. To be more precise, I contend we might characterize their thinking by the following claims.

(1)   Wealth should be re-conceptualized and thought increasingly in terms of wealth production, understood as industry (labor) and the well-being of the populace. Focusing on the people – especially through full employment – leads to wealth in a nation.

(2)   Wealth requires an emphasis on specialization, knowledge, and institutional roles in economic development.

(3)   Political convergence: England must be made to see Ireland and the Irish as British. To facilitate this end, one must avoid economic rivalry with Britain.

James Livesey notes that there were additional connections. For example, Dobbs' father, who had been a correspondent of William Molyneux (whose brother Thomas Molyneux was a founding member) was involved in one of the Society's earliest projects concerning a proposed Irish atlas. See Livesey (2012, p. 63).

[10]   In making this claim, I acknowledge that the larger concept of mercantilism is more complicated and diverse. I am purposefully narrowing the concept to make it appropriate for the present context.

[11]   See Vickers (1959, esp. Ch. 8).

These characteristics *modify* their understanding of mercantile wisdom. I draw these claims from an analysis of three central figures who were active in the first half of the eighteenth century. Thomas Prior, founder of the Dublin Philosophical Society and close friend of Berkeley, published his *List of the Absentees of Ireland* in 1729. Samuel Madden, an Anglican clergyman and key proponent of the Dublin Philosophical Society, published his *Reflections and Resolutions Proper for the Gentlemen of Ireland* in 1733 (reprinted in 1738). Arthur Dobbs, Irish MP for Carrick Fergus and later governor of the territory of North Carolina in the American colonies, published his own work on political economy in two volumes between 1729 and 1731. He was not an ongoing central figure in the Dublin Society, but he knew Madden and Prior and all three were familiar with each other's works. Dobb's *Essay on the Trade and Improvement of Ireland* is a detailed and comprehensive view of Ireland's economy and its relationship with England. Berkeley's own *Querist* first appeared in 1736[12] and is the most philosophical of this list, but all of them clearly draw from one another both in spirit and through literal references.

There are others who might be included in the group. Archbishop William King (1650–1729) contributed to the *Observations* of the (earlier) Dublin Philosophical Society and his correspondence is rich with economic insights and observations. Francis Hutchinson (1660–1739), Bishop of Down and Connor,[13] contributed similar insights concerning the development of his diocese. One must at least mention Jonathan Swift (1667–1745), whose polemical writings frequently touched on matters of political economy, especially his famous opposition to Wood's halfpence in his *Drapier Letters*. There are others as well who made important contributions.[14] I focus on these three figures primarily because they are relatively tightly focused in their thinking and they are closely connected in time and space.

Let us start with an analysis of our Irish thinkers and the extent to which they are orthodox mercantilists. They observe explicitly the central role of hard currency reserves; 'The Riches of every Country is principally estimated by the Quantity of its Gold and

---

[12]   It is worth noting that Samuel Madden edited and published the anonymous edition of the *Querist*.

[13]   Not to be confused with Francis Hutcheson (1694–1746), the Irish-born philosopher associated with the Scottish Enlightenment.

[14]   David Bindon, John Browne, Richard Cox, Alexander Macaulay, Philip Skelton, Daniel Webb, to name a few.

Marc A. Hight

Silver...'.[15] They are all consistent in *recognizing* the importance of balance of trade as a guiding principle. Thomas Prior notes, for instance, that:

> Countries that abound in Mines of Gold and Silver, are enabled by the Bounty of Nature, to bear an Exportation of their Bullion; but others, which want this natural Produce, and have no other way of getting or keeping Money, but by having the Ballance of Trade in their Favour, suffer extreamly, when ever they want Coin sufficient for circulating their Business (Prior, 1729, p. 20).

Prior's complaint is that the prevalence of absenteeism amongst the landowners (individuals who collect rents in Ireland but live outside of Ireland) effectively robs Ireland of the currency it needs to sustain commerce and hence a favorable balance of trade. Later in the same book he gives rules for judging whether trade is favorable or not. The first rule is elegantly mercantile, demonstrating the centrality of the concept of balance of trade.

> I. That is the most advantageous Trade, which takes off the greatest Quantity of the Produce of a Country, and especially of its Manufactures, and which imports fewest Commodities, and those capable of farther Improvement; in which Case there will be the greatest Return in Specie to make up the Balance (Prior, 1729, p. 56).

According to this rule, since England takes off more than 500,000 *l.* yearly (as Prior notes, nearly half of all of the exports of Ireland), mostly in wool and linen, they constitute Ireland's most important trading partner. Yet he also notes that England exports to Ireland 'near the full Value of all we Export to them' (Prior, 1729, p. 57).[16] The point is otherwise quickly passed over. Interestingly, Prior's argument shields England from any blame.

> We are apt to complain of the Hardships laid upon us by *England* in respect to our Trade, and when we are pinch'd, and in Distress charge our Misfortunes to the Account of other People; but if we truly examine all Circumstances, we shall find, that to *our selves* we owe most of the Misfortunes, and Inconveniences we labour under; we owe them to our immoderate Consumption of Foreign

---

[15] See Prior (1729, p. 82).

[16] This is, of course, the error of mercantilist thinking. Today political economists typically believe that voluntary trade is mutually beneficial. Negative balances of trade are neither good nor bad so long as trade occurs.

Commodities at home, and extravagant spending abroad (Prior, 1729, p. 28).

Prior is well aware of the dependent relation, arguing that Irish exports produce considerable profit for the English. This happens first in the case of woolen and linen raw materials that are turned into manufactured goods at great profit for the English. Additionally, Prior keenly notes that the majority of the shipping is done through the English merchant fleet to the considerable advantage of English interests (Prior, 1729, pp. 60–61). And to make matters worse, the English profit handsomely from the large number of Irish absentees who spend much of their coin in England. But the remedies proposed – to be discussed shortly – focus on the behavior of the Irish and not the English.

Samuel Madden similarly emphasizes the necessity of increasing Ireland's trade, but primarily with an emphasis on correcting moral defect. The gentlemen and gentlewomen of Ireland should consume domestic products, avoid unnecessary luxuries, and spend their wealth in Ireland. The poor need to learn how to be industrious and avoid idleness. Just perusing some of the titles of his resolutions (which are exhortations to the gentlemen of Ireland) makes this emphasis clear.

> *Resolution I:* That, as Landlords in this poor Kingdom, we will do our utmost in our little spheres, to remove the defects and difficulties which we find our people and country, and particularly our own estates and tenants, lie under.
> *Resolution V:* That we will oppose and discourage all ill Customs, that destroy frugality, thrift and industry in our Tenants.
> *Resolution X:* That as Masters of Families we will banish from our Tables that luxurious way of living, which is so common and pernicious to the Gentlemen of Ireland.

Like Prior, Madden takes great pains to make it clear that his prescriptions are made in careful deference to England. The fifteenth resolution states 'That we will be so true to ourselves as never to hurt the trade or interest of Great Britain' (Madden, 1738, p. 84). Again, the concept of balance of trade colors the entire analysis.

With Dobbs we find much the same. Dobbs spent considerable time studying the ledgers in the custom houses to provide actual numbers when it came to issues of Anglo-Irish trade.[17] The point

---

[17] Cullen complains about the Irish of the time allegedly making claims without evidence, but he exempts Dobbs and Prior as exceptions to the rule. See Cullen (1967).

Marc A. Hight

was to be able to make fact-based claims about the balance of trade between Ireland and England. His stated intent was to 'restore the Ballance which is now visibly against us [Ireland]' (Dobbs, 1729, p. 4). Near the end of his study Dobbs argues that aiding Ireland requires addressing its poor balance of trade.

> 'Tis highly necessary for us to consider how we may increase our Exports and lessen our Imports, that we may not sink through vast Draughts upon us from thence (Dobbs, 1729, p. 73).

The point, again, is to highlight that these individuals are in the larger part still beholden to the core claims of mercantilist thinking.

Nonetheless, as a group they also introduced new ways of thinking about political economy that demonstrably contributed to the eventual rejection of mercantile thinking. The point should not be overstated, however. My contention is that Dobbs, Madden, and Prior were mercantilists. However, they were *Irish* mercantilists and the difference matters. In short, the political dependence of Ireland on Britain in the eighteenth century forced these capable individuals to revisit the core claims of conventional economic wisdom. I argue that the key changes are twofold. First, the Irish mercantilists slowly and subtly argued for a conception of wealth that emphasized its generation as opposed to its simple nature as piles of metal (which is not to say that they were the *only* individuals who so argued; I am simply focusing on this collection of able minds in Ireland). This first contention is more controversial than one might initially suspect. A rival reading is also plausible, namely that these Irish thinkers did *not* believe that trade created wealth, but instead were making simple pragmatic arguments about how to keep specie within Ireland. I engage this concern below. Second, I argue that they, perhaps in a manner that was not entirely reflective, introduced avowedly institutional concerns into economic thinking in principled ways. They emphasized full employment, the treatment of the working poor, the educational environment, and legislative incentives as a part of their reforms. To the degree that their proposals implicitly, and sometimes explicitly, undermined the assumption that balance of trade was the end-all and be-all of economic policy, they constitute an important moment in the history of the philosophy of political economy.

4. Irish Mercantilism

One striking feature of the Irish mercantilists was their consistent emphasis on *judging* the wealth of a state in terms of the conditions of their working poor. The distinction here is a subtle one. Wealth was still viewed ultimately in terms of stocks of metals, but a good *guide* to such wealth ought to be measured by the welfare of the people. Sir Richard Cox, the 2nd Baronet, expressed the point clearly in a published letter to Prior.

> Every Nation has the Reputation of being rich or poor, from the Condition of the lowest Class of its Inhabitants. If they are plentifully and wholesomely fed; warmly and decently cloathed; neatly and comfortably lodged; that Country, which they dwell in, is esteemed wealthy and happy: Because, all these Conveniencies proceed from a Surplus, remaining to their own Use, after all Demands upon them are satisfied (Cox, 1749, p. 11).

If a nation's poorest are relatively well off, that is a signal that there is a 'surplus', by which Cox is implying a balance of trade surplus for that nation. The assumption that wealth is essentially a balance of trade issue remains; but the emphasis changes.

Years earlier Berkeley gave voice to the same position in the *Querist*. 'Whether a people can be called poor where the common sort are well fed, clothed, and lodged?' (Berkeley, 1736, vol. 6, Query 2, p. 105). Much has been made of the arguments of Berkeley and others to the effect that money was a ticket or counter and could serve good ends without being a precious metal. Berkeley emphasizes not simply money, but the *role* it plays in generating wealth by exciting industry. 'Industry is the natural sure way to wealth.... Money is so far useful to the public as it promoteth industry, and credit having the same effect is of the same value with money...' (Berkeley, 1736, vol. 6, p. 71). We find the Irish mercantilists discussing wealth in terms of its 'foundations' and the mechanisms for generating wealth instead of simple appeals to trade surpluses and stocks of metals. Madden writes, in defending the proposal for an Irish national bank, 'Eighthly, because it will not only double our money, but also treble our industry (*the sole foundation of national wealth*) by enlarging our business, and cause such a quick circulation of our cash...'.[18] Appeals to industry and the generation of wealth are emphasized over the nature of the wealth itself.

At this point one might reasonably use Madden's claim to advance a rival hypothesis. Perhaps, one might argue, Madden is not defending some importantly new conception of wealth. Instead, he is defending traditional mercantilist principles more deeply than I am admitting. Madden's claim (like those of others, including

---

[18] See Madden (1738, p. 173), my emphasis.

Marc A. Hight

Berkeley) that industry is the font of wealth, can reasonably be read as the claim that increasing productivity alters the balance of trade favorably and keeps specie in the country. After all, Madden concludes in the passage I cite by noting that industry ultimately causes 'a quick circulation of our cash'. This and other comments makes it more likely that these Irish thinkers were simply trying to find pragmatic ways to keep wealth (read as specie) within Ireland.

The objection is a good one. I contend that in fact it is partly true. Madden and others *were* thinking in precisely those terms and most certainly did see one of the advantages of their proposals to be the increase of specie within Ireland. But the two explanations are not mutually exclusive. My contention is that these Irish thinkers were breaking away from mercantilist thought, but such conceptual breaks are rarely neat and clean. They are, *in addition to* concerns about specie, opening the path for more modern views of wealth.

As a politically dependent populace, the Irish had to think creatively about wealth in a system that was avowedly determined to keep them in a subservient position. As trade was still considered essentially a zero-sum game, any advantage accruing to the Irish was immediately perceived as a threat to the English. The Irish mercantilists accordingly combatted this response in two ways. First, they argued that promoting trade and industry in Ireland would have the result of increasing industry and trade in England as well. If such proposals were accepted, it is likely that Ireland would indeed enjoy more specie staying and circulating within its borders. Their proposals also signal a more expansive sense of both industry and the benefits of trade. The arguments advanced are subtle and forward thinking for the period. Second, they sought entrance to the 'in-group' by trying to persuade England that the Irish were (or ought to be) British too.

The first strategy demanded, in effect, the argument that a *better* way towards wealth (including concepts of wealth as specie) was simply to increase the size of the proverbial economic pie through strategic trading. If trading is zero-sum, then increasing trade in Ireland could only benefit England if the total amount of trade also expanded, with England taking the larger share of that increase. But such an increase requires surrendering the assumption that trade is zero-sum in the first place. Thus, I argue that the Irish were in effect proposing *new* mutually beneficial trades with England and 'selling' it to them with the promise that England would take the lion share of the benefits. Without perhaps fully understanding the underlying point, the Irish were undermining the mercantilist assumption that trade is zero-sum.

86

What produces wealth is nothing other than industrious labor. Thus, in this first strategy we see a two-pronged approach from the Irish mercantilists. On the one hand, they advocate for full employment on the grounds that more people engaging in productive labor will produce more value to trade and hence more wealth for all involved. On the other hand, they advocate for measures to remedy whatever defects might exist in the populace (rich and poor alike) that might frustrate the goal of growing the proverbial pot. Adam Smith would later tie productive labor, high wages, and population growth together, arguing that one proximate cause of growth and wealth was nothing other than the proportion of the population engaged in productive labor.[19] The latter approach resonated with English mercantilists, who held similar views. Daniel Defoe in 1705 writes scathingly about the poor of *England,* noting there is a 'taint of slothfulness upon our poor', and

> I make no difficulty to promise on a short summons, to produce above a thousand families in England, within my particular knowledge, who go in rags, and their children wanting bread, whose fathers can earn their 15 to 25 s. per week, but will not work, who may have work enough, but are too idle to seek after it....[20]

The Irish, however, introduced *other* remedies for inefficient or lackadaisical work in addition to berating the poor.

One efficient remedy for poverty and lack of wealth was full employment, directed by careful policy. This end would first require the English allowing the development of industry in Ireland. But it would also require a will in Ireland to compel the able to work when moral defect otherwise precludes it. Madden advocates the revival of a 1636 law that built work houses to 'employ all rogues,

---

[19] Smith writes, 'The liberal reward of labour, by enabling them to provide better for their children, and consequently to bring up a greater number, naturally tends to widen and extend those limits.... The liberal reward of labour, therefore, as it is the effect of increasing wealth, so it is the cause of increasing population' (Smith, 1776, I.viii.40 and 42, pp. 98–99). 'The liberal reward of labour ... as it is the necessary effect, so it is the natural symptom of increasing national wealth. The scanty maintenance of the labouring poor, on the other hand, is the natural symptom that things are at a stand, and their starving condition that things are going fast backwards' (Smith, 1776, I: viii.27, p. 91).

[20] See Defoe (1705). For additional period complaints see Hutchison (1953, esp. pp. 56–57).

vagabonds, and study beggars' (Madden, 1738, p. 118). It is only the failure to properly enforce the law that provides an obstacle.

> I have made the fuller abstract of this law, as it is plain it is wholly owing to our own neglect in executing it, that we want proper work-houses, and are therefore presented with such swarms of lazy, useless vagrants in every county in the kingdom. It is certainly one of the worst instances of our being happy in good laws, and miserable by our letting them sleep forgotten and neglected…. (Madden, 1738, p. 149).

Generally the proposals centered on developing new industries that would not be rivalrous with England. Dobbs makes precisely this aim central to his work.

> To this Purpose, I have made some Inquiry into the Numbers and Employment of the People; and have propos'd some Heads, which, if improv'd and reduc'd into proper Laws by our Legislature, I hope will contribute to make us frugal, employ our Poor, improve our Country, extend our Trade, and consequently increase our Numbers and add considerably to His Majesty's Revenue.
>   I am, convinced, we may do this and at the same Time add to the Power, Wealth, and Trade of *Britain*, by employing our Poor in those Branches of the several Manufactures that it is the Interest of *England* we should deal in…. (Dobbs, 1729, pp. ii-iii, Dedication).

All of our Irish mercantilists (to include Berkeley) were staunch advocates of the burgeoning linen industry and of developing new manufactures, from hemp to glassware. The driving point, however, was to increase wealth through increasing productive labor.

Another remedy for poverty and the lack of wealth production was education. Madden in particular was keen to point out the ignorance in Ireland's industries. The emphasis on improving skills and knowledge is, to my mind, a characteristic feature of the Irish mercantilists not pervasive elsewhere. Rashid, in commenting on the emphasis, notes that the Irish mercantilists probably 'had a somewhat better perspective' than Adam Smith did on the relative importance of knowledge with respect to specialization in the growth of productivity (Rashid, Ph.D. dissertation, p. 10). The claim is likely overstated, since Smith was clearly an advocate of public schooling precisely because of the perceived benefits.[21] But the Irish are pushing the

---

[21] See Thomas (2018) and West (2010).

point earlier in the century. Consider a characteristic passage from Madden on the impact of ignorance with respect to tillage.

> A third great obstruction to our tillage is, our downright negligence or ignorance in many material articles belonging to it, and our retaining several old customs which are very prejudicial to it (Madden, 1738, p. 104).

Madden discusses different kinds of ploughs that might be used to greater effect in differing situations, something the English had mastered and the Irish had not. Merely introducing innovations in ploughs, of course, is not enough. Madden calls for programs of instruction. 'But we work our ploughs as ill as we make them' (Madden, 1738, p. 105). In short, the Irish mercantilists are calling for systemic vocational education. The Dublin Society would, after 1731, work to promote the dissemination of this kind of knowledge. But this was directly the result of these men and their recognition that wealth generation was tied *broadly* to the dissemination of knowledge and skills in the workforce. Madden's vision was sweeping, as we find suggested in his nineteenth resolution.

> We resolve to do all we can to introduce all new improvements in husbandry to Ireland, which are likely to be of real profit and advantage, and especially the culture of hops, madder, weld, woad, saffron, liquorice, clover and other grass seeds (Madden, 1738, p. 117).

The idea is to produce wealth through putting the population to work in new industries, fueled both by education and training on the one hand, and legal compulsion on the other.

All this said, the Irish mercantilists were also nonetheless admittedly advocates of the moral defect theory. Even here, however, differences emerge in the complaints about the nature of the poor. The goal was to effectively promote industry. 'Industry' as a concept entails productive effort. But the Irish were more consistent in equally applying moral correctives to the poor and the rich.[22] Stockjobbing and gambling were well-known pastimes for those able to afford it. Although spending on foreign luxuries was universally frowned upon regardless of the nation, the Irish mercantilists were amongst the most zealous in pursuing the point. Prior's *List of Absentees* was an explicit attack on the behavior of the Protestant

---

[22] Berkeley, for instance, had a dim view of the work ethic of the Irish poor (for examples, see *Querist*, Q 19, 106, and Q 357, 134), and chastised the rich for their pursuit of luxury (see *Ruin*, 74–75 and *Querist*, Q103, 113).

Ascendancy in Ireland, echoed by all our Irish mercantilists and many others besides.

In addition, and unlike their English counterparts, the prosecution of the poor for moral defects was more nuanced. Their position in Ireland enabled them to see better that there was another relevant factor in the behavior of the poor, namely that of institutional incentives. In short, one cannot expect the poor to be eager to labor unless they live in situations where they can reasonably expect to benefit from that added labor, either in terms of intensity or longer hours. Prior diagnoses the problem of laziness sharply, even inside his mercantilism.

> ...for Poor we must *ever* be, so long as all the Advantages, we can make by our Industry and Trade, fall so much short of our Remittances Abroad. If we must be always Poor, 'tis better to enjoy Poverty with Ease, than to sweat, and toil, without any Hopes of mending our Condition, and without any other Effect than that of supporting the Vanity of our Gentlemen Abroad, who treat their Country with Contempt, and ruin it without Remorse (Prior, 1729, p. 73).

The passage rings true, but with an odd tone. Basically Prior argues that unless the labor of the Irish outstrips the negative factors against Irish balance of trade (such as the drain absentees place on the nation), then the poor have no good reason to work. Surely, he opines, it would be easier to address the problem of absenteeism than to try and encourage the poor to work to no advantage.

Prior generalizes the problem slightly earlier.

> Our Case is much the same with the *Plantations*, the Produce, and Profit of all our Labour issues constantly to the People of *England*, and therefore 'tis its Interest to give the People of *Ireland* full Employment, to encourage their Industry in every Branch of Trade, and not to stop any Inlett through which Treasure may come into it, since every Acquisition and Profit that we can make, will at last center among them; if they would look upon us with the same Favour, and in the same Light as they ought to do their *Plantations*, they would justly reckon us, a main Foundation of their Wealth and think it not consistent with the Interest to cramp our Industry, or render out Labour trifling and insignificant (Prior, 1729, p. 65).

Because of Ireland's dependent nature, England reaps benefits from everything Ireland does. Prior discusses in the surrounding text not only the advantages of tax revenue, tariffs, and the like, but also the generalized benefits of a *larger economic system*. He uses the example of plantations to make the point. Britain was investing heavily in plantations around the globe, largely in the belief that the production from those plantations would generate more wealth via trade. Prior implores his readers to see that the same applies to what Ireland produces as well. If Ireland were made to be more productive – if it were made possible to trade *more* with Ireland – the *economic pie would grow.*

This brings us full circle on the first strategy employed to promote the generation of wealth. By pursuing full employment through education, moral correction, and the opportunities of new manufactures, the Irish hoped to partake in a share of the overall growth in wealth.

Yet the Irish mercantilists understood that these arguments would likely not be enough, so they engaged in a parallel line of argument. The idea is simple: persuade the English that the Irish should be included in the 'in-group'. If the English would only understand that the Irish were in fact British, they would see that what helps Ireland helps themselves as well. The pleas for understanding ranged from simple exhortations to plans for union along the lines of the 1707 union with Scotland. Madden is customarily politic, arguing for union as an inevitability.

> Nothing but the plain expediency, and benefit of an union could have made Cromwell (who studied to please the people, where he hurt not his own interest by it) take such paces as we all know he did in this matter, and surely the day will yet come, when we shall not hang like a dead limb, on Great Britain, when we might do such good work for it, if our bandages were removed entirely. The Saxon heptarchy, was hardly more a disjointed heap of states than England, Wales, Scotland, and Ireland, seemed before Wales, and Scotland, were so happily united to her; and as Ireland has greatly the advantage of both the last in extent and goodness of soil, trade and number of people, it is not improbable, she will one day have the same happiness and honour (Madden, 1738, p. 95).

Madden goes on to immediately anticipate and refute objections, in particular emphasizing that Ireland would gain little in terms of *political* power to threaten the interests of the rest of the proposed union. Ireland would provide more food, more soldiers, and less trouble were her citizens proper Britons.

5. The Failure of Irish Mercantilism

With a better sense of mercantilism and the key components that make the Irish version importantly distinctive, I turn now to defend two more philosophical and speculative theses. The first of these is that, for all of its innovative spirit, the political proposals of the Irish were essentially doomed to failure, even had robust versions of them somehow been enacted in Ireland.

I dismiss for the sake of argument concerns about how such proposals would have been passed given the dependent nature of the Irish Parliament. None of the laws in Ireland could be put into effect without the approval of the English Parliament. Even so, my assertion here is that the core logic of mercantilism would have undermined the very progress these Irish thinkers were focused on making. In short, my claim is they did not separate themselves enough from the core claims of mercantilism to have a completely coherent economic plan. None of this should be taken to diminish their ingenious and important conceptual advances in political economy. Yet there are reasons Ireland would labor under oppressive restriction for the remainder of the century.

The argument is fairly simple. Mercantilism emphasizes the accumulation of wealth via favorable balances of trade. Ireland was not considered either English or British. Hence, no proposal to significantly advance the wealth of Ireland would be allowed by England (as that would entail less for England). No doubt the logic of the argument is obvious, but there are lessons to be gleaned by seeing the argument applied to the historical case of Ireland.

Perhaps the exemplar of the proposals the Irish mercantilists wanted to advance was the development of the linen and flax industries in Ireland. Prior, Madden, Dobbs, and many others all enthusiastically pushed for public and private funding to employ Irish workers in these new endeavors. The Irish linen industry already existed in the early eighteenth century, but it grew and eventually employed many people. What is instructive, however, is how this proposal was received – and resisted – by others in England. The resistance starts well before the formation of the Dublin Society, and our Irish political economists were well aware of it.

One opponent to the cause of developing Irish industry was Charles Davenant (1656–1714), a classical English mercantilist who wrote an influential book *The Balance of Trade* in 1699 and others besides. He was a prolific pamphleteer in the 1690s and his arguments were engaged into the 1720s and 1730s. Like his mercantilist compatriots, he defined wealth as a favorable balance of trade and argued against the practice of foreign luxury spending. Unlike some others he did advocate for population growth, but mainly at home and in specific cases such as plantation-style colonies. Davenant opposed any measures designed to aid Irish linen and hempen manufacturing. Dobbs takes on Davenant directly.

> By this we may see the Falsity of Dr. *Davenant's* Argument, when we were depriv'd of the Benefit of the woolen Manufacture here, he reasons against setting up the Linnen and Hempen Manufactures in *Ireland*; alleging, if we supply'd *England* with Linnens, the *Hamburgh* Trade would be lost in great Measure by their having no sufficient Return they could make (Dobbs, 1729, p. 67).

Dobbs rightly sees what other mercantilists miss: the entire argument rests on the assumption that trade is zero-sum. Dobbs continues.

> Now it is plain from this way of Reasoning, that he must mean that either that Trade must always against *Britain* upon the Ballance, or that they could not expect to Trade with them if they receiv'd a Ballance from *Hamburgh*; and consequently that Trade, as then carried on, was of no Benefit to *Britain*; for if *England* consumed at home as many *Hamburgh* Linnens or more than the Value of the Goods carried there, then we were either barely Savers or lost by that Trade, and *Hamburgh* must have a Ballance in return from *England*, which would not be poured back again any other way as it would from *Ireland*; thus the benefits would redound to *Hamburgh* instead of *England*, and the foreign Poor be employ'd instead of those under our Government; whereas by the established Maxims of Trade, a wise and prudent Nation should endeavor to procure fewer Importations than Exportations, that a Ballance in Case might be brought into it (Dobbs, 1729, pp. 67–68).

Dobbs understands Davenant's point reasonably well. English mercantilists worried that promoting Irish linens would shift England's trade to Ireland and away from Hamburg, who was then a supplier of linens for the English fleet. But if England stopped buying linens from Hamburg, then Hamburg, in order to right the balance of trade, would stop buying goods from England. Hence England would suffer. In the case of Ireland, however, since Ireland is a dependent colony, England has other avenues from which it can extract value (taxes, requiring Ireland to pay for army garrisons, etc.) and so the resultant losses would be lessened if not avoided. Thus, according to Davenant, England has an interest in maintaining trade with Hamburg but not with Ireland. Dobbs criticizes him for inconsistency, since in a previous similar case concerning competition from muslin producers in the East Indies Davenant made no objection. But Dobbs' response essentially misses the underlying issue. The problem is the inflexible assumption that trade is a zero-sum game. Whereas our Irish innovators see the possibility of wealth generation through wealth *creation*, traditional mercantile thinking does not allow for the possibility.

One might thus read many of the arguments and proposals from the Irish with a sad sort of humor. They clearly see that they must persuade the English that they are not economic rivals. 'We must therefore endeavor', writes Madden, 'to the utmost of our power to make Great Britain see we will never not only rival, but even in any sort interfere with her interest in every branch of trade that can affect her people' (Madden, 1738, p. 85). And then Madden undermines his own point by suggesting a variety of industries where Ireland could excel and undercut production elsewhere. A particularly painful example concerns spirits, ale, and beer, where Madden enthuses,

> I shall mention but one particular more of a different nature, which our merchants may contribute greatly to the improvement of, and that is our brewing in the best perfection possible, the finest and strongest mum, ale, and beer. If once we could come to rival Brunswick, Bristol, and Wales, in the strength and beauty of those liquors which are in so much request abroad, we might save what, to our shame, we import from them, and by their help once we get coals of our own, to boil them with, export great quantities of them at reasonable rates to other nations, to the great increase of his majesty's customs and the full encouragement of our husband-man (Madden, 1738, pp. 166–67).

To be fair to Madden, he is trying to argue that, if considered a part of Britain, Ireland could greatly contribute to the wealth and well-being of all Britons. But I can only imagine that this read to his mercantilist contemporaries as a direct threat to the liquor industries in Bristol and Wales, which, as Madden explicitly says, Ireland would 'rival'. One might apply a similar logic to the arguments for the linen trade. As the Irish linen industry grew, English linen interests would be threatened. The Irish were in a difficult situation so long as the dominant views were mercantilist and they were politically under the thumb of the English.

I conclude that the political and policy proposals of the Irish mercantilists were doomed to less effect until the following century, when conventional wisdom was slowly changed by the success of Smith and others to understand the concept of trade as wealth generation. Union with England also helped – but arguably did not entirely solve – some of the economic problems as well. In turn, however, this leads me to my second point, which is to note the importance of the Irish mercantilists in nonetheless helping to bring about precisely this shift in thinking. Their emphasis on knowledge and other institutional features as impacting employment and productivity, as well as their subtle nudging of economic thinking towards wealth production and away from wealth accumulation, critically moved later eighteenth-century philosophers and political economists out of the mercantilist mindset. Although I have not the space to argue for the claim here, I nonetheless suggest that without the Irish mercantilists, Smith would not have the fullness of his own insights nor the ability to present them as effectively as he did.[23]

References

Jonathan Barth, 'Reconstructing Mercantilism: Consensus and Conflict in British Imperial Economy in the Seventeenth and Eighteenth Centuries', *William and Mary Quarterly*, 73 (2016) 257–90.

George Berkeley, '*An Essay towards preventing the Ruin of Great Britain*', in *The Works of George Berkeley, Bishop of Cloyne*, 9 vols. (London: Thomas Nelson and Sons, 1948–1957).

George Berkeley, '*The Querist*', in *The Works of George Berkeley, Bishop of Cloyne*, 9 vols., (First published 1736, reprinted London: Thomas Nelson and Sons, 1948–1957).

Sir Richard Cox, *A Letter from Sir Richard Cox, Bart. To Thomas Prior, Esq. Shewing, from Experience, A sure Method to establish the Linen Manufacture...* (Dublin: Peter Wilson, 1749).

L.M. Cullen, 'Problems in the Interpretation and Revision of Eighteenth-Century Irish Economic History', *Transactions of the Royal Historical Society*, 17 (1967), 1–22.

Daniel Defoe, *A Second Volume of the Writings of the Author of the True-Born Englishman* (London, 1705).

Arthur Dobbs, *An essay on the trade and improvement of Ireland* (Dublin: A. Rhames, 1729).

The Dublin Society's Weekly Observations (Dublin: R. Reilly, 1739), reprinted in Glasgow as *The Dublin Society's Weekly Observations for the Advancement of Agriculture and Manufactures* (Glasgow: R & A Foulis, 1756).

[23] I would like to thank Byron Carson, Eric Schliesser, Alex Cartwright, and Anthony Carilli for their thoughtful assistance on this article.

Marc A. Hight

T.W. Hutchison, 'Berkeley's *Querist* and Its Place in the Economic Thought of the Eighteenth Century' *British Journal for the Philosophy of Science*, 4 (1953), 52–77.

Charles King, *The British Merchant* (London: 2nd edition 1721).

James Livesey, 'A Kingdom of Cosmopolitan Improvers: The Dublin Society, 1731–1798', in *The Rise of Economic Societies in the Eighteenth Century: Patriotic Reform in Europe and North America* (New York: Palgrave Macmillan, 2012), 52–72.

Samuel Madden, *Reflections and Resolutions Proper for the Gentlemen of Ireland, as to their Conduct for the Service of their Country as Landlords...* (Dublin: R. Reilly, 1738 [1733]).

Hiroshi Mizuta, ed. *Adam Smith's Library* (New York: Oxford, 2000).

Thomas Mun, *Englands Treasure by Forraign Trade, or The Balance of our Forraign Trade is The Rule of our Treasure* (London: J.G. for Thomas Clark, 1664).

George Augustine Thomas O'Brien, *The economic history of Ireland in the eighteenth century* (Dublin: Maunsel and company, 1918).

Steve Pincus, 'Rethinking Mercantilism: Political Economy, the British Empire, and the Atlantic World in the Seventeenth and Eighteenth Centuries', *William and Mary Quarterly*, 69 (2012), 3–34.

Thomas Prior, *A List of the Absentees of Ireland and the Yearly Value of their Estates and Incomes Spent Abroad with Observations on the present Trade and Condition of that Kingdom* (Dublin: R. Gunne, 1729).

Salim Rashid, 'The Irish School of Economic Development: 1720–1750' *The Manchester School*, (1988), 345–69.

Salim Rashid, *The Irish School of Economic Development: 1700–1750*. PhD. Dissertation.

Adam Smith, *An Inquiry into the Nature and Causes of the Wealth of Nations* (Indianapolis: Liberty Fund, 1976 [1979, 1776]).

Philip Stern and Carl Wennerlind, 'Introduction', in *Mercantilism Reimagined: Political Economy in Early Modern Britain and Its Empire* (Oxford: Oxford University Press, 2014), 3–22.

Alex Thomas, 'Adam Smith on the Philosophy and Provision of Education', *Journal of Interdisciplinary Economics*, 30 (2018), 105–116

Douglas Vickers, *Studies in the Theory of Money: 1690–1776* (Philadelphia: Chilton Co., 1959).

E.G. West, *Education and the State*, 3rd edition (Indianapolis: Liberty Fund, 2010).

Berkeley's Criticisms of Shaftesbury and Hutcheson

SAMUEL C. RICKLESS

Abstract
In this paper, I attempt to clarify the nature and purpose of Berkeley's criticisms of Shaftesbury's and Hutcheson's ethical systems in the third chapter of *Alciphron*, explaining the extent to which those criticisms rely on the truth of idealism and considering whether Berkeley or his philosophical opponents have the better of the arguments. In the end, I conclude that some of Berkeley's criticisms are based on confusion and misunderstanding, others are likely contradicted by the empirical evidence, and yet others are unconvincing. At the same time, the criticisms reveal that Berkeley's metaphysical and ethical views are, perhaps surprisingly, significantly intertwined.

My aim is to clarify the nature and purpose of Berkeley's arguments in the third chapter of *Alciphron*. Most read the chapter as an attack on Anthony Ashley Cooper, the Third Earl of Shaftesbury. This makes sense, given that Berkeley goes to the trouble of quoting, sometimes directly, sometimes in mosaic fashion, from Shaftesbury's *Characteristics of Men, Manners, Opinions, Times*, both in the main text and in the footnotes. But some think – as I will argue, mistakenly – that Berkeley takes aim at two different Shaftesburys, an early Shaftesbury and a late Shaftesbury. Others fail to recognize the near explicit references to Francis Hutcheson's elaboration of some of the main themes of Shaftesbury's moral theory, assuming, perhaps from the fact that Hutcheson is not quoted, that Shaftesbury is the *sole* intended target of Berkeley's criticisms. Less well understood, as well, is the nature of Berkeley's criticisms of Shaftesbury and Hutcheson, and the extent to which they depend for their success on the truth of idealism. I will concentrate on elucidating the mistakes that Berkeley attributes to both of his opponents, and then ask whether, and to what degree, they are guilty of the errors Berkeley lays at their door.

1. Shaftesbury's Moral Theory and Hutcheson's Elaboration

Shaftesbury's philosophical output was published in pieces over the course of many years, and eventually collected in his *Characteristics*,

doi:10.1017/S1358246120000119   © The Royal Institute of Philosophy and the contributors 2020

Samuel C. Rickless

published in 1711. *Characteristics* is a sprawling and meandering
work that moves, sometimes within a single essay, through various
topics, including history, literary theory, aesthetics, and moral philosophy. My focus here is on Shaftesbury's ethics.

It is in the second essay, *Sensus Communis, An Essay on the Freedom
of Wit and Humour*, that Shaftesbury first turns, somewhat abruptly,
to the topic of 'morality and religion' (Shaftesbury, 1999, p. 37).[1]
There he proposes numerous criticisms of an approach to morals
he associates with Epicurus among the ancients and with Hobbes
among the moderns. According to the Epicurean/Hobbesian
picture, there are no moral requirements, rules, or virtues that
apply or exist antecedent to the social compact. Moreover, our motivation and obligation to morality or virtue stem from what is in
our own interests. But for Shaftesbury, virtue, which he connects
to 'a social feeling or sense of partnership with humankind'
(Shaftesbury, 1999, p. 50), is natural. Indeed, 'faith, justice,
honesty and virtue must have been as early as the state of nature',
for otherwise there would have been no obligation to obey the
social contract (Shaftesbury, 1999, p. 51). And what is natural, in
the relevant sense, *'in any creature or any kind…is that which is preser-
vative of the kind itself and conducing to its welfare and support'*
(Shaftesbury, 1999, p. 51).

Regarding the motive to be moral, Shaftesbury distinguishes
between 'the mere vulgar of mankind' and the 'man of a liberal education' (Shaftesbury, 1999, p. 59) or 'good breeding' (Shaftesbury,
1999, p. 60): whereas the latter is motivated to be virtuous for its
own sake (since virtue is 'estimable in itself' – (Shaftesbury, 1999,
p. 46)), the former 'often stand in need of such a rectifying object
as the gallows before their eyes' (Shaftesbury, 1999, p. 59). Well-
bred humans, he tells us, act 'from nature, in a manner necessarily
and without reflection': they never deliberate about whether to
commit 'rude or brutal' actions on the basis of 'prudential rules of
self-interest and advantage' (Shaftesbury, 1999, p. 60).

In the *Soliloquy*, Shaftesbury recommends the process of dividing
oneself into two persons, in such a way as to have a critical dialogue
with oneself (Shaftesbury, 1999, p. 83) and examine one's own affections and passions. The end result of soliloquizing, he tells us, is that
one 'must undoubtedly come the better to understand a human
breast, and judge the better both of others and [one]self', and this

---

[1] All references to Shaftesbury are to *Characteristics of Men, Manners,
Opinions, Times*, edited by Lawrence E. Klein (Cambridge: Cambridge
University Press, 1999).

judgment will help in the 'regulation and government of those passions on which the conduct of life depends' (Shaftesbury, 1999, p. 132). Self-criticism, Shaftesbury concludes, will make us 'grow wiser, prove less conceited and introduce into our character that modesty, condescension and just humanity which is essential to the success of all friendly counsel and admonition' (Shaftesbury, 1999, p. 162).

In the first part of *An Inquiry Concerning Virtue or Merit*, which (unlike the other essays) takes the form of a philosophical treatise, Shaftesbury deepens his account of goodness and virtue. One of the guiding questions of the *Inquiry* is whether atheists can be virtuous. To answer this question, Shaftesbury finds it necessary to give an account of atheism and then of the nature of virtue, which he does by first providing an account of the nature of goodness.

Perfect atheism is the belief that there is 'nothing of a designing principle or mind nor any cause, measure or rule of things but chance, so that in nature neither the interest of the whole nor of any particulars can be said to be in the least designed, pursued, or aimed at'. Perfect theism, by contrast, is the view that 'everything is governed, ordered or regulated for the best by a designing principle or mind, necessarily good and permanent' (Shaftesbury, 1999, p. 165).

To define goodness, Shaftesbury begins by pointing out that parts of larger natural systems are good or ill inasmuch as they make for the good or ill of the systems of which they are the parts, and whether an animal is a part of a larger system depends on whether 'there be anything which points beyond himself and by which he is plainly discovered to have relation to some other being or nature besides his own' (Shaftesbury, 1999, p. 168). Thus, animals that may appear ill or bad, when considered in isolation, may indeed be good when considered as parts of larger systems.

But what makes *human beings* good or bad? Shaftesbury argues that diseases and convulsive fits cannot make humans bad, and that being hindered from doing the mischief they desire or abstaining from executing an ill purpose through fear of punishment or the allurement of reward does not make humans good (Shaftesbury, 1999, p. 169). Instead, what makes human beings good or bad is the state of their affections or passions. Thus, '*a good creature is such a one as by the natural temper or bent of his affections is carried primarily and immediately, and not secondarily and accidentally, to good and against ill*', whereas 'an ill creature is...*one who is wanting in right affections of force enough to carry him directly towards good and bear him out against ill or who is carried by other affections directly to ill and against good*', where the relevant good or ill is thought of as the public good or ill, the good or ill of the species (Shaftesbury, 1999, p. 171–172).

But goodness, says Shaftesbury, is not sufficient for *virtue*. Non-human animals can have all manner of good affections, i.e., affections that conduce to the public good, such as generosity, kindness, constancy, and compassion (Shaftesbury, 1999, p. 173). But they are incapable of virtue, because they lack the ability to form 'general notions of things' or to reflect on their affections (Shaftesbury, 1999, p. 172). Virtuous human beings, by contrast, are humans who are good (i.e., their affections carry them, primarily and immediately, towards the public good) by virtue of the fact that they disinterestedly approve upon reflection of their good affections and either have no ill affections or counter such ill affections as they have by disinterested disapproval of those affections (Shaftesbury, 1999, pp. 172–177). Shaftesbury thinks of what is agreeable or disagreeable in our affections as a matter of harmony or dissonance (Shaftesbury, 1999, p. 173), so that the second-order discernment involved in being affected by one's affections is a kind of responsiveness to moral beauty.

Shaftesbury goes on to claim that all human beings are both naturally good (inasmuch as they naturally possess affections, such as pity, love, and kindness, that tend to the public good) and naturally virtuous (inasmuch as they have a natural liking for their good affections and a dislike of their contraries) (Shaftesbury, 1999, p. 178). In this way, all human beings have what Shaftesbury calls 'the sense of right and wrong' (Shaftesbury, 1999, p. 177 ff.), which he also identifies as a 'natural moral sense' (Shaftesbury, 1999, p. 180). And he theorizes that, in order to become ill or vicious, human beings must either be corrupted by 'the force of custom and education in opposition to' their natural moral sense (Shaftesbury, 1999, p. 179) or find themselves unable to withstand their own selfish affections or 'sudden, strong and forcible passion' (Shaftesbury, 1999, p. 182), even as they retain their moral sense.

The role of religion in Shaftesbury's theory of virtue is complicated. On the one hand, false religions sometimes teach the love and admiration of an ill deity (Shaftesbury, 1999, p. 180), so that their adherents lose the proper understanding of the public good and become ill or vicious as a result. And if religions teach that one should submit to the will of a deity, even a good deity, 'through hope merely of reward or fear of punishment', then 'there is in this case...no virtue or goodness whatsoever' (Shaftesbury, 1999, p. 183). But on the other hand, religion sometimes portrays God as

Berkeley's Criticisms of Shaftesbury and Hutcheson

a 'true model and example of the most exact justice and highest good-ness and worth' (Shaftesbury, 1999, p. 182), in which case religion serves the cause of virtue. And even hope of divine reward and fear of divine punishment can support virtue by counteracting selfishness and other ill affections (Shaftesbury, 1999, p. 185). Moreover, reli-gion can sustain virtue in a way that atheism cannot, for the theist who recognizes that all is for the best exhibits greater patience, con-stancy, and acquiescence in the face of ill accidents than does the atheist, who tends instead towards 'a natural kind of abhorrence and spleen' (Shaftesbury, 1999, pp. 190–91). But ultimately Shaftesbury insists that, even if true religion can be supportive of virtue, it is possible for atheists to be virtuous.

In the second part of the *Inquiry*, Shaftesbury defends the classical Socratic/Stoic position that virtue is sufficient for happiness. The central claim is that social love and other natural affections that tend toward the public good, which are active and not suppressed in virtuous human beings, naturally result in 'community or partici-pation in the pleasures of others and belief of meriting well from others'; and out of these arises 'more than nine-tenths of whatever is enjoyed in life' (Shaftesbury, 1999, p. 205). In addition, rational creatures are naturally self-reflective, and, in their soliloquizing moments, experience self-reproach regarding any of their affections that conduce to ill. They will therefore be happier if those affections are extinguished or counteracted (Shaftesbury, 1999, p. 208).

In *The Moralists*, Shaftesbury brings all of the themes discussed in the previous essays together in the shape of a wide-ranging and sprawling dialogue, with the addition of an argument by design for the existence of a deity (Shaftesbury, 1999, pp. 274–76) and criti-cisms of versions of the cosmological argument (such as Locke's) that appeal to 'a first cause, a first being and a beginning of motion' (Shaftesbury, 1999, p. 278). Shaftesbury's version of the design argument presupposes that the universe is beautiful, in the sense that all of its parts are carefully designed to work in harmony so as to form a 'universal system and coherent scheme of things' (Shaftesbury, 1999, p. 275). This assumption, which Shaftesbury thinks would be obvious to 'any fair and just contemplator of the works of nature' (Shaftesbury, 1999, p. 275), also grounds a theodicy. For, as one of his characters in the dialogue puts it, 'if nature herself be not for man but man for nature, then must man, by his good leave, submit to the elements of nature and not the elements to him' (Shaftesbury, 1999, p. 280). We can therefore understand the bad things that happen to good or innocent people (especially natural evils, such as earthquakes) as necessary by-products of a universe

Samuel C. Rickless

that is the best of all possible worlds. (It is not for nothing that Leibniz, writing of Shaftesbury's *Characteristics* in 1712, says: 'I found in it almost all of my *Theodicy* before it saw the light of day...If I had seen this work before my *Theodicy* was published, I should have profited as I ought and should have borrowed its great passages.')[2]

In five *Miscellaneous Reflections* on the five essays that comprise the *Characteristics*, Shaftesbury recapitulates yet again, in the same order but in the same loose manner of 'rambling from subject to subject, from style to style' (Shaftesbury, 1999, p. 393), some of the main themes of the book. It is clear that Berkeley read these reflections carefully, for in both the first (1732) and second (1752) edition of *Alciphron* 3 he quotes (more or less accurately) from several passages in the third and fifth *Miscellanies*.

In 1725, Francis Hutcheson published *An Inquiry into the Original of our Ideas of Beauty and Virtue* (in two treatises, one on beauty and one on virtue) in large part 'to recommend the Lord Shaftesbury's Writings to the World' (Preface).[3] One of Hutcheson's most important contributions takes the form of a defense of Shaftesbury's claim that we are all endowed with a moral sense, distinct from a sense of our own self-interest or advantage. According to Shaftesbury, 'it is full as impossible to conceive that a rational creature, coming first to be tried by rational objects and receiving into his mind the images or representations of justice, generosity, gratitude or other virtue, should have no liking of these or dislike of their contraries...Coming therefore to a capacity of seeing and admiring in this new way, it must needs find a beauty and a deformity as well in actions, minds and tempers as in figures, sounds or colours' (Shaftesbury, 1999, p. 178).

Hutcheson offers various arguments for the existence of a moral sense, a 'perception of moral good [that] is not deriv'd from custom, education, example, or study' (Hutcheson, 2004, p. 99). The most important argument for our purposes appears in the following passage:

[2] See (Leibniz, 1768, p. 45): 'J'y ai trouvé d'abord presque toute ma *Théodicée* (mais plus agréablement tournée) avant qu'elle eut vu le jour...Si j'avois vu cet ouvrage avant la publication de ma *Théodicée*, j'en aurois profité comme il faut, & j'en aurois emprunté de grands passages'.
[3] References are to the second (1726) edition: Francis Hutcheson, *An Inquiry into the Original of our Ideas of Beauty and Virtue*, edited and with an introduction by Wolfgang Leidhold (Indianapolis: Liberty Fund, 2004).

A covetous man shall dislike any branch of trade, how useful soever it may be to the publick, if there is no gain for himself in it; here is an aversion from interest. Propose a sufficient premium, and he shall be the first who sets about it, with full satisfaction in his own conduct. Now is it the same way with our sense of moral actions? Should any one advise us to wrong a minor, or orphan, or to do an ungrateful action toward a benefactor; we at first view abhor it: assure us that it will be very advantageous to us, propose even a reward; our sense of the action is not alter'd. (Hutcheson, 2004, p. 95)

Hutcheson is providing reasons to accept Shaftesbury's claim that our representations of vicious actions in particular elicit from us a sense of moral deformity. Sense, here, is opposed to reason, which is conceived as an instrument used to calculate what is to one's own advantage. Hutcheson's argument is that if the sense of deformity were simply the manifestation of rational self-interest, then our evaluation of particular acts of injustice (such as wronging minors or orphans) would become positively, rather than negatively, valenced. But we do not experience such a change: if you explain that wronging a child will be advantageous to me, my evaluation of the act of wronging does not change from negative to positive. So, the sense of moral deformity, like the sense of taste or hearing, must be a faculty distinct from the faculty of instrumental rationality.

2. Berkeley's Criticisms of Shaftesbury and Hutcheson

In the third chapter of *Alciphron*, Berkeley takes aim at Shaftesbury's *Characteristics*, but also at Hutcheson's elaboration of Shaftesbury's moral sense theory. I will discuss Berkeley's central criticisms in the order in which they are presented.

First, a note about the characters in *Alciphron*. Lysicles and Alciphron are described as 'free-thinkers' (Berkeley, 1950, Alciphron, Ch. 1.1, p. 32), hostile to superstitious prejudices and religious beliefs that are used to keep ordinary people in subjection to despotic government, and ultimately hostile to theism itself, treating atheism as 'the very top and perfection of free-thinking' (Berkeley, 1950, *Alciphron*, Ch. 1.9, p. 44).[4] Lysicles keeps fairly consistently to the views defended by Bernard Mandeville in *The Fable of the Bees*,

---

[4]   References to *Alciphron* are to *The Works of George Berkeley, Volume 3*, edited by A. A. Luce and T. E. Jessop (London: Thomas Nelson and Sons Ltd, 1950).

and plays no role in the discussion that will occupy us. Alciphron appears to move from one free-thinking philosophy to another, in keeping with Berkeley's claim that free-thinkers are 'writers of different opinions' (Berkeley, 1950, *Alciphron*, Ch. 1.1, p. 32). Euphranor and Crito are friends, with the former speaking for philosophy and the latter for religion. And the reason Berkeley describes them as friends is precisely that, as he sees it, philosophy, using reason, helps the cause of religion, which is virtue and salvation.[5]

Berkeley's central criticism begins with an exposition of a moral theory in section 3 that is recognizably Shaftesbury's. Alciphron tells us, among other things, that 'infidels' can be just as virtuous as theists, perhaps even more so because if they are virtuous then it is not through 'fear or hope', the kind of motivation that is

---

[5]   Euphranor is described (Berkeley, 1950, *Alciphron*, Ch. 1.1, p. 31) as uniting 'in his own person the philosopher and the farmer' and as having been to 'university'. He has 'a good collection, chiefly of old books' and 'hath read much, and thought more' (Berkeley, 1950, *Alciphron* Ch. 1.1, p. 32) His major contributions to discussion throughout *Alciphron* are philosophical. Crito says that 'religion is the virtuous mean between incredulity and superstition. We do not therefore contend for superstitious follies, or for the rage of bigots. What we plead for is, religion against profaneness, law against confusion, virtue against vice, the hope of a Christian against the despondency of an atheist' (Berkeley, 1950, *Alciphron*, Ch. 5.6, pp. 179–180). Later, he says that although there is natural religion that can be discovered by reason, 'precepts and oracles from heaven are incomparably better suited to popular improvement and the good of society than the reasonings of philosophers' (Berkeley, 1950, *Alciphron*, Ch. 5.9, pp. 182–183) The very long Fifth Dialogue, which is all about the benefits of Christianity and why evils are not the products of Christianity *per se*, is almost completely driven by Crito. In the Sixth Dialogue, Crito works hard to establish the probative nature of the evidence for Christianity and the authority of Scripture, exhibiting great erudition and a detailed understanding of the history of Christianity. He says that 'what we contend for at present' is 'the general faith taught by Christ and His apostles, and preserved by universal and perpetual tradition in all the churches down to our own times' (Berkeley, 1950, *Alciphron*, Ch. 6.29, p. 276). A little later he says that 'the principles of faith seem to me points plain and clear' and delivers a long speech about this (Berkeley, 1950, *Alciphron*, Ch. 6.30, pp. 278–280). He also says: 'Who ever supposed that scientifical proofs are necessary to make a Christian? Faith alone is required' (Berkeley, 1950, *Alciphron*, Ch. 6.31, p. 280). In the Seventh Dialogue, Euphranor takes over the conversation when it turns to philosophical matters, such as the use of language and personal identity and freedom, before Crito returns to the defense of Christianity.

inconsistent with virtue; that 'there is an idea of Beauty natural to the mind of man', that men are naturally delighted by the contemplation of it, and that it 'attracts without a reason' as a matter of 'untutored judgment'; that beauty is a function of order and symmetry perceived by 'a certain interior sense', whether in the case of 'corporeal things' or in the case of the 'moral world' (all of which explains why 'men's first thoughts and natural notions are the best in moral matters'); that the ability to sense this beauty depends on 'a delicate and fine taste', of which every rational creature has more or less; and that systems of rational beings are formed and held together by 'mutual sympathy', a 'propension towards doing good to our kind' and a 'delight in behold-ing the virtuous deeds of other men, or in reflecting on our own' (Berkeley, 1950, *Alciphron*, Ch. 3.3, pp. 116–118).

Berkeley's first criticism of Shaftesbury's moral theory appears in section 4. There Euphranor tries to tie Shaftesbury's conception of moral beauty (*'to kalon'*) to the Platonic concept of the profitable (*ophelimon*), and to the Aristotelian concept of the laudable (*epaine-ton*) (Berkeley, 1950, *Alciphron*, Ch. 3.4, p. 118).[6] After some brief skirmishing, Alciphron replies that he does not identify moral beauty with either the Platonic or the Aristotelian conception of it (Berkeley, 1950, *Alciphron*, Ch. 3.4, p. 119).

Prompted by Euphranor to give a better explication of moral beauty (Berkeley, 1950, *Alciphron*, Ch. 3.4, p. 119), Alciphron refuses on the grounds that it is 'an object, not of the discursive faculty [i.e., reason], but of a peculiar sense, which is properly called the *moral sense*', in the way that the eye is adapted to the

---

[6]   Plato often describes the virtues (and virtue), which are admirable or beautiful (*kalon*), as 'beneficial' (or: 'useful', 'advantageous', 'profitable') (*ophelimon*). Examples include *Charmides*, where temperance is described as beneficial (174d) and admirable (159c); *Republic* 589c, where justice de-serves praise whether one looks at it from the point of view of pleasure, good reputation or advantage; and *Meno* 87e, where virtue is described as making us good, from which it is inferred, given that everything good is beneficial, that virtue is something beneficial. Plato also sometimes charac-terizes whatever is good and admirable (such as a just action, 476e) as being either pleasant or beneficial (*Gorgias* 477a). In the *Nicomachean Ethics*, which Berkeley had read carefully (*Alciphron*, Ch. 6.12, p. 242), Aristotle claims that we praise (or laud) just and brave individuals, and in general good individuals and virtue itself, and hence identifies virtue with what is laudable or praiseworthy (*epaineton*) (NE 1101b12-14). In the *Eudemian Ethics*, Aristotle says that fine or admirable (*kalon*) ends are laudable (*epai-neton*), and these include justice, temperance, and the other virtues (EE 1248b20 ff.).

perception of colors and the ear is adapted to the perception of sounds (Berkeley, 1950, *Alciphron*, Ch. 3.5, p. 120). It is at this point that Alciphron comes to represent Hutcheson's elaboration of Shaftesbury's moral theory. For it is not Shaftesbury, but Hutcheson, who emphasizes that moral beauty is the object of a special faculty of sensing. In his *Inquiry Concerning Beauty, Order, Harmony, Design*, Hutcheson provides two main arguments for this conclusion. The first is that the pleasure deriving from our perception of beauty 'does not arise from any knowledge of principles, proportions, causes, or of the usefulness' of objects, 'nor does the most accurate knowledge increase this pleasure of beauty' (Hutcheson, 2004, p. 25). The second is that 'the ideas of beauty and harmony, like other sensible ideas, are necessarily pleasant to us, as well as immediately so; neither can any resolution of our own, nor any prospect of advantage or disadvantage, vary the beauty or deformity of an object' (Hutcheson, 2004, p. 25).

Berkeley's immediate response (in the mouth of Euphranor) is that our natural affections (such as compassion for the distressed and tenderness for our own offspring) are not equally distributed among human beings: some of these affections are 'strongest and uppermost in one mind, others in another' (Berkeley, 1950, *Alciphron*, Ch. 3.5, p. 120). Among commentators, there is, I believe, some confusion about Berkeley's point here. According to Paul Olscamp, Berkeley is trying to tell us that 'given the variation in men's appetites and passions, the moral sense theory leads to moral anarchy and relativism' (Olscamp, 1969, p. 168). According to Laurent Jaffro, Berkeley's point is that a moral sense 'would be subjective – and as such arbitrary – insofar as it is identical with "passion or inward feeling"'. Jaffro also claims that Berkeley is here reusing an argument from *Passive Obedience*, to the effect that 'tenderness and benevolence of temper' should not be 'the sole rule of our actions', because 'they may possibly betray us into as great enormities as any other unbridled lust' (Berkeley, 1950, Vol. 6, p. 23; Jaffro, 2007, p. 168). Adam Grzelinski thinks that Berkeley is accusing Shaftesbury of utopianism: 'Berkeley...stresses the utopian nature of this way of thinking, and accuses Shaftesbury of excessive optimism...The sublime beauty of the human spirit and heroic virtue are not accessible to all. Such experience...is but the emotional disposition, which is too labile and impermanent to serve as a foundation for ethics' (Grzelinski, 2015, p. 218).

But none of these commentators has quite understood *why* Berkeley thinks that the unequal distribution of natural affections constitutes a problem for Shaftesbury. Berkeley is not here worried about anarchy, or relativism, or subjectivity, or arbitrariness, or great enormities, or lability, or impermanence. What worries Berkeley is that if moral conduct is a function of natural affection, then the fact that some affections are stronger in some minds and other affections are stronger in others entails that the rule that one should follow one's natural affections will be 'a very uncertain guide in morals', given that it will 'infallibly lead different men different ways, according to the prevalency of this or that appetite or passion' (Berkeley, 1950, *Alciphron*, Ch. 3.5, p. 120). Thus, for example, strong compassion for the distressed in some will lead them to help those in dire need, while weak compassion in others will lead them to ignore the needs of others; strong tenderness for offspring will lead some to care for their children, while weak tenderness will lead others to neglect them; and strong patriotism will lead some to fight for their country, while weak patriotism will lead others to avoid military service. Berkeley's presupposition here is that moral theory should offer us universal and consistent moral guidance. A true account of morality should not recommend opposite courses of conduct to two persons who are in exactly the same situation.

How successful is this criticism? As I see it, Berkeley is either confused or treating Shaftesbury unfairly. (I suspect the former.) Recall that Shaftesbury's theory provides for two levels of affection. The first-order affections that matter to virtue and vice are affections toward the good or ill of others, affections such as generosity, compassion, and love (and their opposites: stinginess, malice, and hatred). To possess affections that tend to the public good is to be a good human being, but not yet to be a virtuous human being. Virtue requires second-order affections directed at first-order affections, namely, approval of affections that tend to the public good, and disapproval of affections that tend to the public ill. Moral beauty (or deformity), according to Shaftesbury, lies in the first-order affections and the actions that those affections produce. Perception and appreciation of this beauty (or deformity) is what our moral sense delivers, at the second-order, not at the first-order. So, whether our first-order affections, such as those Berkeley discusses (fellow-feeling, tenderness toward offspring, affection towards friends, indignation against injustice) are unequal in strength across the human population is irrelevant to the truth or falsity of Shaftesbury's theory of virtue, thought of as the approval of good and the disapproval of bad first-order affections. Presumably, Shaftesbury is aware that some people feel more compassion for strangers than do others, that some people are more patriotic than others, and so on. But first-order affections are not the ultimate moral guide. What matters, for Shaftesbury, is virtue. For example, I might find in myself a certain degree of misanthropy (a first-order affection). Reflecting on this, I experience disapproval of this misanthropy. This disapproval (a second-order affection) leads me to counteract the misanthropy in various ways, perhaps by informing myself about the needs of others and about the ways in which their lives are similar to mine. This is virtue in action, and what Shaftesbury recommends. It is not Shaftesbury's view that we should simply follow whatever first-order affections we find in ourselves. I conclude that Berkeley's 'uncertain guide' criticism of Shaftesbury in *Alciphron* 3.5 fails.

It is at this point in the exchange that Alciphron offers an argument for the view that the second-order perception of moral beauty (in particular) issues from a sensing, rather than from a reasoning, faculty:

> Make an experiment on the first man you meet. Propose a villainous or unjust action. Take his first sense of the matter, and you shall find he detests it. He may, indeed, be afterwards misled by arguments, or overpowered by temptation; but his original, unpremeditated, and genuine thoughts are just and orthodox. How can we account for this but by a moral sense, which, left to itself, hath as quick and true a perception of the beauty and deformity of human actions as the eye hath of colours? (Berkeley, 1950, *Alciphron*, Ch. 3:6, p. 121)

As I have already noted, this argument belongs to Hutcheson, rather than to Shaftesbury. In response, Berkeley (speaking through Euphranor), answers as follows:

> May not this be sufficiently accounted for by conscience, affection, passion, education, reason, custom, religion; which principles and habits, for aught I know, may be what you metaphorically call a moral sense? (Berkeley, 1950, *Alciphron*, Ch. 3.6, p. 121)

There is confusion among commentators about the substance of this reply. Grzelinski, for example, argues that Berkeley is worried that 'the passions can be partial' when 'deprived of the guidance of reason', and that 'in reality altruism too frequently shows a certain partiality' (Grzelinski, 2015, 219). But there is no sign of concern about the excessive partiality of first-order or second-order affections in Euphranor's reply. Stephen Darwall claims that Berkeley's point is that 'the reflective responses that Shaftesbury attributed to a 'natural moral sense' could be explained better on other grounds' (Darwall, 2005, 317). But this doesn't seem quite right, given that Euphranor doesn't explicitly suggest that conscience, education, reason, custom, and religion do a *better job* of explaining why it is that people react with horror when one proposes that they commit some unjust act. Jaffro claims that Berkeley's criticism of Alciphron's argument for the existence of a moral sense is that 'such a hypothesis is superfluous' (Jaffro, 2007, p. 205). This is closer to the truth of the matter. Berkeley's point is that because reason, embodied in religious conscience, is *sufficient* to explain the initial reaction of horror at the prospect of committing an injustice, it is not *necessary* to hypothesize a special moral sense to explain the reaction.[7] Jaffro goes on to say that 'the point against the moral sense is that it does not explain how morality can be enforced; it even seems to exempt us from the necessity of any enforcement of morality' (Jaffro, 2007, p. 205). But there is no sign of any concerns about the enforcement of morality in Euphranor's response to Alciphron's Hutchesonian argument.

How good is Berkeley's 'superfluity' response to Hutcheson? Berkeley is suggesting that one's reaction of horror at the thought of committing an atrocity might well be the product of reason and education, and that the immediacy of the reaction, the lack of deliberation involved in rejecting it as an option, might simply be the product of custom. It must be granted that this is possible. But Hutcheson might reply by pointing to the same horror and lack of deliberation in young children who understand that they are being given the option to wrong a friend, but who have not yet demonstrated the laws of nature (see footnote 7) or experienced a religious upbringing that emphasizes the rewards of heaven and the punishments of hellfire in an afterlife. It is an empirical question whether Hutcheson is right about this, and in the absence of relevant data, it is difficult to say who has the better of the argument.[8]

[7]   In *Passive Obedience*, Berkeley writes that the laws of nature, which derive their obligation from God, are *'stamped on the Mind'* or *'engraven on the Tables of the Heart'* because 'they are well known to Mankind, and suggested and inculcated by Conscience'; they are also 'termed *Eternal Rules of Reason*, because they necessarily result from the Nature of Things, and may be demonstrated by the infallible deductions of Reason' (Berkeley, 1950, Vol. 6, p. 23).

[8]   Interestingly, recent research tends to vindicate Hutcheson. See Kiley, Hamlyn, Wynn, and Bloom (2007, p. 557): 'Infants prefer an individual who helps another to one who hinders another, prefer a helping individual to a neutral individual, and prefer a neutral individual to a hindering individual'; Van de Vondervoort and J. Kiley Hamlin (2016, p. 143): 'Consistent with an intuition-based view of morality, infants evaluate prosocial individuals positively and evaluate antisocial individuals negatively';

Samuel C. Rickless

This brings us to the most important and central criticism of Hutcheson's version of Shaftesbury's moral theory. After a brief interlude in section 7, Euphranor shifts his attention to the Hutchesonian conception of beauty, focusing first on the beauty of sensible objects (in sections 8 and 9), and turning next to the beauty of a moral system (in section 10). In section 8, Euphranor offers an argument that beauty in sensible things 'is an object, not of the eye, but of the mind', that is, an object of reason rather than of a hypothesized moral sense (Berkeley, 1950, *Alciphron*, Ch. 3.8, pp. 123–24). The argument is straightforward, and I reconstruct it as follows:

1. Beauty in sensible objects consists in a certain symmetry or proportion.
2. Proportion in a sensible object implies a mutual relation of size and shape in the object's parts that makes the whole complete and perfect in its kind.
3. An object is perfect in its kind when it answers the end for which it was made.
   So,
4. Determining whether a sensible object is beautiful requires comparing its parts one with another, considering them as belonging to one whole, and referring this whole to its use or end. (from 1, 2, 3)
5. Comparing parts, considering them as belonging to a whole, and referring this whole to a use or end is the work, not of sight only, but of reason through sight.
   So,
6. Determining whether a sensible object is beautiful is the work, not of sight only, but of reason through sight. (from 4, 5)

Tomasello & Vraish, (2013): 'Young children are surprisingly skilled collaborative and cooperative partners' (p. 240); 'By 14 to 18 months of age, [young children] readily engage in instrumental helping such as picking up an object that an adult has accidentally dropped or opening a cabinet door when an adult cannot do so because his hands are full' (p. 241); 'Toddlers even help others at some cost to themselves' (p. 241); '[Some findings suggest] that young children's motivation to help is intrinsic and not dependent on concrete extrinsic rewards, and indeed it is undermined by such rewards' (p. 241–42); 'Young children not only distribute resources equally themselves but also distinguish equal from unequal distributions and prefer equal distributors and distributions' (p. 243).

Berkeley's Criticisms of Shaftesbury and Hutcheson

At the end of section 8, and throughout section 9, Berkeley illustrates and defends the conclusion of this argument by looking at examples of human artifacts (chairs, doors, clothes, pillars, and entablatures). In each case, Euphranor argues that the beauty of the artifact is a function of whether the relation of its parts to each other (i.e., its proportions) is subservient to the end for which it was made (offering a convenient seat in the case of a chair, a convenient entrance in the case of a door, the freedom, ease, and convenience of the body in the case of clothing, supporting a building in the case of a pillar, and giving firmness and union to a building, as well as protecting it from the elements, in the case of an entablature).

In section 10, Berkeley extrapolates from his discussion of sensible beauty to the case of *moral* beauty. For most commentators who pay attention to this argument (not all do), the extrapolation is straightforward.[9] Just as the beauty of a sensible object is a function of the end for which it was made, so the beauty of a moral system is a function of the end for which it was made. And wherever there are ends, there must be an end-setter. In the case of a moral system, Berkeley supposes that the relevant setter of ends is God. So, determining whether a moral system is beautiful is the work of reason, working out how the parts of that system, namely human beings, are parts of a unified whole that is subservient to some divine goal or purpose. Because God is good, his purposes must be so too, and thus his aim in creating the moral system is 'the common benefit of the whole' (Berkeley, 1950, *Alciprhon*, Ch. 3.10, p. 129). Two things appear to follow from this. First, moral beauty, like the beauty of sensible objects, is perceived by reason, rather than by sense, contrary to Hutcheson's version of moral sense theory. And second, because in this life it is evident that many of the wicked are not punished and many of the virtuous are not rewarded, the beauty of a moral system depends on the implementation of divine justice in an afterlife, and thus requires, as Crito puts it early in the dialogue, 'Providence, the Immortality of the Soul, and a future Retribution of rewards and punishments' (Berkeley, 1950, *Alciphron*, Ch. 3.3, p. 118). It will not do, then, to suppose, as Shaftesbury does, that virtue, which involves approval of moral beauty and disapproval of moral deformity, is possible for atheists or for those who treat 'the great points of Faith' as 'exploded conceits' (Berkeley, 1950, *Alciphron*, Ch. 3.7, p. 122).

Before asking whether Berkeley's central criticism of Hutcheson and Shaftesbury succeeds, I want to emphasize an aspect of the

---

[9]   Op. cit. note 5, (pp. 168–70); see also, Flage (2015, pp. 64–65).

criticism that seems to have escaped commentators. Consider that Shaftesbury is not bereft of resources to respond to Berkeley's criticism. Like Berkeley, Shaftesbury thinks that human beings are parts of a greater whole, 'a system of all animals'; and this system of all animals is itself 'comprehended in one system of a globe or earth', which system is itself part of a larger system that is itself part of 'a system of all things' (Shaftesbury, 1999, p. 169). Moreover, Shaftesbury believes that a design argument establishes something that is central to Berkeley's criticism, namely the existence of an intelligent deity who created and maintains the universe for certain purposes. So, Shaftesbury could accept a great deal of what Berkeley says, including the thesis that beauty is a matter of rational proportion that is fitting to an end and the thesis that there is a supreme intelligence guiding and disposing the universe according to its own purposes, without going as far as to accept that moral beauty presupposes rewards and punishments in an afterlife or that virtue requires instrumental reasoning to determine which forms of behavior will be rewarded, and which punished, after death. For, according to Shaftesbury, there is no reason to suppose that the good of the system of all things, the good of the universe as a whole, requires that the virtuous be rewarded and the wicked punished: the good of the universe is compatible with the ill of the solar system, the good of the solar system is compatible with the ill of the planets, the good of the planets is compatible with the ill of the Earth, the good of the Earth is compatible with the ill of the system of animals, the good of the system of animals is compatible with the ill of humanity, and the good of humanity is compatible with the ill of particular human beings. Shaftesbury, like Leibniz, thinks that the universe is the best of all possible worlds, but that it is possible that the best universe might well require the ill of certain parts.[10]

So, we need to think about why Berkeley and Shaftesbury part ways where they do, especially given how many assumptions they share. The central question is why 'the beauty of a moral system, with a supreme Intelligence at the head of it', necessarily requires protection of the innocent, punishment of the wicked, and rewarding of the virtuous (Berkeley, 1950, *Alciphron*, Ch. 3.10, p. 129). According to all the commentators of whom I am aware, there is no clear answer to this question. We have hit rock bottom. Berkeley looks at the universe that Shaftesbury describes, and finds it

---

[10] This is also a major theme in William King's *De Origine Mali*, as Kenny Pearce helpfully pointed out to me in his comments a previous draft of this article.

deformed. As Crito puts it: 'Is it not, I beseech you, an ugly system in which you can suppose no law and prove no duty, wherein men thrive by wickedness and suffer by virtue?' (Berkeley, 1950, *Alciphron*, Ch. 3.11, p. 130). Shaftesbury looks at the same kind of universe, designed by a supreme deity for its own purposes, and finds it beautiful, indeed sublime. The disagreement has all the marks of a stalemate, one to which the proper response on either side appears to be an incredulous stare.

But in actual fact Berkeley and Shaftesbury have sharply differing conceptions of the universe's denizens. Shaftesbury, like his ex-tutor Locke, is a materialist. He simply takes for granted that the universe is composed of material substances existing outside of our minds, that rocks, plants, animals, the Sun, the Moon, the galaxy, and the vast proliferation of stars in the firmament are all out there in an external world. But, as we know from the *Treatise* and the *Three Dialogues*, Berkeley denies that matter exists, indeed he denies that matter is even possible (Berkeley, 1950, PHK p. 9), concluding that all physical objects are nothing more than collections of ideas (because they are collections of qualities, all of which, whether primary or secondary, are ideas – (Berkeley, 1950, DHP, p. 175, p. 187, p. 194)), and consequently, because ideas do not subsist by themselves and hence fail to be substances (Berkeley, 1950, PHK p. 89), that the only substances that exist in the universe are minds (including God) (Berkeley, 1950, PHK p. 33). So, the moral system of which Berkeley speaks is, as Crito emphasizes, 'a system of spirits' (Berkeley, 1950, *Alciphron*, Ch. 3.11, p. 129).[11] It is a system of spirits, not because Berkeley thinks that only minds are relevant to the question of moral beauty, but because he thinks that *minds are the only substances in the universe*. It is on the strength of this thesis that Berkeley can confidently deny what Shaftesbury affirms, namely, that it is possible for the good of the universe to require the collective ill of human minds. For in Berkeley's universe there is no system of substances greater than the system of minds, no greater system whose good might best be served by the ill of all or most of those minds. The good of the universe just *is* the good of those minds, and the good of human minds simply consists in those minds getting what they justly deserve (rewards in the case of virtue, punishment in the case of vice).

There is therefore no stalemate here between Shaftesbury and Berkeley, and the debate does not reduce to a battle of incredulous

---

[11]   Note that Berkeley uses the terms 'mind' and 'spirit' interchangeably (see, for example, Berkeley (1950), PHK p. 2 1950, DHP p. 240).

Samuel C. Rickless

stares. Whether Berkeley is right or wrong about the necessary connection between the existence of moral beauty and 'the great points of Faith' hinges in large part on whether idealism is true or false. It is here, perhaps more than anywhere else, that the systematicity of Berkeley's philosophy becomes manifest. Metaphysics and morals are not autonomous in Berkeley's worldview. And this fact is, if I may say, one of the most beautiful aspects of his philosophical corpus.

It is now appropriate to ask whether Berkeley's criticism of Shaftesbury succeeds. As to the main point of difference between them, the answer is that which of them has the better of the other depends in large part on whether Berkeley's arguments for idealism, and against materialism, are persuasive.[12]

But this is not the only place where one might object to Berkeley's argument. Hutcheson, in particular, who is far more concerned than Shaftesbury is to establish that beauty is perceived by sense, rather than by reason, refuses to accept that beauty always requires proportion, or at least the kind of proportion that is subservient to an end. In a footnote added to the fourth edition of section IV of the *Inquiry Concerning Beauty, Order, Harmony, Design* (1738), Hutcheson responds directly to Berkeley's criticism:

> 'Tis surprising to see the ingenious author of *Alciphron* alledging, that all beauty observed is solely some use perceived or imagined; for no other reason than this, that the apprehension of the use intended, occurs continually, when we are judging of the forms of chairs, doors, tables, and some other things of obvious use; and that we like those forms most, which are fittest for the use. Whereas we see, that in these very things similitude of parts is regarded, where unlike parts would be equally useful: thus the feet of a chair would be of the same use, tho' unlike, were they equally long; tho' one were strait, and the other bended; or one bending outwards, and the other inwards: a coffin-shape for a door would bear a more manifest aptitude to the human shape, than that which artists require. And then what is the use of these imitations of nature, or of its works, in architecture? Why should a pillar please which has some of the human proportions? Is the end or use of a pillar the same as of a man? Why the imitation of other natural or well-proportioned things in the entablature? Is there then a

---

[12] I have argued in previous work that these arguments, though dialectically far better than they are commonly supposed to be, are not conclusive, see Rickless (2013, Conclusion).

sense of imitation, relishing it where there is no other use than this, that it naturally pleases? Again; is no man pleased with the shapes of any animals, but those which he expects use from? The shapes of the horse or the ox may promise use to the owner; but is he the only person who relishes the beauty? And is there no beauty discerned in plants, in flowers, in animals, whose use is to us unknown? (Hutcheson, 2004, p. 210, note 17)

As Hutcheson sees it, then, similarity of parts is required for beauty, even when the proportions of shape and size (as in the case of the legs of a chair) are sufficient for the relevant object's purpose. It follows that proportionality that subserves a given end is not sufficient for beauty. A coffin-shaped door is better suited to permit the entry and exit of human bodies, and yet is counted ugly by comparison to rectangular doors. It follows that proportionality that subserves the end of ingress and egress is not what makes doors beautiful. Pillars are thought to be more beautiful if they have human proportions, but human proportions do not subserve the end of a pillar, which is to support a floor or roof of a building. The beauty of an entablature, which is connected to its imitation of natural or well-proportioned things, has nothing to do with its purpose, which is to give firmness and union to a building and to protect it from the weather. We recognize the beauty of animals that are not in any way useful to us, and we recognize the beauty of plants and animals without being able to refer them to any use at all. All of these remarks, taken together, suggest a different account of beauty than that of proportionality subserving an object's end or purpose. Hutcheson himself proposes that beauty consists in uniformity in variety, a theory of beauty that is designedly non-teleological. But even if Hutcheson's theory is mistaken, it will be difficult for Berkeley to argue that his own teleological theory is compatible with widely-held commonsensical ascriptions of beauty and ugliness to sensible things.

We have looked at Berkeley's central criticism of the Hutchesonian version of Shaftesbury's moral theory. But Berkeley has one additional criticism, placed in the mouth of Crito in section 13 of *Alciphron* 3, a section in which aspects of Shaftesbury's ethical views are summarized as belonging to a character called 'Cratylus'. This feature of the criticism has misled at least one commentator, Laurent Jaffro, who infers from the fact that Alciphron offers two different expositions, one in section 3 and the other in section 13, that 'Berkeley was well aware that Shaftesbury had changed his mind concerning the moral sense and that in the *Soliloquy* he had substantially modified the views he had expressed formerly in his *Inquiry concerning Virtue*' (Jaffro, 2007, p. 206). As Jaffro sees it, the Shaftesbury of the *Inquiry* defends a Hutchesonian conception 'that regarded the sense of right and wrong as analogous to our sensory organs', whereas the Shaftesbury of the *Soliloquy* 'had developed a quite different conception, according to which the moral sense, as a moral *taste*, has to be developed and trained' (Jaffro, 2007, p. 206). Jaffro then reads Berkeley's criticism as an accusation of elitism 'insofar as [Shaftesbury's *Soliloquy* conception of the moral sense] supposes a personal achievement', a 'matter of refined education and some kind of connoisseurship' (Jaffro, 2007, p. 208).

Jaffro's reading, according to which Berkeley has realized that the views of early Shaftesbury and late Shaftesbury, despite being published all together at the same time in 1711, contain different conceptions of the moral sense, is mistaken. The most important piece of textual evidence that Berkeley doesn't take Shaftesbury to have changed his mind in the way Jaffro suggests is that according to the earlier section 3 exposition, the appreciation or 'relish' of moral beauty requires 'a delicate and fine taste' (Berkeley, 1950, *Alciprhon*, Ch. 3.3, p. 117). So, even if Shaftesbury did change his mind regarding whether the moral sense is acquired by means of a refined education, Berkeley shows no signs of having picked up on the change. Furthermore, as I will explain, Berkeley's criticism of Cratylus has nothing to do with elitism.

Still, Jaffro's question, why Berkeley would provide two different expositions of Shaftesbury's ethics, is a good one. The answer, as I see it, is that the views represented as belonging to Cratylus, are supposed to constitute the *practical*, rather than the *theoretical*, aspect of Shaftesbury's moral outlook. We can see this in Crito's summary of Cratylus's views in section 13. Crito begins by telling us that Cratylus 'did, under the pretence of making men heroically virtuous, endeavour to destroy the means of making them reasonably and humanly so' (Berkeley, 1950, *Alciprhon*, Ch. 3.13, p. 132). The problem, Crito tells us, is that Shaftesbury's view that we should leave it to 'taste or relish' to be 'what will influence' moral conduct is a practical recipe for disaster: it is 'as if a monarch should give out that there was neither jail nor executioner in his kingdom to enforce the laws, but that it would be beautiful to observe them, and that in so doing men would taste the pure delight which results from order and decorum' (Berkeley, 1950, Alciphron, Ch. 3.13, p. 133). The better alternative, according to Crito, is the inculcation of religious beliefs, including belief 'of a future state of rewards and punishments', to motivate virtuous conduct in the citizenry, something that Shaftesbury however apparently dismisses as 'children's tales and amusements of the vulgar' (Berkeley, 1950, *Alciphron*, Ch. 3.13, p. 133; see Shaftesbury, 1999, p. 414).

But Berkeley is not being fair to Shaftesbury here. For Shaftesbury *is* an elitist, in the sense that he thinks that there should be different rules for the common folk on the one side and the educated elite on the other. This comes through in a few places in the *Characteristics*. Recall that in *Sensus Communis*, Shaftesbury writes: 'I know, too, that the mere vulgar of mankind often stand in need of such a rectifying object as the gallows before their eyes. Yet I have no belief that any man of a liberal education, or common honesty, ever needed to have recourse to this idea in his mind, the better to restrain him from playing the knave' (Shaftesbury, 1999, p. 59). And in the third *Miscellany*, he says this:

> Thus, we see, after all, that it is not merely what we call *principle* but a *taste* which governs men…Even conscience, I fear, such as is owing to religious discipline, will make but a slight figure where this taste is set amiss. Among the vulgar, perhaps, it may do wonders. A devil and a hell may prevail where a jail and gallows are thought insufficient. But such is the nature of the liberal, polished and refined part of mankind…[that they do not apply] the notion of a future reward or punishment to their immediate behavior in society, [looking] on the pious narrations to be indeed no better than children's tales or the amusement of the mere vulgar. (Shaftesbury, 1999, pp. 413–14)

So, when taste in the educated person is set amiss, Shaftesbury doesn't offer religion as a corrective, but rather philosophy, part of the aim of which is to point out that 'the proportionate and regular state is the truly prosperous and natural in every subject' (Shaftesbury, 1999, p. 414; see also Book II of *An Inquiry Concerning Virtue or Merit*). But in the case of the vulgar, Shaftesbury is happy not only with the threat of jail and execution to deter vicious conduct, but also dissemination and inculcation of the religious story that vicious conduct will ultimately be punished by the devil in hell, even if not in this life. So, it is not that Berkeley accuses Shaftesbury of elitism for offering us a moral theory that is true only of elite connoisseurs of moral beauty. Instead, Berkeley accuses Shaftesbury, unfairly, of promoting a moral practice that will bring about anarchy and vicious conduct.

But Shaftesbury's elitism does present a problem, even if it is not a problem to which Berkeley draws our attention. One of Shaftesbury's

Samuel C. Rickless

recurring refrains is that every human being, whether educated or uneducated, recognizes that certain forms of conduct (killing, maiming, betraying, cheating, stealing, and so on) are morally deformed and naturally recoils from the deformity. There is a fellow-feeling in all of us, a beneficent disposition towards the downtrodden and the desperate. We have a natural love for our offspring. All of these phenomena convince Shaftesbury that we are designed and born to promote the good of the human species, and of the larger systems of which humanity is a part. So why, then, would fear of the gallows or of a hellish afterlife ever be needed to keep the common folk in check? The answer, I imagine – though this is speculative because Shaftesbury does not consider the objection – is that philosophical reasoning about the pleasures and satisfactions of virtue is likely to be lost on the unrefined and the uneducated whose natural moral sense, for one reason or another, has been corrupted or overwhelmed by passion or selfishness. This is, indeed, an unfortunate, uncomfortably undemocratic position to hold. Whether it is true depends on empirical facts about the degree to which the underprivileged are open to the philosophical cultivation of their moral affections.[13]

University of California San Diego
srickless@ucsd.edu

References

Aristotle, *he Complete Works of Aristotle*, edited by Jonathan Barnes (Princeton: Princeton University Press, 1984).

[13] I would like to thank Kenny Pearce and Takaharu Oda for organizing the conference on Irish Philosophy in the Age of Berkeley to which part of this article was a contribution in April 2019, and for their comments on an earlier draft of this article. A previous version was presented at two conferences, one at the National Autonomous University of Mexico in May 2018, and one at the University of Wisconsin-Milwaukee organized in October 2018. I am particularly indebted to the participants at all three conferences, and in particular to Margaret Atherton, Ruth Boeker, Seth Bordner, Enrique Chávez-Arvizo, Lisa Downing, Manuel Fasko, Keota Fields, Melissa Frankel, Marc Hight, Benjamin Hill, Michael Jacovides, Alberto Luis López, Ville Paukkonen, Eric Schliesser, Tom Stoneham, and Peter West for their constructive critical comments.

Berkeley's Criticisms of Shaftesbury and Hutcheson

George Berkeley, *The Works of George Berkeley, Volume 3*, edited by A. A. Luce and T. E. Jessop (London: Thomas Nelson and Sons Ltd, 1950).

Stephen Darwall, 'Berkeley's Moral and Political Philosophy', in *The Cambridge Companion to Berkeley*, edited by Kenneth P. Winkler (Cambridge: Cambridge University Press, 2005), 311–38

Adam Grzelinski, 'George Berkeley's Understanding of Beauty and his Polemic with Shaftesbury', in *Berkeley Revisited: Moral, Social and Political Philosophy*, edited by Sébastien Charles (Oxford: Voltaire Foundation, 2015), 209–226.

J. Kiley Hamlin, Karen Wynn, and Paul Bloom, 'Social Evaluation by Preverbal Infants', *Nature* 450 (2007), 557–59.

Francis Hutcheson, *An Inquiry into the Original of our Ideas of Beauty and Virtue*, originally (1726), edited by Wolfgang Leidhold (Indianapolis: Liberty Fund, 2004).

Laurent Jaffro, 'Berkeley's Criticism of Berkeley's Moral Theory in *Alciphron III*', in *Reexamining Berkeley's Philosophy*, edited by Stephen H. Daniel (Toronto: University of Toronto Press, 2007), 199–213.

Gottfried Wilhelm Leibniz, *Opera Omnia*, vol. 5 (Geneva: de Tournes, 1768).

Paul Olscamp, *The Moral Philosophy of George Berkeley* (The Hague: Martinus Nijhoff, 1969).

Plato, *Complete Works*, edited by John M. Cooper (Indianapolis: Hackett, 1997).

Samuel C. Rickless, *Berkeley's Argument for Idealism* (Oxford: Oxford University Press, 2013).

Daniel Flage, 'Ethics in *Alciphron*', in *Berkeley Revisited: Moral, Social and Political Philosophy*, edited by Sébastien Charles (Oxford: Voltaire Foundations, 2015), 53–68.

Anthony Ashley Cooper, Third Earl of Shaftesbury, *Characteristics of Men, Manners, Opinions, Times*, edited by Lawrence E. Klein (Cambridge: Cambridge University Press, 1999).

Michael Tomasello and Amrisha Vaish, 'Origins of Human Cooperation and Morality', *Annual Review of Psychology* 64 (2013), 231–55.

Julia W. Van de Vondervoort and J. Kiley Hamlin, 'Evidence for Intuitive Morality: Preverbal Infants Make Sociomoral Evaluations', *Child Development Perspectives* 10 (2016), 143–48.

Francis Hutcheson on Liberty

RUTH BOEKER

Abstract

This paper aims to reconstruct Francis Hutcheson's thinking about liberty. Since he does not offer a detailed treatment of philosophical questions concerning liberty in his mature philosophical writings I turn to a textbook on metaphysics. We can assume that he prepared the textbook during the 1720s in Dublin. This textbook deserves more attention. First, it sheds light on Hutcheson's role as a teacher in Ireland and Scotland. Second, Hutcheson's contributions to metaphysical disputes are more original than sometimes assumed. To appreciate his independent thinking, I argue, it is helpful to take the intellectual debates in Ireland into consideration, including William King's defence of free will and discussions of Shaftesbury's views in Robert Molesworth's intellectual circle. Rather than taking a stance on the philosophical disputes about liberty, I argue that Hutcheson aims to shift the focus of the debates towards practical questions concerning control of desire, cultivation of habits, and character development.

1. Introduction

Francis Hutcheson (1694–1746) is best known for his mature works on aesthetics and moral philosophy. It may be surprising that these works contain little direct engagement with questions of liberty, especially since many of his predecessors and contemporaries in Britain and Ireland are involved in controversial debates about liberty and necessity.[1] Hutcheson does not entirely neglect questions of liberty[2], but to gain insight into his understanding of liberty it is informative to turn to a Latin textbook on metaphysics, entitled *Metaphysicae Synopsis: Ontologiam, et Pneumatologiam, Complectens [A Synopsis of Metaphysics Comprehending Ontology and Pneumatology*, hereafter short '*Metaphysics*'],[3] that he prepared for the instruction of students

---

[1]   For instance, see Locke (1975); King (1702). King's *De Origine Mali* has been translated by Edmund Law into English (King, 1781). For further discussion and background, see Harris (2005); Pearce (2019).

[2]   In the following I use the terms 'liberty' and 'freedom' interchangeably. Most of the primary texts that this paper focuses on were originally written in Latin. The Latin term 'libertas' can be translated as 'liberty' or 'freedom' into English.

[3]   This work was not translated into English until 2006. The English translation is included in Hutcheson (2006).

doi:10.1017/S1358246120000120   © The Royal Institute of Philosophy and the contributors 2020

Royal Institute of Philosophy Supplement **88** 2020

and probably composed in the 1720s during his time in Dublin. Yet a note of caution is in order from the outset. The first edition of *Metaphysics* was published without his consent in 1742 and although a second revised edition was published during his lifetime in 1744, he never fully endorsed the work.[4] This textbook was first and foremost a manual for teaching students and its content is constrained by the curriculum at the University of Glasgow. Despite Hutcheson's ambivalence about *Metaphysics*, I believe that it deserves more attention than it has received so far. First, the fact that he prepared a textbook on metaphysics sheds light on his role in the education of students in Ireland and Scotland, as I explain in more detail in section 2. Growing up as a Presbyterian in Ireland, Hutcheson, like many fellow Irish Presbyterians, had to travel to Scotland to earn a university degree and the intellectual and social context in both Ireland and Scotland shape his intellectual development and philosophical thinking. Second, I believe that *Metaphysics* despite being a textbook is more original than sometimes assumed. Although *Metaphysics* offers in the first instance a critical commentary on a textbook by the Dutch metaphysician Gerard de Vries and Hutcheson certainly draws on John Locke's philosophy to challenge the positions presented in de Vries's textbook, it is helpful to take the intellectual context in Ireland into consideration to better appreciate Hutcheson's own contributions to the philosophical debates. In section 3, after briefly providing further background about Hutcheson's textbook *Metaphysics* and its importance for the instruction of students, I examine closely how Hutcheson understands liberty and the will in *Metaphysics*. By showing that his view departs both from de Vries's and Locke's views, I intend to bring to light the independence of his thought. I propose that Hutcheson rather than trying to take a stance on metaphysical disputes about liberty aims to shift the focus of the debates and emphasizes the importance of controlling desires and cultivating right habits. Since these practical tasks do not presuppose a particular understanding of liberty, we can see why he is not very invested in settling the theoretical disputes about liberty. In section 4, I turn to his mature philosophical writings. His *An Essay on the Nature and Conduct of the Passions, with Illustrations on the Moral Sense* includes a critical response to William King's defence of libertarian free will. Although Hutcheson can be seen as more critical about libertarian freedom in this work than in his textbook, his overall strategy is to show that as far as practical considerations

---

[4]   See Moore (2006, Introduction; 1990).

are concerned there is no need to adopt the libertarian view that freedom requires an agent's choices be entirely undetermined, meaning that the agent is in a position to both choose an action and its opposite, since attributions of merit and praise are not grounded in free rational choice. Instead we are better advised to focus on character development.

2. Education in Ireland and Scotland

Francis Hutcheson was born in 1694 in Drumalig near Saintfield, County Down, in Ulster. Both his father John Hutcheson (d. 1729) and grandfather Alexander Hutcheson (d. 1711) were Presbyterian ministers.[5] Hutcheson's family, like many other Presbyterians in Ireland, had roots in Scotland.

Although Scottish settlers had migrated to Ireland, and Ulster in particular, for centuries, an organized colonization process during the reign of King James I (who was formerly King of Scotland as James VI) brought many Scots to Ulster at the beginning of the seventeenth century, where they were granted land.[6] These Scottish settlers established Presbyterian congregations in Ulster. Although Presbyterians were initially happy to be part of the Church of Ireland due to their shared Protestant heritage, rifts between Irish Presbyterians and the Church of Ireland started to grow during the middle of the seventeenth century as the episcopal Church of Ireland became less tolerant of non-Anglican Protestants, whom it termed 'dissenters'. The Church of Ireland, as the established church, started to apply penalties for religious non-conformity to Presbyterians and other dissenting Protestants; thereby they expanded practices that formerly targeted only Catholics. The exclusion of Presbyterians, other Protestant dissenters, and Catholics under the suite of Penal Laws had political motivations and meant that those who did not belong to the Church of Ireland were not in a position to hold public offices. Furthermore, they were excluded from attending Trinity College Dublin, the only University in Ireland during the seventeenth and eighteenth centuries.[7] Political, economic, and educational affairs in Ireland were predominantly in the hands of members of the Church of Ireland, and the Westminster Parliament

---

[5] See Moore (2008).
[6] For further details, see Bartlett (2010, pp. 99–109).
[7] For further details, see Bartlett (2010, pp. 163–67); Brown (2016, pp. 112–17); Foster (1989, pp. 124–25).

too sought to exert its claim to rule. It is worth adding that those in political power in Ireland were not representative of the Irish population as a whole. At least three quarters of the population in Ireland was Catholic, and the much smaller Protestant part of the population was split into Presbyterians, who were mainly based in Ulster and Dublin, and Anglicans, who belonged to the Church of Ireland.[8] Although Presbyterians in Ireland were not prevented from religious worship (as were Catholics), they lacked political rights. Since they could not acquire a university degree in Ireland, many moved to Scotland for study and for many the University of Glasgow was the university of choice.[9] As of 1691, anyone who intended to become a Presbyterian minister needed to have a university degree, which commonly meant matriculation at a Scottish university for an arts degree.[10] The four-year degree included training in logic, metaphysics, moral philosophy, and natural philosophy. Preparation for the Presbyterian Ministry required further four years of studies in Divinity after the completion of the arts degree.[11] Since study outside Ireland was costly, several dissenting academies – called 'philosophy schools' in their day – were established that were meant to prepare students for study at Scottish universities and made it possible for them to abridge their studies in Scotland for the arts degree.[12]

This religious and political context shapes Francis Hutcheson's upbringing and education. From 1702 until 1707 he attends a local School in Saintfield, County Down, and then continues his education at a dissenting academy in Killyleagh, County Down, between 1707 and 1710. His training in Killyleagh made it possible to enter the fourth and final year when he starts his studies at the University of Glasgow in 1710/11. There he joins the natural philosophy class of John Louden. After his graduation Hutcheson remains in Glasgow and studies classical literature for a year before beginning training in Divinity in 1712/13 to become a minister in the Presbyterian church.[13]

[8] See Bartlett (2010, pp. 143–58). For an accessible overview of the issues, see C. M. Barry, 'Toleration in 18th Century Ireland', *Irish Philosophy Blog*, http://www.irishphilosophy.com/2016/11/17/toleration-18th-century/.
[9] See McBride (1993, p. 74); Moore (2008, p. 74; 1990, p. 43).
[10] See Steers (2012, p. 62).
[11] This was decided by the General Synod in 1702. See Steers (2012, p. 64).
[12] For helpful further discussion and insight into the curriculum of dissenting academies, see Steers (2012).
[13] See Moore (2008).

In 1718 Hutcheson returns to Ulster with the intention of becoming a Presbyterian minister. However, his career path changes in 1719 when he accepts an invitation to run a dissenting academy in Dublin, which is the beginning of his career as a teacher. The Toleration Act of 1719 gave more protection to Presbyterians and other Protestant dissenters and made it possible for them to run schools like the dissenting academy that was founded in Dublin.[14] His role at the academy in Dublin involves preparing the next generation of students for study in Scotland, and Glasgow in particular, like the training he received in Killyleagh that prepared him for study at Glasgow.[15] This means that the courses that he teaches in Dublin are meant to resemble the courses that other students attend at Glasgow so that the Irish-based students can abridge their subsequent studies in Scotland. Thus, we can assume that his teaching included logic, metaphysics, and moral philosophy. It is further very probable that he composed textbooks on logic and metaphysics during the 1720s while he teaches at the Dublin academy.[16] Although neither of these textbooks were published during these years, Hutcheson did not teach logic and metaphysics courses again after he left Dublin to take up the chair of moral philosophy at the University of Glasgow, to which he was appointed in December 1729 as Gershom Carmichael's successor.[17]

Hutcheson's teaching in Dublin is certainly constrained by the curriculum at Scottish universities. In his inaugural lecture, delivered at Glasgow in 1730, he recalls being 'involved in laborious and tedious business' (Hutcheson, 2006, p. 191) during the years in Dublin, but this reflection seems overshadowed by modesty. Hutcheson has fond memories of his formative years as a student at Glasgow and is genuinely delighted to return to his alma mater as professor of moral philosophy.[18] Yet the years that he spent in Ireland during the 1720s were no less important for his intellectual development and he is very productive and intellectually creative during this time of his life. He published two major works, namely *An Inquiry into the Original of our Ideas of Beauty and Virtue* (1725) and *An Essay on the Nature and Conduct of the Passions and Affections, with Illustrations on the Moral Sense* (1728) during these years. Furthermore, the intellectual milieu in Dublin and Ireland informs

[14]   See Carey (2006, p. 155).
[15]   See Moore (1990, p. 45).
[16]   English translations of both textbooks can be found in Hutcheson (2006).
[17]   See Moore (1990, pp. xxii–xxiii).
[18]   See Hutcheson (2006, pp. 191–92).

the development of his philosophical views and helps him find his own philosophical voice.[19]

In the following I want to pay particular attention to his views on liberty and situate them within intellectual debates in Ireland. First, Hutcheson is well aware of William King's libertarian defence of free will. William King (1650–1729), who was Bishop of Derry from 1691 until being appointed as Archbishop of Dublin in 1703, publishes *De Origine Mali* in 1702. In this work, which examines the origin of evil, King argues that it is important to distinguish between natural and moral evil and that humans are responsible for moral evil in the world. Moral evil occurs because humans have free will. Although God could have created humans without free will and arranged the world such that they would only do good actions, King believes that free will is essential for human moral development, despite the fact that it can lead to moral evil.[20]

Moreover, Robert Molesworth (1656–1725), who was an intellectual, merchant, and influential politician, was one of Hutcheson's associates in Dublin.[21] Molesworth supported Hutcheson's intellectual development, and probably helped him as he began publishing his works, in a place where Hutcheson was seen as a dissenter and in need of political protection.[22] Molesworth was friends with several intellectuals, whose views were considered radical at that time, including John Toland and Anthony Collins. Molesworth was also a close friend of Anthony Ashley Cooper, the Third Earl of Shaftesbury (1671–1713) and we can assume that Hutcheson had the opportunity to engage with Shaftesbury's works through Molesworth's intellectual circle.[23] Shaftesbury's philosophy aims to revive ancient philosophical views, and emphasizes that philosophy should be practical and help us improve our lives. It offers a stark contrast to the natural law tradition that shaped university courses in moral philosophy. By encountering intellectual views that diverge from the standard university curriculum and that many would have

[19] For further details, see Brown (2002).

[20] For additional details of Hutcheson's and King's relationship, see Brown (2002, Ch. 6).

[21] It is not known how Hutcheson and Molesworth first met. Molesworth's influence was not restricted to Dublin, but rather he also had an influence on student affairs in Glasgow in the 1720s. For further discussion, see McBride (1993, pp. 82–86).

[22] For further details, see Brown (2002, Ch. 1). See also Moore (1990, pp. 46–47).

[23] See Carey (2006, pp. 152–61; 2015, pp. 37–38); McBride (1993, pp. 82–84).

regarded as radical Hutcheson had the opportunity to step back from the views that his teachers in Glasgow advanced and to broaden his understanding of the intellectual debates of his day. This no doubt aided him to develop his own philosophical voice.

3. Liberty and the will in Hutcheson's *Metaphysics*

Hutcheson's most detailed commentary on philosophical debates concerning liberty and the will can be found in his Latin textbook *A Synopsis of Metaphysics*. Although we cannot be confident that it reflects his considered views, it was influential for university teaching in Scotland throughout the eighteenth century.[24] According to James Moore, Hutcheson's *Metaphysics* offers a critical commentary on the Latin textbook *Determinationes Ontologicae et Pneumatologicae* by the Dutch metaphysician Gerard de Vries.[25] De Vries's textbook was regularly assigned at the University of Glasgow during the first half of the eighteenth century and recommended by John Louden in his metaphysics classes. Moore maintains further that Hutcheson draws on John Locke's philosophy to challenge de Vries's metaphysical views.[26] In the following, I aim to show that Hutcheson's approach to metaphysics is more original than this; it not only builds on de Vries's and Locke's works, but also the intellectual debates in Ireland and beyond inform Hutcheson's views and help him add his own voice to metaphysical debates.

Hutcheson's *Metaphysics* is divided into three parts. The first part focuses on being and the common attributes of things, the second on the human mind, and the third on God. For present purposes, the second part is most relevant. There Hutcheson adopts the common distinction between the understanding and the will and the second chapter on the will offers insight into his thinking about liberty. He introduces the understanding and the will as powers of the mind and claims that 'the faculty of understanding and the faculty of willing … are concerned respectively with knowing things and with rendering life happy' (Hutcheson, 2006, II.i.2, p. 112). Although other philosophers of his day would agree with his characterization of the understanding, his claim that the will is concerned 'with

---

[24] Two editions were published during Hutcheson's lifetime in 1742 and an altered and enlarged edition in 1744, followed by five posthumous editions in 1749, 1756, 1762, 1774, and 1780.

[25] See Moore (2006, pp. xiii–xvii).

[26] See Moore (2006, pp. xv–xvi).

rendering life happy' diverges from their accounts of the will. Neither de Vries nor Locke introduce the will in these terms. According to de Vries, the intellect concerns knowledge and the will concerns freedom.[27] Locke introduces the will as follows:

> The Power of Thinking is called the *Understanding*, and the Power of Volition is called the *Will*, and these two Powers or Abilities in the Mind are denominated *Faculties*. (Locke, 1975, II.vi.2, p. 128)

> This *Power* which the mind has, thus to order the consideration of any *Idea*, or the forbearing to consider it; or to prefer the motion of any part of the body to its rest, and *vice versâ* in any particular instance is that which we call the *Will*. (Locke, 1975, II.xxi.5, p. 236)

This means that for Locke the will is a power of the mind, which is exercised in mental acts of volition. If a subsequent action (or its forbearance) is performed (or not performed) in accordance with the volition, the action (or its forbearance) is called voluntary.[28] Since Hutcheson's characterization of the will departs from both de Vries's and Locke's views, it is worth exploring further as to why he introduces the will in terms of happiness.

According to Hutcheson, the will 'seeks (*appetens*) every kind of pleasant sensation and all actions, events, or external things which seem likely to arouse them, and shuns and rejects everything contrary to them' (Hutcheson, 2006, II.ii.1, p. 126). In a passage added to the second edition, Hutcheson explains that this is possible, because all humans constantly desire (*appetitio*) happiness, which he takes to be an innate feature of our human constitution.[29] He further elaborates that 'the mind, so long as it maintains a calm and provident motion[30], is formed to seek every good thing in itself and to shun every evil; and when several things come before it which it cannot

---

[27] See de Vries (1718, p. 106). The Latin reads as follows: 'Sicuti de natura Intellectus est Conscientia, absque qua intellectio non foret talis, sic de natura Voluntatis est Libertas, absque qua nec volitio talis esset, sed brutus impetus. Estque, ejus, aeque ac ipisus voluntatis, adeo mens nostra sibi conscia, ut nullius rei magis'.

[28] See Locke (1975, II.xxi.5, p. 236).

[29] See Hutcheson (2006, II.ii.1, p. 126).

[30] The Latin expression is 'motu fertur et provido'. The Latin adjective 'providus', which is here translated as 'provident', can also be translated as 'prudent'.

have all at the same time, it turns to those which seem greater and more excellent' (Hutcheson, 2006, II.ii.1, p. 126).

His view that humans constantly seek happiness further rests on a distinction between two different kinds of desires.[31] First, Hutcheson argues that there is *sensual desire*. We share this kind of desire with non-human animals and it 'directs us toward pleasure by a kind of blind instinct' (Hutcheson, 2006, II.ii.1, p. 127). This means that the mind 'is driven by a quite violent emotion of the mind to obtain certain sensual goods and to avoid sensual ills' (Hutcheson, 2006, II.ii.1, p. 127). By contrast, the other kind of desire can be called *rational desire* and can be seen as *will* in the proper sense. It involves a 'calm emotion which calls in the counsel of reason and pursues things that are judged, in the light of all the circumstances, to be superior, and are seized by a nobler sense' (Hutcheson, 2006, II.ii.1, p. 127).

Since rational desire, can be seen as the will properly understood, let us consider how rational desire operates. First, Hutcheson argues, there is spontaneously arising desire or aversion, which is often followed by a process of deliberation during which the arguments for getting the things we desire and for avoiding the things that we dislike are carefully considered. After the process of deliberation is completed, 'there follows an *intention* (*propositum*) or *determination* (*consilium*) to do those things that seem most likely to achieve the end' (Hutcheson, 2006, II.ii.1, p. 127). Following the scholastics, the initial desire or aversion can be called 'simple wanting' and the intention to act, which follows the deliberative process, 'efficacious volition' (Hutcheson, 2006, II.ii.1, pp. 127–28).

At first sight, it may appear that Hutcheson here adopts a version of Locke's account of the suspension of desire.[32] As Locke prepares the second edition of his *Essay*, which was published in 1694, he heavily revises the chapter 'Of Power', which is chapter xxi of Book II. As part of the revisions he adds his so-called doctrine of the suspension of desire. In the second edition Locke explicitly distinguishes between desire and volition.[33] While a volition to do action *A*, commonly leads to the performance of *A*, desires are better understood as wishes and not all desires lead to action. Indeed, there can be multiple and conflicting desires. Commonly our strongest and most pressing desire results in a volition, which in turn leads to action, provided

[31] See Hutcheson (2006, II.ii.1, p. 127)
[32] See Locke (1975, E2–5 II.xxvii.47, 50-52 pp. 263–64, 265–67).
[33] See Locke (1975, E2–5 II.xxi.30 pp. 249–50).

there are no external impediments preventing the action.[34] However, the path from desire to volition is not an automatic process. Locke's second edition view is that intelligent beings have the power to suspend any of their desires until they have properly examined the good or evil of the desired things in question. This means that we can 'hold our *wills* undetermined, till we have *examin'd* the good or evil of what we desire' (Locke, 1975, E2–5 II.xxi.52, p. 267).

Despite the apparent similarities between Locke's account of suspension of desire and Hutcheson's understanding of rational desire, I believe that it is important to acknowledge that Hutcheson does not wholeheartedly endorse Locke's views on agency, liberty, and motivation. Differences between their views come to light if we consider how they each understand motivation. Overall, Hutcheson offers a more intellectual account of motivation than Locke. In the first edition of the *Essay* Locke argues that the greater good alone determines the will.[35] Locke was prompted by William Molyneux and William King to rethink his first edition account, who worry that his first edition view is too intellectual. For instance, Molyneux in a letter, dated 22 December 1692, challenges Locke's position by claiming that 'you seem to make all Sins to proceed from the Understanding, or to be against Conscience; and not at all from the Depravity of our Wills' (Locke, 1989, letter no 1597, vol. 4, p. 601). Molyneux here shares a concern that King has expressed in remarks that King prepared upon Molyneux's request on Locke's *Essay* and which Molyneux sent to Locke appended to a letter, dated 15 October 1692.[36] King, who believes that moral evil exists, because God has created humans with free will, since he regards free will as essential for moral development, criticizes Locke's view, because King is concerned that on Locke's view God would be responsible for sin and evil. Locke changed his view concerning motivation and rather than assuming that the greater good alone motivates, his new revised view is that only uneasiness determines the will.[37]

Hutcheson does not share Locke's second edition account of motivation. Instead Hutcheson's understanding of motivation comes closer to Locke's first than his second edition account. Furthermore, Hutcheson emphasizes the importance of controlling desires and cultivating right habits. To see how Hutcheson's view

---

[34]   See Locke (1975, E2–5 II.xxi.40, 47, pp. 257–58, 263–64).

[35]   See Locke (1975, E1 II.xxi.29, pp. 248-51).

[36]   See Locke (1989, letter no 1544, vol. 4, p. 541). For further discussion, see Storrie (2019).

[37]   See Locke (1975, E2–5 II.xxi.29, 31–40 pp. 249, 250–58)).

differs from Locke's and other influential views of his day, it is helpful to turn to his views on liberty and humans' ability to control their desires.

Hutcheson, like de Vries and Gershom Carmichael, acknowledges that his predecessors have grappled with the difficult question of how liberty is best understood.[38] The controversial question, Hutcheson maintains, concerns whether liberty is a power '*to set* [oneself] *to will a thing or its contrary equally*, which is called the *liberty of contrariety* (as if one were to say that he can desire and pursue either that which seems to him pleasant or that which appears harmful and annoying),' or is it '*at least the power to set* [oneself] *to act or not to act, to will or not to will*, which is the *liberty of contradiction*' (Hutcheson, 2006, I.iv.6, p. 97). The former kind of freedom requires a subject to be both able to will an action and its contrary, which means that it is an indifferent power of the mind to turn in any direction. The latter concerns a subject's ability to enter into an act of willing or not willing, or of doing what one wills or omitting what one does not will. Hutcheson invokes these different definitions of liberty also in a subsequent section that addresses the question 'Where liberty lies'. Since this section sheds light on Hutcheson's thinking, it is worth citing the first paragraph in full:

> Since the sentiment of the mind after completing its deliberation does not depend on the will, but necessarily follows the evidence of truth which is put before it, and [since] no previous command of the will arouses simple wishing or the initial desire or aversion, there is no question of *liberty* here at all, whether liberty is taken as *the power of doing what we wish and omitting what we do not wish*, or *a certain indifferent power of the mind to turn equally in any direction*. If therefore *liberty* is *a faculty which, given all the conditions for action, may act or not act, do one thing or its contrary*, it will only have place in an actual intention to act or in an efficacious volition, according to whether we can initiate [the volition] or suppress it by a previous decision of the will. But if this power pays no attention to the appearances of good or evil which are put before it or fails to follow them, it would seem to be a useless and capricious [power]. Anyone, therefore, who finds it absurd that our minds should be endowed with a power which in no way certainly follows our judgment will have to define it to mean merely *a power of doing what we wish and of refraining*

---

[38] See Hutcheson (2006, I.iv.6, pp. 97–99, II.ii.3, pp. 129–31). See also de Vries (1718, 38, pp. 106–10); Carmichael (2002, pp. 34–38).

Ruth Boeker

when we do not wish, however much the mind may have been constrained to wish or not. (Hutcheson, 2006, II.ii.3, p. 129)

While Hutcheson does not offer a new and original definition of
liberty, he shifts the focus of the debates by emphasizing the importance of acting in accordance with 'the evidence of truth'. This means
that once the process of deliberation of the various desires is completed, one should identify the ultimate intention or efficacious
volition guided by truth. This means that if one deliberates which
desire to pursue, say the desire to do *A* or the desire to refrain from
doing *A*, then one should pay attention to the good or evil that are
inherent in or result from the action or omission of the action.
Thus, for Hutcheson the primary question is not to settle which definition of liberty is to be preferred, but rather that deliberation is
guided by moral truth. This is not meant to suggest that he regards
the different positions on liberty to be equally plausible.

In the second edition of *Metaphysics* Hutcheson adds commentaries that outline how Stoic philosophers and Peripatetic philosophers
would engage with the textbook questions concerning liberty.[39] The
fact that he consults sources that find no explicit treatment in de
Vries's textbook and Locke's *Essay* is another indication that he
moves beyond their views. Stoic philosophers argue that '*nothing*
arises *without a cause*' (Hutcheson, 2006, I.iv.6, p. 98). Since causes
cannot go in opposite directions, they believe that totally indifferent
causes are impossible. Thus, Stoics would reject freedom of contrariety. Rather their view is 'that the will is constrained and directed by
each man's character' (Hutcheson, 2006, II.ii.3, p. 129). By contrast,
Peripatetic philosophers offer critical responses to determinism, as
defended by Stoic philosophers, and argue that 'the nature of *rational
causes* [is such] that they can move in any direction, and that this characteristic is theirs by nature' (Hutcheson, 2006, I.iv.6, p. 98).[40] In the
first instance Hutcheson outlines the views of Stoic and Peripatetic
philosophers, as one may expect in a textbook designed for students.
However, is he merely a neutral commentator, or does he add his own
voice to the debates? First, it is worth noting that the Stoic position
receives more detailed consideration than the views of the
Peripatetics, which could be seen as intimating that he leans

[39] See Hutcheson (2006, I.iv.6, 97–98, II.ii.3, pp. 129–31). Hutcheson
was especially interested in the works of the Stoic philosopher Marcus
Aurelius and contributed to a translation of his *Meditations*. Aurelius's
views on liberty can be found in Hutcheson and Moor (2008, X.33,
pp. 129–33).

[40] See also Hutcheson (2006, II.ii.3, pp. 130–31).

towards the Stoic position. Yet there is no clear indication that he aims to defend one position against the other. This opens another interpretive option, namely that he does not regard the views as rival theories and thus he sees no need to settle the dispute.[41] Just as he does not clearly argue in favour of one definition of liberty against another, he does not clearly take a stance regarding the disputes between Stoics and Peripatetics. Instead of seeing this as a weakness of his contribution to the debates, I want to propose that he intends to shift the focus of the debate. Hutcheson emphasizes the importance of making choices and forming intentions, or efficacious volitions, that are guided by truth and that will promote goodness and happiness, but in order to make choices guided by truth, he does not have to settle philosophical disputes about liberty that are in the focus of student textbooks such as the question whether liberty is better understood as liberty of contrariety or liberty of contraction. On the one hand, if our will is indifferent and both options are equally open, it would be irrational to form the volition to perform an action that is evil or has evil consequences. On the other hand, if choices are determined, it will be important to cultivate right habits and to train the mind in such a way that it can control desires. Hutcheson's engagement with Stoic and Peripatetic views helps prepare the next issue to which he turns, namely the question of what control humans have over their desire.[42]

Hutcheson not only argues that calm desires are superior, since they correspond to goods, but also that we are able to direct our mind to suppress desires for bad things and to pursue superior desires:

> Whatever men's freedom may be, if adequate signs of superior goods are put before them, anyone who has carefully examined the things which arouse desire, and has directed the powers of his mind to this thing, [will find that] all his appetites and desires will be stronger or milder in proportion to the goods themselves. Everyone, therefore, who has seriously done this will be able to make all his desires for superior goods and aversion from the graver evils so strong that he will easily be able at need to suppress weaker desires for bad things and his aversion to lesser evils. Thus he will be able to shape the whole pattern of his life, so that he will pursue all the nobler goods and ignore all the lower

---
[41] According to Moore (2006, pp. xxv–xxvii), Hutcheson can be seen as attempting to reconcile Stoic and Peripatetic views.
[42] See Hutcheson (2006, II.ii.3, p. 131).

133

things which are incompatible with them. (Hutcheson, 2006, II.ii.3, p. 131)

For Hutcheson the important task is that humans properly control their desires, but to do so, it is not relevant to quibble about the different definitions of liberty that his contemporaries offer. To see how exactly humans can control their desires it is helpful to turn to another passage where Hutcheson argues that violent emotions or lower desires gain force due to incautious association of ideas.[43] It is not uncommon that we erroneously associate happiness with certain things and pain and evil with other things. For instance, assume that Sarah was planning to help her friend, but on her way to her friend broke her leg. Since then she associates helping friends with evil and has stopped helping friends. In this example Sarah mistakenly associates helping friends with evil. Hutcheson believes that there are many other examples of incautious associations of ideas, but that we can gain control over violent emotions if we carefully examine our associations of ideas and separate the ideas or notions we combined erroneously and carelessly.[44] He writes:

> If we are to achieve a just command of these desires and true freedom of mind, it would be very helpful to separate and take apart these notions which we have so carelessly put together, and take a long, hard look at those things that stimulate the appetite, stripping them of these stolen colors; so that we may discover and learn for ourselves what real good and evil is in each of them, and so that we may not seek or shun them beyond the measure of true good and evil. (Hutcheson, 2006, II.ii.6, pp. 136–37)

On this basis, it can be said that Hutcheson's contribution to debates about liberty that received attention in textbooks used in Scottish universities lies in his shift of focus towards practical questions of how we are best able to attain goodness and happiness. He believes that we are able to control our desires and through the cultivation of right habits and proper examination of association of ideas we can train our mind to pursue superior desires. Since these practical aims are consistent with different ways of understanding liberty, there is no need to settle the dispute as far as practical purposes are concerned.

[43] See Hutcheson (2006, II.ii.6, pp. 136–37).

[44] See also Hutcheson (2002, pp. 20–21, 28, 65–86, 92–93, 104–5, 108–12, 131–32). For further discussion, see Gill (1996). I have also learned from forthcoming work by Kathryn Tabb and John P. Wright on association in eighteenth-century Scottish philosophy.

This shift towards practical questions of self-control has roots in ancient philosophy, but can also be found in Shaftesbury's philosophy.[45] Shaftesbury, like Hutcheson, has great admiration for ancient philosophy. In his major work *Characteristicks of Men, Manners, Opinions, Times* he argues that philosophy should be practical and help us improve our lives and criticizes purely speculative philosophical disputes. In *Soliloquy, or Advice to an Author* – one work included in *Characteristicks* – Shaftesbury emphasizes the importance of becoming an author of one's own life, of governing one's passions, and cultivating a true and noble character. In his *Inquiry concerning Virtue or Merit* – another work included in *Characteristicks* – he regards pleasures of the mind as superior to those of the body and holds that mental enjoyments are the only means to attain certain and solid happiness.[46] Shaftesbury's philosophical ideas were debated in Robert Molesworth's circle and thus we can assume that Hutcheson has had the opportunity to engage with Shaftesbury's philosophy during his years in Dublin. This intellectual context in Dublin certainly played a role in Hutcheson's intellectual development and presumably stimulated him to move beyond the issues presented in textbooks and to add his own voice to debates about liberty.

4. Liberty and the will in Hutcheson's mature writings

Since Hutcheson does not devote a chapter or section in his mature writings to philosophical debates about liberty, we have limited textual resources to reconstruct his mature thinking about liberty. The mere fact that he has little to say about liberty can be seen as further evidence that he does not see the need to settle the philosophical debates that concerned his predecessors and contemporaries. Instead he is more concerned with debates about human nature and aims to show that humans are not merely self-interested beings, but have also benevolent affections towards others that are not reducible to self-love.[47] As he advances his own views concerning human nature he anticipates potential objections. In particular, he intends to show that William King's understanding of liberty does not

---

[45]   See Boeker (2019). Among the ancient sources, Hutcheson is well acquainted with Marcus Aurelius's philosophy and contributed to an English translation of his *Mediations*, which was submitted for publication in 1742.

[46]   See Shaftesbury (2001, vol. 2, p. 58).

[47]   See Hutcheson (2004; 2002).

Ruth Boeker

undermine his philosophical position.[18] I will examine Hutcheson's response to King more closely below, but first let me comment on how Hutcheson advances philosophical studies of the human mind and our mental capacities.

Hutcheson defends the view that there are not only the five well-known external senses, sight, hearing, touch, smell, and taste, but that we are also constituted with several other senses. By a sense he understands the mind's independent capacity to receive ideas '*and to have Perceptions of Pleasure and Pain*' (Hutcheson, 2002, p. 17). Besides external senses, he asserts that we have an internal sense, which concerns the pleasures of the imagination and makes it possible to have '*Pleasant Perceptions* arising from *regular, harmonious, uniform* Objects' (Hutcheson, 2002, p. 17), a public sense, which concerns '"our Determinations to be pleased with the *Happiness* of others, and to be uneasy with their *Misery*"' (Hutcheson, 2002, p. 17), a moral sense, 'by which "we perceive *Virtue*, or *Vice* in our selves, or others"' (Hutcheson, 2002, p. 17), and a sense of honour, '"which makes the *Approbation*, or *Gratitude* of others, for any good Actions we have done, the necessary occasion of Pleasure; and their *Dislike, Condemnation*, or *Resentment* of Injuries done by us, the occasion of that uneasy Sensation called *Shame*, even when we fear no further evil from them"' (Hutcheson, 2002, p. 18).

Hutcheson further argues that corresponding to each type of sense there is a particular type of desire. Desires are part of our human constitution and they arise 'upon Apprehension of Good or Evil in Objects, Actions, or Events, to obtain for our *selves* or *others* the *agreeable Sensation*, when the Object or Event is good; or to prevent the *uneasy Sensation*, when it is evil' (Hutcheson, 2002, p. 18). He identifies the following classes of desire:

> 1. The Desire of *sensual Pleasure*, (by which we mean that of the external Senses); and Aversion to the opposite Pains. 2. The Desires of the *Pleasures of Imagination* or Internal Sense, and Aversion to what is disagreeable to it. 3. Desires of the Pleasures arising from *Publick Happiness*, and Aversion to the Pains arising from the *Misery of others*. 4. Desires of *Virtue*, and Aversion to *Vice*, according to the Notions we have of the Tendency of Actions to the Publick Advantage or Detriment. 5. Desires of *Honour*, and Aversion to Shame. (Hutcheson, 2002, pp. 18–19)

---

[18]   See Hutcheson (2002, pp. 178–82).

The distinction that Hutcheson draws between different senses, on the one hand, and different desires, on the other hand, mirrors the distinction between the understanding and the will.[49] The different senses that he identifies are mental capacities that enable us to receive ideas, while the various desires enable us to attain good and to avoid evil. Identifying several different senses and corresponding desires helps Hutcheson establish his view that humans are not merely self-interested beings, but also benevolent and that benevolence is an inherent part of human nature.

Hutcheson is interested in understanding human action and examines what excites us to choose one action over another. He distinguishes between the reasons that excite actions from the reasons that justify actions and claims 'that all *exciting Reasons* presuppose *Instincts* and *Affections*; and the *justifying* presuppose a *Moral Sense*' (Hutcheson, 2002, p. 138).[50] This thesis enables Hutcheson to challenge rationalist views about motivation. If this is correct, it follows that reason alone cannot motivate or excite action, but rather the presence of instincts or affections is required. He elaborates:

> As to *exciting Reasons,* in every calm rational Action some *end* is desired or intended; no end can be intended or desired previously to some one of these Classes of Affections, *Self-Love, Self-Hatred,* or desire of private Misery, (if this be possible) *Benevolence* toward others, or *Malice:* All Affections are included under these; no *end* can be previous to them all; there can therefore be no *exciting Reason* previous to *Affection.* (Hutcheson, 2002, p. 139).

Yet Hutcheson anticipates that his thesis that reason alone cannot excite actions and always presupposes some instinct or affection will be questioned by his contemporaries, like King, who defend libertarian free will and argue that we can freely determine our actions and who take this to be crucial for merit and praiseworthiness.[51] According to King, free will consists in a faculty of election.[52]

---

[49] This reading is supported by the following statement: 'Whereas *Desire* is as distinct from any *Sensation,* as the *Will* is from the *Understanding* or Senses' (Hutcheson, 2002, pp. 28–29).

[50] According to Garrett, (2002, p. xvii), Hutcheson borrows the distinction from Hugo Grotius (2012, II.i.1) to challenge rationalist accounts of motivation.

[51] See Hutcheson (2002, pp. 178–82)

[52] See King (1702, 5.1.3). King describes the faculty of election as follows: 'if then we suppose such a power as this, it is plain, that the agent endowed with it cannot be determined in its operations by any pre-existent goodness in the object; for since the agreeableness between it and the

Hutcheson asks whether '*determining our selves freely* ... mean[s] *acting without any Motive or exciting Reason*'. If it does not mean that one acts without a motive or exciting reason, then 'it cannot be opposed to *acting from Instinct or Affections, since all Motives or Reasons* presuppose them' (Hutcheson, 2002, p. 179). Alternatively, it could mean that only actions done without any motive or exciting reason are meritorious. Such actions would be actions done 'by *mere Election* without prepollent *Desire* of one *Action* or *End* rather than its opposite, or without *Desire of that Pleasure* which some do suppose follows upon any *Election*' (Hutcheson, 2002, p. 179). This means that one could not prefer an action over its opposite. Hutcheson asks us to consider whether anyone ever acts in this way, namely merely by election without any prior desire. Furthermore, he asks whether we would approve of such an action.

> Upon seeing a Person not more disposed by *Affection, Compassion, or Love or Desire,* to make his Country happy than miserable, yet choosing the one rather than the other, from no *Desire of publick Happiness,* nor *Aversion to the Torments of others,* but by such an *unaffectionate Determination,* as that by which one moves his *first Finger* rather than the *second,* in giving an Instance of a *trifling Action;* let any one ask if this Action should be *meritorious:* and yet that there should be no *Merit* in a *tender compassionate Heart,* which shrinks at every *Pain* of its *Fellow-Creatures,* and triumphs in their *Happiness;* with *kind Affections* and *strong Desire* labouring for the publick Good. If this be the Nature of *meritorious Actions;* I fancy every honest Heart would disclaim all *Merit in Morals,* as violently as the old *Protestants* rejected it in *Justification.* (Hutcheson, 2002, pp. 179–80)

This leads Hutcheson to question the view that he ascribes to King, namely that merit or praiseworthiness is founded on unaffectionate

---

objects, at least in most of them, is supposed to arise from the determination, the agreeableness cannot possibly be the cause of that determination on which itself depends. But the congruity of the object with the faculty is all the goodness in it, therefore there is nothing good in regard to this power, at least in those object to which it is indifferent, till it has embraced it, nor evil till it has rejected it: since the determination of the power to the object is prior to the goodness and the cause of it, this power cannot be determined by that goodness in its operations' (King, 1781, 5.1.3.5). For further discussion, see Pearce (2019).

choice, or mere election.[53] He proposes, '[b]ut perhaps 'tis not the *mere Freedom of Choice* which is approved, but the *free Choice of publick Good,* without any *Affection.* Then *Actions* are approved for *publick Usefulness,* and not for *Freedom*'(Hutcheson, 2002, p. 180). Alternatively, it is possible that neither mere election alone nor public usefulness alone are meritorious, but rather both are jointly required for merit. However, could we praise a manufacturer whose work is publicly useful? Hutcheson believes that in the absence of a kind affection or desire of public good such actions are not meritorious.[54]

According to Hutcheson, philosophers who defend libertarian free will and emphasize the importance of rational choice often fail to acknowledge that in addition to violent passions and desires there are calm desires and affections; and that they confound reason with calm desires and affections. Since violent passions often lead to negative consequences not just for individuals but also for society, Hutcheson believes that they must be properly managed and we should focus on cultivating a calm temper or character. Again, we see that Hutcheson believes that upon closer inspection arguments by defenders of free will prove irrelevant and instead it is more important to focus on character development and the cultivation of right habits.[55]

University College Dublin
ruth.boeker@ucd.ie

---

[53] It is questionable whether Hutcheson's reading of King accurately represents King's account of election. For a more sophisticated interpretation, see Pearce (2019).

[54] See Hutcheson (2002, pp. 180–81).

[55] Earlier versions of this paper were presented at the Center for the Scottish Enlightenment Conference on Science in the Scottish Enlightenment at the Princeton Theological Seminary in March 2017 and the Irish Philosophy in the Age of Berkeley Conference at Trinity College Dublin in April 2019. I would like to thank both audiences for helpful feedback. I am also grateful to Takaharu Oda, Kenneth Pearce, and Katherine O'Donnell for their useful comments on a draft of this paper.

Ruth Boeker

References

C. M. Barry, 'Toleration in 18th Century Ireland', *Irish Philosophy Blog*, http://www.irishphilosophy.com/2016/11/17/toleration-18th-century/.

Thomas Bartlett, *Ireland: A History* (Cambridge: Cambridge University Press, 2010).

Ruth Boeker, 'Shaftesbury on Liberty and Self-Mastery', *International Journal of Philosophical Studies* 27 (2019), 731–52.

Michael Brown, *Francis Hutcheson in Dublin, 1719–1730: The Crucible of His Thought* (Dublin: Four Courts Press, 2002).

Michael Brown, *The Irish Enlightenment* (Cambridge, MA: Harvard University Press, 2016).

Daniel Carey, *Locke, Shaftesbury, and Hutcheson: Contesting Diversity in the Enlightenment and Beyond* (Cambridge: Cambridge University Press, 2006).

Daniel Carey, 'Francis Hutcheson's Philosophy and the Scottish Enlightenment: Reception, Reputation, and Legacy', in *Scottish Philosophy in the Eighteenth Century: Morals, Politics, Religion*, ed. Aaron Garrett and James A. Harris (Oxford: Oxford University Press, 2015), 36–76.

Gershom Carmichael, *Natural Rights on the Threshold of the Scottish Enlightenment: The Writings of Gershom Carmichael*, ed. James Moore and Michael Silverthorne (Indianapolis: Liberty Fund, 2002).

Gerard de Vries, *Rerum Attributis Determinationes Ontologicae. Et De Natura Dei Et Humanae Mentis Determinationes Pneumatologicae*, 6th ed. (Edinburgh: M. J. McEuen, J. Paton, & W. Broun, 1718 [1690]).

R. F. Foster, *Modern Ireland 1600–1972* (London: Penguin Books, 1989).

Aaron Garrett, 'Introduction', in *An Essay on the Nature and Conduct of the Passions and Affections, with Illustrations on the Moral Sense, by Francis Hutcheson*, ed. Aaron Garrett (Indianapolis: Liberty Fund, 2002).

Michael B. Gill, 'Fantastick Associations and Addictive General Rules: A Fundamental Difference between Hutcheson and Hume', *Hume Studies* 22 (1996), 23–48.

Hugo Grotius, *On the Law of War and Peace*, ed. Stephen C. Neff (Cambridge: Cambridge University Press, 2012).

James A. Harris, *Of Liberty and Necessity: The Free Will Debate in Eighteenth-Century British Philosophy* (Oxford: Clarendon Press, 2005).

Francis Hutcheson, *An Essay on the Nature and Conduct of the Passions and Affections, with Illustrations on the Moral Sense*, ed. Aaron Garrett (Indianapolis: Liberty Fund, 2002 [1728]).

Francis Hutcheson, *An Inquiry into the Original of Our Ideas of Beauty and Virtue*, ed. Wolfgang Leidhold (Indianapolis: Liberty Fund, 2004 [1725]).

Francis Hutcheson, *Logic, Metaphysics, and the Natural Sociability of Mankind*, ed. James Moore and Michael Silverthorne (Indianapolis: Liberty Fund, 2006 [1742]).

Francis Hutcheson and James Moor, *The Meditations of the Emperor Marcus Aurelius Antonius*, ed. James Moore and Michael Silverthorne (Indianapolis: Liberty Fund, 2008 [1742]).

William King, *De Origine Mali* (London: Printed by Benj. Tooke, 1702).

William King, *An Essay on the Origin of Evil. To Which Is Added, a Sermon by the Same Author, on the Fall of Man.*, ed. Edmund Law, trans. Edmund Law, fifth ed., revised ed. (London: Printed for R. Fauldner and T. and J. Merril, 1781).

John Locke, *An Essay Concerning Human Understanding*, ed. Peter H. Nidditch (Oxford: Clarendon Press, 1975 [1690]).

John Locke, *The Correspondence of John Locke*, ed. E. S. de Beer, 8 vols. (Oxford: Clarendon Press, 1976–1989).

Ian McBride, 'The School of Virtue: Francis Hutcheson, Irish Presbyterians and the Scottish Enlightenment', in *Political Thought in Ireland since the Seventeenth Century*, ed. D. George Boyce, Robert Eccleshall, and Vincent Geoghegan (London and New York: Routledge, 1993) 73–99.

James Moore, 'The Two Systems of Francis Hutcheson: On the Origins of the Scottish Englightenment', in *Studies in the Philosophy of the Scottish Enlightenment*, ed. M. A. Stewart (Oxford: Clarendon Press, 1990), 37–59.

James Moore, 'Introduction', in *Logic, Metaphysics, and the Natural Sociability of Mankind, by Francis Hutcheson*, ed. James Moore and Michael Silverthorne (Indianapolis: Liberty Fund, 2006).

James Moore, 'Hutcheson, Francis (1694–1746)', in *Oxford Dictionary of National Biography* (Oxford: Oxford University Press, 2008).

Kenneth L. Pearce, 'William King on Free Will', *Philosophers' Imprint* 19 (2019) 1–15.

Anthony Ashley Cooper, Third Early of Shaftesbury, *Characteristicks of Men, Manners, Opinions, Times*, ed. Douglas J. den Uyl, 3 vols. (Indianapolis: Liberty Fund, 2001 [1711]).

Ruth Boeker

David Steers, '"The Very Life-Blood of Nonconfirmity Is Education": The Killyleagh Philosophy School, County Down', *Familia* 28 (2012) 61–79.

Stefan Storrie, 'William King's Influence on Locke's Second Edition Change of Mind About Human Action and Freedom', *International Journal of Philosophical Studies* 27 (2019) 668–84.

'Plainly of Considerable Moment in Human Society': Francis Hutcheson and Polite Laughter in Eighteenth-Century Britain and Ireland

KATE DAVISON

Abstract

This article focuses on Francis Hutcheson's *Reflections Upon Laughter*, which was originally published in 1725 as a series of three letters to *The Dublin Journal* during his time in the city. Although rarely considered a significant example of Hutcheson's published work, *Reflections Upon Laughter* has long been recognised in the philosophy of laughter as a foundational contribution to the 'incongruity theory' – one of the 'big three' theories of laughter, and that which is still considered the most credible by modern theorists. The article gives an account of Hutcheson's text but, rather than evaluating it solely as an explanation of laughter, the approach taken is an historical one: it emphasises the need to reconnect the theory to the cultural and intellectual contexts in which it was published and to identify the significance of Hutcheson's arguments in time and place. Through this, the article argues that Hutcheson's theory of laughter is indicative of the perceived significance of human risibility in early eighteenth-century Britain and Ireland and, more broadly, that it contributed both to moral philosophical debate and polite conduct guidance.

1. Laughter in History

The question 'why do we laugh?' has occupied minds in the western world since antiquity. From Plato to Sigmund Freud – via Aristotle, Thomas Hobbes, René Descartes, Immanuel Kant, and more – the list of those who have interrogated the causes, nature and consequences of human laughter is long and it reads like a roll call of canonical European philosophers. These centuries of scrutiny have generated what are known as the 'big three' theories of laughter (Carroll, 2014).[1] First is the 'superiority' theory: it can be traced back to Aristotle and Plato, but is most commonly associated with Thomas Hobbes. His description of laughter in *Leviathan* cast it as a grimace

---

[1]   On theories of laughter, see for example, Rockelein (2002); Morreall (ed.) (1987); Morreall (2009); Martin (2006).

doi:10.1017/S1358246120000132   © The Royal Institute of Philosophy and the contributors 2020

triggered by experiencing 'sudden glory'. We laugh when we perceive ourselves in a superior light: it is a sneering self-applause that expresses contempt for others (Hobbes, 1651). Secondly, the 'relief' theory, which is most often attributed to Sigmund Freud. His 'hydraulic model' of psychology led him to view joking as means to release social tension: jokes operate as a safety valve, allowing a society to let off steam (Freud, 1905). Thirdly, the incongruity theory, which is often thought to have originated with Francis Hutcheson who thus holds a special place in the philosophy of laughter. His theory was set out in a series of three letters to the *Dublin Journal* in 1725, which were republished posthumously in 1750 in Glasgow – where he had been professor of moral philosophy – as *Reflections Upon Laughter*, together with a critique of Bernard Mandeville's *Fable of the Bees* (Hutcheson, 1750). Hutcheson contended that laughter is triggered by the perception of ill-suited pairings of ideas, objects or situations; it is our response to the coming together of things that are incompatible or out of place. Variations on Hutcheson's theory have since been proposed by a number of philosophers and psychologists and, of the three theories of laughter, incongruity is still considered to be the most persuasive (Morreall, 2009, p. 12). Yet, even now, with our rapidly developing understanding of the human brain, laughter retains an element of mystery. It occupies some psycho-somatic space: more than an emotion or feeling, it is a reaction that originates in the mind, but manifests in the body. Hutcheson's struggle to characterise his subject still rings true: 'that sensation, action, passion, or affection', he wrote, 'I know not which of them a philosopher would call it' (Hutcheson, 1750, p. 16). Sometimes we laugh deliberately, and other times involuntarily as an instinctive reaction to a moment. In both cases, though, laughter is part of our communicative repertoire; it is one of the many verbal and gestural strategies we employ while interacting with one another.[2] Moreover, it seems we have been doing so since our earliest beginnings as a species. For our ancestors, laughter was most likely an indication of safety and play: that of pre-verbal infants is thought to be a legacy of this phenomenon (Gervais and Wilson, 2005; Morreall, 2009, pp. 41–42). Of those who have investigated the phenomenon of human laughter, then, few would disagree with Hutcheson's claim that it 'is plainly of considerable moment in human society'

---

[2]   The anthropologist Mary Douglas has been influential in this respect: see her 'Jokes' in Douglas (1975, pp. 90–114), and 'Do Dogs Laugh? A Cross-Cultural approach to Body Symbolism' in Ibid (pp. 165–69). See also Provine (2002).

(Hutcheson, 1750, p. 32), even if consensus on its precise triggers and effects remains elusive.

For an historian, however, the notion that there exists a universal theory of laughter – that what makes us laugh is transcultural and ahistorical – sets alarm bells ringing (Bremmer and Roodenburg, 1997). Historians are driven to uncover the particulars of past societies and cultures, so the question is not 'what makes us laugh?', but what has made people laugh in different times and places? This question has underpinned a subfield of research focusing on the humour of past societies.[3] And with good reason, as Keith Thomas's foundational contribution to the field argued. 'The historical study of laughter', wrote Thomas, 'brings us right up against the fundamental values of past societies. For when we laugh we betray our innermost assumptions' (Thomas, 1977, p. 77). Thereafter the history of humour expanded in line with the development of cultural history through the 1980s and '90s, not least following Robert Darnton's seminal essay on 'The Great Cat Massacre' in an eighteenth-century Parisian printshop. In accordance with Thomas, Darnton saw jokes as a tool with which to prize open past mentalities. An apparent source of historical hilarity that is deeply unfunny to modern readers – in this case the ritualistic slaughter of cats – exposes starkly the distance between past and present. Emphasising that people in the past 'do not think the way we do', Darnton argued that the effort required to explain the episode unravelled the mental world of those involved. In 'getting' the joke, he could 'get' their culture (Darnton, 1984, pp. 2 and 75–104). Now a well-established field, the history of humour has demonstrated that the subjects considered acceptable to laugh at, and how cruelly, sympathetically, exuberantly or cautiously people laugh, have all varied with time, place and culture. This has generated new insights into past cultures and mentalities, along with the values and sensibilities of the day.[4] But the history of what people have *laughed at*, is not – strictly speaking – a history of laughter. Laughing is a physical and often noisy action: it is not synonymous with humour, at which laughter might be targeted (Apte, 1985, p. 14). Laughing engages the body, the face and the vocal chords, but leaves no trace on the historical record: in an early modern context, we simply cannot 'hear the people not just talking but also laughing', as Thomas aspired to do (Thomas, 1977, p. 77). Yet, we do have representations of laughter

---

[3] See the extensive bibliography in Verberckmoes (1997)

[4] Notably in the case of eighteenth-century Britain, Gatrell (2006) and Dickie (2012).

– a great many of them, both written and visual – and we can write a history using those as source material. In this sense, the historical study of laughter has been more precisely defined as the study of how laughter was depicted, debated and interpreted by past societies (Verberckmoes, 1999, pp. 118–9). Studying laughter in this way is distinct from the approach taken in philosophies of laughter, which have discussed historical theories in depth, but often with a view to evaluating their accuracy. An article focused on Hutcheson's *Reflections Upon Laughter* is a case in point: its goal was to identify 'the limitations of Hutcheson's account of the nature of laughter' (Telfer, 1995, p. 359). In contrast, this article takes an historical approach, which aims to account for why Hutcheson was interested in laughter, and to assess the significance of his arguments in time and place. Approaching laughter in this way has already revealed the extent to which it 'mattered' in certain historical cultures (Skinner, 2001). And it also helps historians to tackle new questions in the history of humour, which concern not what people laughed at, but what that laughter *did*. As Mark Knights and Adam Morton have argued, 'laughter and satire played significant roles in political processes and social practices in a range of historical contexts', and exploring this requires a focus on their reception – indeed, their 'power' (Knights and Morton, 2017, p. 1). In this pursuit, an understanding of how laughter was understood and thought about in the past becomes all the more important.

2. Laughter and Eighteenth-Century Politeness

Eighteenth-century Britain is particularly fertile ground for a history of laughter as it was subjected to an heightened level of investigation and anxiety, which generated abundant material for historians to pore over. Such interest was bound up with the period's well-documented preoccupation with politeness.[5] In the first instance, politeness was a discourse of manners; it denoted refinement of behaviour and personal demeanour, which 'the polite' would exercise when interacting with others. It was discussed and elucidated by the influential essays of Joseph Addison and Richard Steele in *The Spectator* in the early century, and subsequent didactic literature codified polite prescriptions in detail, covering everything from how to converse agreeably to how to stand, dance the minuet, or greet a passer-by on the

---

[5]   See On politeness and its prominence in historical scholarship see Langford (2002) and Klein (2002).

street.[6] Laughter had an ambivalent relationship with such consciously urbane and decorous forms.[7] On the one hand, cheerfulness, wittiness and geniality were crucial to polite encounters, as Jonathan Swift's *Treatise on Polite Conversation* (1738) indicates. In the preface, Swift noted that there was a 'Cause of Laughter which Decency requires' and, when well judged, laughter in conversation was 'undoubted the Mark of a good Taste, as well as of polite and obliging Behaviour' (Swift, 1738, p. v). On the other hand, laughing defied polite aspirations for self-mastery and genteel conversation. Physically, laughter was often an uncontrollable response – and it could be hearty too, shaking the body, crumpling the face and even making the eyes weep. It was such bodily contortions that the fourth earl of Chesterfield famously took issue with in his letters to his son, which subsequently formed the basis of several conduct guides. He wrote,

> Having mentioned laughing I must particularly warn you against it [...] Frequent loud laughter is the characteristic of folly and ill manners; it is the manner in which the mob express their silly joy at silly things; and they call it being merry. In my mind there is nothing so illiberal, and so ill-bred, as audible laughter.

He continued in the same vein, observing 'how low and unbecoming a thing laughter is: not to mention the disagreeable noise that it makes, and the shocking distortion of the face that it occasions'.[8] In a later letter, Chesterfield dwelled upon another concern regarding laughter's compatibility with polite behaviour: its targets. Registering his distaste for the 'silly things' that triggered much laughter, he warned that,

> Horse-play, romping, frequent loud fits of laughter, jokes, waggery, and indiscriminate familiarity, will sink both merit and knowledge into a degree of contempt. They compose a most merry fellow; and a merry fellow was never yet a respectable man.[9]

Sure enough, even a passing acquaintance with eighteenth-century satirical literature, jestbooks or caricature reveals how crude the period's comic tastes could be.[10] Sexual, scatological and cruel

---

[6] See, for example, Anon (1762).

[7] For a full discussion, see Davison (2014).

[8] See Dobrée (ed.) (1932, III, pp. 114–18: to this son, 9 March 1748).

[9] Ibid., (IV, pp. 1379–82: to his son, 10 August 1749).

[10] This material has been explored in depth by Gatrell (2006, esp. pp. 178–210), and Dickie (2012).

Kate Davison

humour was as germane to the age as Palladian architecture and
Wedgewood tea services. Along with its uncontrolled physicality
and impolite targets, there was also anxiety about the effects of laughter in social interaction: laughing *at* others was widely understood as
potentially aggressive and thus not conducive to genial encounters.[11]
Given both the intricacy of polite conduct guidance and recognition
of laughter's prevalence in social situations, it is unsurprising to find
so much ink spilled over how to laugh in company, where, when and
what at.

But politeness also reached beyond a narrow concern with external
behaviour, and laughter was implicated in this respect too. In the
hands of Anthony Ashley Cooper, the third earl of Shaftesbury,
politeness embraced questions of inner morality and virtue so that
it might, as he put it, 'carry *Good-Breeding* a step higher'
(Shaftesbury, 1711, III p. 161).[12] Shaftesbury's writings from the
early century anchored politeness in philosophy: it was not simply
a matter of superficial social behaviour, politeness concerned the
more profound appreciation of beauty, harmony and good order.
These ideas gained purchase outside scholarly debate through the
elevation of 'taste' in eighteenth-century culture. Described in the
mid-century as 'the darling idol of the polite world', the meaning
of taste extended beyond gastronomy to denote the capacity to
discern and take pleasure in the subtle qualities of practically anything, from a well-proportioned landscape to wallpaper or, indeed,
a witty remark.[13] Taste was aspirational: while in theory everyone
had the capacity for it, only some cultivated it (Brewer, 1997,
pp. 88–92). For Shaftesbury, such aesthetic appreciation was
guided by an internal 'moral sense' that, if trained, enabled humankind to fulfil its natural capability for virtue. Hence a refined taste indicated inner virtue and morality. Hutcheson expanded on
Shaftesbury, especially by setting out a number of internal senses, including beauty, harmony, grandeur, novelty and order, which
operate as reflex responses to the perception of certain objects
(Harris, 2017, pp. 325–37). This theory of internal senses was set
out in his *Inquiry into the Original of our Ideas of Beauty and Virtue*
(1725), but it was also elaborated in a less canonical text: his three
letters to the *Dublin Journal* about laughter. For Hutcheson, laughter
was a reflex that revealed the workings of our internal senses and

[11] See, for example, Smilewell (1774). The ambivalent attitude to
laughter in social encounters is discussed in Shrank (2017).
[12] On Shaftesbury and politeness, see Klein (1994).
[13] *The Connoisseur*, 721 (13 May, 1756).

148

aesthetic judgements. And he was not alone on this front: later in the century James Beattie took up a similar theme (Beattie, 1776), but before Hutcheson's letters even became *Reflections Upon Laughter* in 1750, the German philosopher Georg Friedrich Meier (1718–1777) had gone a step further by explicitly arguing that jesting was a branch of aesthetic philosophy. Meier's *Thoughts on Jesting* was a two-hundred-page exposition on how best to jest in company (Meier, 1765). What he called a 'happy Jest' was 'distinguished from Buffoonery and Indecent Drollery' by its 'Conformity to the Rules of the Beauty of our sensitive Knowledge':

> And thus it is a Part, which is within the Province of the fine Arts: And a Research into the Perfections thereof must be considered as a Branch of what is called the Aesthetic. (Meier, 1765, p. 11)

The combinations of objects that any given person saw fit to laugh at revealed their judgement, morality and, of course, taste.

> As it is always an indication of a vitiated low Taste, either to jest in an insipid Manner oneself, or to approve the low, insipid Jests of others; and on the contrary, always Proof of a refined Taste, never to jest but in a sprightly Manner, and never to approve but sprightly Jests. (Meier, 1765, p. 14)

Discussions of laughter were thus entangled with politeness on several levels. Politeness resided in conversation and laughter was recognised as an important part of sharing one another's company, even if conduct guidance remained ambivalent about its effects on social interaction. More profoundly, laughter offered insights into the questions driving moral philosophers and hence attracted their scrutiny. Laughing aloud was an external behaviour that revealed the workings of the internal senses and aesthetic judgements. Getting it right was not just a matter of being 'polite' in the sense of being an agreeable companion, but also in the sense of expressing refined taste and inner virtue.

In these respects, the culture of politeness in eighteenth-century Britain provides important context in which to read Hutcheson's *Reflections Upon Laughter*. Not least, it is reminder that Hutcheson was not writing in isolation, but as part of – and in response to – ongoing debates about human risibility, its meaning and significance in society. And, furthermore, that these debates were themselves part of both scholarly philosophical inquiry into human nature, and wider cultural commentary on the nature of polite manners. Hutcheson's *Reflections Upon Laughter* was a conscious effort to rescue laughter from the trappings of Hobbesian self-interest by rethinking what

Kate Davison

triggers laughter, but it also upheld moral philosophy's widei ci i-
tique of selfishness as the key human motivation: not for nothing
was it later published with a critique of Mandeville. Far from being
aggressive and haughty, for Hutcheson, laughter spoke of the
natural benevolence of human nature and it was crucial to the workings of a polite society. He cast laughter as a pleasant aspect of sociability, which helped to achieve the mutually pleasing and genial
interactions to which polite society aspired; moreover, it offered a
gentle means to correct foibles and follies without causing offence –
particularly useful when good natured relations were the aspiration.

If the intellectual and cultural context is important for understanding what was at stake for Hutcheson when arguing about laughter, the
contexts of original publication also have implications for how his
theory should be interpreted. The usual citation is the 1750
edition, *Reflections Upon Laughter*, but the original text was written
for an audience of newspaper readers and coffeehouse goers – the
urbane gentlemen of early eighteenth-century Dublin. At the time,
the city was home to a thriving print culture. The printing monopoly
held by the king's printer since the mid-sixteenth century had been
eroded by the end of the seventeenth century, as unlicensed printers
and booksellers operated without challenge. The industry grew
steadily thereafter, partly due to the lack of copyright law (established
in England in 1710) which allowed Dublin printers to prosper by
producing cheaper editions of bestsellers, copied from the originals
exported from London for sale in Ireland (Kennedy, 2005, pp.
76–77; Benson, 2009, p. 371). As the second city in Britain's expanding colonial empire, Dublin was an important urban centre and not
short of spaces of sociability in which the *Dublin Journal* would
have been read. In coffeehouses and taverns, newspapers and period-
icals were available for patrons' perusal. Reading was frequently a
social activity at this time and papers like the *Dublin Journal* were
read aloud, debated, and discussed by those present – typically
gentlemen of the middling and upper sorts.[14] This readership sets
the tone of Hutcheson's writing, as well as the subject matter.
Laughter was a topic of concern for those preoccupied by politeness
and Hutcheson caters for his readers by treating it somewhat playfully, even noting the irony of exploring it with such gravity
(Hutcheson, 1750, p. 26). The text is shot through with his moral
philosophy and his theory of the internal senses, but it is packaged
for a wide reading public of educated gentlemen. It is the definition

[14] On reading practices, see Barry (1997); and on coffeehouses, see
Cowan (2005).

of Addison's aspiration in *The Spectator* to 'have brought Philosophy out of Closets and Libraries, Schools and Colleges, to dwell in Clubs and Assemblies, at Tea-Tables, and in Coffee-Houses'.[15] In these respects, Hutcheson was consciously providing a prompt for coffee-house conversation by wading into ongoing debates about laughter and how to behave politely. He was not describing things as they were, but how he believed they *should* be: his text served a prescriptive purpose. No less than Addison, Steele, Shaftesbury and others, his *Reflections Upon Laughter* was part of the effort to cultivate and refine minds, morals and tempers that was at the heart of the politeness project.

3. Refuting a 'palpable absurdity'

The first of Hutcheson's three letters is concerned with refuting Hobbes's account of laughter, which was well known at the time.[16] 'Mr Hobbes', he begins, 'owes his character of a Philosopher to his assuming positive solemn airs, which he uses most when he is going to assert some palpable absurdity, or some ill-natured nonsense' (Hutcheson, 1750, p. 6). The 'palpable absurdity' in question on this occasion was Hobbes's description of laughter in *Leviathan*, which Hutcheson quotes:

> Laughter is nothing else but sudden glory, arising from some sudden conception of some eminency in ourselves, by comparison with the infirmity of others, or with our own formerly: for men laugh at the follies of themselves past, when they come suddenly to rememberance. (Hutcheson, 1750, p. 6)

While allowing that Hobbes might be onto something in the case of ridiculing others' follies, (Hutcheson, 1750, p. 13, discussed below) Hutcheson has no truck with his theory as a general account of laughter. Reducing laughter to an expression of sneering self-applause was to be expected of a philosopher whose 'grand view was to deduce all human actions from Self Love'. Hobbes had 'over-looked every thing which is generous or kind in mankind' – perhaps, Hutcheson quipped, on account of 'some bad misfortune' – and instead

---

[15]   *The Spectator*, no. 10 (12 March 1711).

[16]   Joseph Addison discussed Hobbes's theory of laughter in *The Spectator*, no. 47 (24 April 1711), which gave it a wider circulation: James Beattie noted that Hobbes's theory 'would hardly have deserved notice' had it not been for Addison's essay: see Beattie (1776, p. 332).

Kate Davison

suspected 'all friendship, love, or social affection, for hypocrisy, or selfish design' (Hutcheson, 1750, p. 6). Such a view of human nature was contrary to Hutcheson's moral philosophy, but Hobbes's theory of laughter could also be undermined on logical grounds. If all laughter springs from a sense of superiority, then Hutcheson notes that two suppositions must be true: first, that there can be no laughter either when there is no comparison being made between ourselves and another object, or when that comparison does not make us feel superior; and, secondly, that we must laugh every time we perceive ourselves as superior to another object. As Hutcheson points out, 'if both these conclusions be false, the notion from whence they are drawn must be so too', and thus he sets about a two-pronged attack to confound Hobbes's position (Hutcheson, 1750, p. 7).

First, he recounts causes of laughter that cannot be attributed to our sense of superiority. The delight we experience when we encounter wit in the writing and speech of others, for example, cannot be attributed self-applause. We might have 'the highest veneration for the writing alluded to, and also admire the wit of the person who makes the allusion'. Were we to compare ourselves, we are more likely to feel 'grave and sorrowful' at our own shortcomings than we are to delight in self-love (Hutcheson, 1750, pp. 9–10). Secondly, Hutcheson argues that we frequently experience moments in life when we perceive our own superiority, but this rarely triggers our laughter. This he describes as 'the most obvious thing imaginable', and indeed it would have appeared so to an elite, white, gentleman living in a deeply unequal society. As he sarcastically notes in his first example,

> It must be a very merry state in which a fine gentleman is, when well dressed, in his coach, he passes our streets, where he will see so many ragged beggars, and porters and chairmen sweating at their labour, on every side of him. It is a great pity that we had not an infirmary or lazar-house to retire to in cloudy weather, to get an afternoon of Laughter at these inferior objects (Hutcheson, 1750, p. 11).

And so it ought to follow that an obedient and faithful Christian 'must always be merry upon heretics, to whom he is so much superior in his own opinion', while 'all true men of sense [...] must be the merriest little grigs imaginable'. Moreover, Hutcheson argues, the greater the gulf between ourselves and the object of our laughter, 'the greater would be the jest'. Thus he wonders playfully,

Strange! that none of our Hobbists banish all Canary birds and squirrels, and lap-dogs and pugs, and cats out of their houses, and substitute in their places asses, and owls, and snails, and oysters, to be merry upon. From these they might have higher joys of superiority, than from those with whom we now please ourselves (Hutcheson, 1750, p. 12).

If superiority alone is not fit to explain laughter, what is? This is the question posed by Hutcheson in his second letter and the answer he gives is as follows:

That which seems generally to be the cause of Laughter, is the bringing together of images which have contrary additional ideas, as well as some resemblance in the principle idea: this contrast between ideas of grandeur, dignity, sanctity, perfection, and ideas of meanness, baseness, profanity seems to be the very spirit of burlesque; and the greatest part of our raillery and jest is founded upon it (Hutcheson, 1750, p. 19).

For Hutcheson, the cause of laughter is found in our response to combinations of objects around us, in particular when contrasting objects are found to bear an unexpected resemblance. In making this argument, Hutcheson develops the ideas of others, notably Joseph Addison to whom he refers directly. In *The Spectator* no. 62, Hutcheson notes, Addison ruminated on John Locke's distinction between judgement and wit. The former Locke had described as the capacity to separate ideas from one another, whereas wit lay in the reverse:

the Assemblage of Ideas, and putting those together with Quickness and Variety, wherein can be found any Resemblance or Congruity thereby to make up pleasant Pictures and agreeable Visions in the Fancy (Hutcheson, 1750, pp. 18–19).[17]

In *The Spectator*, Addison described Locke's account as 'the best and most philosophical Account that I have ever met with of Wit', but added the importance of unexpectedness: not every resemblance is witty, 'unless it be such an one that gives *Delight* and *Surprize*'. And he illustrated his point with an example:

Thus when a Poet tells us, the Bosom of his Mistress is as white as Snow, there is no Wit in the Comparison; but when he adds with a Sigh, that it is as cold too, then it grows to Wit.[18]

[17] See also *The Spectator*, no. 62 (11 May 1711) and Locke (1690, p. 68).
[18] *The Spectator*, no. 62 (11 May 1711).

Kate Davison

For Addison, as for Hutcheson, comic amusement results from a surprising similarity between two ostensibly divergent objects.

Hutcheson differs, however, by extending his theory to encompass our perception more generally of things out of place – a straightforward coming together of contrasting objects with incompatible ideas attached to them. This provides an explanation for why we laugh at things that could not be described as witty in the Addisonian sense. To demonstrate his point, he amasses observations from everyday life. 'Any little accident to which we have joined the idea of meanness, befalling a person of great gravity, ability, dignity', he writes, 'is a matter of Laughter'. This includes, 'the strange contortions of the body in a fall, and the dirtying of a decent dress' or even 'the natural functions which we study to conceal from sight', especially if observed in 'persons of whom we have high ideas' (Hutcheson, 1750, p. 21). He is swift to add that slip-ups are amusing no matter who the perpetrator, since the human form is generally associated with lofty ideas, but the joke is all the better in proportion to the gravity and dignity of those involved. A second example Hutcheson gives of a ludicrous incongruity is when violent passions are raised in response to a minor concern, and a third when writing that 'has obtained an high character for grandeur, sanctity, inspiration or sublimity of thoughts' – such as scripture or ancient philosophy – is applied to 'low, vulgar, or base subjects'. In both cases, the combination 'never fails to divert the audience, and set them a-laughing' (Hutcheson, 1750, pp. 19–22). An example of what Hutcheson might have had in mind here is offered by a ballad called *The Tippling Philosophers*. The work of the prolific and popular satirist, Edward 'Ned' Ward (1666–1731), it was originally published in 1710, but remained popular throughout the century; indeed, James Beattie used what he called 'that excellent English ballad' to illustrate one variety of laughter-triggering incongruity (Beattie, 1776, pp. 360–1). Each verse gleefully asserted that the wisdom of ancient thinkers owed much to wine: 'Aristotle, that Master of Arts', began one, 'Had been but a Dunce without Wine,/ And what we ascribe to his Parts,/ Is but due to the Juice of the Vine' (Ward, 1710, pp. 14–15). And another, in full:

Old *Socrates* ne'er was content,
Till a bottle had heighten'd his Joys,
Who, in's Cups, to the Oracle went,
Or he ne'er had been counted so Wise.
Late Hours he certainly lov'd,
Made Wine the delight of his Life,

Or *Xantippe* would never had prov'd,
Such a damnable Scold of a Wife (Ward, 1710, pp. 4–5).

In the preface, Ward described the tavern sociability in which the ballad was first extemporised, before it was embellished and published for others to sing while enjoying a drink of their own. The dignity of ancient philosophy humbled by the more lowly subject of drinking: this was exactly the kind of incongruous juxtaposition of ideas that Hutcheson identified as ludicrous.

Hutcheson's theory of laughter thus has a wide remit, covering words and actions to explain why we laugh in diverse situations, but in each case the perception of incongruity between two objects is crucial. In this respect, it leans heavily upon his notion of the internal senses, which held that certain ideas occur to us whenever we perceive objects or scenes. This becomes clear in the opening passages of his second letter. Referring specifically to the workings of the internal senses, as he saw them, he argues that human nature has 'a great number of perceptions, which one can scarcely reduce to any of the five senses, as they are commonly explained; such as either the ideas of grandeur, dignity, decency, beauty, harmony; or, on the other hand, of meanness, baseness, indecency, deformity'. These different ideas are associated in our minds with material objects, people, and actions, as a result of education, culture, or their natural resemblance. As Hutcheson put it,

> For instances of these associations, partly from nature, partly from custom, we may take the following ones; sanctity in our churches, magnificence in public buildings, affection between the oak and ivy, the elm and vine; hospitality in a shade, a pleasant sense of grandeur in the sky, the sea, and mountains [...] solemnity and horror in shady woods. An ass is the common emblem of stupidity and sloth, a swine or selfish luxury [...] Some inanimate objects have in like manner some accessary ideas of meanness, either for some natural reason, oftener by mere chance and custom. (Hutcheson, 1750, p. 18)

Laughter is triggered when we perceive associations that are incongruous or unexpected, either in their contrast between 'high' and 'low' – sanctity and profanity, say – or by their surprising similarity. When this occurs to us, it is not our sense of beauty or harmony that is excited, but another internal sense: our 'sense of the ridiculous' (Hutcheson, 1750, p. 27). For Hutcheson, we experience the world through learned patterns, and laugh when we perceive some

Kate Davison

disruption to our expectations, or to the routine ways in which we apprehend objects around us.

Modern theorists have described Hutcheson's explanation of laughter as an 'incipient incongruity theory' (McDonald, 2013, p. 49) – the precursor, or first attempt, at one of the 'big three' theories of laughter, and that which is still considered most credible by philosophers and psychologists. It is commonplace in philosophies of laughter to trace a direct line between Hutcheson and modern contributions to the debate. One recent survey, for example, gave a brief account of Hutcheson's contribution before describing the incongruity theory in terms he would have well understood:

> According to the incongruity theory, what is key to comic amusement is a deviation from some presupposed norm – that is to say, an anomaly or an incongruity relative to some framework governing the ways in which we think the world is or should be. (Carroll, 2014, p. 17)

Yet, if we set aside the perspective of hindsight, a different picture emerges. It becomes clear that, for Hutcheson, laughter was a vehicle for his broader philosophical arguments. Logical observation demonstrated that laughter could not be reduced to self-love: there was a good-natured variety that ran counter not just to Hobbes's comments on laughter, but to his brutish notion of human nature more generally. By explaining what *did* cause laughter, Hutcheson also interjects an account of the internal senses. His theory of laughter, therefore, is freighted with significance to contemporary philosophical debates beyond questions of human risibility. Moreover, by writing for an audience of gentlemen coffeehouse goers, he was projecting his ideas outside the confines of scholarly debate. There was more at stake than an explanation of laughter; in the context of eighteenth-century philosophy, Hutcheson's theory was an argument about human nature, and he was writing to persuade a wide audience.

4. The 'proper use' of Laughter

Having dismissed Hobbes, and set out what later became known as the 'incongruity' theory, in his third letter Hutcheson turns to laughter's consequences. These too have important ramifications in their eighteenth-century context, especially concerning the maintenance of politeness in society. 'It may be worth our pains', he begins, 'to consider the effects of Laughter, and the ends for which it was implanted in our nature' (Hutcheson, 1750, p. 27). These two considerations address what laughter is *for* in human society and his findings fall into three arguments: first that laughter is a means of procuring pleasure; secondly, that it facilitates goodwill and amicable social encounters; and thirdly, that it can persuade people to correct their foibles without causing offence. Together, these comprise what Hutcheson describes as 'the proper use' of laughter, (Hutcheson, 1750, p. 26) but he is at pains to add a number of caveats, especially concerning laughter's targets and who is laughing.

Beginning with the first of Hutcheson's arguments, he considers laughter to have a reciprocal relationship with pleasure. The act of laughing is a pleasurable act, and feeling pleasure renders us more apt to laugh:

> Laughter is an easy and agreeable state, that the recurring or sug-
> gestion of ludicrous images tends to dispel fretfulness, anxiety, or
> sorrow, and to reduce the mind to an easy, happy state; as on the
> other hand, an easy and happy state is that in which we are most
> lively and acute in perceiving the ludicrous in objects: anything
> that gives us pleasure, puts us also in a fitness for Laughter.

Hence, he continues, our 'sense of the ridiculous' provides 'an avenue to pleasure, and an easy remedy for discontent and sorrow' (Hutcheson, 1750, pp. 26–27). That this was the first of laughter's purposes for Hutcheson is characteristic of eighteenth-century thought. Whereas Classical and Christian philosophical traditions had been uneasy about the morality of seeking pleasures of the body and mind, Hutcheson was part of a new way of thinking that accepted pleasure as a natural means to fulfilment. In particular, he contributed to the philosophical reworking of how human motivation was understood, which gave these new ideas about pleasure momentum. The Hobbesian conception of human nature held people to be driven primarily by self-preservation, leading inevitably to competition and conflict, but moral philosophers saw in human nature a natural benevolence. Pleasure is not found in egoistic hedonism, but in altruism, sympathy and sociability: it could therefore be virtuous and gratification of the senses is not reserved for the afterlife, but could, and should, be sought in this world (Porter, 1996, pp. 4–10).

Laughter is particularly beneficial, though, because it is not a lonely pleasure. Modern studies have shown that we are more likely to laugh when we are with other people (Martin, 2006, p. 113; Provine, 1996), but Hutcheson too observes that laughing is primarily something we do together, and it is infectious. As he argued, laughter 'is very contagious; our whole frame is so sociable, that

Kate Davison

one merry countenance may diffuse cheaifulness to many'. In this respect, it fosters good nature and geniality:

> It is a great occasion of pleasure, and enlivens our conversation exceedingly, when it is conducted by good nature. It spreads pleasantry of temper over multitudes at once; and one merry easy mind may by this means diffuse a like disposition over all who are in company. There is nothing of which we are more communicative than a good jest. (Hutcheson, 1750, p. 32)

This passage casts laughter as a vital tool in the service of sociability, which was one of the most commendable activities in the pursuit of politeness. As the government of the self and of social relations, politeness was situated above all in the realm of interaction and exchange. Meeting and mixing with fellow humans was thought to have a refining influence on manners and morals (Borsay, 1989, p. 267; Klein, 1994, pp. 3–8 and 96–101). As Shaftesbury put it in *The Characteristicks of Men, Manners, Opinions, Times*, 'We polish one another, and rub off our Corners and rough Sides by a sort of amicable Collision' (Shaftesbury, 1711, I, p. 53). His reference to 'amicable collision' is significant because politeness aspired not just to social interaction, but specifically to social accord. To this end, it called for an open, natural and easy personal manner that rested between the two extremes of frivolous hypersociability and frigid unsociability. The perfect demeanour was neither flighty and frolicsome nor grave and serious. *The Spectator* captured this sentiment when it argued for the benefits of cheerfulness over mirth. The former it considered to be 'an Habit of Mind' that was 'fix'd and permanent' and much preferable to the latter, which was 'short and transient':

> Mirth is like a Flash of Lightning, that breaks thro a Gloom of Clouds, and glitters for a Moment; Chearfulness keeps up a kind of Day-light in the Mind, and fills it with a steady and perpetual Serenity.

As such, a 'chearful Temper' would be 'pleasing to ourselves' and 'those with whom we converse'.[19] This is the same sentiment that underpinned Swift's comments on well-judged laughter in his treatise *On Polite Conversation* discussed above; indeed, the desirability of cheerfulness elaborated on an enduring tradition of thought that rested upon the Aristotelian golden mean. Moral behaviour was found through carving a 'middle way' between two extremes and,

[19]   *The Spectator*, no. 381 (17 May 1712).

where laughter was concerned, 'tact' and 'wittiness' were desirable and they lay between buffoonery and boorishness (Aristotle, *Nichomachean Ethics*, quoted in Morreall (1987), pp. 14–16). This was retained in the European civility tradition and, in England, scholars have traced a marked upswing the cultural prestige attached to wit from the turn of the seventeenth century. In English translations of European conduct guidance, the old English term 'wit' – pertaining to the powers of the mind – was conflated with ingenuity, meaning inventiveness and imagination. It came to signify a celebrated ability to be entertaining, especially in terms of humorousness (Withington, 2010, pp. 186–98).[20] The ability to sparkle in company continued to be advocated in eighteenth-century polite conduct guidance, and it also permeated less esteemed genres of print. Jestbooks, for example, were commonly published with tips for the delivery of their contents. The title page of *The Nut-Cracker* (1751) advertised its contents of 'an agreeable Variety of well-season'd Jests', along with 'Such Instructions as will enable any Man to [...] crack a *Nut* without losing the *Kernel*', i.e. tell the jests successfully (Anon. 1751, title page). When Hutcheson claimed that laughter could 'diffuse chearfulness' and spread a 'pleasantry of temper', he was expanding on a point widely made: that laughter was not just an important part of sharing one another's company, but – with its power to cultivate good humour – it also had a crucial role to play in fostering the social accord and agreeableness to which politeness aspired. To master the art of pleasing in company, a gentleman ought to have a certain cheerfulness and turn of wit.

Thus far in his third letter Hutcheson attended to laughing *with* others, but what should that laughter be targeted *at*? On this point, he contributed to deliberations about the ethics of ridicule and its rhetorical uses.[21] The notion that laughter could correct behaviour had its roots in the satirists of Ancient Greece and Rome; by the early eighteenth century, it was an oft-repeated defence of the satirical mode (Marshall, 2013, pp. 38–53). Writers repeatedly argued that satire upheld morality by subjecting vice to ridicule and Hutcheson agrees. 'If smaller faults [...] be set in a ridiculous light', he wrote, 'the guilty are apt to be made sensible of their folly, more than by a bare grave admonition'(Hutcheson, 1750, p. 31). Poking fun at foibles

[20] On wit, see also O'Callaghan (2007), and on civility in early modern England, Bryson (1998).

[21] For debates about ridicule in the eighteenth century, see Klein (2002) and Lund (2012).

would alert offenders to their foolishness and, so the theory goes, they would adjust their behaviour accordingly. Yet, it was not just that people's behaviour could be corrected in this way; it was that doing so was more effective than other means. The common explanation given was that satire entertained as it instructed, but Hutcheson elaborates further. He argues that if we are challenged directly on our faults, we tend to entrench our positions as we defend ourselves; gentle ridicule, on the other hand, puts us at ease and we are more minded to change. The keyword, however, is gentle. Only if our faults are made ridiculous 'with good nature', he argues, can it be 'the least offensive, and most effectual, reproof' (Hutcheson, 1750, p. 31).

Further caveats are littered throughout Hutcheson's third letter, not least as he discusses 'rules to avoid abuse of this kind of ridicule' (Hutcheson, 1750, p. 35). First, ridicule must target only our minor flaws, or habits that are alterable. 'The enormous crime or grievous calamity of another', or 'a piece of cruel barbarity, or treacherous villainy', are not fit subjects for ridicule. Similarly, laughter should not be targeted at 'imperfections, which one cannot amend'. Were we to be caught laughing on such occasions, it would raise disgust at the 'want of all compassion' or 'hardness of heart, and insensibility' such laughter expressed (Hutcheson, 1750, pp. 30–31). A further tranche of prohibited targets for ridicule are those categorised as being 'every way great', whether a great being, character or sentiment. Primarily, the discussion here revolves around religion. Laughter targeted at divine objects or sentiments was a persistent source of anxiety in early modern society,[22] but Hutcheson's theory of laughter also contains a logical rationale for its inappropriateness. If our 'sense of the ridiculous' relies on the perception of surprising resemblances, objects that are 'every way great' cannot bear a resemblance to meanness and thus cannot be brought into a ludicrous pairing.

Stepping back from Hutcheson's text, however, it is hard to escape evidence suggesting that people *did* find plenty of hilarity in the targets Hutcheson condemns. In surviving jestbooks from the period, jokes at the expense of the poor, the disabled, and the otherwise unfortunate come thick and fast. There are tales of tricks played on blind people or amputees, or people with dwarfism gleefully thrown down chimneys or hung on tenterhooks.[23] One jestbook was divided into subsections, including 'Of Crookedness and Lameness', 'Of Faces and Scars', and 'Of Beggars' (Anon, 1760),

---

[22] For an exploration in the context of the European renaissance, see Screech (1997). See also Gilhus (1997).

[23] Examples discussed in Dickies (2012, esp. chapters 1 and 2).

while a dictionary of slang hinted at the verbal assault suffered by the physically impaired: defining the term 'Lord' as slang for 'a crooked or hump-backed man', it went on to say the following:

> These unhappy people afford great scope for vulgar raillery; such as, 'Did you come straight from home? If so, you have got confoundedly bent by the way' 'Don't abuse the gentleman', adds a by-stander, 'he has been grossly insulted already: don't you see his back's up? (Grose, 1785)

This is to say nothing of the sexual and scatological content.[24] Material such as this was once explained away by classifying it as 'popular' humour, with the implication that it was not for the politer sorts, but this has been difficult to sustain in the face of evidence to the contrary. On the basis of price alone, these texts must have been produced for customers of means: ranging from 1 shilling and 6 pence to as much as 5 shillings, they were beyond the purchasing power of the lower orders. Ownership is more problematic to establish but, where discovered, it is further proof that jestbooks were read by men and women of the middling sort (Dickie, 2012, pp. 30–32).[25] The presence of rude and cruel humour in polite society has often been explained in terms of hypocrisy: this was 'an impolite society that talked a great deal about politeness' (Knights and Morton, 2017, p. 21).[26] Knowledge of what people *were* laughing at certainly reinforces the need to interpret Hutcheson's comments as prescriptive, but it is also worth recognising that he was under no illusions: his effort to delineate appropriate targets for laughter was driven partly by his recognition of 'the impertinence, and pernicious tendency of general undistinguished jests' (Hutcheson, 1750, p. 34). By setting out moral and refined behaviour with respect to laughter, then, Hutcheson was knowingly offering conduct guidance.

Hutcheson's second caveat to the merits of ridicule concerns who was doing the ridiculing. He wrote:

> Ridicule, like other edged tools, may do good in a wise man's hands, though fools may cut their fingers with it, or be injurious to an unwary by-stander. (Hutcheson, 1750, pp. 34–35)

Polite conduct literature routinely instructed readers to adjust their behaviour according to their company (Davison, 2014), and this

---

[24] This has been discussed in Davison (2014, pp. 937–38) and Gatrell (2006, pp. 178–209).

[25] On jestbooks as a genre, see also Munro and Prescott (2013).

[26] See also Dickie (2012, pp. 1–15) and Gatrell (2006, pp. 176–77).

approach also underpins Hutcheson's advice. Speaking directly to his audience of gentlemen coffeehouse goers, he warns that 'we ought to be cautious of our company'. With 'men of sense' Hutcheson considers it acceptable to venture 'the boldest wit', but around 'people of little judgement' much more care is needed, as they may fail to spot the ludicrous nature of the comparison and take the similarity at face value, hence being 'led into neglect, or contempt, of that which is truly valuable' (Hutcheson, 1750, p. 35). Ridicule in the presence of 'weak company' was to be avoided, as they lack a 'just discernment of true grandeur' and are thus apt to misjudge appropriate targets of laughter. In this respect, Hutcheson carves out a distinction in society on the basis of intellectual capacity and judgement. That much is in line with conventional ideas about the aesthetic appreciation possessed by those with refined taste: taste was, after all, nothing of not a marker of status. But Hutcheson's distinction is also about gender. Just as his theory omits society's lower orders and skims over the existence of impolite humour, he is also silent on the question of women's laughter. This was an omission he shared with ridicule's great advocate, Shaftesbury, who had written 'in defence only of the liberty of the Club, and of that sort of freedom which is taken among gentlemen' (Shaftesbury, 1711, I, p. 75). Hutcheson and Shaftesbury's exclusion of women points to anxieties generated not just by laughter, but by women's laughter in particular. This is a topic that has received little scholarly attention, but it is clear that moral philosophers were not alone in advising against women's use of laughter and wit.[27] Women's conduct guidance was as intricate as that targeted at men and showed a similar concern for moderation, poise and self-restraint.[28] For women, however, chastity and passivity were essential and laughter was thought to jeopardise both. One conduct book noted that women's laughter could be read as a sign of licentiousness. Laughing aloud revealed a knowingness that belied modesty: when a young woman laughs, wrote the author, 'she is believed to know more than she should do' (Gregory, 1774, p. 59). Another conduct book – one of the most prominent for women in the period and also written by a man – advised that 'men of the best sense have been usually averse to the thought of marrying a witty female'; domestic harmony required ease, 'But we cannot be easy where we are not safe. We are never safe in the company of a critic'. And continued, 'Who is not

---

[27]   Two works exploring women's laughter specifically are Brown (2002) and Bilger (1998).

[28]   For an exploration of women and politeness see Ylivuori (2018).

shocked by the flippant impertinence of a self-conceited woman, that wants to dazzle by the supposed superiority of her powers?' (Fordyce, 1766, pp. 192–93). The anxiety here is rooted in laughter's perceived force: a wife laughing at her husband could be a moment of challenge to the patriarchal power relations that pervaded society. Hutcheson was one among many to prescribe carefully who ought to wield the power of ridicule.

The discussion of 'the effects of Laughter' in Hutcheson's third letter makes a robust case for its importance in the service of genial sociability and for the power of ridicule to correct minor foibles, thus investing laughter with a key role in the maintenance of politeness in society. Nevertheless, his confidence in laughter's merits was tempered with qualifications, especially regarding the targets of ridicule and *who* was doing the ridiculing. He concluded, 'it may be easy to see for what cause, or end, a sense of the ridiculous was implanted in human nature', but also – crucially – 'how it ought to be managed' (Hutcheson, 1750, p. 32).

5. Conclusion

Since the publication of Hutcheson's *Reflections Upon Laughter* in 1750, philosophers have repeatedly explained human risibility in terms of our perception of incongruities. Later in the eighteenth century, James Beattie's essay 'On Laughter and Ludicrous Composition' invited readers to 'incline to Hutcheson's theory', which he considered 'the best' of those he discussed, before adding his own slight refinement:

> Laughter arises from the view of two or more inconsistent, un-suitable, or incongruous parts or circumstances, considered as united in one complex object or assemblage, or as acquiring a sort of mutual relation from the peculiar manner in which the mind takes notice of them. (Beattie, 1776, pp. 346–47)

For Beattie, we laugh when we perceive a fleeting compatibility between two otherwise incompatible objects, but the contrast between 'dignity and meanness' so important to Hutcheson was set aside. The connection between laughter and incongruity can also be found in the writings of Immanuel Kant. In his *Critique of Judgment*, he described laughter as 'an affection arising from the sudden transformation of a strained expectation into nothing': we laugh when we are prepared for one thing, but meet with another. The sudden shift experienced when we hear a joke generates a sensory pleasure, which 'gives a wholesome shock to the body' (Kant (1790), quoted in Morreall (1987, p. 45)). Into the nineteenth century, Arthur Schopenhauer argued that the 'source of the ludicrous is always paradoxical': it is found in a mismatch between our expectations and an experienced reality. 'The phenomenon of laughter', he wrote, 'always signifies the sudden apprehension of an incongruity between the abstract and the concrete object of perception', that is, between our idea of things and our sensory experience of them (Schopenhauer (1819), quoted in Morreall (1987, p. 51)). Reflecting on this tradition in 1987, the founder of the International Society for Humor Studies, John Morreall, recognised the merits of an incongruity theory of laughter and argued that 'with proper refinement it can account for all cases of humorous laughter' (Morreal, 1987, p. 130). Over and above superiority and relief theories, then, incongruity theories of laughter are still considered the most persuasive, so it is little wonder that Hutcheson's place in the philosophy of laughter remains secure.

Construing Hutcheson's *Reflections Upon Laughter* solely as an 'incipient incongruity theory', however, detaches the text from its historical context and consequently overlooks what was at stake when arguing about laughter in the early eighteenth-century. Reconnecting it to its contemporary cultural and intellectual debates addresses this blind spot and opens up three further concluding points. First, *Reflections Upon Laughter* emphasises that laughter mattered in eighteenth-century Britain and Ireland. For Hutcheson, it was a subject of fascination, which came with a long tradition of philosophical scrutiny and offered insights into his theories about human nature. It was also a source of unease: an everyday aspect of sharing one another's company, but one with a power that was all too easily abused. With careful management, however, he believed laughter was integral to the maintenance of politeness in society. Hutcheson was also confident that his subject would be of interest – and use – more widely among the newspaper readers of early eighteenth-century Dublin. He knew, as well as historians do now, that the polite world shared both his intrigue and ambivalence about laughter. Secondly, the arguments Hutcheson makes are instructive. In order to rescue laughter from the hostile characterisation bequeathed by earlier thinkers, he implicitly reveals polite aspirations: his effort to identify and define laughter's role in agreeable sociability points to a desire for mutually pleasing social interactions, while his support for ridicule on the grounds that it corrected minor foibles expresses an ambition for conformity to a shared sense of acceptable conduct. His anxieties are equally telling. The condemnation of 'undistinguished jests' reveals an awareness that much humour of the time was anything but polite, while fears about women's laughter, or about ridicule among 'weak company', point to the inequalities of gender and status that permeated his society. Thirdly, all this emphasises that Hutcheson's text should be interpreted as more than a theory of laughter; it was a contribution to eighteenth-century moral philosophy and polite cultural commentary. Its first purpose was to challenge Hobbesian conceptions of the innate selfishness of human nature and, in doing so, Hutcheson made a case for his theory of internal senses. Its second goal was to set a standard for how laughter ought to be used in society, and by whom. In this respect, it sat comfortably among the swathes of prescriptive literature published in the period, which attempted to refine minds and morals in the pursuit of politeness. Hutcheson argued his case through a focus on laughter, but his underlying intentions ran deeper than accounting for human chortles and chuckles.

Laughter is an human universal, but it is also culturally and historically contingent: what makes us laugh has changed over time, and so too has how we think about and explain that laughter. The question 'why do we laugh?' will go on being asked, as it has done since antiquity, and new answers will be found, especially as scientific disciplines make their presence felt in a debate once dominated by philosophers.[29] From an historical perspective, however, what matters is not what *actually* causes laughter, but why certain answers have been given at certain times. Taking this perspective, any 'limitations' to Hutcheson's *Reflections Upon Laughter* are less important than what it reveals about culture and society in early eighteenth-century Britain and Ireland.[30]

University of Sheffield
kate.davison@sheffield.ac.uk

References

Anon., *The Nut-Cracker* (London, 1751).
Anon., *The Laugher; or, the Art of Jesting* (London, 1760).

[29] See for example, Lavan et al. (2017).
[30] The research in this article was supported by the Wolfson Foundation. I would also like to thank Kenneth L. Pearce and Takaharu Oda for their comments on previous drafts, and participants at the Irish Philosophy in the Age of Berkeley Conference for their questions and discussion.

Kate Davison

Anon., *The Polite Academy, or School of Behaviour for Young Gentlemen and Ladies* (London, 1762).

Mahadev L. Apte, *Humor and Laughter: An Anthropological Approach* (London: Cornell University Press, 1985).

Jonathan Barry, 'Literacy and Literature in Popular Culture: Reading and Writing in Historical Perspective' in Tim Harris (ed.), *Popular Culture in England, c.1500–1850* (London: Macmillan, 1997), 76–79.

James Beattie, 'On Laughter and Ludicrous Composition' in *Essays* (London, 1776).

Charles Benson, 'The Irish Trade' in Michael F, Suarez SJ, and Michael L. Turner (eds), *The Cambridge History of Book in Britain, Volume 5: 1695–1830* (Cambridge: Cambridge University Press, 2009), 366–82.

Audrey Bilger, *Laughing Feminism: Subversive Comedy in Frances Burney, Maria Edgeworth and Jane Austen* (Detroit: Wayne State University Press, 1998).

Peter Borsay, *The English Urban Renaissance: Culture and Society in the Provincial Town* (Oxford: Clarendon, 1989).

Jan Bremmer and Herman Roodenburg, 'Introduction' in Jan Bremmer and Herman Roodenburg (eds), *A Cultural History of Humour: From Antiquity to the Present Day*, (Cambridge: Polity, 1997).

John Brewer, *The Pleasures of the Imagination: English Culture in the Eighteenth Century* (London: Harper Collins, 1997).

Pamela Allen Brown, *Better a Shrew than a Sheep: Women, Drama, and the Culture of Jest in Early Modern England* (Ithaca: Cornell University Press, 2002).

Anna Bryson, *From Courtesy to Civility: Changing Codes of Conduct in Early Modern England* (Oxford: Clarendon Press, 1998).

Noël Carroll, *Humour: A Very Short Introduction* (Oxford: Oxford University Press, 2014).

Anthony Ashley Cooper, third earl of Shaftesbury, *The Characteristicks of Men, Manners, Opinions, Times* (3 vols, London, 1711).

Brian Cowan, *The Social Life of Coffee: The Emergence of the British Coffeehouse* (London: Yale University Press, 2005).

Robert Darnton, *The Great Cat Massacre and other Episodes in French History* (London: Allen Lane, 1984).

Kate Davison, 'Occasional Politeness and Gentlemen's Laughter in 18th Century England', *The Historical Journal*, 57 (2014), 921–945.

'Plainly of Considerable Moment in Human Society'

Simon Dickie, *Cruelty and Laughter: Forgotten Comic Literature and the Unsentimental Eighteenth Century* (London: University of Chicago Press, 2012).

Bonamy Dobrée (ed.), *The Letters of Philip Dormer Stanhope 4th earl of Chesterfield*, (6 vols, London: Eyre and Spottiswoode, 1932).

Mary Douglas, *Implicit Meanings: Essays in Anthropology*, (London: Routledge and Kegan Paul, 1975).

James Fordyce, *Sermons to Young Women*, 2nd edn. (2 vols, London, 1766), I, 192–93.

Sigmund Freud, *Jokes and their Relation to the Unconscious* [1905], trans. James Strachey (New York: Penguin, 1974).

Vic Gatrell, *City of Laughter: Sex and Satire in Eighteenth-Century London* (London: Walker and Company, 2006).

M. Gervais and D. S. Wilson, 'The Evolution and Functions of Laughter and Humor: A Synthetic Approach', *The Quarterly Review of Biology*, 80 (2005), 395–430.

Ingvild Saelid Gilhus, *Laughing Gods and Weeping Virgins: Laughter in the History of Religion* (London, Routledge, 1997).

John Gregory, *A Father's Legacy to his Daughters*, 4th edn. (London, 1774).

Francis Grose, *A Classical Dictionary of the Vulgar Tongue* (London, 1785).

James A. Harris, 'Shaftesbury, Hutcheson and the Moral Sense' in Sacha Golob and Jens Timmermann (eds), *The Cambridge History of Moral Philosophy* (Cambridge: Cambridge University Press, 2017), 325–37.

Thomas Hobbes, *Leviathan* [1651], /ed. C. B. Macpherson (London: Penguin, 1968).

Francis Hutcheson, *Reflections Upon Laughter, and Remarks Upon the Fable of the Bees* (Glasgow, 1750).

Immanuel Kant, *Critique of Judgment* [1790], trans., James Creed Meredith (Oxford: Clarendon Press, 1911).

Máire Kennedy, '"Politicks, Coffee and News": The Dublin Book Trade in the Eighteenth Century', *Dublin Historical Record*, 58 (2005), 76–85.

Lawrence E. Klein, *Shaftesbury and the Culture of Politeness: Moral Discourse and Cultural Politics in Early Eighteenth-Century England* (Cambridge: Cambridge University Press, 1994).

Lawrence E. Klein, 'Politeness and the Interpretation of the British Eighteenth Century', *The Historical Journal*, 45 (2002), 869–98.

Lawrence E. Klein, 'Ridicule as a Tool for Discovering Truth' in Paddy Bullard (ed.), *The Oxford Handbook of Eighteenth-Century Satire*, (Oxford Handbooks Online, 2019).

Kate Davison

Mark Knights and Adam Morton, 'Introduction' in Mark Knights and Adam Morton (eds), *The Power of Laughter and Satire in Early Modern Britain: Political and Religious Culture, 1500–1820* (Woodbridge: The Boydell Press, 2017), 1–26.

Paul Langford, 'The Uses of Eighteenth-Century Politeness', *Transactions of the Royal Historical Society,* series 6, 12 (2002), 311–32.

Nadine Lavan, Georgia Rankin, Nicole Lorking, Sophie Scott, Carolyn McGettigan, 'Neural Correlates of the Affective Properties of Spontaneous and Volitional Laughter Types', *Neuropsychologia,* 95 (2017), 30–39.

John Locke, *An Essay Concerning Human Understanding* (London, 1690).

Roger Lund, *Ridicule, Religion and the Politics of Wit in Augustan England* (Farnham: Ashgate, 2012).

Rod A. Martin, *The Psychology of Humor: An Integrative Approach* (Elsevier Science & Technology, 2006).

Ashley Marshall, *The Practice of Satire in England, 1658–1770* (Baltimore: Johns Hopkins University Press, 2013).

Paul McDonald, *The Philosophy of Humour* (Penrith: Humanities-Ebooks, 2012).

Georg Friedrich Meier, Gedanken von Scherzen [Hemmerde, 1744], trans. Anon., *The Merry Philosopher; or, Thoughts on Jesting* (London, 1765).

John Morreall (ed.), *The Philosophy of Laughter and Humor* (Albany, NY: State of New York Press, 1987).

John Morreall, *Comic Relief: A Comprehensive Philosophy of Laughter* (Wiley-Blackwell, 2009).

Ian Munro and Anne Lake Prescott, 'Jest Books' in Andrew Hadfield (ed.), *The Oxford Handbook of English Prose 1500–1640* (Oxford: Oxford University press, 2013), 343–58.

Michele O'Callaghan, *The English Wits: Literature and Sociability in Early Modern England* (Cambridge: Cambridge University Press, 2007).

Roy Porter, 'Enlightenment and Pleasure' in Roy Porter and Marie Mulvey Roberts (eds), *Pleasure in the Eighteenth-Century* (Basingstoke: Macmillan, 1996).

Robert Provine, 'Laughter', *American Scientist,* 84 (1996), 38–45.

Robert Provine, *Laughter: A Scientific Investigation* (London: Faber, 2002).

J. Roecklein, *The Psychology of Humor: A Reference Guide and Annotated Bibliography* (Westport, CT: Greenwood, 2002).

'Plainly of Considerable Moment in Human Society'

Michael A. Screech, *Laughter at the Foot of the Cross* (London: Allen Lane, 1997).

Arthur Schopenhauer, *The World as Will and Idea* [1819], trans., R. B. Haldane and J. Kemp, 6th edn. (London: Routledge and Kegan Paul).

Cathy Shrank, 'Mocking of Mirthful? Laughter in the Early Modern Dialogue' in Knights and Morton, *The Power of Laughter and Satire in Early Modern Britain: Political and Religious Culture, 1500–1820* (Woodbridge: The Boydell Press, 2017), 48–66.

Quentin Skinner, 'Why Laughing Mattered in the Renaissance', *History of Political Thought*, 22 (2001), 418–47.

Samuel Smilewell, *The Art of Joking* (London, 1774).

Jonathan Swift, *A Treatise on Polite Conversation* (London, 1738).

Elizabeth Telfer, 'Hutcheson's Reflections Upon Laughter', *The Journal of Aesthetics and Art Criticism*, 53 (1995), 359–69.

Keith Thomas, 'The Place of Laughter in Tudor and Stuart England', *Times Literary Supplement* (21 January 1977), 77–81.

Johan Verberckmoes, 'Humour and History: A Research Bibliography' in Jan Bremmer and Herman Roodenburg (eds), *A Cultural History of Humour: From Antiquity to the Present Day*, (Cambridge: Polity, 1997), 242–252.

John Verberckmoes, *Laughter, Jestbooks and Society in the Spanish Netherlands* (Basingstoke: Macmillan, 1999).

Ned Ward, *Wine and Wisdom; or, the Tipling Philosophers* (London, 1710).

Phil Withington, *Society in Early Modern England: The Vernacular Origins of some Powerful Ideas* (Cambridge: Polity, 2010).

Soile Ylivuori, *Women and Politeness in Eighteenth-Century England: Bodies, Identities, and Power* (New York: Routledge, 2018).

What the Women of Dublin Did with John Locke

CHRISTINE GERRARD

Abstract

William Molyneux's friendship with John Locke helped make Locke's ideas well known in early eighteenth-century Dublin. The *Essay Concerning Human Understanding* was placed on the curriculum of Trinity College in 1692, soon after its publication. Yet there has been very little discussion of whether Irish women from this period read or knew Locke's work, or engaged more generally in contemporary philosophical debate. This essay focuses on the work of Laetitia Pilkington (1709–1750) and Mary Barber (1685–1755), two of the Dublin women writers of the so-called 'Triumfeminate', a literary and intellectual circle connected to Jonathan Swift which met and discussed ideas at the home of Patrick Delaney. Pilkington and Barber were particularly influenced by Locke's ideas on obstetrics and childhood in his *Some Thoughts Concerning Education* and especially by his discussion of memory in the *Essay Concerning Human Understanding*. Both authors engage playfully and imaginatively with Locke's theories, especially in a domestic context. Not all philosophical debates took place in the public male spaces of school, coffee house and university. This essay attempts to recreate the contexts in which intellectually curious women of the 'middling sort' encountered and engaged with philosophical ideas, especially those of Locke, and how these shaped their writing.

One of the most endearing traces of Locke's influence on Dublin women writers can be seen in a small poem published in 1735, 'Written for My Son, and spoken by him in School, upon his Master's first bringing in a Rod' (Barber, 1734, pp. 36–37). The schoolboy speaking the poem complains bitterly about the grim prospect of school beatings, then turns to praise 'that great Sage', 'Who taught to play us into Learning, / By graving Letters on the Dice'. The 'Sage' is John Locke, who in his 1693 *Thoughts Concerning Education* recommends that children should enjoy learning their alphabet by playing with a polygon with letters engraved on each face. The child ends by showering praise on Locke:

> May Heav'n reward the kind Device.
> And crown him with immortal Fame,
> Who taught at once to read and game!

....

doi:10.1017/S1358246120000144   © The Royal Institute of Philosophy and the contributors 2020

Royal Institute of Philosophy Supplement **88** 2020   171

Christine Gerrard

O may I live to hail the Day,
When Boys shall go to School to play!
To Grammar Rules we'll bid Defiance
For Play will then become a Science.

The poem's author is Mary Barber (1685–1755). Her son
Constantine, or 'Con', for whom she wrote the poem, grew up to
become President of the College of Physicians in Trinity College
Dublin. In its blend of humour, domesticity, and light-hearted engagement with education and philosophy, the piece is characteristic
of the writings of a group of Dublin women to which Barber belonged, often known as Swift's 'Triumfeminate' through their associations with their more famous mentor Jonathan Swift. The group
comprised, at various points, Barber (also known as the 'Citizen's
Housewife poet' because of her humble origins as a draper's wife),
the poet and scandal memoirist Laetitia Pilkington, daughter of a
Dublin doctor and obstetrician, the classicist, poet and printer
Constantia Grierson, and the critic Elizabeth Sican.[1] Of these four
women, the two most active and publicly prominent were Barber
and Pilkington, whose work will form the focus for this essay's discussion. Far less is known about the other two women, Grierson
and Sican. The prodigiously talented classicist and poet Constantia
Grierson (nee Crawley) died at 27, leaving behind only a few
poems, most of them posthumously published by Pilkington and
Barber. Less still is known about Elizabeth Sican, wife of a prosperous grocer connected to Swift through the Wood's halfpence trial
over the *Drapier's Letters*, other than from a poem 'On Psyche'
which Swift wrote on her domestic, cultural and intellectual
virtues.[2] To identify these women merely as Swift's protégés (or, as
Swift's friend Orrery snidely suggested, his 'Seraglio'), is, of course,
reductive. Though Swift undoubtedly helped promote Barber's
and Pilkington's well-documented careers, there were other intellectual and literary influences at work in their development as writers.[3]
The cultural background these women shared reveals a more complex
engagement with philosophical ideas current in Dublin at the time,

[1]   For recent work on this circle, see Barnett (2006, pp. 73–97), Gerrard
(2016), and Ingrassia (2016).
[2]   Swift thought that Sican's 'taste was almost refined as her wit'. See
Ehrenpreis (1983, p. 637).
[3]   For a reading of the circle outside Swift's influence, see (Backscheider,
2004). Mary Barber's friendship with the Bluestocking Mary Pendarves,
who married Patrick Delany in 1743, predated her friendship with Swift
by at least 13 years.

such as questions of identity, consciousness and memory, gleaned through their connections with brothers, husbands and fathers at Trinity College Dublin, family book collections, as well as the literary gatherings held by Patrick Delany on Thursday afternoons, nick-named the 'Dublin Thursday Society', at his suburban Dublin villa, Delville, at Glasnevin.[4] As their writings indicate, these women appear to have been familiar with Locke, Berkeley, and pos-sibly other earlier philosophical authors such as Montaigne.

Recent scholarship has paid considerable attention to Locke's 'feminisms', particularly Locke's critique of Robert Filmer's patri-archalism and the extent to which his contract theory includes or ex-cludes women.[5] Yet most studies of Locke's influence on contemporary women writers have been confined to the feminist Mary Astell's somewhat hostile response to Locke's contract theory, his close friendship and correspondence with Damaris Cudworth, and his admiration for Catharine Trotter Cockburn, whose high-minded 1702 defence of Locke's *Essay Concerning Human Understanding*, aligning Locke's moral philosophy with Christian theology, represents one end of a spectrum of women's re-sponses to Locke's thought.[6] At the other end of the spectrum we find female readers and enthusiasts for Locke whose engagement with him was of a more mediated, domestic kind. Of this kind were the women of the Dublin circle, whose exposure to Locke came through daily do-mestic contact, conversations and book borrowing from fathers, brothers and sons who studied or taught at Trinity College Dublin, where Locke had been on the curriculum since 1692. One of the ways in which Locke was disseminated among a wider range of women readers was via popular miscellanies on philosophy and edu-cation aimed at women readers. The young George Berkeley, future Bishop of Cloyne, compiled in 1714 *The Ladies Library*, which in-cluded excerpts from Locke, Astell and Fenelon, among others, for the purposes of educating female readers.[7] This domestic, or 'second-hand' exposure to intellectual ideas in an age when most

[4]   See esp. Hall, ed. (2011, p. 518), and Meaney et al. (2013, pp. 19–20, 24–25); Elias Jr., ed. (1997, vol. 1, pp. 283, 387, vol. 2, p. 674 n. 283: 13).
[5]   For a range of feminist readings, especially of the *Two Treatises*, see especially Hirschman and McClure (2007).
[6]   See Cockburn (1702), Ready (2002), Sheridan (2007) and Parageau (2017).
[7]   See Meaney et al. (2013, p. 17). Although no Irish edition of this text has yet been found, Berkeley's compilation of educational texts printed both in Dublin as well as London indicates a flow of ideas about education between London and Dublin.

Christine Gerrard

women were denied access to formal education and certainly to the study of philosophy, is a process worth studying as evidence of female acculturation to complex philosophical ideas. The women of the Triumfeminate redeployed Locke through a distinctively female, sometimes feminist lens, whilst engaging thoughtfully – yet also playfully – with some of the larger questions of understanding, education and memory raised by texts such as the *Essay Concerning Human Understanding* and *Some Thoughts Concerning Education.*[8]

Cultural historians have shown the long reach which Locke's writings had on early eighteenth-century Ireland.[9] Locke's association with Ireland began properly through his friendship with Sir William Molyneux, founder of the Dublin Philosophical Society and the first translator into English of Descartes' *Meditations*, although Locke had also previously known William's younger brother Thomas when both were studying medicine in Leiden. William's praise of Locke in the dedication of his *Dioptrica Nova* (1692) sparked an intimate, intellectual and personal correspondence that ended only when Molyneux died in 1698. It was Locke's closeness to Molyneux, whose wife Lucy Domville tragically became irreversibly blind in the first year of their marriage, that led him to include a discussion of the so-called 'Molyneux's problem' in his *Essay* – whether a man born blind but restored to sight could visually distinguish between shapes such a cube and a sphere which he had previously known only by touch.[10] The publication in 1708 of Molyneux's *Some Familiar Letters between Mr Locke, and Several of his Friends*, was key to getting Locke known in Dublin, and a source of local pride. The *Familiar Letters* were primarily concerned with the education of Molyneux's son Samuel, but also contained extensive correspondence between Locke and Molyneux over the manuscript of what was published as *Some Thoughts concerning Education*, particularly Molyneux's very liberal responses to some of Locke's strictures on child discipline. 'Such a work as this I desire', wrote Molyneux, 'and that too, at the request of a tender father, for the use of his only son'.[11] *Some Thoughts Concerning*

---

[8]   The idea of 'play' within the reception of philosophical ideas might be fruitfully explored further in relation to this circle. Molyneux memorably used the word 'jocose' to describe his famous 'Molyneux's problem'. See Molyneux et al. (1708, pp. 37–38).

[9]   See especially Kelly (1989).

[10]   See Molyneux (1708, pp. 37–38).

[11]   See Molyneux (1708, p. 35).

What the Women of Dublin Did with John Locke

Education, published in London in 1693, was first published in Dublin in 1728, and there were five Irish reprints of the text (2 editions in 1728), 1737, 1738 and 1778. As Gerardine Meaney has shown, Berkeley used extensive passages from the text, alongside excerpts from Astell and Fenelon, for his 1714 anthology and educational guide, *The Ladies Library*.[12] Locke's engaging, modern treatise on child rearing, adopting a rational, humane, common sense approach to motherhood and infancy, proved one of the most popular guides in England for parents and tutors on how to educate children in an enlightened fashion. It proved no less popular in Dublin. Although Berkeley in his *The Querist* saw Locke's treatise primarily as the key to developing an educated gentry class who would take a paternalistic responsibility for improving their localities, there is no doubt that Barber and others like her focused their attention on education for children of lower social status, including children from trading and mercantile classes.

Locke's privileged position in Dublin intellectual circles also stemmed from the early inclusion on the Trinity College curriculum of his *Essay Concerning Human Understanding* which became a set text in 1692 after William Molyneux recommended it to the provost, St George Ashe. Locke as a political thinker and writer on economics was less widely known in Ireland. Although Jonathan Swift owned copies of, and drew on Locke's treatises on money in his *Drapier's Letters* (1724), and Molyneux drew on Locke's *Two Treatises* for his inflammatory 1698 *The Case of Ireland*, it was not until 1798 that the *Two Treatises* were added to the Trinity College Dublin university curriculum.[13]

Thus early eighteenth-century Dublin knew Locke not primarily as a political or economic writer, but as a philosopher interested in the development of human perception and understanding, and perhaps even more importantly, as an educational writer, with an interest in childhood development and how children learn, and also in parent/child relationships, maternity and childbirth. Insightful recent scholarship has shown how Locke's experience as medical practitioner intersects with and shapes his role on writing for and about women. As Joanne Wright has shown, during his period of political exile in the Netherlands between 1683–88, Locke was part of a close-knit circle of Dutch medical scholars and practitioners, with a particular interest in male midwifery. It was in Leiden that some of

---

[12] See Meaney et al. (2013, p. 17).
[13] See Kelly (1989, pp. 20–24).

Christine Gerrard

Locke's early connections with Dublin were formed, such as with Thomas Molyneux, William's younger brother, who was studying medicine there. Leiden was a hub for European medical training.[14] John Van Lewen, Laetitia Pilkington's father, also studied medicine at Leiden and worked with Boerhaave (he was there slightly after Locke but almost certainly became familiar with his work at this time).[15] The Molyneux family had close links with the Van Lewen family in Dublin: Thomas Molyneux was a colleague of John Van Lewen at the College of Physicians. Thomas's son Daniel Molyneux was very close friends with Laetitia's younger brother Meade.

Like Locke, Van Lewen was very interested in obstetric practice, and when he returned to Dublin from Leiden, 'there then being but one Man-Midwife in the Kingdom; my Father made himself Master of that useful Art, and practis'd it with great Success, Reputation, and Humanity'. It was this reputation as a male midwife that first attracted the bookish and precociously scholarly Constantia Crawley to the Van Lewen household, where she lodged in order to study professional midwifery under Van Lewen. *The Dublin Scussles, or the hungry poets petition* praises one 'Miss Crawley, a lady of notable abilities... no less famous for her Poetical Prowess than her skill in Midwifery'. Born in Kilkenny to humble parents, Constantia Crawley, later Grierson, was a child prodigy who mastered Latin, Greek and Hebrew and French, much of it self-taught. She married the printer George Grierson and shared the honour of being King's Printer, acting as editor and compositor for many of the works his press published. She died aged 27 after acquiring a formidable reputation as editor and classical scholar. Constantia and Laetitia, who lived in the same house for a period of time, became very close friends, sharing an interest in philosophical and scientific ideas, as well as affectionate youthful exchanges of poems.[16]

Laetitia Pilkington and Constantia Grierson both became friends with the significantly older Mary Barber, who by the early 1720s had started to become well known in Dublin. Barber, a highly

[14]   See Elias Jr, ed. (1997, pp. 369–70, n. 12: 40).
[15]   See Wright (2007). She notes that Locke's writings on midwifery reveal his most engaged thoughts about the role of the maternal, the importance of the mother upon early childhood development, and the rational role of education
[16]   See 'To Mrs Van Lewen at a Country Assize', and 'To the Same on the Same Occasion', in Elias Jr., ed. (1997, vol. 1, pp. 18–20).

intelligent, independent-minded woman, who struggled to overcome adversity (marriage to a failing linen draper, four dependent children and poor health), had been friends with Patrick Delany since 1719, long before her association with Swift. She was also close friends with the independent-minded widow Mary Pendarves, her great supporter, who married Delany in 1743. Barber's son Rupert, who became a famed portrait painter, married Delany's niece. They were all part of the group that met regularly, along with Matthew Pilkington, Swift and the Carterets, at Delville, where they discussed philosophical and literary topics. Barber showed a keen interest in Locke's work, and makes explicit, often playful reference, to his ideas, especially on education, child rearing, and man in a state of nature. Barber's *Poems on Several Occasions* of 1734 (in fact published in 1735), aided by Swift's support, attracted a huge subscription list of over 900 subscribers including peers and distinguished literati in both Ireland and England.[17] Her relationship with her four surviving children, particularly her two older sons, Constantine and Rupert, was often the stimulus for and the very subject of her poems. At least fifteen of her poems are explicitly written for her children, and the role of the maternal in education, as well as within marriage, reflects a reading probably not just of Locke but also of Mary Astell, whose *Some Reflections Upon Marriage* may have been introduced to her by Mary Pendarves.[18]

Despite Locke's assumption that authority in marriage should fall to the man as the 'abler and stronger', he by no means undervalued

---

[17]   See O'Flaherty (2013).

[18]   There is no conclusive evidence that Barber and her circle were familiar with Locke's *Two Treatises*, with their attacks on Filmerian patriarchy, but they were certainly familiar with Mary Astell, whose *Some Reflections on Marriage* was reprinted in a Dublin edition in 1730 and suggests an interest by the Dublin literati in the circle around Mary Delany in her distinctive views on the status of women in society. Astell criticised women's entrapment in forced marriages and decried misogyny; 'if a man could respect his own wife when he has a contemptible opinion of her and her sex? When from his own elevation he looked down on them as void of understanding, full of ignorance and passion, so that folly and a woman are equivalent terms with him'. In her poem 'A Conclusion of a Letter to the Reverend Mr C' Barber draws on both Astell and possibly Locke (who challenged Filmer's presumptions of familial authority based on patriarchal rule and the implicit subjection of women). The Irish vicar who Barber mocks in her poem vilifies a rational, intelligent and educated wife like Mrs Barber, seeking instead a domestic slave who will 'serve and obey, as she's bound by her Vows'.

Christine Gerrard

the mother's role in the marriage contract, especially as an educator of her children. In the *Two Treatises*, following a rather unorthodox discussion of polyandry, Locke notes that 'In those parts of America where when the Husband and the Wife part, which happens frequently, the Children are all left to the Mother, follow her, and are wholly under her care and Provision'.[19] In the more domesticated home environments described in *Thoughts on Education* he advocates that all children should be initially be educated at home, rather than at school – a mode customary to the education of girls, rather than boys. In his version of home schooling, Locke sees mothers as essential. He praises the role of mother as early educator in literacy and language: 'and indeed whatever stir there is made about getting of *Latin*, as the great and difficult business, his Mother may teach him herself, if she will but spend two or three hours a day with him'.[20] Locke's strong belief in the power of mothers as early educators found an embodiment in Mary Barber, who invested an extraordinary level of effort and responsibility – as well as genuine pleasure – in her children's education. In her Preface to her *Poems* Barber claims that the education of her children was her chief reason for writing and publishing verse: she wrote her poems 'To form the Minds of my children' as 'I imagined that Precepts conveyed by verse would be easier remembered': 'What has the public to do with verses written between a mother and her son? I answer, that as nothing can be of more use to society than the taking every care to form the minds of youth, I publish some of the verses written by me with that view, when my son was a schoolboy, as the best apology a woman could make for writing at all' (Barber, 1734, pp. xvii-xviii). Barber's interest in education went far beyond the modest female defence of writing to improve or enhance the financial prospects of one's family that women writers often had to adopt to sanction and legitimise their appearance in print. Many of Barber's poems embody a rational, practical approach to childhood learning, inculcated by maternal instruction. The pleasure that Barber took in this role is evident from one of the early poems in *Poems on Several Occasions*, 'A True Tale', which depicts her sitting at home with her children:

> A mother, who vast Pleasure finds
> In modelling her Childrens Minds;
> With whom, in exquisite Delight,
> She passes many a Winter Night;

[19] See Locke (1690, Ch. VI).
[20] See Locke (1693, p. 211).

What the Women of Dublin Did with John Locke

Mingles in ev'ry Play, to find
What Byass Nature gave the Mind. (Barber, 1734, p. 7)

Barber's role as a closely involved home educator of her own children is remarkable for its time, and shows the influence which Locke's ideas on education had on Irish readers. In her 'Conclusion of a Letter to the Reverend Mr C', a poem in which she mimics a misogynistic Irish cleric who deliberately wants to marry an uneducated wife who will cook and sew, and who he can master and control, she passes down this advice to her son when he comes to have children of his own: choose a wife who will be both an intellectual companion and tutor of their children.

Yet still, let her principal Care be her Mind:
In forming her Children to Virtue and Knowledge,
Nor trust, for that Care, to a School, or a College. (Barber, 1734, p. 61)

Barber had clearly assimilated Locke's *Thoughts on Education* closely. Although the earliest Irish edition of 1728 was aimed at an elite – 'Published at the request of several of the nobility of the kingdom' – in line with Berkeley's ideal in *The Querists* of an educated, responsible and paternalistic Irish gentry who would provide a lead in the improvement of their localities, Barber expands Locke's text to appeal to a broader social audience. The Dublin subscription list for the 1728 edition included many ordinary local tradespeople. Excerpts from it were printed in the 1735 Dublin reprint of *The Apprentices' Vade Mecum*, whose author, Samuel Richardson, drew heavily on *Thoughts on Education* in his second 'Pamela' novel, *Pamela in Her Exalted Condition* (1742), devoted to the servant Pamela's rearing and education of her children with the aristocrat Mr B (Richardson, 2012). Samuel Richardson, a friend of Mary Barber and publisher of her *Poems on Several Occasions*, would undoubtedly have approved of her educational aims and poems drawing on Locke's theories on education, designed to improve the minds of her children.

Barber uses her closeness to her oldest son Con to comment on his daily life at school, his relationship with his school friends, and especially his school masters. She ventriloquizes Con's voice to explore and critique contemporary educational practices and other social ills from a child's viewpoint. The poem with which I opened, 'Written for My Son, and spoken by him in School, upon his Master's first bringing in a Rod', echoes one of Locke's abiding concerns in education, the role which corporal punishment should, or

Christine Gerrard

ideally should not, play at home and in school. Locke himself was se-
verely beaten at Westminster school under the notorious Dr Busby,
and in the preface to *Thoughts on Education* he suggests that his
friend Edward Clarke might send his own recalcitrant son there for
a short period of time to instil in him gratitude for the more benevolent regime of home schooling. *Thoughts on Education* is regularly
punctuated by Locke's protests against the inefficacy and cruelty of
beating, for example, 'Beating then, and all other Sorts of slavish
and corporal Punishments, are not the Discipline fit to be used in
the Education of those who would have wise, good, and ingenuous
Men' (Locke, 1693, pp. 50–51). Locke believed that persuasion and
argument were far more effective than the rod in teaching a child.
In the *Familiar Letters* Molyneux discussed Locke's fondness what
we would now describe as 'educational toys', 'the contrivances you
propose for teaching them to read and write' including games to
teach the alphabet and /writing skills (Molyneux et al., 1708,
p. 53). In 'Upon his Master's first bringing in a Rod', Con echoes
Locke's opinion that education should involve fun and play, rather
than whipping and beating.

> That Sage* was surely more discerning
> Who taught to play us into Learning,
> By graving Letters on the Dice:
> May Heav'n reward the kind Device.
> And crown him with immortal Fame,
> Who taught at once to read and game! (Barber, 1734, pp. 16–17)

The asterisk is footnoted with a reference to 'Mr Locke', who advocates that 'Play will then become a Science'. The reference to 'graving
Letters on a Dice' refers to section 149–50 of *Thoughts on Education*:

> Thus Children may be ... *taught to read*, without perceiving it to be
> any thing but a Sport, and play themselves into that which others
> are whipp'd for ... I have therefore thought, that if *Play-things* were
> fitted to this purpose, Contrivances might be made *to teach
> Children to Read*, whilst they thought they were only playing.
> For example, What if an *Ivory Ball* were made like that of the
> Royal-Oak lottery, with Thirty two sides, or one rather of
> Twenty four or Twenty five sides; and upon several of those
> sides pasted on an A, upon several others B, on others C, and on
> others D? I would have you begin with but these four Letters, or
> perhaps only two at first; and when he is perfect in them, then
> add another; and so on till each side having one letter, there be
> on it the whole Alphabet. (Locke, 1693, pp. 178–79)

What the Women of Dublin Did with John Locke

Locke's *Thoughts on Education* also inspired Barber's most frequently anthologised poem, 'Written for my Son, and spoken by him at his first putting on Breeches'. In this imaginative, unusual poem, Barber projects herself into the mind of a little boy who is made to wear tight-fitting masculine clothes after an infanthood in gender-neutral frocks, when, at the age of seven or eight, as was customary, boys were 'breeched'.[21] Con's protests against the discomfort and dangers of stiff, formal and tight-fitting clothing, including trousers, shoes, waistcoats and hats, are expressed with an eloquence and philosophical sophistication humorously incongruous for a little boy, albeit a precocious one.

> WHAT is it our Mamma's bewitches,
> To plague us little Boys with Breeches?
> To tyrant *Custom* we must yield,
> Whilst vanquish'd *Reason* flies the Field. (Barber, 1734, p. 13)

Mary Barber's adult voice can be heard behind that of her son. The critic Christopher Fanning claims that Barber is using her son covertly to ventriloquize typical female grievances against society's demands for women to subject themselves to discomfort and pain in the service of conformity to fashion or in order to please men (Fanning, 2001). The small boy vocalises the type of complaint more often made by eighteenth-century women forced into tight bodices and stays to attract potential suitors.[22] Yet it is clear to anyone who has read *Thoughts on Education* that Barber is also echoing both Locke's, and even earlier, Montaigne's, radical hostility to oppressive forms of 'Custom' in dress which damage the development of the human body, and that she is engaging with a larger philosophical debate about what is 'natural' and what is socially determined.[23]

Among the evils in dress about which Barber's son complains, tight shoes are the most vivid and visceral:

> Our Legs must suffer by Ligation,
> To keep the Blood from Circulation;
> And then our Feet, tho' young and tender,
> We to the Shoemaker surrender;
> Who often makes our Shoes so strait,
> Our growing Feet they cramp and fret;
> Whilst, with Contrivance most profound,

---

[21] See Lavoie (2015).
[22] See Chico (2005).
[23] See especially Mankin (2005).

Christine Gerrard

> Across our Insteps we are bound;
> Which is the Cause, I make no Doubt,
> Why Thousands suffer in the Gout. (Barber, 1734, p. 13)

Barber's description of the deliberate 'cramping' and 'binding' of 'growing Feet' evokes Locke's horrified account of Chinese female infant foot-binding in *Thoughts on Education*. 'The Women of *China*, by bracing and binding them hard from their Infancy (imaging I know not what kind of Beauty in it) have very little Feet'. He complains about their stunted growth and short lives, which he attributes to 'the unreasonable binding of their Feet; whereby the free Circulation of the Blood is hindred, and the Growth and Health of the whole Body suffers. And how often do we see, that some small part of the Foot being injured by a Wrench or a Blow, the whole Leg and thigh thereby lose their Strength and Nourishment, and dwindle away?' (Locke, 1693, p. 12). Locke's account (one of the earliest), later taken up by Mary Wollstonecraft, was almost certainly an influence on Barber, who also includes in her poem references to other barbaric patriarchal oriental practices, such as nooses made of bow-strings by the 'Grand Turk' by which Turkish sultans murdered disobedient wives and enemies (Barber, 1734, p. 14).

Barber's foot obsession might stem in part from her painful attacks of chronic gout. Yet her hostility to tight footwear and her preference for bare feet echo many of Locke's ideas on bare-foot health. Locke advises that the young children of the gentry should have their '*Feet to be washed* every night in cold water and to have his *Shooes* so thin, that might leak and *let in Water*' (Locke, 1693, p. 5); and he even advocates that well-bred children should walk barefoot in the cold and wet to make them hardier like 'the poor People's children'. This is part of Locke's ongoing advocacy in *Some Thoughts* with the hardy and robust as opposed to the over-refined and over-bred.

> Those who have been bred nicely, will wish he had, with the poor People's Children, gone *Bare-foot*; who, by that means, come to be so reconciled, by Custom, to Wet in their Feet, that they take no more Cold or Harm by it, than if they were wet in their Hands. And what is it, I pray, that makes this great difference between the Hands and the Feet in others, but only Custom? I doubt not, but if a Man from his Cradle had been always used to go bare-foot, whilst his Hands were constantly wrapped up in warm Mittins, and covered with *Handshooes*, as the *Dutch* call *Gloves*; I doubt not, I say, but such a Custom would make

taking Wet in his Hands, as dangerous to him, as now taking Wet in their Feet is to a great many others (Locke, 1693, pp. 5–6).

As Robert Mankin has shown, Locke's attack on 'custom' derives in part from Montaigne's essay 'De l'usage de se vestir', or 'Of the Custom of Wearing Clothes', in which Montaigne argues that even in cold northern climates nature has equipped us to live with more exposure to cold and wet then we endure, and that only the force of custom limits us and makes us behave (and dress) as we do (Mankin, 2005). Although Locke never visited Ireland, he must have been familiar from his conversations with Molyneux about the Irish practice of walking barefoot everywhere, with only upper stocking covering the ankles and calves – a practice common into the nineteenth and even twentieth centuries, the barefoot Irish were viewed in different ways by Irish philosophers and 'improvers'. Berkeley, Swift and Samuel Madden often used the barefoot Irish peasant to typify Irish poverty and degradation. Berkeley often alludes to Irish shoelessness in *The Querist*. In his *Short View of the Present State of Ireland* (1728) Swift described 'The families of farmers who pay great rents ... without a shoe or stocking to their feet'. Samuel Madden in 1738 complained of the 'poor Natives so low ... fed with wretched scraps and cloath'd with Rags; numbers of them going bare-legg'd and barefooted, or at best wearing Brogues (as they call their Shoes) so wretched and vile, they are little better than the Wooden Shoes of France, or those of the Peasants in Spain'.[24] Yet Mary Barber radically follows Locke, and before him, Montaigne, in defending bare feet and Irish brogues as a positive type of hardy primitivism.

From the medical perspective which informs all his writings on obstetrics and the raising of children, Locke abhors the deformities of body and the illnesses caused unnecessarily, he believed, by the constricted apparel favoured by 'custom'. He advises parents to make sure that

... your Son's *Cloths* be *never* made *strait*, especially about the Breast. Let Nature have scope to fashion the Body as she thinks best: she works of herself a great deal better, and exacter, than we can direct her ... Narrow Breasts, short and stinking Breath, ill Lungs, and Crookedness, are the Natural and almost constant Effects of *hard Bodice*, and *Cloths that*

[24] See Lucas (1956, pp. 334–36). Lucas identifies a large number of references throughout literature of both the 18th and 19th centuries on the practice of going barefoot in Ireland.

pinch. That way of making slender waists, and fine shapes, serves but the more effectually to spoil them. Nor can there, indeed, but be disproportion in the parts, when the nourishment, prepared in the several offices of the body, cannot be distributed, as nature designs. (Locke, 1693, pp. 10–11)

Locke (somewhat playfully) adopts a politicised language of captivity and liberty when he condemns the widespread practice of swaddling babies: 'The poor Thing lies on the Nurse's Lap, a miserable little pinioned Captive, goggling and staring with its Eyes, the only organ it has at Liberty, as if supplicating for Freedom to its Fetter'd Limbs'. Barber goes much further than Locke himself in drawing on Montaigne's essay on clothing in her attacks on the tyrant '*Custom*'. The animals and birds all dress in perfect proportion to their wants and needs, so why can't we? Montaigne argues that 'as plants, trees, and animals, and all things that have life, are seen to be by nature sufficiently clothed and covered, to defend them from the injuries of weather:

Proptereaque fere res omnes ant corio sunt, Aut seta, ant conchis, ant callo, ant cortice tectae [And that for this reason nearly all things are clothed with skin, or hair, or shells, or bark, or some such thing. – Lucretius, iv. 936.] so were we: but as those who by artificial light put out that of day, so we by borrowed forms and fashions have destroyed our own. And 'tis plain enough to be seen, that 'tis Custom only which renders that impossible that otherwise is nothing so (Montaigne, 1574).

Mary Barber's poem expands Montaigne's account with imaginative liberty.

The wild Inhabitants of Air
Are cloath'd by Heav'n, with wond'rous Care;
Their beauteous, well-compacted Feathers
Are Coats of Mail against all Weathers;
Enamell'd, to delight the Eye,
Gay, as the Bow that decks the Sky.
The Beasts are cloath'd with beauteous Skins,
The Fishes arm'd with Scales and Fins;
Whose Lustre lends the Sailor Light,
When all the Stars are hid in Night.

O were our Dress contriv'd like these,
For Use, for Ornament, and Ease!
Man only seems to Sorrow born,
Naked, Defenceless, and Forlorn.

Yet we have Reason, to supply
What Nature did to Man deny:
Weak Viceroy! Who thy Pow'r will own,
When *Custom* has usurp'd thy Throne?
In vain did I appeal to thee,
Ere I would wear his Livery;
Who, in Defiance to thy Rules,
Delights to make us act like Fools.
O'er human Race the Tyrant reigns,
And binds them in eternal Chains:
We yield to his despotic Sway,
The only Monarch All obey. (Barber, 1734, pp. 15–16)

The *Memoirs of Laetitia Pilkington,* published between 1748 and 1754 by Mary Barber's Dublin friend, and later rival, Laetitia Pilkington, also testify to a domestic familiarity with Locke. Much has been written on Pilkington, whose lively *Memoirs* offer a uniquely intimate domestic account of her mentor Jonathan Swift, her Dublin childhood, and her later descent into poverty in London following her infamous divorce from her clerical poet husband Matthew. Recent scholarly attention has focused more on Pilkington's survival strategies for surmounting a series of abusive relationships with more powerful men than on her intellectual seriousness and engagement with philosophical or scientific debate.[25] Yet it is often forgotten that Pilkington, before she acquired a reputation as a Grub Street demimondaine, was better known as the youngest daughter of a distinguished doctor, John Van Lewen, President of the College of Physicians, and that her mother Elizabeth was an educated and intellectual woman, who also attended the Thursday salon gatherings at Patrick Delany's Delville. Pilkington obviously did not enjoy the benefits of the Trinity College education experienced by her younger brother Meade, but she grew up in a house surrounded by books, ideas and conversation. In December 1731 the intellectual Mary Pendarves, who subsequently married Patrick Delaney, described a Sunday evening to the Van Lewens household.

Spent the evening at Doctor Van Luens. I believe I have mentioned that family to you before: they are sensible and cheerfull. It was proposed by Mrs Van Luen that everybody should own what quality they valued themselvs most for, and afterwards, what they most disliked in themselves: this fancy made us very merry, and made our conversation not unlike some in Clelia

---

25 See, for example, Clarke (2008) and Cook (2012).

Christine Gerrard

[de Scudery's philosophical novel, 1644–1661]. (Elias Jr (ed.), 1997, vol. 2. p. 374 n. 16:23)

Laetitia was also, as Catherine Ingrassia has shown, a voracious reader in Swift's library, and her love of reading, writing and memorising texts started in infancy (Ingrassia, 2016). She also had a serious interest in scientific ideas, striking up a friendship in London with the eminent physiologist Stephen Hales in 1739 (*Memoirs*, 1. 33–34). She was clearly familiar, as we will see, with both *Thoughts on Education* and *The Essay on Human Understanding*. Patrick Kelly notes that undergraduate understanding of the nuances of Locke's *Essay*, part of the curriculum since 1692, were often shaky. More than a century later, the eminent Dublin lawyer Sir Jonah Barrington commented that 'the college course at that time, though a very learned one, was ill-arranged, pedantic, and totally out of sequence. Students were examined in *Locke on the Human Understanding*, before their own had arrived at the first stage of maturity' (Kelly, 1989, p. 22). Arguably a clever, quick and curious young woman like Pilkington, raised in an intellectual Dublin household, might have come to a better understanding of Locke's ideas than many male undergraduates. Pilkington clearly enjoyed playing word games at home which depended on puns and ambiguity. Snippets from diaries and letters of Trinity College students during this period show a familiarity with Locke that anticipates the playful pleasure in the ambiguity of words that we find in the work of another Irish writer, Laurence Sterne. In his autobiographical novel *The Life of John Buncle* (1753), the former Trinity College student Thomas Amory praises his first year encounter with Locke's *Essay* very highly: 'When I was sent to University ... The first book I took in my hand was the Essay of that fine Genius Mr *Locke* ... who shewed me greatly how true knowledge depended on a *right meaning of words*'.[26] In her *Memoirs*, Pilkington engages repeatedly with Locke's *Essay*. She recalls a Lockian conversation with her younger brother Meade over the 'right meaning of words'. Meade 'teiz'd me one Evening to write some verses as a School Exercise for him'. 'I asked him what I should write upon'. 'What should you write Upon', he replies, 'but the Paper?' (*Memoirs*, 1. 45). The ambiguity of the preposition 'Upon' recalls Locke's discussion of 'the doubtfulness or ambiguity of the signification of words'. Pilkington responds to Meade's teasing with a poem, 'O spotless Paper, fair and white', later given the title 'Carte Blanche', which she prints in the

[26] From Amory (1753, p. 6).

What the Women of Dublin Did with John Locke

Memoirs. In his *Some Thoughts on Education* Locke describes the child's mind as 'White Paper, or Wax, to be moulded and fashioned as one pleases'. In her impromptu poem occasioned by her brother's teasing, Pilkington's blank sheet of paper becomes a metaphor for that schoolboy's mind. As Chantel Lavoie notes of this poem, the title 'Carte Blanche' 'may refer not only to the purity of the unspoiled page, but also to the possibilities presented by John Locke on the changeable nature of humanity, and the personality as a *tabula rasa*'. (Lavoie, 1999, p. 208)

It is through the lens of Locke's *Essay* that Pilkington filters her personal memories of her childhood experiences of education and learning. Her rather bitter recollection of her mother's daily beatings owes far less to Locke's benign *Thoughts on Education*, with its general hostility to corporal punishment of children, than to the *Essay on Human Understanding*'s account of childhood memory retention through pain and pleasure. Pilkington's mother clearly did not follow Locke's injunctions against corporal punishment. 'My mother strictly followed *Solomon*'s Advice, in never sparing the Rod … whether I deserv'd it or not, I was sure of Correction every Day of my Life' (Elias Jr (ed.), 1997, vol 1. p. 13). Pilkington relates how her mother prevented her from trying to read books, following a bout of smallpox which had weakened her sight and which threatened her looks and hence marriageability. When she pestered her exasperated mother for the meaning of a word, she 'would tell me the Word, but accompany it with a good Box on the Ear, which I suppose, imprinted it on my Mind'. Her phrase 'imprinted it on my Mind' recalls Locke's terminology in his *tabula rasa* discussion in *Some Thoughts on Education*, showing how ideas are imprinted on the childhood mind through sensory impressions. Pilkington claims that her mother's ear-boxing 'had this Effect on me, insomuch that I never forgot what was ever told me; and quickly arrived at my desir'd Happiness, being able to read before she thought I knew all my Letters'. The enforcement of memory through pain echoes Locke's *Essay Concerning Human Understanding*: '*Attention, repetition, pleasure and pain, fix ideas. Attention* and *repetition* help much to the fixing any ideas in *the memory*. But those, which naturally at first make the deepest and most lasting impressions, are those that are accompanied with *pleasure* or *pain* … pain should accompany the reception of several ideas' (Nidditch (ed.), 1975, II. X: 3). Pilkington ironically equates pain with rapid acquisition of literacy but is very clear that this is not the best way to learn. In her *Memoirs* she contrasts this severe and painful mnemonic tool with the more positive rewards – high praise, commendation, and a shilling – that her father gives her for learning to read.

Christine Gerrard

Pilkington was clearly particularly interested in Locke's theories of memory in the *Essay's* Book II, Chapter X *'Of Retention'*. This is an unusual and early female interest in memory and cognition. Women writers had long been associated with memory, but more often memory as a pious, social and commemorative act – the recording of the passing of life, expressed in the elegy for the dead parent, spouse and most commonly child.[27] Memory as a cognitive function, or as something which related to a sense of individual personal identity and development, did not emerge until far later. Yet in the *Memoirs*, which spend so much time recording the lives of others and how they intersect with her own life, Pilkington is drawn at frequent moments to consider memory as an intellectual faculty, and her conceptual (rather than merely personal or anecdotal) engagement with memory appears to be inspired primarily by Locke. Arguably Locke's interest in consciousness and identity, the joining up of the dots between past and present selves, as well as his interest in memory as a faculty, held a particularly strong appeal to women who were starting to experiment with life-writing and other autobiographical and self-exploratory modes. Locke defined personal identity as consciousness rather than substance. 'And as far as this consciousness can be extended backwards to any past action or Thought, so far reaches the Identity of that Person; it is the same *self* now as it was then, and tis by the same *self* with this present one that now reflects on it, that the Action was done ... So that what-ever has the consciousness of present and past Actions, is the same Person to whom they both belong'.[28] For Locke, consciousness comprises identity, and eighteenth-century philosophers such as Berkeley believed that Locke's theory of personal identity depended upon memory, a reaching forward and backward of consciousness through time in a continued life.[29]

Such concerns shape Pilkington's life-writing. The *Memoirs* are studded with an unusual awareness of the nature and function of memory. In proto-Proustian mode, she remarks that 'I have observed, that the Scent of a Flower, or the Tune of a Song, always conveys to Remembrance the exact Image of the Place in which they were first noticed' (Elias Jr (ed.), 1997, vol. 1, pp. 282–83). Discussing the relationship between wit, memory and the imagination, she disputes an aphorism in Pope's *Essay on Criticism* to argue that that memory is a prerequisite for wit. 'I know not how

27 See especially Mellor (2010) and Gerrard (2018).
28 See Nidditch, ed. (1975, II. 27: 9 and II. 27: 16).
29 See Berkeley (1957, vol. 3, section 7.8).

What the Women of Dublin Did with John Locke

any Person can be witty without a good Memory' (Elias Jr (ed.), 1997, vol. 1, p. 55). Her own retentive textual memory supplied her with material for wit and play. She drew on between 250–300 quotations from memory for the *Memoirs* and loved to play games with Swift in which they matched each other quotation for quotation through the works of Shakespeare and others. Yet Pilkington's obsession with memory was far deeper than textual recall. One day, after reading Locke and speculating 'on that most amazing Faculty of the human Mind, Memory', she writes 'Memory: A Poem'.

In what Recesses of the Brain
Does this amazing Pow'r remain,
By which all Knowledge we attain?

What art thou, Memory? What Tongue can tell,
What curious Artist trace thy hidden Cell,
Wherein ten thousand different Objects dwell?

Surprising Store-house! in whose narrow Womb
All things, the past, the present, and to come,
Find ample Space, and large, and mighty room.
....
Where thou art not, the cheerless human Mind
Is one vast Void, all darksome, sad, and blind;
No Trace of anything remains behind.

The sacred Stores of Learning all are thine;
'Tis only thou record'st the faithful Line;
'Tis thou mak'st Humankind almost divine.
(Elias Jr (ed.), 1997, vol. 1, 54–6)

In its scientific approach and intellectual content, 'Memory' is an unusual poem, especially for an Irish female poet of the early eighteenth century. Pilkington draws primarily on Locke's transitional treatment of memory, which combines earlier ideas of memory as mnemonic system with a more modern, subjective concept of memory that equates memory with identity, individuality and selfhood. It is also possible (as with Barber's knowledge of Montaigne), that the reading of these Dublin women was wider and deeper than we can conjecture, and that Pilkington may have been influenced by other scholastic and Renaissance philosophers on memory she may have encountered in her father's library – or indeed in Swift's library, to which she describes having access. Locke in his *Essay* deploys the traditional spatial metaphors of the Aristotelian and later Renaissance mnemonic tradition, which

Christine Gerrard

views memory, in its ideal form, as a retrieval mechanism for what has been previously stored, memory as a store room, through which the individual moves to retrieve the images placed there.[30] Memory is 'the storehouse of our ideas. For the narrow mind of man, not being capable of having many ideas under view and consideration at once, it was necessary to have a repository to lay up those ideas, which at another time it may have use of'.[31]

Pilkington's apostrophe to memory as the 'surprising Storehouse!' echoes Locke's, and prior to that, the medieval scholars Albertus Magnus and Thomas Aquinas's metaphor of memory as the 'storehouse of ideas'.[32] Pilkington depicts memory as a cabinet of curiosities made up of 'recesses in the brain', 'a hidden Cell, / Wherein ten thousand different Objects dwell'. It is the repository of the 'Sacred Stores of Learning'. Yet, in an original turn, Pilkington transforms the static 'container' into an organic, specifically female container: 'In whose narrow womb / All things, the past, the present and to come / Find ample space and large and mighty room'. This container is paradoxically 'narrow' yet also 'mighty', intimate yet expansive, female and gestational. Pilkington wrote the poem when she was pregnant with her daughter Charlotte: maternal imagery here 'approximates the mind's profound generation of mental associations, extends the day's ruminations. Pregnant with expansive reading and literally pregnant with her daughter Charlotte, Pilkington imagines her wit 'lay'd up till season due and fit'.[33] Pilkington boldly figures memory as the mother of wit. Whereas earlier male writers such as Rochester and Pope equate the maternal imagery of wombs and procreation with dullness, amnesia and vacuity, Pilkington's gestational metaphor for memory is richly productive. Throughout the *Memoirs*, we see Pilkington concerned with both the mnemonic aspects of memory – her ability to learn texts off by heart and to recite them, a foundational part of her early girlhood desire to please and be praised, part of the traditional repertoire of female accomplishment – and with memory as individuated, personal history, a capacity for reflection, a linking of past and present selves. Memory is a function of mind, a capacity to recall at will past perceptions and to renew them again.

The influence of Locke's thought – and indeed, of philosophical thought in general – on the women of eighteenth-century Dublin is

[30]   See Yates (1996) and Whitehead (2009, pp. 53–54).
[31]   See Nidditch, ed. (1975, p. 147).
[32]   See Carruthers (1990, p. 122).
[33]   See Berens (1999, pp. 111–12).

a subject which has barely been touched by scholars. Topics worth pursuing will be the extent to which women associated through fathers, husbands and sons with the academic milieu of Trinity College Dublin, had access to the ideas, books and scholarship which characterised their world. Further work still needs to be done in exploring the links between Locke, Holland, Dublin and the relationship between medical understanding, cognitive philosophy and educational theory. Yet a preliminary study of the writings of at least two of the women of the Dublin Triumfeminate from a philosophical perspective, and, in turn, the writings of other contemporary women who produced poetry on a sometimes amateur or domestic basis, not necessarily to get into print, might encourage us to consider the ways in which ordinary women of the 'middling sort' accessed philosophical ideas in a domestic context and how these might have entered into their works. Not all philosophical debates took place in the public male spaces of school, coffee house and university. The intimacy of Locke's personal correspondence with friends and writers like Molyneux or Cudworth, focusing on maternal and familial relations, sickness and health, care of infants and early education, as well as Locke's personal recollections within his correspondence of the influence of his own father and mother, and his inexhaustible fascination with childhood play and games, might send us back into an examination of the domestic spaces of the period to uncover more about women's engagement with philosophy in the early modern period.

Lady Margaret Hall, Oxford
christine.gerrard@lmh.ox.ac.uk

References

Thomas Amory, *The Life of John Buncle, Esq.* (London, 1753).

Paula Backscheider, 'Inverting the Image of Swift's "Triumfeminate"', *Journal for Early Modern Cultural Studies* 4: 1 (2004), 37–71.

Mary Barber, 'Written for my Son, and spoken by him in School, upon his Master's first bringing in a Rod', *Poems on Several Occasions* (London, 1734) [1735].

Louise Barnett, *Jonathan Swift in the Company of Women* (Oxford: Oxford University Press, 2006).

K. I. Berens, 'The Sword Unsheathed: Wit in Laetitia Pilkington's *Memoirs*', doctoral dissertation, University of California, Berkeley, CA, 1999.

Christine Gerrard

George Berkeley, *Alciphron: Or the Minute Philosopher*, in T. E. Jessop and A. A. Luce, eds., *The Works of George Berkeley, Bishop of Cloyne* (London: Nelson, 1948–1957).

Mary Carruthers, *The Book of Memory* (Cambridge: Cambridge University Press, 1990).

Tita Chico, *Designing Women: The Dressing Room in Eighteenth-Century English Literature and Culture* (Bucknell University Press, 2005).

Norma Clarke, *Queen of the Wits: A Life of Laetitia Pilkington* (London: Faber and Faber, 2008).

Daniel Cook, 'an Authoress to be Let: Reading Laetitia Pilkington's Memoirs', in Daniel Cook and Amy Culley (eds), *Women's Life Writing 1700–1850: Gender, Genre and Authorship* (Basingstoke: Palgrave Macmillan, 2012), pp. 39–54.

Catharine Trotter Cockburn, *A Defence of Mr. Lock's Essay Concerning Human Understanding* (London, 1702).

Michel de Montaigne, "Of the custom of wearing clothes." Trans. Charles Cotton. 1574. *Quotidiana*. Ed. Patrick Madden. 30 Mar 2007. 14 Jan 2020 <http://essays.quotidiana.org/montaigne/custom_of_wearing_clothes/>.

Irvin Ehrenpreis, *Swift: The Man, His Works, The Age* (3 vols., London: Methuen, 1983).

A. C. Elias Jr (ed.), *The Memoirs of Laetitia Pilkington* (2 vols., Athens, Ga: University of Georgia Press, 1997).

Christopher Fanning, 'The Voices of the Dependent Poet: The Case of Mary Barber', *Women's Writing* 8 (2001), pp. 81- 98.

Christine Gerrard, 'Senate or Seraglio: Swift's "Triumfeminate" and the Literary Coterie', *Eighteenth-Century Ireland* 31 (2016), 13–28.

Christine Gerrard, 'Memory and the Eighteenth-Century Female Poet', in *Memory in Western Literature*, 3 vols. (Sivas, Turkey, 2018), vol. 1 1–23.

Augusta Hall, ed., *The Autobiography and Correspondence of Mary Granville, Mrs Delany*, vol. 1 (Cambridge: CUP, 2011).

Nancy J. Hirschman and Kirstie M. McClure, eds., *Feminist Interpretations of John Locke* (University Park, Penn: Penn State University Press, 2007).

Catherine Ingrassia, 'Elizabeth Thomas, Laetitia Pilkington, and Competing Currencies of the Book', *Women's Writing* 23 (2016), 312–24.

Patrick Kelly, 'Perceptions of Locke in Eighteenth-Century Ireland', *Proceedings of the Royal Irish Academy: Archaeology, Culture, History, Literature*, 89 (1989), pp. 17–35.

What the Women of Dublin Did with John Locke

Chantal Lavoie, '*Tristram Shandy*, Boyhood, and Breeching', *Eighteenth-Century Fiction*, 28: 1 (2015), pp. 85–107.

John Locke, *A Second Treatise on Civil Government* (1690), chapter VI, 'Of Paternal Power'.

John Locke, *Some Thoughts Concerning Education* (London, 1693).

A. T. Lucas, 'Footwear in Ireland', *Journal of the County Louth Archeological Society* 13: 4 (1956), pp. 309–394.

Robert Mankin, 'Locke's Education of the Personality', *Études Anglaises* 58: 4 (2005), pp. 387–401.

Gerardine Meaney, Mary O'Dowd and Bernadette Whelan, *Reading the Irish Woman: Studies in Cultural Encounters and Exchange, 1714–1960* (Liverpool: Liverpool University Press, 2013).

Anne K. Mellor, '"Anguish no Cessation Knows": Elegy and the British Woman Poet, 1660–1834', in Karen Weisman (ed.), *The Oxford Handbook of the Elegy* (Oxford, 2010), 442–62.

William Molyneux, et al., *Some Letters between Mr. Locke, and Several of his Friends* (London, 1708).

Peter Nidditch, ed., *John Locke: An Essay Concerning Human Understanding* (Oxford: Clarendon Press, 1975).

Emily O'Flaherty, 'Patrons, Peers and Subscribers: The Publication of Mary Barber's Poems on Several Occasions (1734), PhD. thesis, NUI Galway, 2013.

Sandrine Parageau, '"A Defence of the Essay on Human Understanding" (1702) by Catharine Trotter: Or, How Lockean Theory of Personal Identity suits Women', *Dix-Huitieme Siecle* 275 (2017), 353–69.

Kathryn Ready, 'Damaris Cudworth Masham, Catharine Trotter Cockburn, and the Feminist Legacy of Locke's Theory of Personal Identity', *Eighteenth-Century Studies* 35:4 (2002), 565–76.

Samuel Richardson, *Pamela in Her Exalted Condition*, ed. Albert J. Rivero, (Cambridge: Cambridge University Press, 2012).

Patricia Sheridan, 'Reflection, Nature and Moral Law: The Extent of Catharine Cockburn's Lockeanism in her Defence of Mr. Locke's Essay', *Hypatia* 22 (2007) 131–53.

Anne Whitehead, *Memory* (London: Routledge, 2009), 53–4.

Joanne H. Wright, 'Recovering Locke's Midwifery Notes', in Nancy Hirschbaum and Kirstie M. McClure, eds., *Feminist Interpretations of John Locke* (University Park, Penn: Penn State University Press, 2007), 213–40.

Frances Yates, *The Art of Memory* (London: Routledge and Kegan Paul, 1996).

From Serena to Hypatia: John Toland's Women

IAN LEASK

Abstract
This paper focusses on John Toland's influential *Hypatia* (1720), an account of the neo-Platonist philosopher and mathematician murdered in ancient Alexandria; it also considers segments of his *Letters to Serena* (1704), and suggests various conjunctions between the two texts which confirm Toland's genuine and sustained feminist commitment. As I try to establish, Toland's concern is as much about contemporaneous events as it is about 'disinterested' history: by promoting Hypatia as the representative of philosophy in its perennial struggle with superstition and priestcraft, Toland is able to underscore the wider case for an inclusive and capacious conception of 'enlightenment'.

John Toland's role in shaping the early, radical, Enlightenment is increasingly well appreciated.[1] But Toland's own conception of enlightenment was not focused solely on the role of religion and on 'ungodding' the world[2] – even if the critique of 'priestcraft', superstition and vestigial theocracy was central in his oeuvre. Toland offered sustained arguments against xenophobia and anti-Semitism, for example: his 1714 *Reasons for Naturalizing the Jews*[3] has been lauded for its prescient critique of ethnic 'essentialism', its historically based prognoses, and its full-frontal assault on unthinking prejudice. He also offers a series of arguments and assertions that can be regarded as feminist (or at least proto-feminist) in their intent; it is this aspect of his work that I want to focus upon here. I shall concentrate on Toland's 1720 account of Hypatia (Toland, 1720, pp. 103–136),[4] the

---

[1] See, especially Jacob (1981) *passim*; Israel (2001, pp. 609–14; 2006, pp. 102–4, 112–3, 183–7); Leask (2017).

[2] A term that Toland coins and employs in his *Letters to Serena*. The edition used here is *John Toland's 'Letters to Serena'*, ed. Ian Leask (Dublin: Four Courts, 2013).

[3] See Toland (1714); Champion (2000); Karp (2006); Leask (2018); Lurbe (1999).

[4] Hereafter 'H'. An edition of *Hypatia*, was published, separately from the rest of the *Tetradymus*, in London, by Cooper *et al*, in 1753; this version was also, no doubt, highly important in promulgating Toland's particular take on Hypatia.

doi:10.1017/S1358246120000193   ©The Royal Institute of Philosophy and the contributors 2020
Royal Institute of Philosophy Supplement **88** 2020

Ian Leask

brilliant neo-Platonist of ancient Alexandria, but I shall also consider a segment of his 1704 *Letters to Serena*, and suggest various conjunctions between the two texts – conjunctions which underscore the general case we can make for Toland as a kind of feminist.[5]

For sure, positing Toland's feminist commitment and his religious critique as wholly discrete entities is ultimately artificial – and mistaken. *Hypatia* may present a woman as emblematic of reason, but the particular status that he gives her depends, for its full efficacy, upon a 'theological' contrast: Hypatia's philosophical prestige shines all the more brightly in its polar opposition to the darkness of a famed churchman. Nonetheless, and as I hope to show, here, this same fusion (of feminist commitment and critique of priestcraft) serves to accentuate Toland's intellectual audacity, when we treat it as a thesis that is as much about contemporaneous affairs and attitudes as it is about ancient Alexandria. The implicit yet clear message Toland gives is that 'enlightenment' must mean – at one and the same time – establishing women's equality and overcoming religious tyranny.

*

Born and raised in fourth-century CE Alexandria, Hypatia was the daughter of Theon, a noted astronomer and mathematician, who established herself as an equally important astronomer and mathematician,[6] and also as a learned neo-Platonist philosopher. She built a reputation for her knowledge and wisdom, was highly respected by civic and political figures (as well as academics and scholars), and attracted several generations of followers and students, many of whom would go on to become influential figures themselves in Egypt and beyond. The extent of her career is worth highlighting: although the myth that emerged around Hypatia often depicts her as being

---

[5]   For the purposes of this paper, I am treating 'feminism' as an understanding that – at a foundational, even ontological level – men and women are equal (intellectually, morally, culturally, etc.), but also that – because of sexist, misogynistic and patriarchal attitudes and structures (structures that are cultural, political, socio-economic, etc.) – the aforementioned equality remains unrealized; accordingly, one of feminism's central goals is the critical exposure of those same attitudes and structures. I understand that this is not a 'universal' or univocal definition – some might argue that feminism is more about recognizing the important distinctions between men and women –but it seems appropriate, as a broad definition, for the case I want to make here.

[6]   She produced important commentaries on the mathematical works of Diaphantos and Appollonius, for example, as well as revisions of her father's work on Ptolemy. See Cameron and Long (1993, pp. 39–62 esp. 44–50).

barely into her twenties at the time of her horrific murder, a scholarly consensus has started to emerge that has her being considerably older – probably in her sixties.[7] It seems almost certain, then, that she helped to shape several generations of Alexandrian intellectual and cultural affairs.

In terms of the mythologized picture that built up, Toland, it seems fair to say, played a highly important, formative, role.[8] Nonetheless, he was not quite the first early modern writer to consider Hypatia's significance. The theologian and church historian Schmidt had looked at aspects of her mathematical thought, as part of a study the Greek astronomer Hipparchus;[9] and the pietist scholar Arnold had also given her brief consideration in his (sympathetic) history of heresy (Arnold, 1669, pp. 229–30). More importantly, Gilles Ménage gave Hypatia the single largest entry in his 1690 *History of Women Philosophers* (more of which anon):[10] he synthesised a range of sources to provide an account that would almost certainly prove foundational for Toland's. Yet, whatever the scholarly precedents (and sources), it seems that the rhetorical charge of Toland's treatment ignited a far more partisan line of presentation, one which stretches from Voltaire's *Dictionary*, to Gibbon's *Decline and Fall*, to the Victorian melodrama of Charles Kingsley (Kingsley, 1853) and the 'Parnassian' poetry of Leconte de Lisle,[11] right through to Amenábar's 2009 movie *Agora*. It is Toland who establishes Hypatia as anti-Christian martyr.[12]

Which is not to suggest that Toland's case is some unsubstantial diatribe. On the contrary, and typically, he demonstrates ample (if not quite sober) scholarship by drawing on a range of sources that follow Gilles Ménage's lead and that have become standard for subsequent research on Hypatia:[13] principally, Socrates Scholasticus,

[7] See Dzielska (1995, pp. 67–68). Dzielska draws on the sixth century *Chronographia* of John Malalas to support her case. See, too, Watts (2017, p. 21) and Penella (1984).
[8] See, especially, (Dzielska, 1995, pp. 1–26).
[9] See (Schmidt, 1689, esp. pp. 25–36).
[10] See Ménage (1984, pp. 25–29).
[11] See, for example, 'Hypatie' in de Lisle (1852, pp. 1–7).
[12] For specific treatment of Toland's role, see Dzielska (1995, pp. 1–5), Watts (2017 pp. 135–138). As Watts states, succinctly (at p. 136): 'Toland's treatise had an immediate impact that would help to shape the way that Hypatia was remembered by many of the most important thinkers of the eighteenth and early nineteenth centuries'.
[13] More recent research has also drawn on John of Nikiû's seventh-century *Chronicle* – a text unsympathetic to Hypatia and unknown in Western Europe until the end of the nineteenth century.

Ian Leask

but also Philostorgius of Cappadocia, the fifth century church historians and contemporaries of Hypatia; Damascius, the last scholarch of the Academy, and author of the *Life of Isodore* (most likely composed early in the sixth century); Nicephorus Callistus and Nicephorus Gregoras, Byzantine historians of the 13th and 14th centuries; as well as the *Suda* (or *Suidas*), the 10th century Byzantine encyclopaedia (which itself probably relied on the sixth century historian Hesychius of Miletus for its information about Hypatia). However partial it might be, Toland's account is hardly devoid of historical ballast.

The material circumstances of the events Toland describes are hugely important – whether or not we subscribe to the kind of anti-clerical morality tale that Toland crafts out of them. Drawing on a range of recent and relatively recent scholarship, and bracketing Toland's own account, temporarily, we can present a composite narrative along the lines that follow.[14] Christian hegemony was beginning to emerge, in fifth century Alexandria, from a volatile swirl of rival energies. Crucial to this process seems to have been the action of Theophilus, the patriarch (or pope) of Alexandria, who, at the end of the 4th century CE, made manifest a growing Christian confidence by razing pagan temples to the ground and stamping out any perceived heresy. When he died, in 412, two main players emerged as rivals for his title: Timothy, who had been archdeacon of Alexandria, and Cyril, a zealous hardliner who was also Theophilus's nephew. Timothy may have had more official and ecclesiastical backing, but Cyril could draw on the power of the Alexandrian mob, and – after three days of riots and street fighting – he was duly confirmed as his uncle's successor.

Once in power, Cyril soon made clear that he would outdo Theophilus in terms of missionary zeal. Any supposed heretics (such as the Novatians) were ruthlessly pursued. Perhaps more tellingly, much of the city's Jewish population – a central part of the polity since its foundation – was expelled, after Cyril had deliberately ratcheted up tensions. (Cyril's virulently anti-Jewish sentiments are made explicit in writings from the start of his episcopacy.)[15] Alexandria was being cast, or recast, as 'essentially' Christian. And

[14] The principal sources employed here are: Rist (1965); Cameron and Long (1993); Dzielska (1995); Haas (1997); Wessel (2004); Watts (2006, pp. 143–68; 2017).
[15] See, for example, Cyril's *Sixth Festal Letter,* in Cyril (2008, pp. 101–124). For detailed treatment of Cyril's anti-Jewish position, see Wessel (2004, pp. 33–45).

such a reconfiguration necessarily meant that the patriarch's dominion stretched way beyond sacerdotal and ecclesiastical affairs: one of Cyril's primary concerns became how he might undermine, and ultimately usurp, Orestes, the Roman governor of Egypt.

In the power-play that unfolded, Cyril stirred hundreds of zealous Nitrian desert monks – the so-called *Parabolani*[16] – to take up his cause on the streets of Alexandria. They confronted Orestes and almost managed to murder him; he survived only thanks to ordinary Alexandrians protecting him from this 'holy' mob, after his own guards had fled. In response, Orestes executed Ammonius, the main monkish offender; but, in turn, Cyril tried to trump politics with theology by decreeing Ammonius a martyr deserving veneration. The atmosphere in what for centuries had been a famously cosmopolitan and tolerant city turned increasingly poisonous. And it was within this febrile constellation that Hypatia met her horrific end.

The precise circumstances are hazy. What seems fairly certain is that Hypatia supported Orestes politically, and that – given her status, and given the prestige and power of so many of her former students – this support, in turn, provided Orestes (and his faction) with a force and gravitas to which Cyril could never realistically aspire and of which he was profoundly jealous. Cyril responded by instigating a propaganda campaign that transformed Hypatia's academic pursuits into black magic: the bishop recast the philosopher as a witch. And as these necromantic allegations took root in the collective imagination of Alexandria, so suspicions grew and festered to such a degree that, one fateful day in March 415, a mob led by a minor clergyman, Peter, hauled Hypatia from her chariot, stripped her naked, battered her to death with shards of pottery, and then burned her corpse, outside the city limits. No charges were ever brought; no-one was ever convicted.[17]

Returning to Toland's narrative, we find him unsparing in his condemnation of Cyril as instigator of the murder. 'A Bishop, a Patriarch, nay a Saint, was the contriver of so horrid a deed, and his

---

[16] According to Toland, they were 'the fittest executioners of Cyril's cruelty' (H, p. 129).

[17] See Dzielska (1995, pp. 83–100); Watts (2017, pp. 107–120). Watts points out, however, that advisors to Theodosius II, the eastern emperor, carried out an investigation which resulted in various sanctions against Cyril; the patriarch may only have avoided more serious recriminations thanks to hefty bribes paid to the emperor's lackeys. See Watts (2017, p. 117).

Ian Leask

Clergy the executioners of his implacable fury', he tells us (H, p. 103). And there can be no question, Toland claims, that the Christians of Alexandria somehow acted beyond Cyril's wishes, and that he neither knew of nor could have prevented this 'black deed' (H, p. 131): the evidence in favour of Cyril's direct involvement is overwhelming, Toland states (claiming support from Socrates Scholasticus, Damascius and the *Suda*). In short: political expediency (and sheer personal jealousy) rendered Hypatia 'a sacrifice to the Prelate's pride' (H, p. 129).

Cyril's significance is not only as a directly 'political' figure, however. As well as assuming his central role in Hypatia's murder, Toland emphasizes Cyril's posthumous imprint on the increasingly metaphysical complexion of Christological and Trinitarian discourse during the patristic period; in effect, the figure of Cyril of Alexandria becomes a composite, or cluster, in which political chicanery and violent fanaticism are fused with 'Scholastic fictions' (H, p. 133) and metaphysical hair-splitting. (And, of course, stressing this fusion will be so important for the contemporaneous points that Toland wants to make *via* the figure of Cyril – more of which anon.) Specifically, what Toland focusses on is Cyril's influence on debates regarding Jesus' status as both divine and human, and, even more specifically, on whether Jesus was to be regarded as 'of the *same* substance' as God (*homoousios*), or 'of *similar* substance' (*homoiousios*). The fine details of these bitter, sometimes sophistical, yet ultimately world-historical disputes do not have to concern us, here. We can note, however, that Cyril took a particularly hard line against the Nestorian claim that Jesus had two distinct natures, human and divine, which were connected in the person of Christ; Cyril insisted, instead, that Christ's 'two natures' were fused in the Word of God.

Cyril's campaign culminated in the victory he enjoyed at the Council of Ephesus, in 431, when Nestorius, until then the bishop of Constantinople, was excommunicated and his doctrine condemned as heresy. (Cyril, it seems, positioned himself as opposing Nestorianism in a structurally similar way to how Athanasius, his predecessor as bishop of Alexandria, had opposed Arianism, a century earlier.[18]) We can note, as well, that Cyril's thinking had a profound impact on the Council of Chalcedon of 451 CE, seven years after his death – and that it thus helped shape the character of subsequent Christological and Trinitarian debate.

[18] For detailed treatment, which gives particular attention to rhetorical context, see Wessel (2004, esp. pp. 190–235).

As it happens, Toland pays little attention to the distinction between Arian and Nestorian heresies.[19] Instead, he uses the broader, Alexandrian, context to express his disdain for the kind of theological debate that he associates with the name of Cyril: 'with me', he tells us, 'the *Homoiousion* and the *Homoousion* are of no account, in comparison of the *Bible*, where neither of them are to be found' (H, p. 134). And, regarding the supposed problem of 'ARIAN poyson', Toland scoffs that he is 'not a whit concern'd' (ibid.) The approach is hardly finessed, then; but Toland's principal aim is broad condemnation of how the supposedly pure ethical core of Christian religion became obscured by layers of theological sediment. As such, his position in *Hypatia* is essentially unchanged from that articulated a quarter of a century earlier, in *Christianity Not Mysterious*.[20] There, in order 'to shew *how Christianity became mysterious*,' Toland claims to demonstrate 'how so divine an Institution did, through the Craft and Ambition of *Priests* and *Philosophers*, degenerate into mere *Paganism*' (CNM, p. 96). Pure and straightforward in its first century or so, Christianity was gradually overcome by dubious interest groups and political forces: a self-serving caste of philosopher-priests set itself up as the only possible arbiter of divine truth; the plain message of the gospel was 'absolutely perverted and destroyed' (CNM, p. 97) by ever-more elaborate rituals, rites and metaphysical speculation; and the official adoption of Christianity by the Roman emperors took the religion even further from its marginal origins (as well as producing a swathe of purely expedient conversions).

Toland's treatment of Hypatia is located in the same narrative of decline – although in this case, the focus is on a specific point rather than the wider arc. Proper learning and discourse in the 5th century CE suffered 'irreparable damage', Toland claims, from the vogue for 'metaphysical distinctions about the *Trinity*, and extravagant notions about the essence of GOD (whose majesty they blasphem'd by their profane distinctions)' (H, p. 112). Christianity's

[19] However, it seems important to note that pockets of neo-Arianism and Eunomianism continued to exist in Egypt and the eastern Roman empire well into the fifth century, and that Cyril continued to devote considerable intellectual energy – manifest in various festal letters and scriptural commentaries – to combating them. See Wessel (2004, pp. 57–72), and Hanson (1988, pp. 598–638).

[20] John Toland, *Christianity Not Mysterious: Or, A Treatise Shewing, That there is nothing in the Gospel Contrary to Reason, Nor Above it: And that no Christian Doctrine can be properly call'd A Mystery* (London: Anon., 1696). Hererafter, 'CNM'.

primal significance as a vehicle for promoting a universal ethical code, accessible to all, became increasingly obscured by Trinitarian, eschatological or soteriological disputes. And so, as far as Toland is concerned,

> There's nothing surer, there's nothing truer; but of genuin Christianity there remain'd very little at that time [of Cyril], unless Christianity be made to consist in the bare name and profession... Neither the doctrines nor distinctions then in vogue were ever taught by CHRIST or his APOSTLES; and... the ceremonies injoin'd or practis'd were all utterly unknown to them. (H, p. 133)

To reiterate, though: Toland's Cyril is a composite figure, a fusion of absurdly rarefied theological abstraction, on the one hand, and bloody *realpolitik*, on the other; the metaphorical violence done to Christianity's core becomes causal, it seems, in producing the literal violence committed in the name of the Church (and its rule). Moreover, in the course of his treatment, Toland's rhetorical position broadens – subtly yet distinctly – from historical account and retrospective judgement to *contemporaneous* implication and insinuation; accordingly, Toland is able to raise supposedly perennial theological-political issues (in which, of course, the hyphenation is crucial).

The overall Preface to the *Tetradymus*, the collection within which *Hypatia* appeared, had already located Toland's account of Cyril and Hypatia, quite explicitly, in terms of contemporary events – specifically, a very public clash between Henry Sacheverell, the High Church Tory who argued for the divine right of kings, passive obedience and suppression of dissent (and around whom angry, violent, opposition to Whig ideology coalesced), and William Whiston, Newton's successor as Lucasian professor of mathematics at Cambridge, confirmed Whig, and avowed anti-trinitarian.[21] At the start of 1719, in an act of provocatively passive aggression, Whiston had attended a

---

[21]   Toland had history with both, so to speak. He had published Toland (1710) as an angry response to the incendiary preaching (and publication) that would lead to the minister's trial; he followed this with Toland (1711). (Arguably, so much of Toland's intellectual efforts after 1710 were directed against the 'Sacheverellian' anti-Whig backlash of the second decade of the eighteenth-century.) Unsurprisingly, he was far more favourably disposed to Whiston, and in parts 10 and 11 of the *Pantheisticon* (1720) Toland makes plain his qualified agreement with Whiston's general approach to natural history, as ventilated in the latter's 1696 *New Theory of the Earth*.

service at Sacheverell's church, St. Andrew's in High Holborn, London, and (pointedly) refused to stand during the Athanasian creed – much to the chagrin, not just of the minister, but of most of the congregation; Sacheverell had duly published an attack on Whiston and his 'gross Arianism'.[22] Toland, in his Preface, tells us that he was moved to write his account of Hypatia in response to 'the unlawful and unchristian usage' that Whiston had received from Sacheverell (H, 'Preface', p. vii): Toland mocks High Church indignation and mob denunciations in the name of 'religion' – although he also suggests that it was only 'the good nature of the English people' that prevented Whiston from being 'torn to pieces for all his gown and innocence' (H, 'Preface', p. viii).

In *Hypatia* itself, the indications of contemporary relevance are more subtle and allusive, but probably all the more effective, as a result. For example, and as we have already noted, the register of his comments regarding the *homoiousian* versus *homoousian* debates is designed to suggest that the intrinsic irrelevance of these same debates is ongoing (so to speak). We are also given a barbed abstraction from the particularities of fifth-century Alexandria when Toland asks: 'where was it otherwise [in terms of outcome] when the Clergy where [sic] permitted to share in the government of civil affairs?' (H, p. 127) The absurdity of any continuing reverence for Cyril is made explicit when Toland also asks of his readers: 'how insufferable a burlesquing of God and Man is it to revere so ambitious, so turbulent, so perfidious, and so cruel a man, as a *Saint*?' (H, p. 135) But perhaps the most significant comment, in this respect, and one of the most telling sentences in Toland's account, overall, is his claim that

> ... they were no Christians that kill'd HYPATIA: nor are any Christian Clergymen now to be attack'd thro the sides of her murderers, but those that resemble them; by substituting precarious Traditions, Scholastic fictions, and an usurp'd Dominion, to the salutiferous [or 'health engendering'] Institution of the holy JESUS. (H, p. 133)

With this particular charge, past and present are folded into each other, and the horrors of theological-political thuggery are made manifest as a continuous danger. For Toland, it was not just

---

[22] For an account of the St Andrew's church event, see McDonald (2016, pp. 193–94). For an overall account of Whiston's life and thought, see Force (1985). Force notes, in his account, that '[i]t can have done [the Arian]... aspect of the Newtonian cause little good when such deists as John Toland defended Whiston' (Force, 1985, p. 113).

Ian Leask

ancient Alexandria that faced the consequences of a 'deluge of Ignorance, Superstition, and Tyranny' (H, p. 136): fanaticism remains an ongoing threat to freedom, he tells us.

We can gauge something of the effect of this very particular appropriation of history by turning to one of the first critical responses that *Hypatia* engendered: Thomas Lewis' pointedly titled *The History of Hypatia, A most Impudent School-Mistress of Alexandria: Murder'd and torn to Pieces by the Populace* (Lewis, 1721). Lewis, a High Church Anglican cleric who also published a vitriolic periodical, *The Scourge, in Vindication of the Church of England*, immediately suspected the '*Dis-ingenuity*' of Toland's history, and countered by casting Cyril as 'a zealous *Christian*, or (in vulgar phrase) a *High-Churchman* in those days' (Lewis, 1721, p. 5), and Socrates Scholasticus as 'an Unforgiving, Inflexible *Puritan*' (Lewis, 1721, p. 13); for Lewis, it seems, two could play at Toland's game. Purporting to present the true story of 'this *She Philosopher*', Lewis depicted Toland's account as 'a mere *Lampoon*, dress'd up with malice, prejudice and ignorance', and designed 'to blast the reputation', not only of Cyril, but also of Henry Sacheverell, who, according to Lewis, was '[Cyril's] faithful successor in Zeal, against the Modern *Novations* and Arian Heresie' (Lewis, 1721, p. 3). Lewis's case may be overwrought; nonetheless, it was as clear to him then as it should be to us now that Toland's scholarly efforts were by no means disinterested.[23]

*

As already indicated, above, Toland's account of Hypatia seems to have been all the more historically significant for its rhetorically intensified dualisms: reason and philosophy shining in their virtuous opposition to superstition and brutal clerical ambition. Unsurprisingly, however, the historical actuality is probably a more complex affair. In terms of the specific role attributed to Cyril, for example, there seems little doubt that he was a ruthless operator, envious of Hypatia's popularity, and determined (at just about any cost) to establish Christian hegemony. Nonetheless, and as Dzielska has demonstrated, convincingly, we cannot simply assume, as Toland tends to, that Cyril was directly responsible for her murder (even if he did much to create the climate in which it

---

[23]   A further response worth noting is the anonymous 'Dissertation sur Hypacie, où l'on justifie Saint Cyrille d'Alexandrie sur la mort de cette Sçavante', in the *Continuation des Mémoires de Litterature et d'Histoire* 5.1 (1728, pp. 139–86).

took place): the evidence is equivocal, and there is nothing that suggests an explicit order or directive on his part.[24]

Furthermore, and leaving aside the specifics of Cyril's role, so many other aspects of the more general binary opposition that animates Toland's version of events seem historically questionable. Hypatia was accomplished in mathematics and logic, for sure; but she was also a not untypical neo-Platonist seeking to employ 'philosophy' for an ultimately mystical end. (We know, too, that astrology, alchemy and dream-interpretation were all important concerns for her circle.) Her followers and acolytes included Christians as well as pagans: she may have come emblematically to stand for 'the violent end of classical Greek thought', but her overall milieu was more likely a very eclectic and 'multicultural' affair.[25] (One of her most important students was the Christian neo-Platonist Synesius of Cyrene, who would become bishop of Ptolmais.) Furthermore, in backing the Roman governor, rather than the Alexandrian pontiff, she was not necessarily taking some kind of principled anti-religious stand, in the name of philosophy: Orestes himself was an avowed and committed Christian (a point that Toland omits mentioning). Toland may have done a huge amount to create the legend of Hypatia; but his account is a loaded affair, for sure.[26]

For anyone familiar with Toland's wider project and *modus operandi*, there is little surprise in finding that he is thoroughly partisan and partial in his use of historical sources. Indeed, if there is anything like a consistent Tolandian 'method' to be identified, across his writings, we could say (with only some exaggeration) that it consists of utilizing any possible source, ancient or modern, to further his general campaign of 'ungodding' the world. What I want to focus on for the remainder of my consideration, however, is not so much the lack of historical nuance and subtlety, but the fact that Toland has chosen a woman as emblematic of philosophical enlightenment. Why and how might this be significant?

One could say that Hypatia's status *qua* female intellectual is peripheral to Toland's use, or exploitation, of the horrible events regarding her murder: the main point he wants to make seems to be about religion *versus* reason, in general. And, inasmuch as there is any

[24] See Dzielska (1995, pp. 90–91); see, also Wessel (2004, p. 53).
[25] On Hypatia's relations with Christians, see Watts (2017, pp. 46–50).
[26] Watts (2006, pp. 202–3), suggests that the death of Hypatia served to undermine Cyril's own position: she was far more hospitable to Christianity than the more stridently pagan Iamblichan neo-Platonists who gained more prominence in Alexandria after her murder.

Ian Leask

'gendered' significance to Toland's *Hypatia*, it might seem more dubious than it is anything else: after all, he conjoins Hypatia's knowledge with her 'beauty' and 'innocence'; he tells us that her students were 'powerfully affected by a charming mind in a charming body' (H, p. 108), that she was 'a Lady of such beauty, modesty, wisdom and virtue' that she was 'eagerly sought' in marriage (H, p. 119); and he even pontificates on her sex life and whether or not she died a virgin (H, pp. 121–22). It hardly needs pointing out that these kinds of consideration simply never arise when Toland is writing about male thinkers – even those with whom he is in profound disagreement.[27]

Nonetheless, and without wanting to dispute that Toland is capable of condescension, I want to look at aspects of the opening paragraphs of *Hypatia*, where Toland (once again) makes points that are designed to be simultaneously historical and perennial. Discussing the way in which Hypatia's father, Theon, had ensured that she had a broad education in 'the most abstruse sciences', Toland notes that these are 'reputed [to be] the proper occupation of men, as requiring too much labour and application for the delicate constitution of women' (H, p. 105); against which assumption he immediately replies: 'That this notion is a vulgar prejudice, the vast number of ladies who have in every age distinguished themselves by their professions or performances in Learning, furnishes an un[-an]swerable argument' (ibid.). He adds that 'whole volumes have been written, containing nothing else but the lives of such women, as became eminent in all kinds of literature, especially in philosophy, which, as it is the highest perfection, so it demands the utmost effort of human nature' (ibid.). It seems that we can establish a legitimate and fruitful link between the remarks here and the Preface to Toland's 1704 *Letters to Serena* – specifically, the large chunk of it (sections 4–9) which is taken up with the person of 'Serena', the position of women in history and in philosophy, various manifestations of misogyny, and what we might term 'sexual politics'.

The *Letters* consists of five free-standing yet inter-related essays on a huge range of issues – like the origins of prejudice, the genealogy of the (spurious) idea of an immortal soul, the political abuse of theological notions, and the denial of any transcendent or transitive cause of motion or movement in the wider cosmos. The work emerged from an intense eighteen-month period that Toland spent in the royal courts of Hanover and Berlin, in 1701 and 1702,

---

[27]   Although it seems fair to point out, as well, that these were probably standard discursive tropes, at the time.

during which he became ensconced in the brilliant intellectual circle of Sophia, the empress of Hanover, and her daughter, Sophie Charlotte, the queen of Prussia – a circle that pivoted around the great polymath, and one of the towering figures of Western thought, Gottfried Leibniz. Both of the princesses were devoted to philosophical and theological debate, and it is generally accepted that Leibniz's most important later work (like the *Theodicy* and the *New Essays*) emerged from conversations and correspondence between the three of them (and various other interlocutors): the princesses' probing intellects seem to have forced Leibniz to hone his arguments into the shapes by and in which they have since come to be known.[28]

The first three of Toland's *Letters* were apparently written for the edification of Sophie Charlotte, and were designed to clarify, develop and consolidate the kind of arguments he had offered in person, at court: the princess is never named, but there is little doubt about the identity of the 'Serena' of Toland's title. These three, and two further, more metaphysical essays, were published along with a Preface, which is styled as 'a letter to a gentleman in London', probably Pierre Desmaizeaux, the exiled French Huguenot intellectual who would later write a posthumous biography of Toland (as well as produce a translation of Bayle's *Dictionary*). It is this Preface that bears consideration alongside the account of *Hypatia*.

Here, without identifying Sophie Charlotte, Toland reveals that the first three letters were intended for a female recipient (whom he is styling as 'Serena'). And from the text, it seems that this is a problematic issue for Desmaizeux – Toland says he can immediately imagine what his correspondent is thinking, and (intriguingly) refers to some history between them when he writes: 'You may remember how often I took the part of the other sex against your prejudices rather than your judgement' (Toland, 2013, p. 51).

Toland goes on to recount how he was often forced to describe men as 'rude, unmannerly, ignorant, and rough-hewn monsters'; he poses the question of whether women's exclusion from education is the result of unthinking prejudice or more cynical design; he reminds his correspondent how he had demonstrated 'the parity of the intellectual organs in both sexes' and the way in which women would be 'equally capable of all improvements, had they but equally the same advantages' as those enjoyed by men; and he goes on to catalogue women in history who – despite the social and structural

[28] For fuller treatment of Toland's intellectual relationship with Leibniz, see Leask (2012).

impediments they faced – were able to achieve political and even military success (Toland, 2013, p. 51).

What I want to highlight, here, are some of the precise details of Section Six of the Preface – not least, some of the implications of Toland's reference points. For a start, Toland mentions the significance of Gilles Ménage's 1690 *History of Women Philosophers* – the collection of 65 dictionary-style entries covering the entirety of Western thought, and which (as indicated above) devotes its single largest entry to Hypatia herself. (Ménage also seems to supply Toland with his scholarly leads.) This text is almost certainly uppermost in his mind, in his *Hypatia*, when he tells us about the 'whole volumes' that have been written on the subject. Here, it seems, we have a direct link – in terms of reference as well as subject-matter – between *Hypatia* and the Preface.

Toland goes on to mention, as an example of an important contemporary female philosopher, Catharine Trotter (Cockburn), who had published an incisive appreciation and defence of John Locke's *Essay Concerning Human Understanding* (a text which Toland revered), and who was also known for dramatic and literary works.[29] And, although this is never made explicit in the *Letters*, both of these names – Ménage and Trotter (Cockburn) – are resonant in terms of their wider public reception (and, indeed, public ridicule). Ménage had been satirized by Molière in his play, *Les femmes savantes*; an English version, *The female virtuosos*, by Thomas Wright, had been a great success on the London stage, in 1693. (Ménage is presented in the play as the ridiculous pedant, Vadius.)[30] Three years later, in 1696, Catherine Trotter had been the one of the targets of a grotesque (but anonymous) satire called *The Female Wits; or, The Triumvirate of Poets at Rehearsal*; again, it had been performed on Drury Lane, and was then published in 1704, the same year as the *Letters*. (As well as attacking Trotter, *The Female Wits* satirized two other writers, Mary Pix and, especially, Delariviere Manley. Part of backlash against the growing success, in the 1690s, of women's writing, the play culminated, ominously, in the silencing of women's drama.)[31]

---

[29] See Sheridan (ed.), (2006). For an overview, see Broad (2002, pp. 141–65). For a collection of her literary works, see Kelley (ed.), (2006).

[30] Molière also produced *Précieuses Ridicules*, a play which lampooned what he took to be the preciousness and mannered refinement of the female salon.

[31] See Finke (1984). See, too, Milling (2010).

In the Preface, then, Toland is invoking two names that have very particular resonances; we could even say that Toland is retrieving these names, and the efforts they entail, from misogynistic attack. And it seems that this context (of theatrical derision and critical retrieval) might provide an important clue as to why Toland chose to style Sophie Charlotte as 'Serena' – and, in turn, how this nomination might provide further evidence of Toland's feminist position.

Specifically, I want to consider another dark corner of Restoration satire – two plays by the English dramatist (and Royalist) Edward Howard,[32] both of them published in 1671: *The women's Conquest*, and *The six days adventure, or the new Utopia*. The first of these depicts a group of Amazons whose female-led society is undermined – and so the 'natural order' restored – when they eventually recover their wits and fall in love with men. The second is similar: set on the island of Utopia, it depicts a situation in which – because of an ancient decree – political power shifts from the island's men to its women. In establishing their new regime, the women consider various types of government, but decide on a republic; and the leader who emerges, through good sense and virtue rather than brute power or ambition, is called Serina.[33] (She is depicted as calm and sagacious, and possessing a sort of natural authority.) However, faced with a revolt, when the men threaten to leave the island altogether, the women are forced to end their Utopian experiment, after just six days, and a male monarch takes over again: normal service is resumed. And lest we see this as a sly critique of patriarchy, we should note that Howard tells us, in his preface, that the women in his play are 'made use of to confirm the judgement and practice of the world in rendring them more properly the weaker sex, than to authorize their judgement'.[34]

For sure, there is no conclusive 'proof' that Toland knew the play, never mind that he intended to invoke it. But Toland's erudition was wide; and he certainly knew the work of Edward Howard's brother,

---

[32] Howard's brothers, Robert, Henry and James, were also dramatists; his sister, Elizabeth, was married to John Dryden.

[33] The spelling used in the play is Serina, rather than Serena.

[34] Howard (1671), no page numbers given for preface. Nussbaum (1984), cites Howard's work as exemplifying a particular type of literary misogyny of the period, based around the figure of the powerful Amazon (and the threat that she posed). Nussbaum presents a host of similar cases – works like John Fletcher's *Sea Voyage*, Joseph Weston's *Amazon Queen*, the anonymous *Female Rebellion*, etc. See, especially, Nussbaum (1984, ch.3, pp. 43–56). For a different reading, focussing more on the 'constitutional' issues in the play, see Pankratz (2014, pp. 85–101, esp. 97–99).

Ian Leask

Robert (which had Socinian overtones to it).[35] He lived the bulk of his adult life in London, with an astonishing network of political and literary contacts, and we can take it as read that, in general, he would have been familiar with goings-on of the city's stage – after all, Restoration theatre had a cultural and political significance more like that of television and social media today. It hardly seems outrageous to suggest that Toland appreciated, only too well, the implications carried with the name 'Serena'.

*

In conclusion, we can say that the explicit claims Toland makes in *Hypatia* and in the Preface to his *Letters to Serena* demonstrate a consistent 'feminist commitment':[36] he is not a programmatic or systematic thinker, but it seems clear that his vision of enlightenment is broad and inclusive, and entails what today we would term 'gender equality'. Toland's presentation of Hypatia as a philosophical martyr is meant to underline this commitment: the critique of 'fanaticism' from the point of view of virtuous reason is more than a general claim, and one that posits philosophy as capacious and inclusive (and not solely a male preserve).

Beyond this wider point, I am also suggesting that the theatrical and dramatic resonances in the Preface of the *Letters to Serena* allow us to speculate that Toland's designation – Serena – may be intended as a rebuff to the misogynistic attitudes exemplified by Restoration satire (but reflecting a far wider malaise). And, if this is the case, it again emphasizes the wider, inclusive, culture that Toland is looking to create: Serena has not been 'put back in her place', but – instead – has been directly involved in debating and

[35]   See, for example, Toland (1699, pp. 138–39), where Robert Howard is described as 'a Gentleman of Great Generosity, a Patron of Letters, and a hearty Friend to the Liberty of this Country'.
[36]   It seems worth noting here that, in 1697, Toland had (very probably) written the preface to work titled *A Lady's Religion, in a Letter to the Honourable Lady Howard*, in which he seemed to argue that men and women had an equal capacity for religious understanding – and also for priesthood. Interestingly, the Lady in question was Anne Howard – a member of the same dynasty as Edward. Although anonymous, the preface's author uses the pseudonym 'Adeisidaemon', or 'without superstition', by which name Toland offered his 1700 poem *Clito*, and which he also used as the title of a 1709 work published along with his *Origines Judaicae*; both the *Origines* and the *Adeisidaemon* offered secular and classically-informed approaches to Scripture.

shaping some of the most important issues of the day (as ventilated in Toland's text).

Whether or not we accept that the nomination 'Serena' has the very specific charge that I am suggesting it might have, we can certainly see Toland's writings as being part of a vanguard that was creating new conceptual and cultural possibilities. For Toland, it seems, enlightenment that did not involve women's equality was not enlightenment at all.[37]

Dublin City University
ian.leask@dcu.ie

References

Anon., 'Dissertation sur Hypacie, où l'on justifie Saint Cyrille d'Alexandrie sur la mort de cette Sçavante', in the *Continuation des Mémoires de Litterature et d'Histoire* 5.1 (1728), 139–86.

Gottfried Arnold, *Unpartheyische Kirchen und Ketzer-Historie von Amfang des Neuen Testaments bis auf das Jahr Christi 1688* (Frankfurt: Thomas Fritzschens, 1669).

Jacqueline Broad, *Women Philosophers of the Seventeenth Century* (Cambridge: Cambridge University Press, 2002).

Alan Cameron and Jacqueline Long, *Barbarians and Politics at the Court of Arcadius* (Berkeley: University of California Press, 1993).

Justin Champion, 'Toleration and Citizenship in Enlightenment England: John Toland and the Naturalization of the Jews, 1714–1754', in *Toleration in Enlightenment Europe*, eds. O.P. Grel and R. Porter (Cambridge: Cambridge University Press, 2000), 133–156.

Cyril, *The Fathers of the Church*, vol.118 (Saint Cyril of Alexandria, *Festal Letters* 1–12), trans. Philip R. Amidon, ed. John J. O'Keefe (Washington, D.C.: Catholsic University of America Press, 2008).

Leconte de Lisle, *Poëmes antiques* (Paris: Librairie de Marc Ducloux, 1852).

Maria Dzielska, *Hypatia of Alexandria*, trans. F. Lyra (Cambridge, Ma.: Harvard University Press, 1995).

[37] I should like to thank a variety of interlocutors for their helpful comments on earlier versions of this paper. I am especially grateful to Bartholomew Begley, Moyra Haslett, Jonathan Israel, Darrell Jones, Alissa MacMillan, Kenneth Pearce and Takaharu Oda.

Ian Leask

Laurie A. Finke, 'The Satire of Women Writers in *The Female Wits*', *Restoration: Studies in English Literary Culture, 1660–1700*, 8/2 (1984), 64–71.

James E. Force, *William Whiston. Honest Newtonian* (Cambridge: Cambridge University Press, 1985).

R.P.C. Hanson, *The Search for the Christian Doctrine of God. The Aryan Controversy, 318–381* (Edinburgh: T&T Clark, 1988).

Christopher Haas, *Alexandria in Late Antiquity. Topography and Social Conflict* (Baltimore: Johns Hopkins University Press, 1997).

Edward Howard, *The six days adventure, or the new* Utopia (London: Thos. Dring, 1671).

Jonathan Israel, *Radical Enlightenment. Philosophy and the Making of Modernity, 1670–1750* (New York and Oxford: Oxford University Press, 2001)

Jonathan Israel, *Enlightenment Contested. Philosophy, Modernity, and the Emancipation of Man 1670–1752* (New York and Oxford: Oxford University Press, 2006).

Margaret Jacob, *The Radical Enlightenment: Pantheists, Freemasons and Republicans* (London: Allen & Unwin, 1981)

Jonathan Karp, 'The Mosaic Republic in Augustan Politics: John Toland's *Reasons for Naturalizing the Jews*', *Hebraic Political Studies*, 1, (2006), 462–92.

Anne Kelley (ed.), *Catherine Trotter's 'The Adventures of a Young Lady' and Other Works* (Aldershot: Ashagate, 2006).

Charles Kingsley, *Hypatia or the New Foes with an Old Face* (London: John Parker & Son, 1853).

Ian Leask, 'Unholy Force: Toland's Leibnizian 'Consummation' of Spinozism', *British Journal for the history of Philosophy*, 20 (2012), 499–537.

Ian Leask, 'Speaking for Spinoza? Notes on John Toland's *Origines Judaicae*', in *Reassessing the Radical Enlightenment*, ed. Steffen Ducheyne (London: Routledge, 2017), 143–59.

Ian Leask, 'Only Natural: John Toland and the Jewish Question', *Intellectual History Review*, 28, 4, (2018), 515–28.

Thomas Lewis, *The History of Hypatia, A most Impudent School-Mistress of Alexandria: Murder'd and torn to Pieces by the Populace, in Defence of Saint Cyril and the Alexandrian Clergy. From the Aspersions of Mr Toland* (London: Bickerton, 1721).

Pierre Lurbe, 'John Toland and the Naturalization of the Jews', *Eighteenth Century Ireland*, 14 (1999), 37–48.

Grantley McDonald, *Biblical Criticism in Early Modern Europe. Erasmus, the Johaninne Comma and Trinitarian Debate* (Cambridge: Cambridge University Press, 2016).

Gilles Ménage, *History of Women Philosophers* [*Historia Mulierum Philosopharum*], trans. Beatrice Zedler (Lanham, Maryland: Rowman and Littlefield, 1984).

Jane Milling, 'The Female Wits: Women Writers at Work', in Catie Gill (ed.), *Theatre and Culture in Early Modern England, 1650–1737. From Levaiathan to Licensing Act* (London: Routledge, 2010), 131–42.

Felicity Nussbaum, in *The Brink of All We Hate: English Satires on Women, 1660–1750* (University Press of Kentucky, 1984).

Anette Pankratz, 'Performing Republics: Negotiations of Political Discourse in Restoration Comedies', in Dirk Wiemann and Mahlberg (eds.), *Perspectives on Revolutionary Republicanism* (London: Routledge, 2014), 95–112.

Robert J. Penella, 'When Was Hypatia Born?' *Historia. Zeitschrift für Alte Geschiche*, 33/1 (1984), 126–28.

John M. Rist, 'Hypatia', *Phoenix*, 19 (1965), 214–25.

Johann Andreas Schmidt, *Hipparchus, Theonae doctaque Hypatia in mathesis celebres: Dissertatione Historico-Mathematico* (Jena: Litteris Krebsianis, 1689).

Patricia Sheridan (ed.), *Catharine Trotter Cockburn: Philosophical Writings* (Peterborough, Ontaria: Broadview Press, 2006).

John Toland, *Christianity Not Mysterious: Or, A Treatise Shewing, That there is nothing in the Gospel Contrary to Reason, Nor Above it: And that no Christian Doctrine can be properly call'd A Mystery* (London: Anon., 1696).

John Toland, *Life of John Milton* (London: John Darby, 1699).

John Toland, *Mr Toland's Reflections on Dr Sacheverell's Sermon Preach'd at St Paul's Nov. 5 1709* (London: J. Baker, 1710).

John Toland, *High Church Display'd. Being a Compleat History of the Affair of Dr Sacheverell, In its Origin, Progress, and Consequence* (London: anon., 1711).

John Toland, *Reasons for Naturalizing the Jews of Great Britain and Ireland*, etc. (London: J. Roberts, 1714).

John Toland, *Hypatia: Or the History of a Most Beautiful, Most Vertuous, Most Learned, and Every Way Accomplish'd Lady; who was Torn to Pieces by the Clergy of Alexandria, to Gratify the Pride, Emulation, and Cruelty of Their Archbishop, Commonly But Undeservedly Styled St. Cyril*, in Toland, *Tetradymus* (London: Brotherton, Meadows *et al*, 1720).

John Toland, *John Toland's 'Letters to Serena'*, ed. Ian Leask (Dublin: Four Courts, 2013).

Edward J. Watts, *City and School in Late Antique Athens and Alexandria* (Berkeley: University of California Press, 2006).

Ian Leask

Edward J. Watts, *Hypatia. The Life and Legend of an Ancient Philosopher* (Oxford: Oxford University Press, 2017).

Susan Wessel, *Cyril of Alexandria and the Nestorian Controversy* (New York and Oxford: Oxford University Press, 2004).

Peter Browne on the Metaphysics of Knowledge

KENNETH L. PEARCE

Abstract
The central unifying element in the philosophy of Peter Browne (d. 1735) is his theory of analogy. Although Browne's theory was originally developed to deal with some problems about religious language, Browne regards analogy as a general purpose cognitive mechanism whereby we substitute an idea we have to stand for an object of which we, strictly speaking, have no idea. According to Browne, all of our ideas are ideas of sense, and ideas of sense are ideas of material things. Hence we can conceive of spiritual things – including even our own spirit – only by analogy. One interesting application Browne makes of his theory is an account of how concepts such as knowledge can be correctly applied to beings that have no intrinsic properties in common, such as non-human animals, humans, angels, and God. I argue that this is best understood as what, in the contemporary literature, is known as a 'multiple realizability' problem and that Browne's solution to this problem has important similarities to functionalist theories in recent philosophy of mind.

Peter Browne was a philosopher, theologian, and polemicist belonging to the conservative 'high church' faction of the Protestant Church of Ireland. He was provost of Trinity College Dublin from 1699 to 1710, and bishop of Cork from 1710 until his death in 1735.[1]

Browne's philosophical career began with his 1697 *Letter in Answer to a Book Entitled Christianity Not Mysterious*. The book is, as the title suggests, a reply to John Toland's argument against religious mysteries (Toland, 1696). One strand of this reply is a defense of analogy as a cognitive tool whereby we are able to have a sort of indirect conception of things of which we, strictly speaking, have no ideas. Browne uses the doctrine of analogy to argue against the Lockean thesis that 'we can have knowledge no farther than we have ideas,' (Locke, 1690, §4.3.1) and thereby to undermine Toland's argument for the claim that we cannot believe in religious mysteries like the Trinity.

Analogy is the central theme that runs through all of Browne's philosophical works, up until his last, and longest, work, *Things Divine and Supernatural Conceived by Analogy with Things Natural*

---

[1] For a detailed intellectual biography, see Winnett (1974).

doi:10.1017/S1358246120000156

Kenneth L. Pearce

and Human (1733), usually known (insofar as it is known at all) by the shortened title *Divine Analogy*. This paper will explore Browne's use of the doctrine of analogy to explain the attribution of knowledge to 'brutes' (i.e., non-human animals), humans, angels, and God. The account to be examined is not a theory of epistemology as ordinarily understood: that is, it is not a theory of epistemic justification or the norms of theoretical rationality. Rather, it is a metaphysical account of what knowledge, as a mental state, really is.[2] This account, I will argue, bears interesting resemblances to functionalist theories in recent philosophy of mind.

1. Browne's Theory of Analogy

David Berman has characterized Browne as a 'right-wing Lockean' of the Irish 'counter-enlightenment,' employing Locke's principles for conservative ends (Berman, 2005, p. 82). Browne himself, however, would certainly not take kindly to being described as a Lockean of any sort. In *Divine Analogy*, Browne writes,

> the University…[has been] unhappily poysoned by an *Essay concerning Human Understanding:* Which appeared indeed in the Beauties of Style, and Wit, and Language; but all this was the Glittering of the Serpent, to palliate and disguise a long Series of false Principles of Knowledge, directly destructive of revealed Religion especially; and calculated with no small Labour and Artifice for leading youthful and half learned Minds into all that prevailing Ignorance and Infidelity, which sad Experience hath shewn to be the Consequences of them. (Browne, 1733, pp. 127–28)

Although Browne mostly avoids the use of medieval philosophical jargon, it would be more accurate to describe Browne as a Thomist than as any kind of Lockean.[3] However, like many other early readers of Locke,[4] Browne sees Locke's epistemology as basically

---

[2]   In this respect, Browne's theory to some degree resembles 'knowledge first' approaches in contemporary epistemology. See, e.g., Williamson (2000).

[3]   As we will see, analogy is *the* central concept in Browne's philosophy. Browne credits Aquinas ('the Angelic doctor') as the best theorist of analogy to date (Browne, 1733, p. 93). However, as we will also see, Browne's own conception of analogy has important differences from Aquinas's.

[4]   See, e.g., Leibniz (1704, pp. 47–50).

Peter Browne on the Metaphysics of Knowledge

Aristotelian in orientation and therefore sees large parts of Locke's theory as compatible with his own Thomistic point of view. In trying to express his Thomistic view in the language of modern philosophy, and trying to defend it against modern opponents, Browne often sounds similar to Locke. This may well be intentional. Whether or not Browne himself saw his project this way, the easiest way for us to approach Browne's theory of analogy will be to begin by highlighting four central theses on which Browne is in approximate agreement with Locke, then identify Browne's crucial departure from Locke.

In the first place, then, Locke holds that all ideas are derived from experience. There are two sorts of experience: sensation, which is directed at external objects, and reflection, which is directed at the mind itself (Locke, 1690, §§2.1.1–4). Here, Browne takes a harder line than Locke, endorsing at full strength the Scholastic maxim that there is nothing in the intellect that was not first in the senses (Browne, 1729, pp. 55, 382) and holding that 'we have no Ideas but of sensible Objects' (Browne, 1729, p. 64). Browne argues against Locke's ideas of reflection explicitly and at length (Browne, 1729, pp. 64–69, 102–3, 412–14).[5] The question of how, according to Browne, we manage to think about the mind and its acts in the absence of ideas of reflection will be addressed in some detail in the next section.

Second, Locke holds that '*Words in their primary or immediate Signification, stand for nothing, but the* Ideas *in the Mind of him that uses them*' (Locke, 1690, §3.2.2).[6] Similarly, according to Browne, 'Words…are external, sensible, instituted Signs of Ideas[,] Conceptions or complex Notions in our Mind; which not being *Immediately* communicable, cannot be made known to others without some such Indications' (Browne, 1733, p. 535).

Third, Locke defines 'truth' as '*the joining or separating of Signs as the Things signified by them, do agree or disagree one with another*'. Locke goes on to explain,

> The *joining* or *separating* of signs here meant is what by another name, we call Proposition. So that Truth properly belongs only to Propositions: whereof there are two sorts, *viz*. Mental and Verbal; as there are two sorts of Signs commonly made us of, *viz*. Ideas and Words. (Locke, 1690, §4.5.2)

---

[5] See also Browne (1733, pp. 23–29); for further discussion, see Berman (2005, pp. 94–96).

[6] In chapter 3.7, Locke carves out an exception for the so-called 'particles' (syncategorematic terms), but this exception will not concern us here

Kenneth L. Pearce

As words signify ideas and inherit their reference from the reference of the corresponding idea, so verbal propositions signify mental propositions and inherit their truth value from the corresponding mental proposition. Similarly, according to Browne, 'without some [ideas, notions, or conceptions] affixed to the Words we make use of, we can never form a *Mental* Proposition answering to the *Verbal*: Nor can a Word without some of these annexed to it, be one of the Terms in a Syllogism' (Browne, 1733, p. 511).

Fourth and finally, since, according to Locke, 'our Knowledge...all consists in Propositions,' (Locke, 1690, §2.33.19) and (mental) propositions are constructed out of ideas, it follows that 'We can have *Knowledge* no farther than we have *Ideas*' (Locke, 1690, §4.3.1). Regarding this principle, Browne writes, 'this Assertion may very well be granted to our Freethinkers as true, *That we can have no Knowledge without Ideas*...and yet be very false in *Their* Sence of it, which is *That we can have no Knowledge of things, whereof we have no ideas*' (Browne, 1729, p. 409).

This last point is the crucial one. Browne holds that we have only sensory ideas, and sensory ideas are ideas of material things. Thus, if we cannot have knowledge of things of which we have no ideas, we can have no knowledge of any immaterial things, a consequence Browne regards as disastrous (Browne, 1729, p. 402). Browne must therefore hold that we can after all have 'Knowledge of things, whereof we have no ideas'. But having come so far with Locke, how can Browne get off the boat?

The hidden premise needed to get from the claim that there is no knowledge without ideas to the claim that there is no knowledge *beyond* ideas is what Kenneth Winkler has called 'the content assumption' (Winkler, 1989, p. 39). This is the view that the content of any thought is fully determined by the idea the thinker has. In other words, each idea has its own proper object(s), and to have that idea is to have a thought about that object or those objects, and nothing else. Winkler argues that Locke rejects the content assumption (Winkler, 1989, pp. 39–43). However, this interpretation has been challenged.[7] The fact that Locke appears to rely on the content assumption in the argument that there can be no knowledge beyond ideas is an additional piece of evidence that Locke endorses this assumption. Browne's theory of analogy, however, is precisely a strategy for rejecting the content assumption, thereby permitting knowledge *beyond* ideas while retaining Locke's ban on knowledge

---

[7] See Yaffe (2004); Pearce (2019).

without ideas. Analogical thought does require an idea, but the object the thought is *about* is not the same as the object the idea is *of*.

Regarding our ability to conceive of immaterial things, Browne writes,

> when any thing differs thus totaly in Kind from all things whereof we have any direct Idea or immediate Consciousness; we must either remain utterly Ignorant of its Nature and Properties, without being able either to think or speak of it at all: Or we must form Conceptions of it by substituted Representations, and Analogy with those Beings and Properties whereof we have some direct and immediate Perception or Consciousness. (Browne, 1733, p. 247)

What is crucial here is the notion of 'substituted Representations'. We have no ideas of immaterial things, and we cannot think without ideas. If, therefore, we are to think of immaterial things, we must do it by 'substituting' some sensible idea in place of the missing idea of that thing. Thus, although we have no 'direct idea' of (e.g.) God, we can use some sensory idea to represent God analogically.

This preserves all four of Browne's points of approximate agreement with Locke: the idea we use to represent God is derived from (sensory) experience; the word 'God' signifies this idea; mental propositions like *God is omnipotent* are joinings of ideas, and are true if and only if the things signified by the ideas agree; and no such proposition can be formed without a subject idea and a predicate idea. However, in the case of analogical propositions like *God is omnipotent*, the ideas are *not* used to signify their 'direct and immediate' objects, but rather, by analogical substitution, are used to signify some reality of which we have no idea.

Browne says less than one might like about how this substitution actually works, and real clarity about the theory can only be achieved by examination of his particular examples. The central aim of this paper is the examination of one such example, the concept of *knowledge*. However, before we proceed to the analysis of knowledge, it will be useful to get a slightly better grip on Browne's notion of analogy by seeing how he contrasts it with metaphor.

According to Browne, analogy is a middle path between literal and metaphorical thought and speech (Browne, 1729, p. 13).[8] After

---

[8]   As Manuel Fasko pointed out to me, it is interesting that Browne and other philosophers employing analogy in the aftermath of Toland typically characterize analogy as a middle path between the literal and the metaphorical, whereas Aquinas and the other Medieval philosophers from whom the

Kenneth L. Pearce

Browne's *Letter* against Toland, William King, the archbishop of Dublin, had also employed analogy to answer objections against Christianity (King, 1709). However, as the deist Anthony Collins quickly pointed out, King's account did not adequately distinguish analogy from metaphor and therefore arrived at a view on which, strictly speaking, 'God is neither wise nor good' (these attributes being predicated of God only metaphorically) (Collins, 1710, p. 22).[9] Similar objections were pressed by the conservative Calvinist John Edwards (1710).[10] It was partly in response to these critiques that Browne saw the need for a more thorough exposition and defense of the theory of analogy (Browne, 1729, pp. 11–24).[11] Indeed, according to Browne, the response to King is only one manifestation of a larger intellectual trend: Browne claims that all forms of religious dissent (including Socinianism, deism, freethinking, and even atheism) are based fundamentally on the assumption that there is no middle way between literal and metaphorical speech (Browne, 1729, pp. 28–32). The issue of the distinction between metaphor and analogy therefore receives a great deal of emphasis.

According to Browne, both metaphor and analogy involve the substitution of the idea of one thing to stand for another thing. In the case of metaphor, 'the figurative Words, and Ideas, and Conceptions, are us'd without any *Real Similitude* or *Proportion*, or *Correspondent Resemblance* in the things compared. The Comparison is not founded in the *Real Nature* of the Things, but is a pure Invention of the Mind and intirely *Arbitrary*' (Browne, 1729, p. 106). Examples Browne gives here include the use of 'taste', a word originally referring to one of the five senses, to refer to aesthetic judgment, and the description of a stormy sea as 'angry'. According to Browne,

---

theory is drawn present it instead as a middle path between the univocal and the equivocal (e.g., Aquinas, *Summa Theologica*, Iq13a3, Iq13a5). Browne recognizes this fact in his exposition of Aquinas (Browne, 1733, pp. 94–96), but does not seem to realize that this is different from his own approach.

[9] On the exchange between King and Collins, see Pearce (2018, §12.1).

[10] John Edwards (1637–1716), a Church of England clergyman, should not be confused with another conservative Calvinist, Jonathan Edwards (1703–1758), an American Congregationalist minister.

[11] Browne does not usually name living authors, so it is sometimes difficult to identify his targets. The italicized text at Browne (1729, pp. 18–19) is a series of (near) quotations from Edwards (1710). The italicized text at Browne (1729, pp. 20–22) is a series of (near) quotations from Collins (1710).

in such cases we do indeed substitute not just the word but also the concept for which the word stands, and consider a piece of music as if it were an object of gustatory enjoyment or the heaving waves of the sea as if they were an expression of anger.

A further characteristic of metaphor is that it is not 'absolutely *Necessary* to a *True* and *Real* Knowledge of the Things designed to be expressed or conceived by the substituted Ideas' (Browne, 1729, p. 106). In other words, metaphor is a way of talking and thinking about things of which we have some prior conception: we *choose* to substitute some other idea in place of the direct and proper idea of the thing in question in order to stimulate the imagination or call attention to certain features of the thing, but metaphorical thought and speech, according to Browne, is never strictly necessary. It can always be translated into literal speech without loss of cognitive content. It is for this reason that, although Browne often speaks of metaphor as involving substitution, he also writes that 'Metaphor is rather an *Allusion*, than a real *Substitution* of Ideas': in metaphor, although we make use of 'a very remote and foreign Idea' in thinking about the object, nevertheless some prior non-metaphorical conception of the object is always also present (Browne, 1729, p. 142).

Both of these features contrast with analogy. In analogy,

> Conceptions and *Complex Notions* we already have of Things *Directly* and *Immediately* known, are made use of and substituted to represent, *With some Resemblance, or correspondent Reality and Proportion*, Divine things whereof we can have no *Direct* and *Proper* Idea, or *Immediate* Conception or Notion at all. (Browne, 1733, p. 107)

Browne is here speaking of the particular case of 'divine analogy,' that is, the use of analogy in speaking of God. However, as we will see, he regards analogy as a much broader phenomenon.

Analogy, then, differs from metaphor in that the substitution is not arbitrary but based on a '*Correspondent Reality* or *Resemblance*' (Browne, 1729, p. 141). Further, analogy differs from metaphor in that analogy is a tool whereby we conceive of a 'thing [that] differs...totaly in Kind from all things whereof we have any direct Idea or immediate Consciousness' (Browne, 1733, p. 247). We do this by substituting an idea or conception we do have for the corresponding or resembling thing of which we have no idea. It is because of the lack of any direct idea that Browne says that analogy involves a 'real substitution' and not just an 'allusion' as in metaphor. It is also for this reason that Browne says that 'Analogy [is] us'd to *Inform* the

Kenneth L. Pearce

Understanding, as Metaphor and other Figures are, to *Affect* the *Imagination*' (Browne, 1733, p. 136).

The central puzzle for this kind of account is: what kind of '*Real*...Correspondency and Proportion' (Browne, 1729, p. 143) could possibly exist between things that 'differ[]...totaly in Kind'? (Browne, 1733, p. 247). In the case of religious mysteries, like the Trinity, Browne thinks it is sufficient to say that it is revealed by God that some correspondence or proportion or resemblance exists, although we have no knowledge of this correspondence or proportion or resemblance.[12] However, in other cases Browne thinks we can say something more contentful about the nature of the correspondence. In what follows I will argue that, in the particular case of knowledge attributions, Browne endorses a kind of proto-functionalism in order to allow for a metaphysically real 'proportion' between things utterly different in kind.

2. Analogical Knowledge Attributions

According to Browne, our concept of knowledge and of all other mental states begins from our understanding of ourselves. Browne employs the word 'thinking' to refer to 'the particular way of Knowledge in Man' (Browne, 1729, p. 152).[13] Further, according to Browne, 'it...[is] the *Essence* of a Man to be composed of Soul and Body, and to think by the operation of these two essential Parts in conjunction' (Browne, 1729, p. 80). We know that thinking involves the body because 'we feel [thinking] to be a *Labour* of the Brain, and we find our selves as much wearied with intense Thought, as with hard bodily Labour' (Browne, 1729, p. 150). However, according to Browne, we also know that thinking involves spirit.

Regarding our knowledge of spirit, Browne begins by noting that 'the Standard and Oracle of Ideas in our Age' (Locke) holds 'that we have the clearest Idea of active Power from our Idea of *Spirit*', where 'spirit' is defined as 'a *Thinking Substance*; which [Locke] labours to shew may be *Matter* for ought we know' (Browne, 1729, p. 73; see Locke, 1690, §4.3.6). In response, Browne insists that

---

[12]   See Browne (1729, pp. 302–21); Browne (1733, pp. 4–8, 118–19).

[13]   Browne is oddly insistent that this is the 'proper Acceptation' of the word 'thinking', i.e., the correct use of the word according to the rules of English. He provides no evidence in support of this claim. Since, as Browne himself recognizes, the lexicographic issue is not of much philosophical importance, I will treat Browne's usage as stipulative.

this account cannot be correct, since in fact spirits cannot be material, and we have no ideas of immaterial substances. We cannot derive an idea of active power from our idea of spirit, since we have no idea of spirit.

Browne sometimes says that we 'have an immediate *Consciousness* of the Operations' of the mind (Browne, 1729, p. 66; cf. Browne, 1733, p. 23), which might be taken to suggest that he endorses the view of Malebranche and Berkeley that we know our selves and our actions by 'consciousness' or 'reflection' without the mediation of ideas (Malebranche, 1674–1675, pp. 237–39; Berkeley, 1713, pp. 231–34). In fact, Browne's view is more radical than this.[14] According to Browne, 'The Mind or spiritual Part of us cannot look upon or into itself, by either a direct or reflex Act...We have no Knowledge of our own Spirit, or of any of its Faculties, but from conscious Experience of its several Ways of Acting upon the Ideas of Sensation' (Browne, 1729, pp. 108–9). Although we have a kind of consciousness of our mental operations, this does not allow us to form ideas of them: 'whenever we *Attempt* to frame any *Ideas*, properly speaking, of the Mind's Operations or the *Manner* of them, they prove no more than *Indirect Metaphorical Images* borrowed from Sense and Imagination' (Browne, 1733, p. 25). In order to conceive of our mental operations, we must make use of '*Complex Conceptions*, formed from a *Consciousness* of the Operations themselves, and Ideas of Sense taken together' (Browne, 1733, p. 24). This consciousness, according to Browne, does not allow the mind to think about its operations '*Abstractedly*' because it is no more than the mind's ability to 'observe[] its own *Motions* and *Actions* and Manner of operating upon those [sensory] ideas' (Browne, 1729, p. 66). All of our conceptions of mental operations are conceptions of operations performed *upon ideas*. The ideas form part of the conception and cannot be abstracted away.

[14] There is considerable interpretive dispute about the views of Malebranche and Berkeley on self-knowledge, so perhaps not all interpreters will agree that the view I attribute to Browne is more radical than the views of Malebranche and Berkeley. However, most interpreters of Berkeley (myself included) hold that we are aware of our mental acts *as active*. As Ian Tipton puts it, an action 'is not primarily an object for mind but rather something we are aware of through doing it' (Tipton, 1974, p. 267). See Bettcher (2007, pp. 69–74); Roberts (2007, pp. 36–39); Pearce (2017, pp. 126–28). Browne's view of our ignorance of spirit is stronger than this.

Kenneth L. Pearce

Browne's view, then, is that it is by observing the mind's manipulation of sensory ideas that we come to a conception of the mind. In another text, Browne explains,

> we observe such Effects with regard to things material and sensible, as we conclude cannot proceed from any inherent Power in themselves; and therefore we rightly infer there must be some other Beings *Not material* which have the Power of producing such Effects...So that we come to our Knowledge of Power, not from any *Direct* Knowledge or Idea we have of Spirit; but intirely from our Reasoning upon sensible Objects. (Browne, 1729, p. 74)

Because of Browne's rejection of ideas of reflection, he applies this account even to self-knowledge: I *infer* the existence of an immaterial part of myself because I observe myself performing operations that cannot be accounted for by mere matter (Browne, 1729, pp. 97–8).

Browne holds, then, that all human mental operations (which are the only mental operations of which we have direct knowledge) involve the cooperation of a material part and a spiritual part. The material part is, at least to some extent, an object of direct awareness and is a thing of which we can have ideas. The immaterial part is known only by inference, and we have no ideas of it. Recall that Browne accepts the Lockean view that we cannot think without ideas. How then do we manage to think about these hybrid spiritual-material processes? Enter, once again, the theory of analogy.

In the *Procedure*, Browne describes our acquisition of the concept of spirit as follows:

> WE have not even the least *Direct Idea* or Perception of the purely spiritual Part of us; nor do we discern any more of its *Real Substance* than we do that of an Angel. We are so far from an exact view or intuitive knowledge of it, that we are forced to argue and infer its very *Existence* from our Observation only of such Operations as we conclude could not proceed from mere Matter; and because we have no direct Idea of it, we express the *Nature* of it, as we do that of Spirit in general, by the negative Word *Immaterial*. And as we cannot form one Thought of our Spirit, otherwise than as it is in conjunction with the Body; so neither can we conceive any of its Operations but as performed together with bodily Organs: and therefore it is that we are under a necessity of expressing the *Modus* of them all in Words borrowed from Sensation and bodily Actions. Thus we say the Mind *Discerns, Apprehends, Distinguisheth,* or *Separates* one

thing from another; it *Draws* one thing out of another, which is a *Consequence* or one thing *Following* from another. Nay, when we would *Attempt* to form *Ideas* of *Thinking* and all the various Modes of it, they are imagin'd to be so many *Motions* or Agitations of the Soul, in conjunction with the most refin'd and spiritous Parts of the Body, about the Ideas of sensible Objects. (Browne, 1729, pp. 97–98; Cf. Browne, 1733, pp. 23–28).

It is Browne's view that all of our talk about the mind and its operations is analogical: our conceptions of mental operations are constructed from sensory ideas.[15]

Regarding our concept of spirit in general, Browne writes, 'the Word *Spirit* in its first Propriety is used to signify the most volatile and exalted Parts of *Matter*; and is from thence taken to express an human Soul in *Conjunction* with Matter; and from thence again transferr'd to represent a purely *Immaterial* Substance by Analogy' (Browne, 1729, p. 118). Thus, quite generally, thought about any kind of disembodied spirit involves a two-fold analogy: first, we substitute ideas of sensible things to stand for human mental operations, all of which proceed by spirit in conjunction with matter. This substitution creates an analogical conception which has the sensory idea as an ingredient. This analogical conception is, by a second iteration of analogy, transferred to stand for the operations of a purely immaterial spirit, creating a second analogical conception that contains the first as an ingredient.

Browne's comments on thinking and knowledge follow this pattern: the concept *thinking* is constructed from sensory ideas by means of analogy to stand for a certain joint operation of spirit and matter in a human being. The concept *knowledge* is constructed from the concept *thinking* by a second analogy in order to form a concept that can apply to purely immaterial beings (angels and God) and also purely material beings ('brutes', i.e., non-human animals). Thus, Browne writes,

---

[15]   Browne applies this strategy not only to actions, but also to passions. In fact, Browne would say that the very concepts of action and passion are analogical conceptions arising from the action of one body upon another. In our concepts of passions, we conceive of something *happening to* the mind, and we conceive of this using the analogy of some bodily motion. Thus, for instance, we speak of *falling* in love, employing a sensory idea of a bodily fall from some height. (This example is mine, not Browne's.) See Browne (1733, pp. 27–28). Browne, however, never addresses the question of how or why we conceive some mental goings on as active and others as passive. I thank Samuel Rickless for raising the question about passions.

Kenneth L. Pearce

> we can form no other Notion of *Knowledge* in an Angel or separate [i.e., disembodied] Spirit except by that of *Thinking*; but this is no more than an *Analogical* Conception, which the Mind substitutes instead of the real true manner and kind of Knowledge in Angels which we are utterly ignorant of; and which is as imperfectly represented by Thinking, as their Motion is by the moving of our Feet. (Browne, 1729, p. 150; Cf. Browne, 1697, pp. 42–43)

Because, according to Browne, it is essential to thinking (the human form of knowledge) that it be performed by the cooperation of spirit and matter, it is clear that no purely material or purely spiritual being can, properly speaking, think. There is a second reason, according to Browne, why a purely spiritual being could not think: the knowledge of a pure spirit would be '*Intuitive* and *Instantaneous*' (Browne, 1729, p. 150). Thinking, however is successive and not instantaneous (Browne, 1729, pp. 76, 150). It is for these reasons that a second analogy is needed.

Browne does admit that we correctly apply *knowledge* and other mental state concepts to brutes, although they are purely material. However, their form of knowledge, according to Browne, is only that 'which we call by the Name of *Instinct*; and is realy no other than a Calculation or *Disposition* of their Senses by the Author of Nature' (Browne, 1729, p. 158). Mental state terms like 'knowledge', Browne says, provide 'the best *Analogous* Notions and Words we have, to represent those *Movements* of [brutes] which seem to *Mimick* the *Actions* and Faculties of Men' (Browne, 1729, p. 171). These movements are purely mechanical, and it seems that they ought in principle to be comprehensible within a completed physiology.

The case of pure spirits is quite different: 'we know nothing of the true manner of that operation in them, which is answerable to knowledg in us' (Browne, 1697, p. 42).

It might be thought that a general concept of knowledge, applicable to purely material and purely spiritual things, could be formed by abstraction. However, Browne denies this. Abstraction, according to Browne, consists only in the removal of part of the content of an idea or conception. However, all of our ideas are sensory, hence they are all ideas of material things. Thus, to remove the sensory/material content of an idea or conception would be to remove *all* of the content (Browne, 1729, pp. 196–99; Browne, 1729, pp. 106–8). For this reason,

> If we abstract…intirely from our *Thinking*, which includes the Labour of the Brain; we could form no Notion or Conception

of the *Wisdom* of Spirits in general, much less of the Wisdom of God; and therefore for *Want* of any such abstract Notion or Idea...we are forced to substitute that of our *Thinking*, to represent an inconceivable *Correspondent Perfection* which is in God (Browne, 1729, pp. 196–97).

Thus, regarding God in particular, Browne writes,

there is certainly some inconceivable *Perfection* in God answerable to *Human Knowledge*; which is obtained by the Labour of Thinking and the Operation of Matter and Spirit in essential Conjunction: *Goodness* in God is an inconceivable Excellency of his Nature correspondent to what we conceive and express by the same Word in human Nature; And the *Similis Ratio* or *Proportion* runs thus, *What* Knowledge and Goodness are in the Nature of *Man, That* some inconceivable but correspondent Perfections are in the Nature of God (Browne, 1733, pp. 137–38).

The concept of *thinking* is constructed by the analogical substitution of the ideas of certain bodily motions or operations to stand for certain operations of the human mind, which proceed sequentially and by co-operation of the spiritual and the material, and which are known only by their effects on sensible ideas. The concept of *knowledge* is constructed by a second analogical substitution, whereby we use the concept of *thinking* to stand for either purely material or purely spiritual operations that are 'answerable' or 'correspondent' to thinking in humans. Our basic question still remains, however: if these operations are utterly different in kind, what could this 'answerability', 'correspondence', or 'proportion' possibly amount to?

3. Analogy and Functionalism

To begin to understand the nature of the correspondence between different forms of knowledge, it will be useful to ask: what basis can we have for attributing knowledge to non-humans? That is, what kind of evidence gives us reason to believe that a non-human has knowledge?

Given the fact that Browne's main focus is our thought and speech about God, and given the importance for Browne of such affirmations as *God is omniscient* (all-knowing), it is surprising that Browne says so little about this issue. The *Procedure* does include a chapter with the title '*From the Existence of Things material and human, is inferr'd the necessary Existence of God*' (bk. 3, ch. 8). However, this chapter isn't

Kenneth L. Pearce

really aimed at defending the existence of God against the atheist, but rather (as the title suggests) at describing how human beings (rationally) arrive at belief in God. The primary target here is likely Anthony Collins, who had argued that King's analogical theory of the divine attributes undermined all arguments for the existence of God (Collins, 1710).[16] Browne therefore gives a one paragraph summary of the argument which he takes his opponents already to endorse and spends the remaining ten pages of the chapter criticizing the Lockean account of how we form the idea of God and defending the view that the argument instead supports an analogical conception of God.

Browne summarizes the basis for our belief in God as follows:

> Because the Mind perceives it to be a flat Contradiction that the Beings which have been *Produced*, taken all together or singly, should produce *Themselves*; or that they should possibly be produc'd or preserv'd as they are, otherwise than by the infinite Power and Wisdom of an *Intelligent Agent:* Which first Cause must be *Without* Beginning; since it is likewise flat Contradiction that he should have made himself. (Browne, 1729, p. 447)

This is consistent with Browne's general position on the epistemology of spirit, quoted above, that spirits can only be inferred from their effects (Browne, 1729, p. 74).

King had pressed a similar line in more detail:

> the Descriptions which we frame to our selves of God, or of the Divine Attributes, are not taken from any direct or immediate Perceptions that we have of him or them; but from some Observations we have made of his Works, and from the Consideration of those Qualifications, that we conceive would enable us to perform the like. Thus observing great Order, Conveniency, and Harmony in all the several Parts of the World, and perceiving that every thing is adapted and tends to the Preservation and Advantage of the Whole; we are apt to consider, that we could not contrive and settle things in so excellent a

---

[16] Collins' *official* position in this tract is a Locke-inspired form of deism. However, there is some question about Collins' sincerity. Berkeley alleged that Collins' real intention throughout his officially deistic writings was to insinuate atheism, and David Berman has argued that Berkeley was likely correct about this. See Berman (1990, ch. 3). However, some other scholars have been skeptical. See, e.g., Hudson (2009, pp. 101–102); Waligore (2012, pp. 183–84).

manner without great Wisdom: and thence conclude, that God who has thus concerted and settled Matters, must have Wisdom; and having then ascrib'd to him Wisdom, because we see the effects and result of it in his Works, we proceed and conclude, that he has likewise *Foresight* and Understanding, because we cannot conceive Wisdom without these, and because if we were to do what we see he has done, we could not expect to perform it, without the exercise of these Faculties.

And it doth truly follow from hence, that God must either have these, or other Faculties and Powers equivalent to them, and adequate to these mighty Effects which proceed from them. And because we do not know what his Faculties are in themselves, we give them the Names of those Powers, that we find would be necessary to us in order to produce such effects, and call them Wisdom, Understanding, and Fore-knowledge…Thus our Reason teaches us to ascribe these Attributes to God, by way of Resemblance and Analogy to such Qualitys or Powers as we find most valuable and perfect in our selves (King, 1709, §4).

Both Browne and King hold that we attribute power and wisdom to God because these attributes are necessary for the production of the effects God has in fact produced. Our concepts of power and wisdom are derived from the finite power and wisdom of creatures. We know that the power and wisdom of God are utterly different in kind from these, but we apply these concepts because power and wisdom are the attributes that would be needed in order for creatures to produce similar effects. There is no direct comparison between human attributes and divine attributes. Since we do not know what God is like in Godself, no such comparison is possible for us. The comparison is rather between the 'Order, Conveniency, and Harmony' finitely wise and powerful humans may bring about in some limited domain and the 'Order, Conveniency, and Harmony' God has brought about in the universe as a whole. In this way, God is named from God's effects.

King and Browne do not specify their sources for this view, but the analysis differs markedly from that of Aquinas (*Summa Theologica*, Iq13) and bears a striking resemblance to Maimonides. Further, many Christian philosophers in this period, including Browne, had at least some familiarity with Maimonides.[17] According to

---

[17] See, e.g., Bayle (1696, pp. 134–39); Leibniz (1710, §§262–3); Browne (1733, pp. 136–8). Browne's mention of Maimonides is in his summary of the remarks on the divine attributes in Wollaston (1731, pp. 101, 114–20). Wollaston frequently quotes Maimonides in Hebrew.

Kenneth L. Pearce

Maimonides, the only positive attributes that can be applied to God are those derived from action (Maimonides, *Guide*, p. 71). Maimonides explains:

> Whenever we apprehend one of God's actions, we apply to God the attribute from which this action proceeds, i.e. call Him by a name derived from that action. For instance, we apprehend the tenderness with which He provides for the formation of the embryos of animals...Such action on our part would presuppose affection and tender feeling. That is what we mean by mercy, and we therefore use of God the term Merciful...Of course God is not experiencing the feelings of affection or tenderness but such actions as a father will do for his child through pure love, compassion, and affection do emanate from God with regard to His favourites, though they are not caused by affection or change...In the same manner all Divine acts are actions that resemble human actions in springing from certain affections and psychological states, but with God they do not spring from anything that is in any way superadded to His essence. (Maimonides, *Guide*, pp. 74–75)

According to Maimonides, we describe God accurately when we denominate God from God's actions in this way. The words we use are taken from human attributes that produce resembling actions, although these attributes bear no resemblance to anything in God. Maimonides in fact goes farther: he endorses a very strong form of the doctrine of divine simplicity and therefore holds that there is nothing in God corresponding to any of these attributes because there is nothing 'in' God at all: God is God, and there is really nothing more to be said about the divine essence than this.

King seems not to go as far as Maimonides on this last point, since he holds that 'it doth truly follow from hence, that God must either have these, or other Faculties and Powers equivalent to them, and adequate to these mighty Effects which proceed from them' (King, 1709, §4). Nevertheless, he agrees with Maimonides that the divine attributes are denominated from the resemblances of divine actions to human actions.

Browne's view appears to be similar, since he holds that our observation of the orderliness of the created world is involved, not just in our inference to the actual existence of God, but in the formation of our concept of God. Thus, the divine wisdom is that which produces the orderliness of the universe.

It is here that the comparison with functionalism may be helpful. Functionalism, in contemporary philosophy of mind, is often motivated by consideration of *multiple realizability*. To use a standard example, at the level of neurology there is little or nothing in common between the states of humans and those of octopus, yet both humans and octopus are capable of pain, hunger, etc. As David Lewis suggested, it even seems conceivable that a Martian with a hydraulic 'nervous system' (and, properly speaking, no nerves at all) could experience pain (Lewis, 1983, pp. 122–30). It might be thought that this implies that pain, hunger, and so forth are not physical or neurological states at all, since these states may be had in common by beings that have nothing in common physically or neurologically.

According to the functionalist, this is not so. Instead, mental states can be defined by their *causal profile*, their 'syndrome of most typical causes and effects' (Lewis, 1966, p. 17).[18] Lewis famously drew a comparison to bike locks: the unlocked state is the state in which the lock easily pulls apart, and the locked state is the state in which it doesn't. The internal physical implementation of the lock is no part of the definition of these states, and locks with no physical similarity can be in the same state. Yet these states are nothing over and above the physical (Lewis, 1966, pp. 17–18).

Although functionalism is typically seen as an effort to preserve some form of physicalism, some philosophers have thought that it is an advantage of functionalism that it allows for the possibility that the mind could be either physical or non-physical.[19] According to these philosophers, our mental state concepts do not settle this question and so we ought to be able to provide an analysis that is neutral with respect to it. Functionalism accomplishes this.

The similarity to Browne should be clear. In the first place, Browne's account is motivated by a kind of multiple realizability problem: knowledge can be attributed to beings whose intrinsic states have nothing in common, including beings who are purely material, beings who are both material and spiritual, and beings who are purely spiritual. Further, the term 'knowledge' for Browne appears to be defined in part by its characteristic effects. There is genuine similarity in the effects produced by knowledge in brutes, humans, angels, and God, although there is no genuine similarity in the intrinsic nature of these forms of knowledge themselves.

My interpretive suggestion is, therefore, as follows. 'Knowledge' for Browne refers to the functional role that, in humans, is played

[18] Although Lewis initially characterized his view as a version of psychophysical identity theory, it has subsequently been regarded as an early version of functionalism. See Levin (2018, §3.4). Lewis himself later described his view as 'functionalist' (Lewis, 1983, p. 124).

[19] See, e.g., Putnam (1975, pp. 292–95).

Kenneth L. Pearce

by thinking. This is the role of using information to produce intelligent, goal-directed action.

As Browne frequently emphasizes, thinking is a sequential (temporally extended) process that requires the cooperation of the immaterial spirit with the material brain in order to process the input from the senses and produce the relevant output. This kind of processing does not occur in either brutes or purely spiritual beings. Nevertheless, both brutes and purely spiritual beings engage in intelligent, goal-directed action on the basis of information about the world. Hence *something* must be playing the knowledge role.

In the case of brutes, this role is played by instinct, which is a purely physical/biological process that could in principle be analysed within an adequate account of animal physiology.

In pure spirits (angels and disembodied post-mortem humans), the knowledge role is played by some immaterial and non-sequential spiritual feature. In our embodied earthly state, we are unable to say anything positive about this feature except that it plays the knowledge role.

In God the knowledge role is played by an infinite, immaterial, non-sequential divine attribute, about which we will *never* be able to know anything other than that it plays the knowledge role. Nevertheless, we know *something* in God plays the knowledge role, since we know that creation is an intelligent, goal-directed activity. In this way, Browne develops a kind of proto-functionalist account of knowledge and other mental states that are attributed in common to humans and non-humans, especially God.[20]

There is a theological worry about Browne's view here. As mentioned above, King and Browne seem to depart from Maimonides in allowing that there really is something in God corresponding to these states, contrary to Maimonides' insistence on an extremely robust conception of divine simplicity that would reject any real distinction of states or attributes within God. Historically, in fact, divine simplicity was one of the main motivations for denying that qualities could be predicated univocally of creatures and God: when applied to a human judge, 'justice' and 'mercy' designate two different attributes (which often come into conflict), but as applied to God, both designate God's nature, i.e., Godself.[21] Hence, these predicates cannot be applied in the same way to God and creatures, and the same is true of all other predicates. As mentioned above, Browne seems to see himself as a kind of Thomist, and Aquinas likewise

---

[20] A functionalist analysis of divine mental states has recently been defended by Vandergriff (2018).

[21] See, e.g., Maimonides, *Guide*, 68–71.

strongly insists on divine simplicity, and sees it as a motivation for rejecting univocity (Aquinas, *Summa Theologica*, Iq3a6). However, a key component of functionalism (one of its key points of contrast with behaviorism) is that it posits causal interactions between different mental states as part of the causal profile defining those states. Furthermore, Browne constantly insists that analogy requires some real correspondence or proportion, and not a merely imaginary one. As a result, Browne's view appears to be inconsistent with the strong doctrine of divine simplicity, as understood by classical philosophical theologians such as Maimonides and Aquinas. This is an uncomfortable position for a staunch traditionalist who holds up Aquinas as his philosophical hero.

Browne does comment explicitly on the doctrine of divine simplicity at one point in his *Divine Analogy*, and what he says is surprising. Criticizing some remarks on the doctrine of analogy by John Sergeant,[22] Browne writes,

> He affirms with great positiveness *That Mercy, Justice, Power, Wisdom, &c. are not all distinguished in the divine Nature*. But how doth he know this? Because God is a *Simple* Being. But how doth he know what *Uncompoundedness* or *Simplicity* is in the divine Nature *It self*? All that he or any Man living can know of it, amounts to no more than a Negation only of all Composition discernible in the Creature: All that can be affirmed of God's Attributes in this Respect is, that there is no Distinction between them which is conceivable, as it is in it self, to the Mind of Man; and that if they are actualy distinct in him, it cannot be after the *Same Manner* they are distinct in the Soul of Man. But however they are, or are not realy distinct in him; we are under a necessity of conceiving them distinguished after the same Manner we find them in our selves; for otherwise we could neither think nor speak of God at all. God hath made a Distinction between his own Attributes thro' all the Language of Revelation; and I think it becomes *Divines* to adhere to those Distinctions, and to leave his unintelligible Notion of divine Simplicity to the *Metaphysicians*. (Browne, 1733, pp. 160–61)

Browne stops short of actually rejecting the doctrine of simplicity, but his remarks here amount, essentially, to a defense of his practice of completely ignoring that doctrine. If I am correct that Browne sees the real correspondence needed to distinguish analogy from metaphor

[22] The long passage quoted (without citation, as usual) by Browne (1733, pp. 157–58) is from Sergeant (1700, pp. 365–68).

as (at least in this case) a functional correspondence, and if I am further correct that Browne sees divine simplicity as potentially threatening this correspondence, this would make sense of his discomfort with the simplicity doctrine. Furthermore, it would make sense of why Browne feels the need to criticize that doctrine in his discussion of Sergeant: Browne has just been criticizing Sergeant for failing to distinguish adequately between metaphor and analogy (Browne, 1733, p. 159). For Browne, I suggest, Sergeant's version of the doctrine of divine simplicity is at least partly responsible for that failure.

Browne is committed, at a minimum, to the claim that we cannot conceive how the kind of real correspondence required for analogy could obtain without a real plurality of divine attributes. Insofar as we are extremely limited in our ability to understand God, this might not precisely rule out the strong classical doctrine of divine simplicity, but it does mean that human thought about God necessarily treats that doctrine as false.

4. Conclusion

Analogy is the central theme running through all of Browne's writings. Although this doctrine is, for Browne, primarily of importance for its role in making possible human thought and speech about God, it is a general-purpose cognitive mechanism that is used throughout human thought and speech, including in our thought and speech about human and animal minds. This mechanism works by the substitution of some sensory idea to stand for something that is of a completely different kind from the object of the sensory idea, but nevertheless has a real correspondence to it.

I have argued that, at least in the case of the concept *knowledge*, this 'correspondence' should be understood as functional. Like functionalists in analytic philosophy of mind, Browne is motivated in large part by multiple realizability concerns: there is a state that we want to attribute in common to things that have no intrinsic similarity. Also like functionalists, Browne solves this problem by emphasizing what the states *do*, their 'syndrome of most typical causes and effects' (Lewis, 1966, p. 17).

Despite his rejection of Locke's ideas of reflection, Browne does think that we have more direct insight into the particular nature of human mental states than functionalists typically allow. Further, Browne thinks that this insight shows that the human mind functions by the cooperation of a material substance with an immaterial substance. He is therefore a substance dualist in his conception of the human person – a view contemporary functionalism was specifically designed to avoid. My conclusion, then, is that Browne developed what can aptly be described as a functionalist metaphysics of knowledge and other mental states shared by humans and non-humans. However, he should not be understood as endorsing a functionalist metaphysics of the human mind.[23]

Trinity College Dublin
pearcek@tcd.ie

References

Thomas Aquinas, *The Summa Theologica of St. Thomas Aquinas*, trans. Fathers of the English Dominican Province, 2nd ed. (London: Burns Oates & Washbourne, 1920).

Pierre Bayle, *Historical-Critical Dictionary. Selections*, trans. Richard H. Popkin (1696; repr., Indianapolis; Cambridge: Hackett, 1991).

George Berkeley, *Three Dialogues Between Hylas and Philonous* (1713), in *Philosophical Writings*, ed. Desmond M. Clarke, Cambridge Texts in the History of Philosophy (Cambridge: Cambridge University Press, 2008). Cited by marginal numbers.

David Berman, *A History of Atheism in Britain: From Hobbes to Russell* (London: Routledge, 1990).

David Berman, *Berkeley and Irish Philosophy*, Continuum Studies in British Philosophy (London; New York: Continuum, 2005).

Talia Mae Bettcher, *Berkeley's Philosophy of Spirit: Consciousness, Ontology, and the Elusive Subject* (London: Continuum, 2007).

Peter Browne, *A Letter in Answer to a Book Entitled Christianity Not Mysterious* (Dublin: John North, 1697).

Peter Browne, *The Procedure, Extent, and Limits of Human Understanding*, 2nd ed. (London: William Innys, 1729).

Peter Browne, *Things Divine and Supernatural Conceived by Analogy with Things Natural and Human* (London: William Innys; Richard Manby, 1733).

Anthony Collins, *A Vindication of the Divine Attributes: In Some Remarks on His Grace the Archbishop of Dublin's Sermon, Intituled, Divine Predestination and Foreknowledge Consistent with the Freedom of Man's Will* (London: A. Baldwin, 1710).

[23] Many thanks to all of the participants in the IPAB conference for very helpful and enlightening discussions, and special thanks to Manuel Fasko, Takaharu Oda, and Samuel Rickless for helpful comments on a previous draft of this chapter.

Kenneth L. Pearce

John Edwards, *The Divine Perfections Vindicated: Or, Some Brief Remarks on His Grace William Lord Archbishop of Dublin's Sermon* (London: Jonathan Robinson, John Lawrence, and John Wyat, 1710).

Wayne Hudson, *The English Deists*, The Enlightenment World 7 (London: Pickering & Chatto, 2009).

William King, *Divine Predestination and Fore-Knowledg, Consistent with the Freedom of Man's Will* (Dublin; London: J. Baker, 1709).

G. W. Leibniz, *Theodicy: Essays on the Goodness of God, the Freedom of Man, and the Origin of Evil*, ed. Austin Farrer, trans. E. M. Huggard (1710; repr., La Salle, Ill.: Open Court, 1985).

G. W. Leibniz, *New Essays on Human Understanding*, ed. and trans. Peter Remnant and Jonathan Bennett, Cambridge Texts in the History of Philosophy (1704; Cambridge: Cambridge University Press, 1996)

Janet Levin, 'Functionalism,' in *The Stanford Encyclopedia of Philosophy*, ed. Edward N. Zalta, Fall 2018 (Stanford: Metaphysics Research Lab, Stanford University, 2018), https:// plato.stanford.edu/archives/fall2018/entries/functionalism/.

David Lewis, 'An Argument for the Identity Theory,' *Journal of Philosophy* 63, (1966), 17–25.

David Lewis, 'Mad Pain and Martian Pain,' in *Philosophical Papers*, vol. 1 (Oxford; New York: Oxford University Press, 1983), 122–30.

John Locke, *An Essay Concerning Human Understanding*, ed. Peter H. Nidditch (1690; Oxford: Oxford University Press, 1975).

Nicolas Malebranche, *The Search After Truth*, ed. and trans. Thomas M. Lennon and Paul J. Olscamp, Cambridge Texts in the History of Philosophy (1674–1675; Cambridge: Cambridge University Press, 1997).

Moses Maimonides, *The Guide of the Perplexed*. Abridged, ed. Julius Guttman, trans. Chaim Rabin (Indianapolis: Hackett, 1995).

Kenneth L. Pearce, *Language and the Structure of Berkeley's World* (Oxford: Oxford University Press, 2017).

Kenneth L. Pearce, 'Matter, God, and Nonsense: Berkeley's Polemic Against the Freethinkers in the *Three Dialogues*,' in *Berkeley's Three Dialogues: New Essays*, ed. Stefan Storrie (Oxford: Oxford University Press, 2018), 176–90.

Kenneth L. Pearce, 'Locke, Arnauld, and Abstract Ideas,' *British Journal for the History of Philosophy* 27, (2019), 75–94.

Hilary Putnam, 'Philosophy and Our Mental Life,' in *Mind, Language, and Reality: Philosophical Papers, Volume 2* (Cambridge: Cambridge University Press, 1975), 291–303.

John Russell Roberts, *A Metaphysics for the Mob: The Philosophy of George Berkeley* (Oxford: Oxford University Press, 2007).

John Sergeant, *Transnatural Philosophy, or Metaphysics: Demonstrating the Essences and Operations of All Beings Whatever, Which Gives the Principles to All Other Sciences* (London: John Sergeant, 1700).

I. C. Tipton, *Berkeley: The Philosophy of Immaterialism* (London: Methuen & Co Ltd, 1974).

John Toland, *Christianity Not Mysterious: Or, a Treatise Shewing, That There Is Nothing in the Gospel Contrary to Reason, nor Above It: And That No Christian Doctrine Can Be Properly Call'd a Mystery*, 2nd ed. (London: Sam. Buckley, 1696).

Kevin Vandergriff, 'Naturalism, Theism, and Multiply Realizable Mental States,' *Religious Studies* 54, no. 1 (2018): 91–105.

Joseph Waligore, 'The Piety of the English Deists: Their Personal Relationship with an Active God,' *Intellectual History Review* 22, (2012), 181–97.

Timothy Williamson, *Knowledge and Its Limits* (New York: Oxford University Press, 2000).

Kenneth P. Winkler, *Berkeley: An Interpretation* (Oxford: Clarendon Press, 1989).

Arthur Robert Winnett, *Peter Browne: Provost, Bishop, Metaphysician* (London: SPCK, 1974).

William Wollaston, *The Religion of Nature Delineated*, 5th ed. (London: James and John Knapton, 1731).

Gideon Yaffe, 'Locke on Ideas of Substance and the Veil of Perception,' *Pacific Philosophical Quarterly* 85, (2004), 255–72.

John Austin SJ (1717–84), The First Irish Catholic Cartesian?

JACOB SCHMUTZ

Abstract

Early-Modern Irish Catholics exiled on the European continent are known to have often held prominent academic positions in various important colleges and universities. This paper investigates the hitherto unknown Scholastic legacy of the Dublin-born Jesuit John Austin (1717–84), a famous Irish educator who started his career teaching philosophy at the Jesuit college of Rheims in 1746–47, before returning to the country of his birth as part of the Irish Mission. These manuscript lecture notes provides us first-hand knowledge about the content of French Jesuit education in the middle of the eighteenth century, which does not correspond to its classical reputation of 'Aristotelian' scholasticism opposed to philosophical novelties. While stitching to a traditional way of teaching, Austin introduces positively elements from Descartes, Malebranche, Locke and Newton into the curriculum. The present paper focuses on his conception of philosophical certitude (*certitudo*), which he considered a necessary condition for the possibility of philosophical knowledge.

The history of early-modern Irish philosophy is divided into two almost hermetic temporalities: on one side, we have the Anglo-Irish Protestant tradition, with its hallmark institution Trinity College; on the other side, we have the exiled Catholic Irish tradition, represented by secular clergymen as well as members of regular orders such as Franciscans, Dominicans and Jesuits, mainly active in the vast network of Irish colleges on the continent due to the penal laws restricting Catholic education on Irish soil. Both traditions had one thing in common: a strong and peculiar linkage to France, in particular during the eighteenth century. For the Protestant tradition, it was due both to the English reception of the philosophies of Descartes, Malebranche and Port-Royal, and to the particular input of numerous French Calvinist exiles who settled in Dublin after the revocation of the Edict of Nantes (1685). For the Catholic tradition, it was a somewhat later phenomenon: whereas the first generation of Catholic exiles where mainly linked to Spain and the Habsburg territories of Central Europe, France became the central port of call for eighteenth-century Irish Catholic intellectuals[1].

[1]   A point well established in Whelan (2009, pp. 304–320).

doi:10.1017/S1358246120000168   © The Royal Institute of Philosophy and the contributors 2020

Royal Institute of Philosophy Supplement **88** 2020   239

Jacob Schmutz

For the history of philosophy, this French predicament raises a paradox: it has long been admitted that unlike its Protestant counterparts, open to philosophical novelties of the age – empiricism and experimental philosophy, Cartesian idealism and Malebranchian spiritualism –, the Catholic Irish tradition remained firmly attached to medieval Scholastic traditions and their Aristotelian conceptualism[2]. And whereas most Anglo-Irish scholars from Trinity knew their Aquinas and did not neglect reading some Jesuit courses – Peter Browne for instance discusses sometimes Suárez at length – the Catholic tradition was reputed impervious to anything published in Protestant circles. In this paper, I will argue that such a stark contrast does not apply to the eighteenth century, often presented unilaterally as the 'Golden Age of Anglo-Irish intellectual history'[3]. A number of Irish Catholic scholars active on the continent were increasingly exposed to the 'new philosophies', and integrated Cartesian and Lockean insights into their apparently old-fashioned courses of philosophy. Some of them even managed to return to Ireland, with the progressive loosening of the anti-Catholic restrictions on educational activity.

Although scholarship on the philosophy of early-modern exiled Irish Catholics has made considerable progress, very little, if not nothing, is known about the *return* of this philosophical tradition to Ireland itself. At that time, Catholic education on the Irish soil was restricted to grammar schools for young boys, and almost nothing is known about the intellectual identity of the promoters of these schools. Most of them, however, had received a solid philosophical and theological education on the continent. This was the case of the Dublin-born Jesuit John Austin (1717–84), who will be the focus of this paper. While Austin's educational action is well documented and

---

[2]   We do not have any global history of the *content* of the philosophy and theology of Irish Catholic churchmen on the continent, which is largely due to the fact that they were divided into competing traditions (Jesuits, Franciscans, Dominicans, seculars). But we do have a great number of quality monographs on prominent individual figures such as Luke Wadding, Michael Moore, Luke Joseph Hooke and others. For the institutional aspects, social network and the intellectual role of the Irish colleges, see the seminal Corcoran (1916), still relevant to understanding the penal laws affecting the Catholics, and the classical work of Corish (1985). For a general overview of this diasporic Scholastic tradition, see Robinson-Hammerstein (1971); O'Connor (ed.) (2001); O'Connor and Lyons (eds.) (2006); O'Connor (2009).

[3]   An expression used by Berman (2004, part II, pp. 77–174, part II), reprinting studies dating back to the 1980s; Duddy (2004, p. xiii).

John Austin SJ (1717–84), The First Irish Catholic Cartesian?

acknowledged in most histories of Irish education, we actually do not know anything about the type of philosophy that stands behind his educational enterprise. In this paper, I will attempt to reconstruct Austin's conception of philosophy as 'knowledge of all things accessible to natural light', as it can be found in a hitherto unknown manuscript I recently discovered and identified in a French provincial library.

1. John Austin's Career

John Austin was born in Dublin in 1717, and he received his first education in one of the grammar schools opened by the Jesuits in the northern edges of the city[4]. Like many other Catholic boys, he had to leave Ireland to pursue higher education: at the time, France with its efficient network of Irish Colleges present in major university towns seemed a prime destination[5]. Austin's first port of call was Nancy, where he entered the Society of Jesus in 1735, at the age of eighteen. He is only one of an important community of Irish Jesuits active in the French Jesuit Provinces (the country was then divided into four Provinces, Champagne, France, Aquitania and Lyons), which produced a number of famous figures, such as Bernard Routh SJ (1695–1768), often rumored to have converted Montesquieu on his death bed, as well as a number of other returnees linked to Austin and the development of private schools in Ireland, such as Thomas Betagh SJ (1737–1811, trained in Pont-à-Mousson like Austin) and James Philip Mulcaile SJ (1727–1801, trained in Paris). The emergence of France is itself a noteworthy fact of a shift in intellectual influence: it stands in contrast with the past century, when Irish Jesuits were mainly attracted to places like Salamanca, Santiago de Compostela, Seville, Lisbon, Coimbra, Louvain and Antwerp, almost all Habsburg territories. It will also explain the strong French influence in the emergence of Catholic higher education in Ireland, and it will explain why Austin would show a particular interest in discussing Descartes, Malebranche and others. After his novitiate, he followed a very classical career path

---

[4]   The classical biographical study on John Austin is O'Rahilly (1939), to be complemented by Finegan (1970); O'Neill SJ and Dominguez (ed.) (2001, vol. 1, pp. 271–72). He does not, strangely, have any entry in the *Bibliothèque de la Compagnie de Jésus* by Carlos Sommervogel, nor in Webb (1878).

[5]   The history of Irish Catholic colleges in France is well documented: see Swords (ed.) (1978); Chambers, in O'Connor (2001, pp. 157–74).

Jacob Schmutz

for a Jesuit of his time: he enrols as student of philosophy at the Jesuit University of Pont-à-Mousson (1735–37), and then becomes a professor, first of humanities, then of philosophy, at the College of Rheims[6]. He must then have enrolled for his theological education: first in Rheims for two years (1745–47) – after which he is ordained priest on 22 September 1747 –, and then in Poitiers (1747–49), probably on the instances of Thomas Hennessy SJ, the Superior of the Irish Mission from 1729 to 1750. Poitiers was at the centre of a region which counted a great number of recent Irish immigrants and refugees, but also numerous long-established families with links to the Bordeaux and Cognac wine business[7]. The Irish College of Poitiers was then an important 'hub' for the Irish Jesuits prepared to be sent back to the country as part of the Mission, as Austin himself documents it in his correspondence[8]. There he finished apparently his theological education and ended his French sojourn as Prefect of discipline at the Irish College. In 1750, at the age of 33, he returns to Ireland, as assistant to the parish priest John Murphy at Saint Michael & John in Dublin. It is on Irish soil that he pronounces in 1753 his fourth vow (of 'special obedience' to the pope regarding the Jesuit mission), the ultimate Jesuit oath after the classical vows of poverty, chastity and obedience. Austin starts his educational mission in Dublin, opening a private school at Saul's Court in 1760 which would soon attract a great number of talented and prominent students – dramatist John O'Keeffe (1747–1833) was for instance one of them[9]. Like all Jesuits, his

[6] According to Francis Finegan SJ, he taught philosophy from 1739 to 1744, but O'Rahilly's older study argues that he also repeated philosophy in 1744–45. The date of the manuscript suggests that he still taught this subject in 1746–47, while embarking on his theological studies, which was a very common practice. On the history and culture of the College of Rheims, see Dubois SJ (1956).

[7] The Irish college of Poitiers was one of last Irish colleges opened in France. It was established 1674 by Ignace Browne SJ – only Nantes would follow in 1689. On the history of the College, see Finegan SJ (1954); Delattre SJ (1956). More generally on the Irish presence in Poitiers and their social impact in the region, see the well-documented study Jahan (2013).

[8] See his comments in a letter written from Rheims in 1742 (O'Rahilly, 1939, p. 191).

[9] On the Irish mission during Austin's life, see Fenning (1965); on its role in the development of Catholic education in Dublin, see O'Donnell SJ (1999); Begadon (2009). For a general overview of the history of the Irish Jesuits, see McRedmond (1991).

John Austin SJ (1717–84), The First Irish Catholic Cartesian?

action was strongly impacted by the suppression of the Society in 1773: the Irish Mission had basically always been supported by the network of Irish Jesuits active in France and Spain, and at the time of the suppression, it counted with only 19 members. Austin becomes a secular priest of the diocese of Dublin and finishes his life as reputed preacher. His life-long companion Thomas Betagh becomes vicar general of the archdiocese of Dublin. John Austin dies about ten years after the suppression of the Society, in 1784, and he is buried at St. Kevin's Church in Dublin.

2. Austin's Manuscript in the Context of Irish Diasporic Scholasticism

John Austin's scholastic legacy is a long in-4° manuscript of 319 pages, corresponding to the first part of a course of philosophy taught in 1746–47[10]. It is a typical example of classroom notes, taken down by an anonymous student, clearly dated but unfortunately without any explicit reference to any place of transcription. It very probably corresponds to his last year at the College of Rheims.

Although we know a lot about Irish diasporic *students* in France, thanks to the work of historians such as Laurence Brockliss and Patrick Ferté[11], we still know almost nothing about diasporic *professors*, with the exception of the few figures who managed to get their works printed – such as Michael Moore (†1721)[12] and Luke Joseph Hooke (†1796), who held one of the most prestigious Parisian

---

[10]   J. Au[s]tin, *Philosophiae pars prima. Logica* (no place, 1746–1747), Vire, Bibliothèque Municipale (now Médiathèque de Vire-Normandie), Ms. 36, 319 I wish to thank Mrs Élodie Loup for facilitating my access to the manuscript collections. Hereafter the manuscript will be abbreviated *PPP*.

The classical catalogue of Vire Public Libray by Fédérique (1889, p. 422) mentions it under the name 'Autin' and gives no further identification – the 's' seems indeed to have been added by a different hand. It belonged to the private collection of François-Michel Morin-Lavallée, a nineteenth-century local erudite and mayor of the town, who enriched the local library and had probably bought it elsewhere. This may explain its strange fate of ending up in this collection which has no specific relationship with Irish colleges. The subtitle says: *Tractatum hunc philosophicum accepi a venerando admodum Patre Au[s]tin Societatis Jesu anno Domini 1746 et 1747.*

[11]   See Brockliss and Ferté (1987, pp. 527–72; 2004); O'Connor (2006).

[12]   See the famous anti-Cartesian work by Moore (1692). On Moore and the Parisian context, see Chambers (2000; 2001) and Chambers, in O'Connor and Lyons (2006).

chairs of theology[13]. Our documentary legacy is much more extensive for other Irish exiled traditions, in particular for the Franciscans active in the colleges of Louvain, Prague and Rome[14]. For the specific case of France, all we have are a few notebooks of lectures clearly taken down by Irish students under various French professors[15], and only three or four philosophy manuscript lecture notes effectively taught by Irish professors in France[16].

This documentary scarcity has a strong influence on our perception of the 'enlightened' or 'counter-enlightened' character of Irish Catholic philosophy: as both Éamon Ó Ciosáin and Liam Chambers have recalled, Irish professors in Paris were often associated with the Aristotelian reaction of Parisian college professors against Cartesian novelties[17]. Abstruse scholastic logical distinctions and formalities were even dubbed 'gibier d'Hybernois' ('game for the Irish')[18]. But a close scrutiny of newly discovered eighteenth century courses such as Austin's might well offer a different picture: the Irish professors actually closely followed the path of a typical post-Cartesian scholasticism, that had become mainstream not only in the secular *collèges de plein-exercice* of the University of Paris, but also in the French provinces of the Society of Jesus. From that point of view, Austin's manuscript is not just precious to understand the history of Irish Catholic philosophy, but also French Jesuit philosophy in general: whereas the French Provinces had arranged for the printing of a handful of courses of philosophy during the second half of the seventeenth century, only one complete course was ever printed during the entire eighteenth century, that of Gaspar Buhon

[13]   On Hooke, see O'Connor (1995; 2014, pp. 420–38).

[14]   See the classical study by Millet OFM (1964); Bhreathnach, MacMahon and McCafferty (eds.) (2009); for Prague in particular, see Kuchařová and Pařez (2015).

[15]   A few of them are mentioned by Chambers (2009, pp. 217–18).

[16]   Other complete lecture notes of philosophy taught in France, so far unnoticed by bibliographers, include: O'Keefe SJ, *Physica particularis* (College of Rennes, 1751), cop. Jacques Foucault de la Morinière, Rouen CNDP, Ms. 2006–3205, 279 p.; James McDonogh, *Quarta pars philosophiae seu physica specialis* (Plessis-Sorbonne College, Paris, 1771), cop. James Phelan, Maynooth, Russell Library, Ms. s.n., 411 p.; to be complemented with *Prima pars logicae, de idea seu perceptione* (Plessis-Sorbonne College, Paris, 1755–56), Saintes BM, Ms. 40, 440–652, and probably the anonymous *Prima philosophiae secunda, seu metaphysica* (1756), Saintes BM, Ms. 38, 723 p.

[17]   See Ó Ciosáin (1999, pp. 141–46); Chambers (2009, p. 137).

[18]   See Daniel (1700, p. 130).

John Austin SJ (1717–84), The First Irish Catholic Cartesian?

SJ (†1726) from the Province of Lyons[19]. All the rest of Jesuit teaching is kept in the form of manuscript lecture notes similar to Austin's, and with the exception of François de Dainville's seminal work on natural philosophy, none of them has ever been studied[20]. In particular, we lack precise information about the content of philosophy education in the Province of Champagne – the closest clearly identifiable manuscript course from Pont-à-Mousson I could locate related to Austin's dates back to 1699[21].

3. Austin's Introduction to Philosophy

Philosophy courses in the French provinces of the Society of Jesus were at Austin's time limited to two years[22], and divided into four

[19]   Buhon (1723, 4 vols). On the relationship between printed and manuscript courses in the French Society of Jesus, see Schmutz (2007a), which is a tentative list of the most important printed French Jesuit courses of philosophy.

[20]   On the importance of these manuscript 'cahiers', see again Dainville SJ (1991).

[21]   The Jesuits of the Province of Champagne did not print any normative course of philosophy, and everything we know is kept in manuscript form. Among the few direct points of comparison with Austin's course, one could mention a logic course taught by Edmond Simonnet SJ in Pont-à-Mousson in 1699 (Metz BM, Ms. 1058 – not seen), as well as an anonymous *Cursus philosophicus* taught in Rheims 1713–14 (copied by A.-Fr. Terbarghorst, Gemeentearchief Maastricht, Ms. 264 – not seen), a printed thesis sheet from 1738 (*Theses ex universa philosophia*, def. N.-J. Lombard, Rheims, 1738; copy at the Newberry Library, Chicago, QB42.L5 1738) and a later course of logic taught by Ignatius Nickel SJ, *Principia philosophiae sive logica*, cop. Th.-B. de Pélichy (Ghent University Library, Ms. 367).

[22]   On Jesuit education in France, see the classical studies by Dainville SJ (1991) and for individual records of colleges, see Delattre, *Les établissements des jésuites en France*. For a recent global panorama, see Grendler (2018), featuring also a complete list of Jesuit schools in France. The immense literature on the *Ratio studiorum* and the birth of Jesuit philosophical education is rather useless to understand what was going on already after the 1620s in most provinces. The classical monographs on major institutions such as Clermont College in Paris or the Collège of La Flèche all contain important information on the curriculum, but most focus on the earlier decades. See de Rochemonteix (1889); Dupont-Ferrier (1921). On the pre-Enlightenment context, see Northeast (1991). A thorough

parts: logic, ethics, metaphysics and physics[23]. Such an order departed from the classical Aristotelian-Alexandrian order, which was logic, physics, metaphysics and ethics and to which the Jesuits had long remained faithful. The presence of ethics in the philosophy course was a French peculiarity, since in many other countries, in particular in Spain and Italy, it was replaced by moral theology. The first three parts were usually finished in the first year (logic taking the biggest temporal share), while the second year was dedicated to a long physics course, which at the time integrated largely experimental physics after a general presentation of Aristotelian concepts such as matter, form, time and movement[24]. From Austin, only the first part, corresponding to logic, survives. The whole course was preceded by a long section of general prolegomena (about 100 pages long), under the title *Introductio ad philosophiam*, and this text will be the focus of the present study.

By adding such an *Introductio*, the French Jesuits, to which Austin belonged, mimicked a practice that had been developed in the secular colleges, in particular at the University of Paris, such as Harcourt, Grassins, Plessis, etc. where it was a common practice since the middle of the seventeenth century. Much has been written about the important influence of Jesuit scholasticism on general university education during the seventeenth century, but since the 1720s, at least in France, influence changed sides. The new Parisian *collège*-philosophy of the first decades of the eighteenth century became normative and influenced the way the Jesuits themselves – as well as other religious orders in France – had to present their philosophy. French Jesuit courses of the 1720–50s resemble much more those of secular Parisian professors such as Edmond Pourchot (1651–1734), Jean Du Hamel (often confused with the more

---

appreciation of eighteenth-century Jesuit philosophy and theology in France is still needed.

[23] We don't know how Austin precisely organized his course, since we have kept only the introduction and the first part dedicated to logic. But he indicates himself the following order in his chapter on the division of philosophy: logica, ethics, metaphysics and physics. Cf. (Austin, *PPP*, p. 101). This order had already been followed one decade earlier at the College of Rheims (1738) in the printed *Theses ex universa philosophia* defended by Lombard. On the quadripartite structure of seventeenth century French philosophy courses, see Ariew (2014, pp. 41–105).

[24] On the teaching of Physics among eighteenth-century French Jesuits, see Dainville (1991, pp. 355–91) and some good observations on the 1700 French context by Feingold (2003). For a summary very dependent upon Dainville, see Lécrivain (2016, pp. 486–505).

John Austin SJ (1717–84), The First Irish Catholic Cartesian?

famous Jean-Baptiste Du Hamel, 1624–1706), Guillaume Dagoumer (ca. 1660–1745) and Pierre Lemonnier (1676–1757)[25], than the vast *cursus philosophici* of some of the seventeenth century Jesuit heroes – such as Pedro Hurtado de Mendoza SJ (1578–1641), Francisco de Oviedo SJ (1602–51) or Rodrigo de Arriaga SJ (1592–1661), which were all often reprinted in France and widely read during earlier decades within and outside of the Society[26].

Austin's *Introductio* is organized according to three chapters addressing the nature (ch. 1, *De natura philosophiae*), the existence (ch. 2, *De existentia philosophiae*) and the division of philosophy (ch. 3, *De divisione philosophiae*), with a small appendix on the history and origins of philosophy (*De origine philosophiae*). Most of his contemporaries treated the same matter according to a typified list of questions, inherited both of the Latin medieval reception of Aristotle's *Posterior Analytics*[27] and of the Roman tradition of Cicero and Quintilian, two important references in the traditional education system of the early Society of Jesus and in the scholastic tradition in general. Austin, like most of his French predecessors, proves a bad Aristotelian by starting with the *quid sit* question[28]. He starts by proposing his own definition of philosophy, by making three claims:

> First thesis: philosophy, according to its name, is the love and the study of wisdom. (…). Second thesis: philosophy, according to reality, is the knowledge (*scientia*) of things that can be known by natural light. (…). Third thesis: all things that can be known by the natural light are the object of philosophy[29].

[25] Du Hamel (1678), with reprints; Pourchot (1695) with many reprints; Dagoumer (1703) a rare first edition, reprinted and largely modified in 1746; Du Hamel (1705); Lemonnier (1750), many reprints and with manuscript testimonies going back to the 1720s. On the general context of this post-Cartesian college philosophy, see Brockliss (1987), and more specifically on the role of Pourchot and others, see Brockliss (2006).On their integration of Cartesian elements, see Ariew (2014); for the 1730s, see Hanna (1988) (about Lemonnier, who taught Diderot in 1730–32 at Harcourt College).

[26] On the classical structure of scholastic courses, see Thorndike (1951); and a precious typology in Blum (1998, pp. 158–81). On the impact of these courses, see Schmutz (2020).

[27] See Aristotle, *Anal. Post.* II 1, 89b26-32.

[28] So did also J.-B. Du Hamel, G. Dagoumer and Lemonnier, for instance. J. Du Hamel and G. Buhon SJ started more classically with the *an sit* question.

[29] Austin (*PPP*, pp. 14–15): 'Praenotiones (…) Thesis prima: philosophia secundum nomen considerata [15] est amor studiorumque sapientiae. (…).

Jacob Schmutz

There seems to be nothing really original about this definition, but two points are nevertheless noteworthy: first, Austin follows the medieval tradition in clearly calling philosophy a *scientia* (the Latin scholastic rendering of Aristotle's *episteme*), and thus as the highest possible type of assent, as opposed to mere opinion; second, Austin insists on the fact that philosophy is based on natural light alone. During the late seventeenth century, French academic culture had been rocked by several acts of censorship, the Faculty of Theology reminding the Arts colleges that they should not dispute objects relating to theology. By insisting on philosophy as based on natural light, Austin recalls that what discriminates objects of theology from objects of philosophy is not their intrinsic nature, but the type of habit that allows them to be known: reason (or natural light), and not faith. French Scholastics thus clearly thought that God as the supreme spiritual being and the human soul were proper objects of *philosophy*, since they were accessible to natural reason, and could therefore be studied as part of the metaphysics section of the philosophy course. Metaphysics then usually contained a general section called 'ontology' (*ontologia*), and a special section called 'pneumatology' (*pneumatologia*), dedicated to spiritual being only, which included God and the human soul[30]. We do not, unfortunately, have kept a trace of Austin's lectures on this part of philosophy, but what he says about consciousness in his prolegomena is quite consistent with the common usage of the time.

Austin reminds us of the integration of immaterial beings into the scope of philosophy in his chapter on the division of philosophy, which answers the classical *quotuplex* question. According to its objects, says Austin, philosophy is divided into one part dealing with 'immaterial objects', and another one with 'material things'[31]. Austin does not dedicate a complete chapter on the 'causes' of philosophy, but he reproduces some elements of this classical topic in his appendix on the 'origins of philosophy'. According to a very Augustinian narrative of gift and fall, God was usually seen as the

---

Thesis secunda: philosophia secundum rem considerata est scientia rerum naturali lumine cognoscibilium'; (*Ibid.*, p. 31): 'Thesis [tertia]: res omnes naturali lumine cognoscibiles sunt obiectum philosophiae.'

[30] See for instance the division proposed by Dagoumer (1757, p. 8): 'Metaphysica ratione sui obiecti alia est generalis, quae Ontologia dicitur; alia specialis,quae vocatur Pneumatologia'.

[31] Austin (*PPP*, p. 100) ('De divisione philosophiae'): 'Philosophia (...) dividitur in duas partes, quarum altera tractat de obiectis immaterialibus, altera de rebus materialibus'.

John Austin SJ (1717–84), The First Irish Catholic Cartesian?

first efficient cause of philosophy, since he had impressed perfect philosophical knowledge into Adam's mind[32]. But after original sin, the philosophers were needed to 'restore' or 'repair' philosophy. Austin therefore finishes his introduction with a very short history of philosophy under the title *On the Restorers of Philosophy*[33]. He mentions the six ancient philosophical sects: Thales, Pythagoras, the Academics including Plato and Socrates[34], the Epicureans, the Stoics and the Peripatetics. The medieval Peripatetics are then presented as being the three schools of the Thomists, Scotists and Nominalists. He concludes his catalogue with the Anti-Peripatetics, among which he singles out Descartes ('a man of sublime genius'[35]), Gassendi, Malebranche, and two 'famous Englishmen' Locke and Newton[36]. The only Jesuit author mentioned in his catalogue is the independently-minded Honoré Fabri SJ (1607–88), commonly ranked among the Anti-Peripatetics[37].

The most interesting and the longest part of Austin's introduction is his second chapter dedicated to the *existence* of philosophy. It answered the traditional question *an sit philosophia*, which was often treated as first by his contemporaries (in good medieval Aristotelian fashion, the *an sit* has to precede the *quid sit*)[38]. If philosophy is defined as the *scientia* of things that can be known by natural light, then such a knowledge must be *possible*. This section of the *an sit* was therefore the classical place where the early-modern French Scholastics would discuss the quality of the knowledge accessible to the human intellect: can it reach the level of absolute certitude required for *scientia*? If not, then philosophy in the strictest sense of

---

[32] Austin (*PPP*, p. 101): 'Contendunt vulgo philosophi Adamum habuisse philosophiam, eamque in primo creationis instanti infusam'. Cf. for instance also Du Hamel (1705, vol. I, p. 76); Pourchot (1700, p. 155): '.Deus Philosophiam perfectam infundit Adamo'; Pourchot (1695. Vol. 1, p. 30).

[33] (Austin, *PPP*, pp. 102–104) ('De philosophiae reparatoribus'). Pourchot considered the other philosophers as the 'secondary cause of philosophy'. Cf. Pourchot (1700, p. 159): 'Philosophi omnes dici possunt causa secunda Philosophiae'.

[34] Interestingly, both Plato and Socrates are considered as defendors of academic doubt: 'ambo docebant dubium de omnibus', says Austin (*PPP*, p. 103). Same in Nickel (*Principia philosophiae*, p. 111).

[35] Austin (*PPP*, p. 104): '... vir ingenio sublimi'.

[36] Austin (*PPP*, p. 104): '... celeberrimi Angli'.

[37] On Fabri as a renovator of scholasticism, see Boehm (1965, pp. 305–60); Roux (2005).

[38] See for instance Du Hamel (1705, vol. I, pp. 1–2).

Jacob Schmutz

the word is not possible. If yes, then one must refute those who argue that the human mind must doubt about everything or settle with probability. John Austin's presentation offers an interesting discussion of the Cartesian hyperbolic doubt at the light of traditional scholastic conceptions of degrees of certitude. As we shall see, this will lead him not so much to refute Descartes – as might be expected – but to integrate Cartesian insights into the classical scholastic framework.

4. Austin's Post-Cartesian Foundationalism

In most traditional Scholastic circles of the second part of the seventeenth century, Descartes's philosophy was perceived as a form of radical scepticism because of the argument of the hyperbolic doubt in the first *Meditation*[39]. This certainly stands in stark contrast with our common perception of Descartes today, where we tend to see him rather as a foundationalist or as a 'Conqueror of Scepticism', as Richard Popkin had labelled him in his seminal book on early-modern scepticism[40]. The argument that we must doubt of everything was also at the heart of two of the last condemnations of Cartesian doctrines: first, the royal anti-Cartesian formulary directed to the University of Paris (1691), prohibiting professors from teaching that one must 'doubt everything before being certain of any knowledge'[41]; and second the Jesuit condemnation of Cartesian propositions under General Michelangelo Tamburini (1706), of which the first one argues that 'the human mind can and must doubt

---

[39]   On the first scholastic reactions to Descartes' hyperbolic doubt, see Ariew (1999, pp. 188–205), revised in Ariew (2011, pp. 295–329); Ariew, in Feingold (2003, pp. 157–94). For the reception on Cartesian philosophy among French Jesuits, see also the seminal work, Sortais (1929).

[40]   See Popkin (2003, p. 143).

[41]   Among the 1691 Formulaire, see the following propositions, as translated by Ariew (2014, p. 204): '1. One must rid oneself of all kinds of prejudices and doubt everything before being certain of any knowledge. 2. One must doubt whether there is a God until one has a clear and distinct knowledge of it. 3. We do not know whether God did not create us such that we are always deceived in the very things that appear the clearest'. See also Schmaltz (2017, pp. 51–52) for the full text and context. On the history of Cartesian censorship, see Ariew (1994); Ariew (1999, pp. 155–71); Schmaltz (2002, part III; 2004); Roux (2019).

John Austin SJ (1717–84), The First Irish Catholic Cartesian?

everything except that it thinks and consequently that it exists'[42]. If we look closely at these two condemnations, the Jesuit version seems to be more restrictive than the Parisian formulation: whereas the Parisian Formulaire speaks of *universal* doubt before certitude, the Jesuit condemnation speaks of universal doubt *with one exception*, namely that we think and exist. This means that from the Jesuit perspective, even a position that excludes one's own thought and existence from universal doubt is not acceptable. If our own existence and thought were the only certain objects of natural knowledge, then we would need a divine guarantee or supernatural knowledge for all other objects. The Jesuits saw the absolute certitude of the *cogito* as collapsing into fideism, invalidating thereby all our natural knowledge coming from the senses or from human testimonies[43]. This is clearly the picture John Austin must have had of Descartes: he is not concerned with portraying him as an absolute sceptic, but rather as an 'epistemic idealist'[44] who gives a too strong criterion for knowledge, so strong that it eventually discredits the task of philosophy.

Austin proceeds in two steps. First, to ascertain the possibility of philosophy, he argues that if philosophy is a *scientia*, and since *scientia* entails, in good Aristotelian fashion, truth and certitude, then we must admit that at least some form of certitude is required in order to practice philosophy. Austin argues that at least two things can be considered as absolutely certain:

> There must exist some infallibly true knowledge (*existit aliqua cognitio infallibiliter vera*). Proof: a judgment in which nobody can be fooled (*falli*) is an infallibly true; and there exists some

---

[42] On the elaboration of the list of propositions, see Dainville (1991, p. 372). The text of the censored propositions is easily accessible in Rochemonteix (1889, vol 4, pp. 89–90) with a translation by Ariew (1995, p. 224): '1. The human mind can and must doubt everything except that it thinks and consequently that it exists. 2. Of the remainder, one can have certain and reasoned knowledge only after having known clearly and distinctly that God exists, that he is supremely good, infallible, and incapable of inducing our minds into error. 3. Before having knowledge of the existence of God, each person could and should always remain in doubt about whether the nature with which one has been created is not such that it is mistaken about the judgments that appear most certain and evident to it.'

[43] This is the sense of the fifth proposition in the Jesuit list: '5. Beyond divine faith, no one can be certain that bodies exist – not even one's own body'.

[44] I take this expression from Pasnau (2017, p. 22 in particular).

judgment in the natural order in which nobody can be fooled.
There are two such judgments: first, *I think*; second,
Nothingness has no properties. In those two judgments nobody
can be fooled[45].

The first example of certitude given by Austin is the Cartesian *ego
cogito*. The second is an example that has been regularly used since
the seventeenth century, *nihili nulla est proprietas* ('nothingness has
no properties'): this means that there cannot be thought – a property –
without a thinker, or a mode without a substance, and thus a property
without some existence that sustains it[46]. During Austin's time, both
axioms were clearly identified as properly Cartesian, even if most
Scholastics were aware of patristic and medieval forerunners, especially for the certitude of internal acts. The explicit juxtaposition of
both axioms had also been a commonplace, especially since
Malebranche, whose works enjoyed an even wider readership in scholastic circles than Descartes':

> Nothingness has no properties. I think. Therefore I am. But
> what am I, I who think, at the time when I think? Am I a
> body, a mind, a human being? As yet I know nothing of all
> this. I know only that, at the time I think, I am something that
> thinks (Malebranche, 1997, p. 6)[47].

---

[45]   Austin (*PPP*, p. 36): 'Thesis: existit aliqua cognitio infallibiliter vera.
Probatur: iudicium in quo nullatenus falli possimus est cognitio infallibiliter
vera, atqui existit iudicium aliquod naturalis ordinis in quo nullatenus falli
possumus. Sint ista duo iudicia, primum ego cogito; alterum nihili nulla est
proprietas, atque in his duobus iudiciis nullatenus falli possumus'. A decade
later in Rheims, Ignatius Nickel SJ discusses similar questions not in the
introduction (which he skips), but within the chapter on method, the
fourth operation of logic. See Nickel SJ, *Principia philosophiae sive logica*,
111 sq. ('Utrum detur aliqua cognitio certa?').

[46]   See Descartes (1985, p. 196): '... we should notice something very
well known by the natural light: nothingness possesses no attributes or qualities (*nihili nullas esse affectiones sive qualitates*), there is necessarily some
thing or substance to be found (*necessario inveniri*) for them to belong to'.
For Descartes' use of this axiom, see Gouher (1962, ch. 10).

[47]   For the French text, see *Entretiens sur la métaphysique*, in *Œuvres*,
vol. 12, p. 32: 'Le néant n'a point de propriétés. Je pense, donc je suis.
Mais qui suis-je, moi qui pense, dans le temps que je pense? Suis-je un
corps, un esprit, un homme? Je ne sais encore rien de tout cela. Je sais seule-
ment que, dans le temps que je pense, je suis quelque chose qui pense'. For a
commentary, see Alquié (1974, p. 64).

John Austin SJ (1717–84), The First Irish Catholic Cartesian?

Austin does not mention neither Descartes nor Malebranche by name, but we clearly have here an interesting testimony of the evolution of philosophical references within eighteenth century Jesuit scholasticism. It is striking that Austin does not here use the classical first principle the scholastics had always opposed to the *cogito*, namely the Aristotelian Principle of Non-Contradiction. According to one of its formulations, it uses the language of properties: 'It is impossible for the same thing to belong and not to belong at the same time to the same thing and in the same respect' (Aristotle, *Met.* IV 3, 1005b19-20). The medieval Aristotelian commentators have extracted this principle from its initial semantical context ('if you say A, you cannot mean –A') in order to make it the first and firmest principle of metaphysics: since a substance cannot, for instance, have two contradictory properties at the same time. During the entire seventeenth century, scholastic readers of Descartes had systematically opposed this objective Principle of Non-Contradiction to the subjective *cogito*[48]. To give an Irish Jesuit example, one may recall the testimony of Richard Arsdekin SJ (1620–93), professor in the Flemish-Belgian Province at the colleges of Louvain and Antwerp, who compiled a list of all the classical philosophical axioms taken for certain in his *Tractatus de idea scientifica*, which is a useful summary of seventeenth century scholastic epistemology. Among them, he recalls of course the Aristotelian Principle of Non-Contradiction, and the classical earlier Jesuit Renaissance commentators on it, of which he singles out Pedro da Fonseca SJ (1528–99), and adds: 'this is most evident for everybody, except Descartes (*quod cuivis evidentissimum est, praeter Cartesium*)' (Arsdekin SJ, 1687, p. 270)[49]. Austin belongs thus clearly to a different generation: he is not concerned with portraying Descartes as a sceptic negating Aristotelian principles. On the contrary, Austin clearly seems to *endorse* Cartesian and post-Cartesian principles as sources of infallible knowledge.

---

[48]   For a first presentation of this debate, see Schmutz (2007b).

[49]   For a classical Jesuit discussion of the Principle of Non-Contradiction as first principle of certitude, see for instance Suárez SJ (1597, pp. 81–4). For another pre-Cartesian Jesuit example, see Marcellius SJ (1635, p. 22): '*Quodlibet est vel non est. Est hoc primum principium affirmativum absolutum de esse rei, quo significatur naturalis et necessaria immediatio contradictorie oppositorum; talis nempe, ut impossibile sit, inter illa cadere aliquod medium.*' The Spanish Jesuit de Ulloa SJ (1748, p. 13), also attacks Descartes as a negator of the first principle, quoting Arsdekin.

Jacob Schmutz

In a second step of his discussion on the existence of philosophy, however, Austin formulates his own criticism of Cartesian method: if only such very abstract primary principles as those mentioned above could yield certitude, then the scope of philosophy as natural knowledge would be very limited. It is therefore necessary to investigate further what the conditions of certitude are, and Austin does so in a section entitled *De regulis veritatis,* 'on the rules of truth'. This Patristic expression had been revived by Descartes himself in the *Meditations*[50], in order to qualify his assumption that 'everything which I clearly and distinctly perceive is true'[51]. Austin's key argument is that the absolute or infallible type of certitude produced by the above-mentioned two axioms is the only possible type of certitude. Corporeal and social knowledge can also yield forms of natural certitude: they might be weaker than infallible certitude, but they can still be considered as certitude. This entails that we might well have *degrees* of certitude, rather than one absolute *a priori* certitude on one side and mere opinion or conjecture for the rest. Austin uses here a classical Scholastic distinction between three types of certitude:

> There are three types of certitude (*certitudo*)[52]: metaphysical, physical and moral. Metaphysical certitude is about what cannot be falsified in any possible way (*quod non potest subesse falsum*), not even by God. Physical certitude is about what cannot be rendered false, with the exception of God's [intervention]. Moral certitude is about what in the absolute could be rendered false, but that would only be the case if all honest men became liars[53].

[50] See Descartes (*Meditationes*, V, AT VIII, p. 70, 26) transl. John Cottingham, in: *Philosophical Writings*, vol. 2, 48: 'I was ignorant of this rule for establishing the truth'. The discussion of metaphysical principles under the title of *regula veritatis* quickly became common among Parisian post-Cartesian scholastics, such as in Besoigne (1714, f. 17v ff., in particular f. 21v): 'Evidentia prima est veritatis regula'.

[51] Descartes (*Meditationes*, III, AT VII, 35, 14–15, p. 23): 'So I now seem to be able to lay it down as a general rule (*pro regula generali*) that whatever I perceive clearly and distinctly is true (*illud omne esse verum, quod valde clare et distincte percipio*)'.

[52] I have consistently used the antiquated term of 'certitude', rather than 'certainty' with all its Wittgensteinian connotations, to render the Latin *certitudo*. For an excellent lexicographical synthesis of the emergence of the Latin scholastic meaning of *certitudo*, see Biard (2011).

[53] Austin (*PPP*, p. 57): 'Certitudo triplex, metaphysica, physica et moralis. Certitudo metaphysica ea est cui ne divinitus quidem falsum

254

John Austin SJ (1717–84), The First Irish Catholic Cartesian?

This tripartition is a late-medieval heritage: similar divisions could already be found in authors fourteenth- and fifteenth-century authors such as John Buridan, Peter of Ailly, Jean Gerson or John Mair, and it was a common staple of seventeenth century Jesuit philosophy courses[54]. The expression *quod subesse potest falsum* was common in medieval epistemology: the highest level of certitude, metaphysical certitude, cannot be about something false. Metaphysically certain propositions cannot be falsified by anybody, not even by God. This was the degree of certitude granted since the fourteenth century to the classical axioms of metaphysics, such as the Aristotelian Principle of Non-Contradiction[55]. Austin chooses to illustrate this level of absolute certitude by means of the Cartesian *cogito*. But this absolute type of certitude does not entail that all other forms of epistemic attitudes would simply be considered uncertain, and of no value for philosophy: Austin admits also the existence of 'physical certitude', which corresponds to the normal course of natural events, perceivable by our senses[56], and which only divine intervention could falsify[57]. The same reasoning applies for the third type of certitude, *moral certitude*, which

---

subesse potest; physica est ea cui falsum subesse non potest nisi ab ipso Deo; moralis est ea cui absolute falsum subesse potest, tamen subesse potest supponi nisi (...) omnes probi in mendacium conspirent».

[54] On the medieval distinction between different types of *certitudo*, see Zupko (2001); Biard (2012); Grellard (2015); Pasnau (2017, in particular the notes p. 174 ff). For a presentation of seventeenth century discussion of certitude, see numerous occurrences listed in Knebel (2000) *ad indicem*.

[55] The most radical case being Nicholas of Autrecourt, who considered the absolute condition of *non subesse falsum* as the only condition for science – thereby rejecting all other forms of knowledge into scepticism. See Autrecourt (1994, letter 2 p. 62): 'Excepta certitudine fidei, nulla est alia certitudo primi principii, vel que in primum principium potest resolve. Nam nulla est certitudo nisi illa cui non subest falsum...' On this theory, see Grellard (2005); Denery (2005, pp. 148–49). Reactions to Nicholas' position provoked a vivid debate about *degrees* of certitude.

[56] Cf. Austin (*PPP*, p. 76): 'Sensuum testimonium parit certitudinem physica circa existentiam corporum in particulari.'; Nickel SJ (*Principia philosophiae sive logica*, p. 132): 'Legitimum sensuum testimonium parit certitudinem physicam'.

[57] His definition here is very much in line with fourteenth-century definitions of *certitudo naturalis*. See for instance Buridan (2001), quoted by Zupko (2001, p. 175): '... another sort of human certainty (*certitudo humana*) on the part of the proposition is that of a true proposition which cannot be falsified by any natural power and by any manner of natural

corresponds to our everyday beliefs: the classical example was the love of mothers for their children – they 'almost' all do love their children. The origin of this type of certitude is human authority or more generally testimonial knowledge. Austin says it can be produced by the testimony (*testimonium*) of a small number of wise men, or of a great number of 'prudent and honest men'[58]. Such knowledge is certain, and could only be rendered false in the very unlikely hypothesis that all honest men become liars[59].

The distinction between these three types of certitude was a very common philosophical theme in seventeenth century Jesuit textbooks[60], as well as in French secular college philosophy. It was also rapidly imported into post-scholastic English-language philosophy during the seventeenth and eighteenth centuries, both among Protestant and Catholic authors[61]. Diderot, a former student of Pierre Lemonnier in the 1730s[62], reproduces them in the

---

operation, although it can be falsified by a supernatural power and in a miraculous way. And such certainty suffices for the natural sciences.'

[58] Austin (*PPP*, p. 89); Nickel SJ (*Principia philosophiae sive logica*, p. 139): 'Hominum testimonium parit certitudinem moralem'.

[59] On the emergence of the concept of *certitudo moralis* between Jean Gerson and early-modern scholasticism, see Schüssler (2019, pp. 49–50), with further references; on uses in seventeenth century moral theology, see also Knebel (2000, *ad indicem*).

[60] See for instance de Arriaga SJ (1639, p. 200); de Peñafiel SJ (1673, 55b); Mayr SJ (1745, vol. 1, p. 506). After Austin in Rheims, it is also used by Nickel SJ (*Principia philosophiae sive logica*, p. 120).

[61] See for instance the commonly accepted definitions in Chambers (1751, vol. I, s.v.): 'Further, the schools distinguish three other kinds of *certitude*, with regard to the three different kinds of evidence whence they arise. *Metaphysical* certitude, is that arising from a metaphysical evidence: such is that a geometrician has of the truth of this proposition, 'that three angles of a triangle are equal to two right ones'. *Physical* certitude, is that arising from physical evidence: such is that a man has that there is fire on his hand, when he sees it blaze, and feels it burn. *Moral* certitude, is that founded on moral evidence: such is that a person has, that he has got, or lost a cause, when his attorney and friends, send him express notice of it, or a copy of the judgment, etc.' See for instance the use of the same concept by Toland (1696, p. 17): 'humane authority, is call'd also moral certitude'.

[62] Cf. Lemonnier (1750, vol. I, p. 259): 'Certitudo (…) subdistribuitur in Metaphysicam, Physicam & Moralem. Metaphysica vocatur, quando motivum essentialem habet connexionem cum objecto cognito. Physica dicitur, quando, juxta leges ordinarias, infallibilem habet connexionem cum objecto cognito. Denique vocatur Moralis, quando connexionem

John Austin SJ (1717–84), The First Irish Catholic Cartesian?

Encyclopédie, and Austin's 1746 lectures were thus perfectly in the spirit of the time. But what remains relatively original is the way he understands the *motive* of metaphysical certitude. Austin identifies two distinct sources or motives capable of yielding metaphysical certitude. The first is evidence (*evidentia*), the second is 'consciousness' (*conscientia*), two sources that were again not commonly used in this context among earlier seventeenth century Scholastics, even within the Society.

Evidence, as the first source of metaphysical certitude, is defined by Austin as the natural 'relationship' certain ideas have with each other, and of which we have a *clear and distinct* perception[63]. Whereas medieval uses of the *certitudo* were both subjective and objective (one could speak of the *certitudo* of a thing)[64], early-modern Scholastics have tended to restrict *certitudo* to the subjective attitude of the mind which firmly adheres to a proposition without any possibility of doubt[65], as opposed to the objective 'motives' that yield this attitude. The property of a proposition provoking a certain 'clear and distinct' judgment was then called 'evidence' (*evidentia*), instead of certitude (Descartes' *regula veritatis*), and Austin says that such a clear and distinct perception 'forces the assent in an invincible way' (*invincibiliter rapiat assensum*)[66]. This distinction between objective

---

habet, ita probabilem, ut vir prudens ex illo motivo judicare possit.' See also Pourchot (1695, vol. 1, p. 25).

[63] Austin (*PPP*, p. 59): 'Thesis secunda: evidentia parit certitudinem metaphysicam'.

[64] A duality still present among many early-modern authors – Lemonnier for instance distinguished between the *certitudo ratione subjecti*, defined as the *imperturbabilitas* of the knowing subject, and the *certitudo ratione objecti*, which is the immutability of the object itself. A third type is the *certitudo motivi*, defined as the connexion between both. See Lemonnier (1750, vol. I, p. 259).

[65] See for instance Hurtado de Mendoza (1619, p. 200): 'Evidentia est claritas sive perspicuitas qua intellectus quasi videt obiecta, certitudo est firma determinatio adhaesioque intellectus ad verum ut verum est.'; Arriaga SJ (1639, p. 200): 'Adverto, certitudinem esse adhaesionem intellectus alicui veritati, sine formidine aut dubitatione an aliter se res habeat quam ab ipso cognoscitur.'

[66] Austin (*PPP*, p. 58): 'Thesis prima: datur evidentia. Explicatur: dari evidentiam nihil aliud est, quam dari claram et distinctam perceptionem habitudinis inter terminos'; (*Ibid.*, p. 59): 'Invincibiliter rapiat assensum. Ergo datur clara et distincta etc.' For a later discussion of this expression, see Gigot (1777, vol. 1, p. 183): 'Veteres definiebant evidentiam quemdam fulgorem qui mentem rapiebat: haec autem est vaga oratoris notio, non viri

Jacob Schmutz

evidence and subjective certitude was a typical Jesuit doctrine: and Austin is here clearly in line with the Scholastic tradition of the Society which defined evidence as certitude *plus* clarity and distinction stemming from its object. This leads Austin to distinguish further between objective and formal evidence, using a propositional language: the realm of evidence is constituted by sets of 'evident' propositions, where objective evidence will express the necessary relationship between the terms of the proposition, and formal evidence the act of judgment which is necessitated by this relationship:

> Evidence is either objective or formal. Objective evidence is the relationship (*habitudo*) of one term with the other; formal evidence is the clear and distinct perception of this relationship. Formal evidence comes either from a true or direct judgment, either from a rational or reflexive judgment. The first corresponds to the immediate perception of the relationship (*habitudo*) between two terms, for instance when I say 'human being is rational'; the second is the immediate perception of the relationship between two or more judgments, as for instance when I say 'I think therefore I am'[67]

Medieval Scholastic authors often referred to these 'evident' propositions as *per se nota*, 'known by themselves', i.e. propositions of which the knowledge of the definition of the term would immediately entail a true assent to the proposition itself – and the medieval example of an analytic proposition such as *homo est animal rationale* is still used by Austin to illustrate a 'true and direct judgment'. In a later paragraph, he also gives geometrical and mathematical axioms:

---

philosophantis. Evidentia, est perceptio convenientiae vel disconvenientiae idearum inter se'.

[67] Austin (*PPP*, pp. 57–58): 'Praenotiones. Prima: evidentia alia obiectiva alia formalis. Obiectiva est habitudo unius termini ad alterum, formalis est clara et distincta perceptio illius habitudinis. Secunda: evidentia formalis alia verii iudicii sive iudicii directi, alia iudicii ratiocinativi, sive iudicii reflexi. Prima est immediata perceptio habitudinis inter duo extrema ut cum dicitur homo est rationalis; secunda est immediata perceptio habitudinis inter duo aut plura iudicia ut cum dicitur ego cogito ergo existo.' The distinction between 'direct' and 'reflexive' evidence was already common in Parisian secular scholasticism around 1700–1710: see for instance Besoigne (1713, 19v): 'In evidentia potest distingui duplex sensus, sensus directus et sensus reflexus'; for a later testimony, see Gigot (1777, p. 51). The same applies for the distinction between objective and subjective evidence: see for instance Besoigne (1714, f. 21v).

258

John Austin SJ (1717–84), The First Irish Catholic Cartesian?

totum est maius sua parte, bis duo dant quatuor (Austin, *PPP*, p. 58), classical Scholastic examples of 'evident' propositions provoking metaphysical certitude, still used by many influential Jesuit logic courses of the previous century[68]. What is striking and somewhat original in Austin's presentation, is the unproblematic use he makes of a classical Cartesian proposition, or more exactly of a Cartesian inference (*cogito ergo sum*) in order to illustrate the formal evidence of a reflexive judgment. Obviously, he was certainly not the first to do so: secular college professors in Paris had already associated Aristotelian and Cartesian axioms in their definition of certitude since the 1670s[69], but it took time to be fully accepted by Jesuit authors to make the same use, and it does not appear in any of the classical printed courses that were used in France, only in manuscript notes.

Austin's post-Aristotelian endeavour is even more clearly illustrated in his presentation of the second source of metaphysical certitude, namely *conscientia*. Certitude is here not produced by a judgment of evident propositions, but by an 'interior sentiment (*sensus interior*) which testifies what happens within our soul and thereby signifies the existence of modifications of the soul.'[70] This definition of *conscientia* corresponds to what is rendered in English as 'consciousness', rather than 'conscience'. The complex process which led to use a term initially dedicated to speak of the practical

---

[68] See for instance Arriaga SJ (1639, p. 200): 'Denique certitudo *Metaphysica* est, qua ita proponitur obiectum, ut in ordine ad omnem potentiam non possit aliter esse, ut quam ego habeo de existentia Dei de illis principiis, *Quodlibet est vel non est, Quae sunt eadem uni tertio, sunt idem inter se*, & alii similibus, & de omnibus mysteriis revelatis a Deo, quae non possunt esse falsa etiam in ordine ad potentiam Dei absolutam.' Even the very pro-Cartesian Pourchot stitches to classical scholastic examples form metaphysical certitude, such as *totum est maius sua parte*. Cf. Pourchot (1695, vol. 1, p. 25).

[69] See for instance Besoigne (1714, f. 25r-25v) for a thorough discussion.

[70] Austin (*PPP*, p. 68): 'Conscientia est sensus interior qui nobis attestatur id quod intra animam nostram geritur et ita significat existentiam modificationum animae'. Compare with the definition in Pourchot (1695, vol. 1, p. 47): '... eam perceptionem, qua seipsam suaque cogitationes mens cognoscit, *conscientiam* appellari, quia suarum cogitationum, aut affectionum sibi conscia est, secumque quodammodo scit se cogitare, sive, se cogitantem intimo sensu aut sensione percipit.'; Gigot (1777, vol. 1, p. 176): 'Sensus intimus est illa affectio animae, quae anima intime sibi conscia est de praesenti suo statu. Dicitur etiam *Conscientia*'.

Jacob Schmutz

intuition of right and wrong (the Patristic *synderesis*) to label the internal acts of the mind has been well documented[71]. Austin's Latin is here clearly in line with this new understanding of *conscientia* as self-awareness, and its remote source is once more the Malebranchian definition of conscience, which had been a common staple of Jesuit learning since its integration into the *Dictionnaire de Trévoux* in 1704[72]. It is interesting to see Austin clearly differentiate consciousness from evidence as two *different* sources of metaphysical certitude, whereas earlier Scholastic secular authors simply associated them under the name evidence[73]. Within the Society of Jesus, enshrining the *sensus intimus* or *interior* as a source of metaphysical certitude had already a long history, even anterior to its popularization in the vernacular *Traité des premières vérités* (1724) by the Parisian Jesuit Claude Buffier SJ (1661–1737)[74] – who is not mentioned by Austin.

[71]   A distinction of meanings recalled by another Jesuit perhaps linked to Austin, who taught at the College of Poitiers in 1744: de Laquilhe SJ (f. 11r-v): 'Conscientia seu sensus intimus est animae perceptio qua anima cognoscit se ipsam, facultates, affectiones, propensiones, etc. ubi nota quod multum differat sensus intimus a conscientia de qua in morali, per quam anima sibi conscia est et iudicat quid rectum fit et honestum, quid malum et illicitum.' On the duality between, conscience and consciousness, see the still precious historical development that can be found in Hamilton (1846, vol. 2, pp. 940–45). Among more recent studies, see Glyn Davies (1990); Balibar (1998), for the English-French vocabulary of consciousness; Knebel (2014, pp. 348–54).

[72]   Cf. *Dictionnaire universel françois et latin, vulgairement appelé Dictionnaire de Trévoux* (Paris, 1721), vol. 2, 820: 'En métaphysique, on entend par la *conscience* ce que d'autres appellent *sens intime*, c'est-à-dire le sentiment intérieur qu'on a d'une chose dont on ne peut former d'idée claire & distincte. Dans ce sens, on dit que nous ne connoissons notre ame, & que nous ne sommes assurés de l'existence de nos pensées, que par la *conscience*; c'est-à-dire par le sentiment intérieur que nous en avons, & par ce que nous sentons ce qui se passe en nous-mêmes'. On the influence of this definition, initially formulated in the earlier dictionary by Furetière (1701), see the seminal work by Rodis-Lewis (1950, p. 112 ff), and Ferraro (2019, pp. 92–3).

[73]   See for instance the influential Parisian teacher Besoigne (1713, f. 17v-18r): 'Evidentia in nobis est sensus intimus quo nobis conscii sumus rem ita se habere quomodo a nobis percipitur. Atqui sensus ille intimus est per se notus, quemadmodum sensus doloris, voluptatis, etc., non potest non esse cuilibet manifestus.'

[74]   The role of Buffier had been underlined by Spink (1978, p. 275). For other testimonies on the *sensus intimus* as source of metaphysical certainty, see Schmutz (2007); after Austin, see for instance Gigot (1777, vol. 1,

John Austin SJ (1717–84), The First Irish Catholic Cartesian?

Unlike Buffier, Austin does not restrict the object of this intimate sentiment or feeling to the awareness of one's existence, but opts for a more reflexive approach: we do not primarily perceive our existence, but the 'modifications of our soul', such as thought (*cogitatio*), pain (*dolor*) and joy (*laetitia*) (Austin, *PPP*, p. 68). These modifications resist divine intervention, they are 'mine' in such a certain way that they can produce absolute certitude.

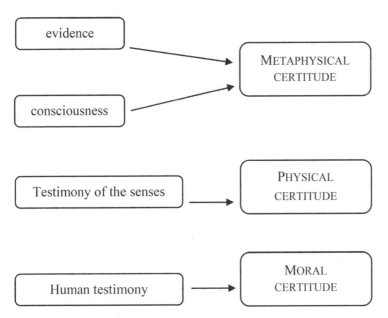

The double criterion of evidence and consciousness, as sources of metaphysical certitude, can be found in several other later courses, both within and outside the Jesuit tradition[75]. The result of Austin's discussion of degrees of certitude – summarized in the above graph – is a peculiar blend of late medieval vocabulary with early-modern Cartesian and Malebranchian insights. From the late

---

p. 182): 'Hoc effatum, *Quidquid intime sentitur, hoc est verum*, est primum certitudinis principium, in his quae pertinent ad praesentem statum animae nostrae'; Caron (1760, p. 79), also identifies consciousness and evidence as the sources of metaphysical certitude.

[75]   One decade after Austin in Rheims, Ignatius Nickel SJ also discusses (in the reversed order) consciousness and evidence as sources of metaphysical certitude: Nickel SJ (*Principia philosophiae sive logica*, p. 120): 'Testimonium conscientiae parit certitudinem metaphysicam'; (*Ibid.*, p. 126): 'Evidentia immediata parit certitudinem metaphysicam'.

Jacob Schmutz

medieval Scholastic tradition, he takes seriously the idea that certitude does not need to be absolute, but admits degrees; from the early-modern philosophical tradition, he looks at certitude from the point of view of the mental acts of the thinking and feeling mind. By putting these *Regulae veritatis* at the core of his general introduction to philosophy, one can also understand how his entire logic course is organized, and how it departs from the late medieval tradition. The proper object of early-modern Scholastic logic are not terms and inferences, as in late medieval terminist logic, but mental concepts, called *perceptions* or *ideas*, mental judgments about them (*iudicia*), and finally reasonings associating judgments (*discursus* and *methodus*)[76]. Ideas (or 'perceptions') can be clear and distinct, or obscure and confused; judgments can be metaphysically, physically or just morally certain. No trace of Austin's metaphysics course survives, but we can be pretty sure that its object and method can be deduced from what he says in the introduction about evidence and consciousness. Since the 1730s, the object of French Jesuit metaphysics courses was not the common being (*ens commune*) of the classical Suarezian tradition (existence and essence, possibility and actuality), but exclusively 'spiritual' or 'immaterial' being, including God, the angels, and the human mind (*mens*). The discussion of metaphysical certitude was therefore essential to provide solid proofs for the existence of the human mind, as separate from the sensory experience[77]. Austin's course stands clearly in the tradition which 'psychologized' both logic and metaphysics within the Scholastic tradition, in a way largely compatible with Port-Royal or the Lockean tradition.

5. Conclusion

Does all this make Austin the 'first Irish Catholic Cartesian', as suggested in the title of this study? John Austin was certainly not the

[76] *Theses ex universa philosophia*, def. Lombard, § 1: 'Logica mentis operationes spectat. Praecipuae sunt perceptio, judicium & discursus.'; Austin (*PPP*, p. 119): 'Operationes mentis sunt obiectum materiale logicae'; Nickel SJ (*Principia philosophiae sive logica*, p.c4), also lists the four operations of *perceptio*, *judicium*, *discursus* and *methodus*. On this general evolution, see Ariew (2014, pp. 43–57).

[77] For a point of comparison, see *Theses ex universa philosophia*, def. Lombard, § 3: 'Metaphysica praecipuè Spiritum contemplatur. (...) Spiritus creatus duplex: Angelus et mens humana: non nisi possibilitatem Angeli nos docet ratio, mentis vero humanae realiter existentis & spiritualitatem & immortalitatem demonstrat'.

John Austin SJ (1717–84), The First Irish Catholic Cartesian?

first Irish Catholic exiled professor to have embraced various elements of Cartesian and post-Cartesian epistemology. As we have seen, Cartesian and Malebranchian insights had penetrated almost all schools of traditional Scholastic philosophy during the first decades of the eighteenth century. In 1732, another Irish exiled scholar from Prague, the Franciscan Peter Arcedeckne (†1738), claimed that in 'France and Belgium', philosophy had become Cartesian, whereas in the rest of Europe, it remained 'Aristotelian' (Arcedeckne OFM. 1732, p. 49).[78] In spite of being schooled in Scotism, Arcedeckne was himself also strongly influenced by French college philosophy, in particular by Dagoumer and Pourchot, and could thus also compete for the title of 'First Irish Catholic Cartesian'. This shows that we should always be very careful when appreciating Scholastic temporalities: during the 'Golden Age of Anglo-Irish Philosophy', even Catholic courses of philosophy did not correspond to the received image of 'Aristotelian', 'Thomistic' or 'Scotistic' textbooks of earlier decades. They all integrated to a various extent innovations that had been developed by non-Scholastic thinkers such as Descartes, Malebranche and Locke. This integration of early-modern philosophy into the textbooks was facilitated by the fact that the classically trained Scholastics such as Austin could recognize, within the philosophy of the 'Anti-Peripatetics', a great number of elements that were compatible with the late-medieval tradition. Their discussion of the degrees of certitude perfectly illustrates this possibility, by relating the *cogito* or the *sensus intimus* with the traditional Scholastic discussion on the grades of certitude and the knowledge of our interior acts, which goes back to late-medieval Augustinianism.

One may finally argue that there is nothing really 'Irish' about Austin's philosophy, and that he is just a typical example of French post-Aristotelian scholasticism. Unlike the Franciscans, who kept a proper Irish Province and greatly contributed to the preservation of the Irish language and the study of its pre-reformation history, the Irish Jesuits were all part of foreign provinces and hierarchies.

---

[78] Arcedeckne's biography remains obscure, as underlined by Derr (2013, vol. 2, p. 2, under 'Archdekin'). He obviously taught at the College of the Immaculate Conception in Prague, and quotes typical Central European references, but his outstanding knowledge of Parisian scholasticism might suggest that he acquired some training there, or perhaps in Louvain. He finished his career as bishop of Killala in Connacht (1736–38). His philosophical relevance has been brought to my attention by a footnote from Knebel (2014, p. 372, note 119), who describes him as a 'well-informed (...) Irish Cartesian'.

Jacob Schmutz

Once back in Dublin, Austin was not even able to teach Scholastic philosophy, but divided his intellectual activity between lower education and religious preaching. But as a typical representative of the Irish diasporic scholasticism in France – which attracted about three quarters of Irish exiled clerics during the eighteenth century – (Whelan, 2009, p. 310), Austin's integration of modern philosophy and traditional scholasticism has nevertheless contributed to shaping the intellectual identity of Irish Catholic culture. One of Austin's most prominent students in Dublin was the young Patrick John Plunkett (1738–1828), who would follow his master's footsteps and acquire further philosophical and theological education in Paris, before being consecrated bishop of Meath (1779). This strong French predicament explains why so many themes typical of the French brand of the Catholic Enlightenment could later be found back in Dublin as well as in the curriculum of Saint Patrick's College in Maynooth – almost exclusively staffed by Irish returnees from France and exiled French clergymen fleeing the Revolution[79]. The scholastic language of 'rules of truth', of degrees of certitude, of 'objective and formal' evidence, etc. became a hallmark of the very rationalistic philosophical education that would survive well into the nineteenth century and even beyond in the tradition of Catholic seminaries[80].

Université Catholique de Louvain
jacob.schmutz@uclouvain.be

References

Ferdinand Alquié, *Le cartésianisme de Malebranche* (Paris: Vrin, 1974).
Peter Arcedeckne OFM, *Cursus philosophicus* (Prague: Joachim Kamenitzky, 1732).
Roger Ariew, 'Damned if you do: Cartesians and Censorship, 1663–1706', *Perspectives on Science* 2 (1994), 255–274
Roger Ariew, 'Bourdin and the Seventh Objections', in: *Descartes and His Contemporaries: Meditations, Objections, and Replies*, ed. Roger Ariew and Marjorie Grene, (The University of Chicago Press, 1995), 208–225.

[79] On this tradition, emphasizing the role of French returnees, see O'Connor (1981); Corish (1995, pp. 1–25).

[80] I wish to thank warmly Kenneth Pearce, Takaharu Oda and Eric Schliesser for their remarks and corrections that helped improving this paper.

John Austin SJ (1717–84), The First Irish Catholic Cartesian?

Roger Ariew, *Descartes and the Last Scholastics* (Ithaca, N.Y.: Cornell University Press, 1999).

Roger Ariew, *Descartes Among the Scholastics* (Leiden: Brill, 2011).

Roger Ariew, *Descartes and the First Cartesians* (Oxford University Press, 2014).

Rodrigo de Arriaga SJ, *Logica*, disp. 16, in Id., *Cursus philosophicus* (Paris: J. Quesnel, 1639 [1st edn 1632]).

Richard Arsdekin SJ, *Tractatus de idea scientifica*, in Id., *Theologia universa*, vol. II (Dinningen: Bencard, 1687).

John Au[s]tin, *Philosophiae pars prima. Logica* (no place, 1746–1747), Vire, Bibliothèque Municipale (now Médiathèque de Vire-Normandie).

Nicholas of Autrecourt, *His Correspondence with Master Giles and Bernard of Arezzo*, ed. and translated by Lambert-Marie de Rijk (Leiden: Brill, 1994).

Étienne Balibar, *John Locke, Identité et différence. L'invention de la conscience* (Paris: Seuil, 1998).

Cormac Stephen Begadon, *Laity and Clergy in the Catholic Renewal of Dublin, c. 1750–1830* (PhD NUI Maynooth, 2009).

David Berman, *Berkeley and Irish Philosophy* (New York: Continuum, 2004).

Jérôme Besoigne, *Logica* (1713), Paris BSG, Ms. 2178.

Jérôme Besoigne, *Metaphysica* (Plessis-Sorbonne College, 1714), Paris BSG, Ms. 2180.

Edel Bhreathnach, Joseph MacMahon OFM and John McCafferty (eds), *The Irish Franciscans, 1534–1990* (Dublin: Four Courts Press, 2009).

Joël Biard, 'Certitudo', in: *Mots médiévaux offerts à Ruedi Imbach*, ed. Iñigo Atucha, Dragos Calma, Catherine König-Pralong and Irene Zavattero (Porto: FIDEM, 2011), 153–162.

Joël Biard, *Science et nature. La théorie buridanienne du savoir* (Paris: Vrin, 2012).

Paul Richard Blum, *Philosophenphilosophie und Schulphilosophie. Typen des philosophierens in der Neuzeit* (Stuttgart: Franz Steiner Verlag, 1998).

Alfred Boehm, 'Deux essais de renouvellement de la scolastique au XVIIe siècle. II. L'aristotélisme d'Honoré Fabri', *Revue des sciences religieuses* 39/4 (1965), 305–360.

Laurence W.B. Brockliss, *French Higher Education in the Seventeenth and Eighteenth Centuries. A Cultural History* (Oxford University Press, 1987).

Laurence W.B. Brockliss, 'The Moment of No Return. The University of Paris and the Death of Aristotelianism', *Science and Education* 15/2–4 (2006), 259–278.

Laurence W.B. Brockliss and Patrick Ferté, 'Irish Clerics in France in the Seventeenth and Eighteenth Centuries: A Statistical Survey', *Proceedings of the Royal Irish Academy*, series 87C, vol. 9 (1987), 527–572.

Laurence W.B. Brockliss and Patrick Ferté, 'Prosopography of Irish Clerics in the Universities of Paris and Toulouse, 1573–1792', *Archivium Hibernicum* 58 (2004), 7–166.

Gaspar Buhon SJ, *Philosophia ad morem Gymnasiorum finemque accomodata* (Lyons: Bruyset, 1723).

John Buridan, *Summulae. De demonstrationibus*, ed. Lambert-Marie de Rijk (Turnhout: Brepols, 2001).

Jean-Charles-Félix Caron, *Compendium institutionum philosophiae. Tomus primus* (Paris: N.M. Tilliard, 1760).

Ephraim Chambers, *Cyclopedia: Or an Universal Dictionary of Arts and Sciences*, 5th edition (London: D. Midwinter etc., 1751).

Liam Chambers, 'Defying Descartes: Michael Moore (1639–1726) and Aristotelian Philosophy in France and Ireland', in: *The Medieval World and the Modern Mind*, ed. Michael Brown and Stephen Harrison (Dublin: Four Courts Press, 2000), 11–26.

Liam Chambers, *The Life and Writings of Michael Moore, c. 1639–1726* (PhD NUI Maynooth, 2001).

Liam Chambers, 'A Displaced Intelligentsia: Aspects of Irish Catholic Thought in Ancien Régime France', in: *The Irish in Europe, 1580–1815*, ed. Thomas O'Connor (Dublin: Four Courts Press, 2001), 157–74.

Liam Chambers, 'Rivalry and Reform in the Irish College, Paris, 1676–1775', in: Irish Communities in Early Modern Europe, ed. T. O'Connor & Mary Ann Lyons (Dublin: Four Courts Press, 2006), 103–129.

Liam Chambers, 'Irish Catholics and Aristotelian Scholastic Philosophy in Early-Modern France, c. 1600-c. 1750', in: *The Irish Contribution to European Scholastic Thought*, ed. James McEvoy and Michael Dunne (Dublin: Four Courts Press, 2009), 312–330.

Timothy Corcoran, *State Policy in Irish Education, 1536–1816* (Dublin: Browne & Nolan, 1916).

Patrick J. Corish, *The Irish Catholic Experience. A Historical Survey* (Dublin: Gill and Macmillan, 1985).

Patrick J. Corish, *Maynooth College, 1795–1995* (Dublin: Gill and Macmillan 1995).

John Austin SJ (1717–84), The First Irish Catholic Cartesian?

Guillaume Dagoumer, *Philosophia ad usum scholae accomodata*, 4 vols (Paris: Pierre Aubouin, Charles Clousier & Barthélémy Girin, 1701–03).

Guillaume Dagoumer, *Metaphysica* (Lyons, 1757 [¹1702]).

François de Dainville SJ, *L'éducation des jésuites, XVIᵉ–XVIIIᵉ siècles*, ed. Marie-Madeleine Compère (Paris: Ed. de Minuit, 1991).

Gabriel Daniel SJ, *Voyage du Monde de Descartes*, vol. 1 (Amsterdam, 1700).

Pierre Delattre SJ (ed.), *Les établissements des jésuites en France depuis quatre siècle. Répertoire topo-bibliographique*, vol. 4 (Enghien: Institut Supérieur de Théologie / Wetteren: Imprimerie de Meester Frères, 1956).

Pierre Delattre SJ, 'Poitiers. Le Collège irlandais (1674–1762)', in Delattre (1956) 57–60.

Dallas G. Denery, *Seeing and Being Seen in the Later Medieval World. Optics, Theology and Religious Life* (Cambridge University Press, 2005).

Eric Derr, *The Irish Episcopal Corps* (PhD NUI Maynooth, 2013).

René, Descartes, *Principia philosophiae*, transl. John Cottingham, in: *Philosophical Writings*, vol. I (Cambridge University Press, 1985).

[Jean-Baptiste Du Hamel, anon.], *Philosophia vetus et nova ad usum scholae accomodata, in Regia Burgundica novissimo hoc biennio pertracta. Tomus primus qui Institutiones logicas, & logicam ipsam continet* (Paris: Etienne Michallet, 1678).

Jean Du Hamel, *Philosophia universalis, sive commentarius in univer sam Aristotelis philosophiam* (Paris: Cl. Thiboust & Esclassan, 1705), 5 vols.

Henri Dubois SJ, 'Reims. Le Collège (1606–1762)', in: Delattre (1956), 278–302.

Thomas Duddy, 'Introduction', in: *Dictionary of Irish Philosophers* (Bristol & New York: Thoemmes & Continuum, 2004).

Gustave Dupont-Ferrier, *Du collège de Clermont au lycée Louis-le-Grand, 1563–1920*, vol. 1: *Le Collège sous les Jésuites, 1563–1762* (Paris: E. de Boccard, 1921).

Charles-Antoine Fédérique (*Catalogue général des manuscrits des bibliothèques publiques de France*, vol. 10, Paris: Plon, 1889).

Mordechai Feingold, 'Jesuits: Savants', in: *Jesuit Science and the Republic of Letters*, ed. M. Feingold (Cambridge, Mass.: The MIT Press, 2003), 1–46.

Hugh Fenning, 'Some Problems of the Irish Mission, 1733–1774', *Collectanea Hibernica* 8 (1965), 58–109.

Angela Ferraro, *La réception de Malebranche en France au XVIIIᵉ siècle. Métaphysique et épistémologie* (Paris: Classiques Garnier, 2019).

Jacob Schmutz

Francis Finegan SJ, 'The Irish College of Poitiers: 1674–1762', *The Irish Ecclesiastical Record* 104 (1954), 18–31.

Francis Finegan, 'Fr. John Austin (1717–1784)', *Jesuit Year Book* 43 (1970), 5–18.

Daniel Gigot, *Institutiones philosophicae ad usum Seminariorum. Tomus primus* (Toul: Joseph Carez, 1777 [¹1763]).

Catherine Glyn Davies, *Conscience as Consciousness: The Idea of Self-Awareness in French Philosophical Writing from Descartes to Diderot* (Oxford: Voltaire Foundation, 1990).

Henri Gouhier, *La pensée métaphysique de Descartes* (Paris: Vrin, 1962).

Christophe Grellard, *Croire et savoir. Les principes de la connaissance selon Nicolas d'Autrécourt* (Paris: Vrin, 2005).

Christophe Grellard, 'Probabilisme et approximation du vrai au XIVe siècle', in: *Vérité et crédibilité. Construire la vérité dans le système de communication de l'Occident (XIIIe–XVIIe siècle)*, ed. Jean-Philippe Genet (Paris: Editions de la Sorbonne / École française de Rome, 2015), 65–79.

Paul F. Grendler, *Jesuit Schools and Universities in Europe, 1548–1773* (Leiden: Brill, 2018).

William Hamilton, 'On the History of the Terms Consciousness, Attention and Reflection', in: Thomas Reid, *The Works*, ed. William Hamilton (Edinburgh: Maclachlan, Stewart & Co., 1846), vol. 2, 940–945.

Blake T. Hanna, 'Diderot: formation traditionnelle et formation moderne', *Recherches sur Diderot et l'Encyclopédie* 5 (1988), 3–18.

Pedro Hurtado de Mendoza SJ, *Universa philosophia*, Mainz 1619 [¹1615].

Sébastien Jahan, 'Les exilés irlandais en Poitou au XVIIe et XVIIIe siècles', *Revue du Nord* 400–401/2 (2013), 451–466.

Sven K. Knebel, *Wille, Würfel und Wahrscheinlichkeit. Das System der moralischen Notwendigkeit in der Jesuitenscholastik 1550–1700* (Hamburg: Felix Meiner, 2000).

Sven K. Knebel, 'Durandus, Quirós, Consciousness', in: *Durand of Saint-Pourçain and His* Sentences *Commentary*, ed. Andreas Speer, Fiorella Retucci, Thomas Jeschke and Guy Guldentops (Louvain: Peeters, 2014), 343–384.

Hedvika Kuchařová and Jan Pařez, *The Irish Franciscans in Prague, 1629–1786*, transl. Jana and Michael Stoddart (Prague: Karolinum Press, 2015).

Guillaume-Joseph de Laquilhe SJ, *Logica* (1744), Princeton University Library, Ms. C0199, n° 1077.

John Austin SJ (1717–84), The First Irish Catholic Cartesian?

Philippe Lécrivain, *Les premiers siècles jésuites. Jalons pour une histoire (1540–1814)* (Namur: Lessius, 2016).

Pierre Lemonnier, *Cursus philosophicus ad scholarum usum accomodatus*, 4 vols (Paris: Louis Genneau & Jacques Rollin, 1750).

Nicolas Malebranche, *Dialogues on Metaphysics and Religion*, transl. David Scott (Cambridge University Press 1997).

Henricus Marcellius SJ, *Armamentarium scientificum* (Paris: Michel Soly, 1635).

Anton Mayr SJ, *Philosophia peripatetica antiquorum principiis et recentiorum experimentis confirmata*, vol. 1: *Logica* (Venice: N. Pezzana, 1745 [^{1}1739]).

Louis McRedmond, *To the Greater Glory of God. A History of the Irish Jesuits* (Dublin: Gill and Macmillan, 1991).

Benignus Millett OFM, *The Irish Franciscans, 1651–1665* (Rome: Gregorian University Press, 1964).

Michael Moore, *De existentia Dei et humanae mentis immortalitate secundum Cartesii et Aristotelis doctrinam disputatio in duos libros divisa* (Paris: Charles Robustel, 1692).

Catherine M. Northeast, *The Parisian Jesuits and the Enlightenment, 1700–1762* (Oxford: Voltaire Foundation, 1991).

Éamon Ó Ciosáin, 'Attitudes Towards Ireland and the Irish in Enlightenment France', in: *Ireland and the Enlightenment, 1700–1800*, ed. Graham Gargeli and Geraldine Sheridan (London: Macmillan, 1999).

Priscilla O'Connor, *Irish Clerics at the University of Paris, 1570–1770* (PhD NUI Maynooth, 2006).

Rhoda F. O'Connor, 'The Growing Demand for Catholic Education leading to the Establishment of St Patrick's, Maynooth 1795', *Irish Educational Studies* 1 (1981), 216–307.

Thomas O'Connor, *An Irish Theologian in Enlightenment Europe: Luke Joseph Hooke 1714–1796* (Dublin: Four Courts Press, 1995).

Thomas O'Connor (ed.), *The Irish in Europe, 1580–1815* (Dublin: Four Courts Press, 2001).

Thomas O'Connor, 'La solidarité contre-réformée: les réseaux de collèges irlandais dans l'Europe catholique, 1578–1793', in: *Étudiants de l'exil. Migrations internationales et universités refuges (XVIe–XXe siècles)*, ed. Patrick Ferté and Caroline Barrera (Toulouse: Presses Universitaires du Mirail, 2009), 71–80.

Thomas O'Connor and Mary Ann Lyons (eds.), *Irish Communities in Early Modern Europe* (Dublin: Four Courts Press, 2006).

Thomas O'Connor, 'Luke Joseph Hooke: Theological Tolerance in an Apologetic Mold', in: *Enlightenment and Catholicism in Europe: A*

Transnational History, ed. Jeffrey D. Burson and Ulrich L. Lehner (University of Notre Dame Press, 2014), 420–438.

Edward E. O'Donnell SJ, *The Jesuits in Dublin, 1598–1998* (Dublin: Wolfhound, 1999).

Charles O'Neill SJ & Joaquín M. Domínguez SJ (eds.) *Diccionario histórico de la Compañía de Jesús*, (Roma & Madrid: Institutum Historicum S.I. / Universidad Pontificia de Comillas, 2001).

Alfred O'Rahilly, 'Father John Austin S.J. (1717–1784)', *The Irish Monthly* 67/789 (1939), 181–196.

Robert Pasnau, *After Certainty. A History of Our Epistemic Ideals and Illusions* (Oxford University Press, 2017).

Leonardo de Peñafiel SJ, *Disputationes scholasticae et morales de virtute fidei divina* (Lyons: Pierre Chevalier, 1673).

Richard H. Popkin, *The History of Scepticism: From Savonarola to Bayle*, Revised and Expanded Edition (Oxford University Press, 2003).

Edme Pourchot, *Institutiones philosophicae ad faciliorem veterum ac recentiorum philosophorum lectionem comparatae*, 4 vols (Paris: J.-B. Coignard, 1695).

Edme Pourchot, *Exercitationes scholasticae in varias partes philosophiae* (Paris: Jean-Baptiste Coignard, 1700).

Helga Robinson-Hammerstein, 'Aspects of the Continental Education of Irish Students in the Reign of Elizabeth I', *Historical Studies* 8 (1971), 137–153.

Camille de Rochemonteix, *Un collège de jésuites aux XVIIe et XVIIIe siècles. Le Collège Henri IV de La Flèche*, Le Mans: Leguicheux, 1889, 4 vols.

Geneviève Rodis-Lewis, *Le problème de l'inconscient et le cartésianisme* (Paris: PUF, 1950).

Sophie Roux, 'La philosophie naturelle d'Honoré Fabri (1607–1688)', in: *Les Jésuites à Lyon, XVIe-XXe siècles*, ed. Étienne Fouilloux and Bernard Hours (Lyons: ENS-LSH Editions, 2005), 75–94.

Sophie Roux, 'The Condemnations of Cartesian Natural Philosophy Under Louis XIV (1661–91)', in: *The Oxford Handbook on Descartes and Cartesianism*, ed. Steven Nadler, Tad M. Schmaltz and Delphine Antoine-Mahut (Oxford University Press, 2019), 755–779.

Tad M. Schmaltz, *Radical Cartesianism. The French Reception of Descartes* (Cambridge University Press, 2002).

Tad M. Schmaltz, 'A Tale of Two Condemnations: Two Cartesian Condemnations in 17th-Century France', in: *Descartes e i suoi Avversari. Incontri cartesiani II*, ed. Antonella Del Prete (Florence: Le Monnier Università, 2004), 203–221.

John Austin SJ (1717–84), The First Irish Catholic Cartesian?

Tad M. Schmaltz, *Early Modern Cartesianisms: Dutch and French Constructions* (Oxford University Press, 2017).

Jacob Schmutz, 'L'invention jésuite du "sentiment d'existence", ou comment la philosophie sort des collèges', *XVIIe siècle* 59/4 (2007a), 613–631.

Jacob Schmutz, 'L'existence de l'ego comme premier principe métaphysique avant Descartes', in: *Généalogies du sujet, de saint Anselme à Malebranche*, ed. Olivier Boulnois (Paris: Vrin, 2007b), 215–268.

Jacob Schmutz, 'Pedro Hurtado de Mendoza, the Scholastic Godfather of Early-Modern Philosophy. Teachers, Students, Manuscripts, and the Making of a Philosophical Classic in Early-Modern Europe', in: *Pedro Hurtado de Mendoza (1578–1641). System, Sources and Influence*, ed. Lukaš Novák and Daniel D. Novotný (Leiden: Brill, 2020), forthcoming.

Rudolf Schüssler, *The Debate on Probable Opinions in the Scholastic Tradition* (Leiden: Brill, 2019).

Gaston Sortais, *Le cartésianisme chez les Jésuites français au XVIIe et au XVIIIe siècle* (Paris: Beauchesne, 1929).

John S. Spink, 'Les avatars du sentiment d'existence de Locke à Rousseau', *XVIIIe siècle* 10 (1978), 268–98.

Francisco Suárez SJ, *Disputationes metaphysicae* (Salamanca: J. & A. Renaut, 1597).

Liam Swords (ed.), *The Irish-French Connection, 1578–1978* (Paris: The Irish College, 1978).

Lynn Thorndike, 'The *Cursus philosophicus* before Descartes', *Archives internationales d'histoire de la science* 4 (1951), 16–24.

John Toland, *Christianity not Mysterious*, 2nd edition enlarged (London: S. Buckley, 1696).

Juan de Ulloa SJ, *Prodomus, seu prolegomena ad scholasticas disciplinas. Editio secunda* (Madrid: Antonio Marín, 1748 [¹1711]).

Alfred Webb, *A Compendium of Irish Biography* (Dublin: M.H. Gill & Son, 1878).

Kevin Whelan, 'A Nation in Waiting? The Irish in France in the Eighteenth Century', in: *Franco-Irish Connections. Essays, Memoirs and Poems in Honour of Pierre Joannon* (Dublin: Four Courts Press, 2009), 304–320.

Jack Zupko, 'On Certitude', in: *The Metaphysics and Natural Philosophy of John Buridan*, ed. J.H.H.M. Thijssen and Jack Zupko (Leiden: Brill, 2001), 165–182.

Index of Names

Index of Names